CALLOT'S ETCHINGS

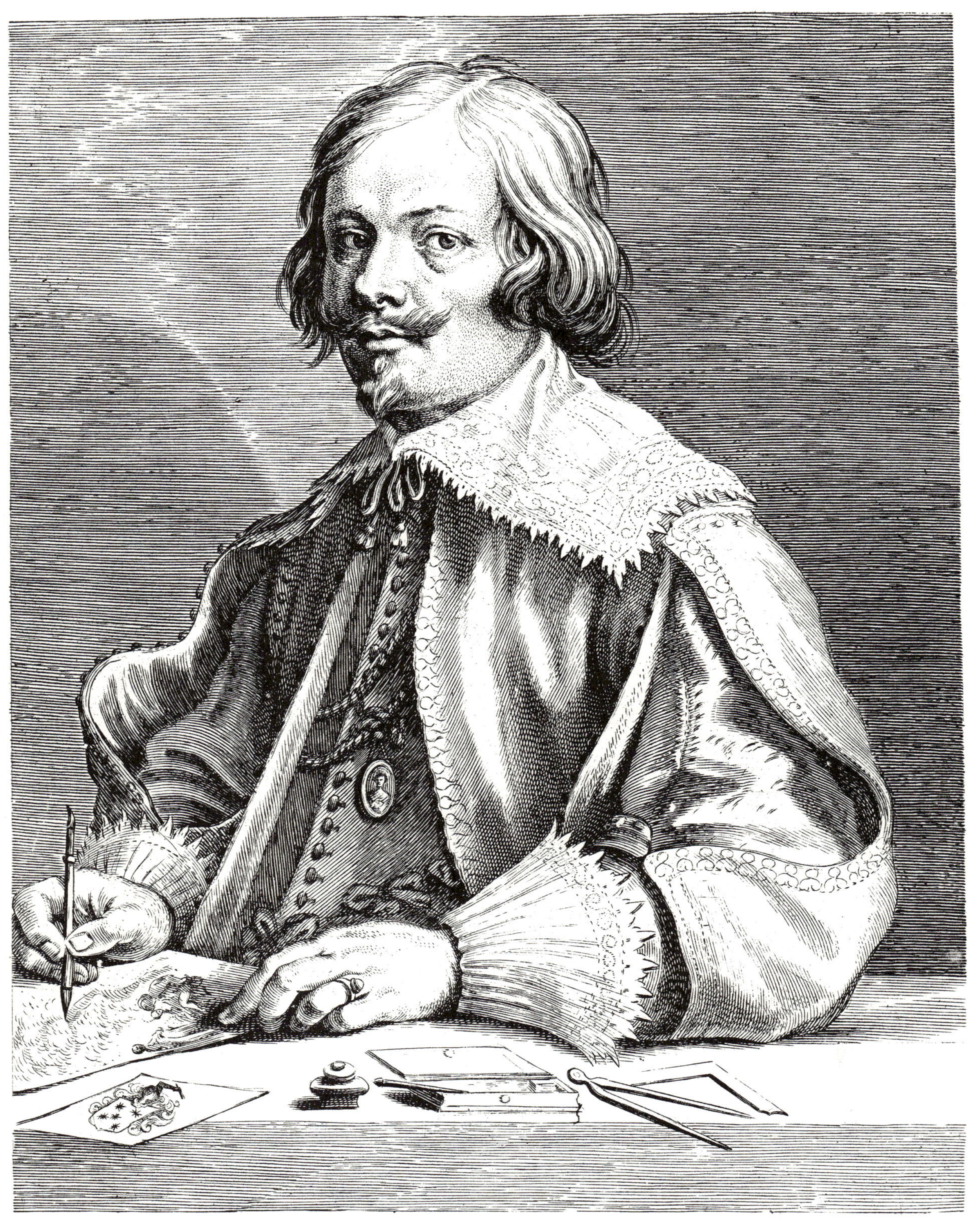

"Jacques Callot, Noted Etcher in Nancy, Lorraine." Engraved by Lucas Vorsterman the Elder from a painting by Anthony Van Dyck. (Howard Daniel Collection)

CALLOT'S ETCHINGS

338 PRINTS

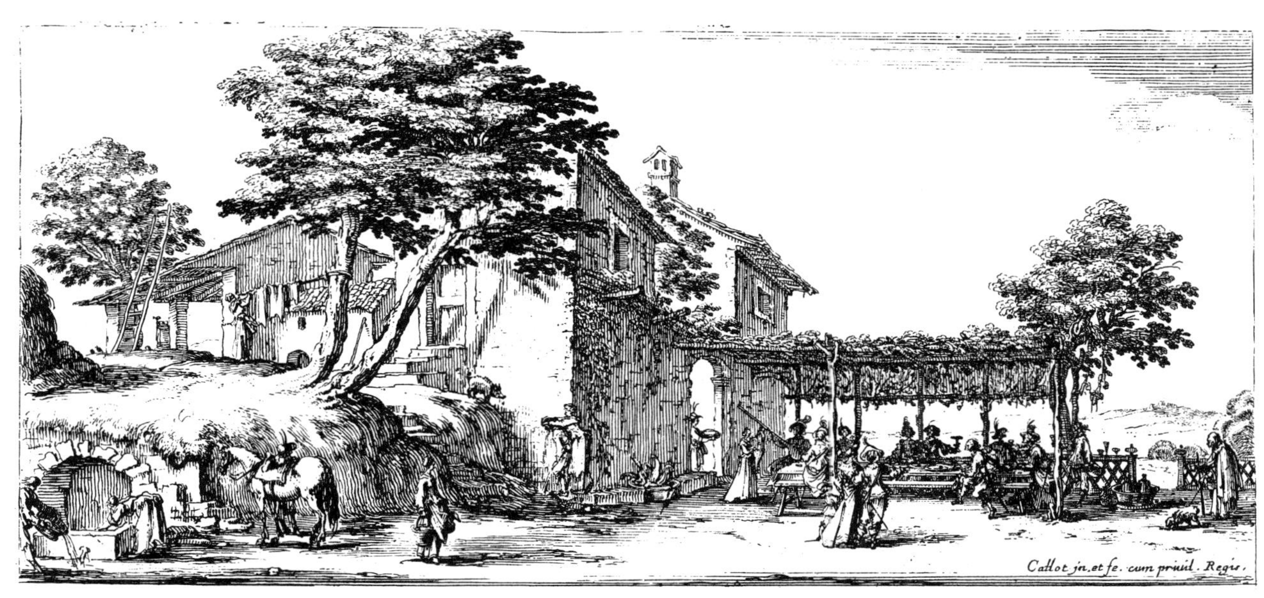

EDITED BY HOWARD DANIEL

Dover Publications, Inc., New York

Published in Canada by General Publishing Company, Ltd.,
30 Lesmill Road, Don Mills, Toronto, Ontario.
Published in the United Kingdom by Constable and Company, Ltd.,
10 Orange Street, London WC 2.

Callot's Etchings: 338 Prints is a new work, first published by Dover Publications, Inc., in 1974.

International Standard Book Numbers:
0-486-23073-2 (paper edition)
0-486-23081-3 (cloth edition)

Library of Congress Catalog Card Number: 73-81506

Manufactured in the United States of America
Dover Publications, Inc.
180 Varick Street
New York, N.Y. 10014

This book is for the Davies family

Acknowledgments

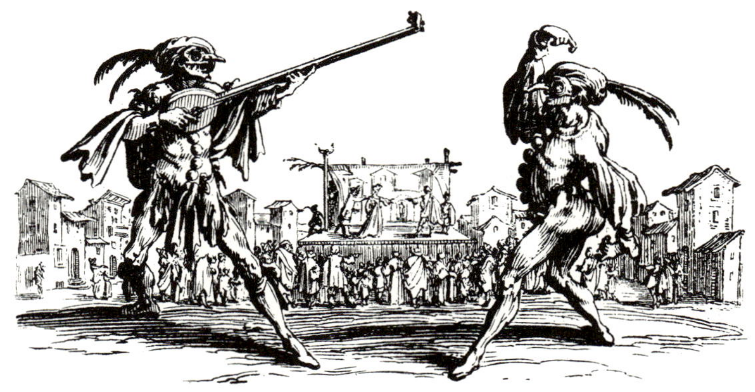

Most of the illustrations in this book were reproduced directly from original prints in the Lessing J. Rosenwald Collection of the National Gallery of Art in Washington, D.C. Several others are from originals in the National Gallery's R. L. Baumfeld Collection. Special thanks are due to Messrs. Rosenwald and Baumfeld for their personal participation and cooperation. At the National Gallery, Miss Kathleen T. Hunt and Dr. H. Diane Russell were most helpful in arranging the loan of the prints, and Mr. Fred Cain devoted many hours of his professional skill to the project.

A number of other illustrations were reproduced from originals in the possession of Mr. Howard Daniel, who made the picture selection for this volume and wrote the introductory text.

A few illustrations are from photographs furnished by the British Museum, London, and the Bibliothèque Nationale, Paris.

The illustrations and text were printed by The Murray Printing Company at Forge Village, Massachusetts. The interest and craftsmanship of their staff were essential to the successful completion of the book.

Dover Publications, Inc.

Contents

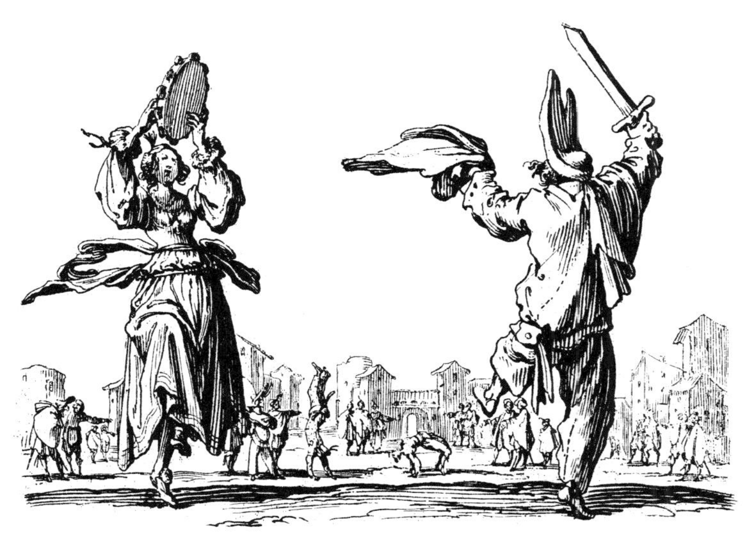

INTRODUCTION

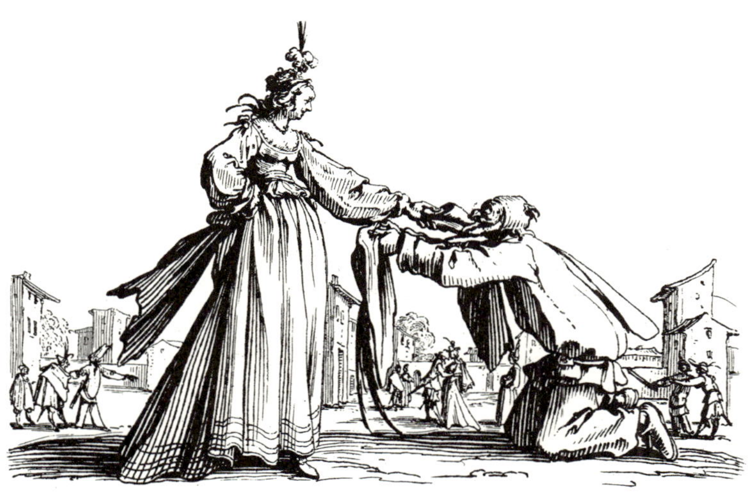

The late sixteenth-century world into which Jacques Callot was born—in Nancy, capital of the independent Duchy of Lorraine, in 1592—was entering what historians have recently diagnosed as a great economic and political crisis. This crisis culminated in his lifetime in the destruction and horrors of the Thirty Years' War. Since Callot was the first great artist to reflect so directly and immediately the historical as well as the everyday events of his time, some consideration of this crucial moment of western and central Europe is necessary for a fuller understanding of his work.

This period saw a drop in general production and a decline in commerce. At the same time there was a steady and continuous rise in the price of all basic commodities. On top of this, Europe was stricken by a resurgence of epidemic diseases of particular virulence. Phenomenally cold weather was largely responsible for recurrent famines, particularly in France.

The sixteenth-century ambitions of the Spanish kings to dominate most of Europe—a predominant cause of the crisis in Callot's time—had given way in the seventeenth century to the bitter rivalry between two other absolute monarchies, the Holy Roman Empire of the Hapsburgs and Bourbon France. This conflict, which is seen today as the chief issue at stake in the Thirty Years' War, called for large armies, financed by brutal taxation that weighed most heavily on the peasants. Not unnaturally they reacted, and France in particular witnessed a series of violent and destructive, but futile, uprisings. The enormous cost of maintaining the royal courts of the period was another factor in the economic depression.

Callot, his family, and his native Lorraine were part and parcel of this whole development.

The dukes of independent Lorraine had established Nancy as their capital as early as the middle of the twelfth century, and had faced their critical test in the fifteenth century when they overcame the invading Burgundians (1477). During the Hundred Years' War, Lorraine fought alongside the French against the English. Because of its geographical location between France and the Hapsburg lands, Lorraine was brought into prominence by the Reformation and its consequences. From the sixteenth-century religious struggles Lorraine emerged intensely Catholic. This is an important fact in the background and life of Jacques Callot, whose ties with militant Counter-Reformation Catholicism were close and strong. Five of his seven brothers and sisters were members of one or another part of the Franciscan Order.

The period of greatest prosperity for Lorraine came during the 63-year reign (1545–1608) of Duke Charles III, who devoted himself magnificently to the arts of peace after his quarrel with French King Henri IV was terminated by the latter's conversion to Catholicism in 1594. Charles greatly favored the bourgeoisie, who during his reign established or operated important mining and manufacturing industries that were ruined in the wars that followed.

Duke Henri II, the son of Charles III, reigned for a period of sixteen reasonably peaceful and uneventful years (1608–1624). His successor, Charles IV, was a nephew of Henri who married Henri's daughter. In a particularly troubled time Charles IV was not a particularly able ruler, and his political intrigues led to the invasion of Lorraine and the occupation of Nancy in 1633 by Richelieu and Louis XIII. During the Thirty Years' War, half a dozen armies marched over, fought over, and plundered much of Lorraine, which lost at least half its population.

Moreover, the disasters of this period drove the bulk of the survivors deeper into irrational beliefs, and there was an extraordinary recrudescence of witch-burning. Contemporary accounts based on eye-witness reports claim that Lorraine was reduced to an almost animal life characterized by robbery, murder, and even cannibalism.

The Callot family were well established in and around Nancy for several centuries before the birth of Jacques Callot in 1592. Scholars who have burrowed into the archives of the *département* of Meurthe-et-Moselle have uncovered plentiful evidence of an able and vigorous family of small independent landowners with Church connections. Jacques Callot's immediate forebears have most relevance for us. His grandfather Claudon Callot was an archer in the bodyguard of Duke Charles III. He must have come from a respectable family for in 1559 he married Claude de Fricourt, thought to be a grandniece of Joan of Arc. Being a member of the duke's bodyguard was no ordinary post. Claudon's job in the immediate entourage of the duke called for discretion, intelligence, and a certain polish. Clearly he had these qualities for the records show that he was also used as a confidential messenger. Indeed it is reasonable to assume that the confidence of the duke made it possible for him to operate as a sideline activity a large and profitable inn in Nancy, the Three Kings. The archives show that many of the guests of the inn were the duke's business or diplomatic agents or visitors, whose bills were settled from the ducal purse.

Claudon Callot took advantage of the swift and constant rise in prices during his life and invested his savings and the profits from his inn in real estate. He acquired considerable estates in the village of Bainville-sur-Madon in the district of Toul. He also speculated in real estate in the town of Nancy, which expanded greatly during the reign of his master, Charles III. Such were his services to the duke that in 1584 he was ennobled. He had to pay a considerable sum into the duke's coffers for the honor, but it had its compensation. He secured a complete exoneration from taxes. Selling his inn, he then acquired a seigneurial property at Bainville-sur-Madon. As a noble he was now able to exercise certain feudal rights in the small town which had probably been the cradle of the Callot family.

Claudon Callot profited in other ways from his ducal connections. He arranged the marriage of his four daughters to court officials. Two sons became monks and he obtained for his eldest son, Jean, then eleven, the living of the church of Bainville. Next, Claudon secured Jean's entry into the duke's corps of archers, and some years later Jean became court herald and organizer of functions. In this capacity he had an altogether courtly life free from the commercial activities of his father. At the age of 25, abandoning his ecclesiastical benefice, he made one of those good bourgeois marriages common among court officials. His bride, Renée Brunehaut, was the daughter of a distinguished medical doctor at the ducal court. Jacques Callot was the second son of the marriage.

When Claudon Callot died in 1594, Charles III, obviously grateful for the faithful services of his former archer-messenger, saw to it that the "bourgeois noble" (as they were called in Lorraine) was buried in the Church of the Cordeliers in Nancy among the first families of the land. But seven years before the death of old Callot, father and son experienced one of those checks not uncommon at the time. Duke Charles was still asserting Lorraine's claim to the French throne in opposition to Henri of Navarre (Henri IV), and as a direct consequence, the German and Swiss mercenaries recruited by De Bouillon, chief of the French Protestant armies, destroyed some fifty Lorraine villages as they traversed the country. One of them was Bainville-sur-Madon, which was burned in 1587.

There is no doubt that tales of the rapine, plunder, and destruction of the village which was then the main source of the Callot family's prosperity must have constantly regaled the early childhood of Jacques Callot. But his earliest years were a period of peace and great prosperity for Lorraine. The journal of a ducal official, Jacques Vuarin, records that the years 1595–1598 were "fertile and abundant to the great happiness of the people who were able to recover from the serious losses caused by the wars."

We see then that Jacques Callot was born into a prosperous family of ennobled bourgeoisie and that his earliest years were spent in an ambiance of pomp and ceremony. There was a popular saying in the early seventeenth century that the most impressive sights in Europe were the coronation of the French king at Rheims, the crowning of the German emperor at Frankfurt, and the burial of the Duke of Lorraine at Nancy. The funeral arrangements for Charles III, who died in 1608, lasted for about two months and were directed by Jacques Callot's father. Several thousand notables participated in the ceremonies, which reached their climax in the funeral procession and interment. It might well be assumed that the young Jacques, already apprenticed to an engraver of precious metals attached to the court, assisted his father. What is important is that at an early age Jacques Callot was brought into the closest contact with pomp and ceremony of a highly theatrical nature. This so conditioned him that nearly all of the more than 1400 plates he engraved or etched bear to a greater or lesser extent this theatrical quality.

Fêtes, ceremonies, and pageants played an extremely important role in diverting the feudal aristocracy from their customary grappling with power. In a sense they served as a sort of opium of the upper class. The scholar Alewyn has shown the enormous importance of the tournament and court fêtes and, related to this, a reason for the great success of such works as *Orlando Furioso* and *Jerusalem Delivered*. The tournament was a colorful and sometimes bloody ritual in which a now largely powerless aristocracy could act out its power fantasies. The two great poems reveal a rich and exotic world in which the feudal nobility could, in their imagination, perform feats of chivalry no longer remotely possible in real life.

A sort of romantic legend grew up about the early years of Callot. Hard-nosed scholars in recent years have tended to pooh-pooh the more romantic aspects of the legend (but perpetuate it by repeating it; they seem too fascinated by it to ignore it). What we do know for certain is that Jacques Callot went to school near the ducal palace intended for the sons of court officials. Here the Abbé Didier Breton taught reading, writing, arithmetic, music including singing, church decoration, a little astronomy and geometry, and the elements of grammar. At the age of fourteen or fifteen Jean Callot apprenticed his son Jacques to the court jeweler and goldsmith Demenge Crocq, paying him the sum of 4000 francs to cover his tuition, board, and lodging.

The story which tradition has handed down to us fills in the gaps with a truly romantic flourish. The sources are Callot's earliest biographers,

Baldinucci and Félibien. These two scholarly writers apparently based their works on verbal accounts of the early life of Callot told to them by close personal friends of the artist, or by other acquaintances of his. Each writer wrote seemingly without knowledge of the other. The legend, whose main elements might well be fact, relates that from his earliest years the young Jacques Callot was fascinated by drawing and filled his school books with his sketches. Baldinucci reports that Callot, at the age of twelve, ran away from the comfort of the paternal home and made a long and dismal journey to Rome; that in order to realize his dreams he subjected himself to the pangs of a poor and hard life. He is said to have joined a band of Gypsies and to have made his way over the Alps, first to Florence. Here an officer of the grand duke, impressed by the appearance and manner of the young traveler, directed him to the court engineer and organizer of fêtes, Cantagallina, who taught him drawing. Shortly afterwards the young man left Florence to satisfy his desire to see Rome. It is possible that this second flight was triggered by arrangements in Florence to return the young truant to Nancy, the relations between the two grand-ducal courts being close. The wife of Grand Duke Ferdinand I was Christine of Lorraine, daughter of Charles III. Callot's stay in Rome was short. Some Nancy merchants—probably warned to look out for the boy—found him and brought him back to his parents. Two years later he took to the road again, this time for Turin. His elder brother went in hot pursuit and brought him back shortly afterwards. Convinced by these flights of the serious intention of their son to be an artist (so the legend goes on), his parents finally accepted his choice of vocation. His father arranged for the lad to join the entourage of a Lorraine ambassador being sent to the Pope. On his arrival in Rome Callot studied engraving with the burin under the French artist Philippe Thomassin. His studies with this master did not last long. The older man feared that his handsome pupil was becoming too attractive to his young wife. Thomassin encouraged Callot to leave Rome and continue his studies in Florence. Here he was well received and given lodging in the Uffizi.

Perhaps the boyhood adventures of Jacques Callot were exaggerated and romanticized in the telling. But the essential facts are quite likely to be true. Both Baldinucci and Félibien were serious writers and the French scholar Ternois reminds us that the "flight to Rome" was very much in the air in the early seventeenth century. He cites the youthful journeys, flights, or attempts to reach Italy by Poussin, Claude Lorraine, Perrier, François de Nôme, and Claude Deruet. What is clearly untrue is that the family of Jacques Callot objected to their son becoming an artist. Their connections with the ducal court and the religious orders guaranteed a reasonable standard of living for their artistically gifted child. After all, an engraver was a part of the apparatus of feudal power. An important function of such a court official—and they were such—was the recording of genealogies, fêtes, ceremonies, and other evidences of status and power. The work generally thought to be Callot's first is in fact a portrait of Duke Charles III (Plate No. 1). The apprenticing of the lad for a then considerable sum to Demenge Crocq at the age of fourteen or fifteen would suggest strongly their approval of his future profession.

It is fairly well established that the young Callot left for Italy late the following year (1608). His Nancy apprenticeship therefore lasted less than two years. Most of his formation, then, was Italian. The obviously precocious student had already in Nancy the opportunity to familiarize himself with the work and style of court artists influenced by the School of Fontainebleau and by the Mannerists in general. The two outstanding Lorraine artists Bellange and de La Tour had not reached their maturity during Callot's early years in Nancy, and the slight influence they had on his art came later.

The exact length of Callot's stay in Rome with Thomassin is uncertain, but he was probably there for a little more than three years. Philippe

Thomassin came from Troyes in France, where he had been a gold and silversmith. In that craft he was an extremely competent artist with one of the essential tools of engraving, the burin. With that mastery he had applied himself to the engraving of prints. In Rome he worked as an engraver and print dealer. Under his guidance the young Callot mastered the technique of the burin, a tool calling for great skill and control. Of almost equal importance in his artistic education was the opportunity to familiarize himself with prints that living among Thomassin's stock made possible. This stock was probably large and varied in subject matter. The importance of engravings in the sixteenth and seventeenth centuries was considerable. From the two great print markets of Antwerp and Rome engravings were disseminated over much of Europe. They formed an important part of the pictorial stock of ideas of many painters.

About the works engraved by Callot in Rome we lack precise information. Scholars generally credit him with a few undistinguished engravings of religious subjects. They also credit him with two series of engravings, *The Months* and *The Seasons*. These works are artistically uninspired—they borrow greatly from Northern European engravings undoubtedly seen in Thomassin's stock—but show considerable technical mastery for a young apprentice.

On the death of Margaret of Austria, Queen of Spain, the Florentine court commissioned the painter-engraver Antonio Tempesta to make 29 etchings of the *Pompe funèbre de la Reine d'Espagne*. The urgency of the commission required Tempesta to seek the help of other artists including the young Callot who, as a result, got his first experience in etching. That experience directly or indirectly prompted Callot's early departure for Florence. The city must have attracted him greatly. The competition there was far less keen than in a Rome overcrowded with artists. In all likelihood Callot counted on the patronage of the dowager grand duchess, Christine of Lorraine. He probably left Rome for Florence at the end of 1611 or the beginning of 1612.

Ternois's researches have shown that Callot's first years in Florence bear none of the marks of special favor from the court. It is true he had lodgings in the Uffizi, but so did many other humble court employees. He was in fact a junior artist, still studying to master his craft. The Florence where Callot established himself was culturally, politically, and economically only a shadow of its former self. As we have seen, Rome was the magnet which attracted the talented and ambitious. The Church had recovered from the staggering blows delivered to its power, prestige, and purse by the Protestant Reformation of the previous century. Stimulated by that able and extraordinarily energetic new order of Spanish origin, the Jesuits, and with the political and military backing of Spain, the Church was girding itself for its great counteroffensive, the Catholic Counter-Reformation. The intellectual and spiritual strain in the Counter-Reformation strongly influenced Callot, as we shall see later. But by nature he was not a militant and the hurlyburly of Rome was not to his liking. The quieter atmosphere of the quasi-backwater court of the Medicis at Florence was more suitable for his development and maturity.

The Grand Duchy of Tuscany was politically little more than a satellite of Spain, which largely dominated the entire Italian Peninsula. The Medici family ruled a state whose area had been greatly enlarged since the days of Cosimo and Lorenzo. Although far less powerful, the Medici were still one of the richest families in Europe. Indeed that fact, rather than political power based on territory, had been responsible for a network of Medici marriages through which the family still exercised considerable influence. The high point in that area in Callot's time was the marriage of Maria dei Medici (Marie de Médicis) to Henri IV of France. While the Medici court no longer attracted the most outstanding artists and literary figures, some of its wealth was still employed to maintain the outward appearance of splendor. Among the gifted people attracted to Florence were scientists and technologists who were used partly as teachers of the Medici children and partly as designers and organizers of court fêtes and festivities. The greatest names among these were Galileo, Cantagallina, and Giulio Parigi. The latter was one of those many-sided talents not uncommon at the time: architect, surveyor, military engineer, engraver, and designer, creator, and director of court spectacles, fêtes, and ceremonies. Of particular importance in Callot's education under Parigi in Florence was his study of drawing, particularly with the pen. It may well be assumed that he also obtained from his coworker in the ducal court, Galileo, some rudimentary instruction in mathematics and science. From some of his later works, particularly of battle scenes and sieges, and of crowds, it has not unreasonably been inferred that he was acquainted with Galileo's practical experiments with the recently invented telescope. But undoubtedly of even far greater importance was the thorough instruction he received from Parigi in the technique of etching. His first essays in that field—for Tempesta—in Rome were uninteresting. The researches of the scholar Ternois in the Uffizi collections have revealed how much Callot owed to Parigi. Indeed, so much of what we consider the essence of Callot's style—the precise drawing in minuscule, the graceful arrangement in his plates of very small figures, the pushing back of the space in his pictorial world to a great distance by insertion of tiny figures in the background—all of this came from Parigi. But he soon far surpassed his master.

Such were the main technical influences of the Florentine artists and craftsmen on Jacques Callot. These were to stand him in good stead for the rest of his relatively short life. After a few brief years in Florence he was a superb and outstanding master of the two principal printmaking techniques, engraving and etching. But mastery of technique alone was only one aspect of Callot's genius. The far more important aspect was the subject matter and pictorial content of his work. His taste, curiosity, and deep humanity were stimulated and developed during his years in Florence. Although his last years were spent in Lorraine and France, in all truthfulness he was essentially a product of Florence. After he left Florence to return to the north, he never ceased to dream of the city. From one of his few surviving letters—to a Florentine friend—we know that the possibility of returning to Florence was always in the back of his mind.

Nancy at the time of Callot, notwithstanding the muted brilliance of its small court, was a provincial backwater compared to Florence. While Florence itself was a backwater compared to Rome, it could live well off the enormous intellectual and artistic capital accumulated during the fifteenth and sixteenth centuries. It could live well materially, too. Ferdinand I, the last of the great Medici bankers, had expanded the family business. He had his trading stations all over the Mediterranean and his banking branches in most of the larger European cities. Such was the authority given by his wealth that he arranged without difficulty the marriage of his niece Maria dei Medici to Henri IV of France. The death of Ferdinand in 1609 brought the Medici economic expansion to a halt, but the fortune he left to his son Cosimo II was so vast that that well-educated and cultured weakling could indulge his taste for brilliant fêtes and pageants for more than a decade.

For the young Callot, living with fellow artists and scholars right in the Uffizi, the horizons expanded enormously. The daily access to the fabulous artistic treasure trove of the Medici family must have intoxicated the mind and senses of the gifted young artist. He had an opportunity to travel in and about the Tuscan realms of his master. He commemorated the semi-military aristocratic order of the Knights of St. Stephen which the Medicis had created and based on their newly developed port of Livorno. The knightly façade of this order, like that of the more famous and older Spanish orders of Calatrava, Alcántara, and Santiago, and like that of St. John of Jerusalem in Malta, was a respectable covering for keen economic interests. It is believed that Callot accompanied for a time one of the Medici naval forces which protected the family shipping and trade interests in the Mediterranean, particularly against the Turks. Such works as "The Slave Market" (No. 102) and *The Combat of Four Galleys* (No. 9) are thought to stem from that experience. These and works such as *The Medici Battles* (No. 2) and the landscapes (Nos. 76–82), particularly the *Medici Landscapes* (Nos. 78–82), were the competent professional bread-and-butter products of a paid retainer who celebrated the status and grandeur of his employers.

The works which ended his Florentine apprenticeship—the large "Ecce Homo" based on a Flemish engraving influenced by a work of Bosch, the "Hell" after Poccetti, and *The Great Passion* (Nos. 83–85)—were a reflection of the Baroque theatrical taste which the young Cosimo II was indulging to the utmost. These works were an appropriate introduction to other works directly connected with pageantry and the theater. During 1616 Callot etched a series of plates known as *The War of Love* (No. 3). The etchings record an elaborate pageant which took place in and around the Arno. The pageant included exotic vessels and machines designed by Parigi and a ballet featuring armed troops.

In 1616 Callot also produced another series known as *The War of Beauty* (No. 5). This work recorded a most elaborate opera full of extraordinary mythological floats and machines, also designed by Parigi. The work celebrated the engagement of Prince Federigo of Urbino to the Grand Duke Cosimo's sister, Claudia dei Medici. The same year Callot etched his *Intermèdes* (No. 6), three scenes from an opera-spectacle produced in the Pitti Palace for the marriage of Claudia and Federigo. These works and others done at about the same time, such as *The Tragedy "Soliman"* (No. 101) and "The Massacre of the Innocents" (No. 103) have increasing artistic interest. Already visible in them are the brilliant, witty, and completely theatrical ideas which shortly thereafter appeared in two of his first great works, *The Seven Deadly Sins* (Nos. 91–97) and the first version of "The Temptation of St. Anthony" (No. 8). At about this time, too, Callot produced the small engraving which some scholars consider be his self-portrait (No. 7).

It was during these years of rapidly maturing talent that Jacques Callot's pictorial imagination was enormously stimulated by the *commedia dell'arte*. This uniquely Italian phenomenon—a sort of popular street theater—reached its heyday during Callot's stay in Florence. The distinguishing characteristic of the *commedia dell'arte*, or "theater of the professionals," is that the players used an outline plot or scenario, but improvised all the dialogue. Many of the plots were rough descendants of the comedies of Terence and other Roman dramatists. The improvised dialogue was topical, satirical, and often extremely bawdy. There was a set of stock characters: Harlequin, Punchinello, Pantalone, Sylvia, the Doctor, the Captain, the Lovers, the Dirty Old Men, the Scheming Women, etc. It was truly a theater of professionals, for great skill was required to be effective in pieces which called for the multiple talents of dancer, singer, acrobat, juggler, and improvising satirical artist. We know from the Medici archives that many *commedia dell'arte* companies played in Florence during Callot's years in the city. This vital, popular theater, which inspired so many of the comedies of Molière, fascinated Jacques Callot. It stimulated him to etch many dozens of plates which give us the most complete pictorial record of its visual appearance. Its dance aspects had a special fascination for him. They inspired his early "Two Pantaloons" (No. 4); all 24 plates of one of his greatest works, the *Balli di Sfessania* (Nos. 104–127); and all of the *Gobbi*, or Dwarfs (Nos. 128–148). The last-named plates are not strictly part of the *commedia dell'arte* series but are based on the companies of performing dwarfs popular at the Medici court in Callot's time. Their performances, as we can see from Callot's etchings, imitated certain of the ballet and theatrical aspects of the *commedia*. Some writers see in one etching of the series (No. 139) a satirical self-portrait of the artist. In his plates called *Three Actors* (Nos. 86–88) he recorded the key characters of the *commedia*—Pantalone, the Lover, and the Captain. These are three of the greatest theatrical prints ever made.

During the middle period of his stay in Florence—1616 or 1617—Callot experimented with and brought to perfection a technique for engraving used by silversmiths and jewelers. This was the technique of etching silver with an acid which bit through lines drawn through a very hard varnish. Callot applied the technique to a copper plate and discovered that he was able to obtain the precision of the burin (the tool used to engrave metal directly) and the fineness of line permitted by the hard varnish. Scholars believe that during a visit to Siena he studied the black *graffiti* which Duccio, and later Beccafumi, had executed on the white part of the floor of the Cathedral. He was able to capture in his etching the variable widths of line which those earlier artists had achieved in their *graffiti*.

Callot's first series of etchings using these techniques was *The Caprices* (Nos. 26–75). The fifty plates in this set, each about the size of a visiting card, were etched through hard varnish. Such is the fineness and delicacy of the tiny figures in the middle ground and background of the etchings that it is generally assumed that Callot worked with a double magnifying glass. The series was Callot's first great success. It was dedicated to the seventeen-year-old Prince Lorenzo. Such was the delight of his Medici employers in this completely original work that they paid him a handsome cash bonus.

What Callot set out to do in the *Caprices*—some scholars consider the sixteen plates of the *Varie Figure* (Nos. 10–25) as a sort of dry run for the exercise—was to portray scenes of everyday life in and around Florence. The French scholar Sadoul, who has examined the plates with extraordinary affection and care, notes that the one depicting "Handball on the Piazza Santa Croce" (No. 75) manages to include in the general scene four or five hundred figures, twenty horses, and ten carriages or wagons. And all of this in a space which could be covered by four postage stamps! The series was truly a mirror of Tuscan modes and manners in the early seventeenth century, as Sadoul states.

A number of Soviet critics starting with Glikman have found in the *Caprices* a record of the contemporary class struggle, and in their author a precursor of "socialist realism." It is true that Callot's etchings show some of the miseries of a Tuscany in decline and decadence. But they show equally the common people enjoying themselves, in their own dances or as spectators of the sumptuous Medici pageants. There is no question concerning the wide-ranging eye of Callot. But it is misleading and unprofitable to endow this superb craftsman—at the same time both devout Christian and uncomplicated courtier—with a critical, analytical, and political mind.

Art historians and scholars have gone to great lengths to fit Callot into a neat and tidy niche as a Mannerist or as an Early Baroque artist. While his art has clear elements of each style, the tying of a label on Callot is by no means the last word on the subject. If we accept Arnold Hauser's summary of the socio-political bases of Mannerist and Baroque style—and it is difficult not to—how markedly Jacques Callot's art reflects the principal characteristics of these styles! In his seminal *Social History of Art*, Hauser writes:

> Mannerism is the artistic style of an aristocratic, essentially international cultured class, the early baroque the expression of a more popular, more emotional, more nationalistic trend. The more mature baroque triumphs over the more refined and exclusive style of mannerism, as the ecclesiastic propaganda of the Counter-Reformation spreads, and Catholicism again becomes a people's religion. The court art of the seventeenth century adapts the baroque to its specific needs; on the one hand it works up baroque emotionalism into a magnificent theatricality, and on the other, it develops its latent classicism into the expression of an austere and clear-headed authoritarianism. But in the sixteenth century mannerism is the court style par excellence. At

all the influential courts in Europe it is favoured against every other trend . . . . The mannerism of the courts is, especially in its later form, a uniform and universally European movement—the first great international style since the Gothic. The source of its universal influence is the absolutism which spreads all over Western Europe and the vogue of the intellectually interested and artistically ambitious court households. . . . By spiritualizing the human figure, the Gothic took the first great step in the development of modern expressionism, and now mannerism takes the second by breaking up the objectivism of the Renaissance, emphasizing the personal attitude of the artist and appealing to the personal experience of the onlooker.

In his last years in Florence Callot produced two more works inspired by popular festivities, "The Fan" (No. 89) and "The Fair at Impruneta" (Nos. 98–100). The former depicts, inside the extremely Baroque frame of a fan, a popular festival in and along the Arno. But this, too, was a sort of dry run for his "Impruneta," one of the greatest plates in the history of etching. In the small town of Impruneta, some eight miles south of Florence, a festival is held each 18th of October. The festival takes the form of a pilgrimage to worship a portrait of the Virgin Mary allegedly by St. Luke which is hung in the church constructed in the village by the rich Florentine family of the Buondelmonti. There is evidence that Callot was the guest of this family at a pilgrimage. It was the fair accompanying the pilgrimage which attracted Callot. A studious art historian has counted in Callot's large plate 1138 men and women, 45 horses, 67 asses, and 137 dogs (curiously he has omitted a not inconsiderable number of birds!). The "Impruneta" was dedicated to Cosimo II and was an enormous success. The grand duke gave Callot a medal as a mark of his esteem for this work. The artist clearly treasured this decoration for it appears in his engraved portrait by Van Dyck (frontispiece).

The "Impruneta" was the last major large work executed by Callot in Florence. Shortly after finishing it, he produced the small and exquisite etchings *Four Banquets*. But Callot's prospects in Florence were shortly to take a turn for the worse. Cosimo II died on 28 February 1621 after a series of illnesses. Already for some years the affairs of the Medicis had not thrived. The assassination of Concini, their man in Paris, was followed by a complete cessation of the repayment of the substantial loans which had accompanied Maria dei Medici when she married Henri IV. The beginning of the Thirty Years' War suddenly affected the Medici house in its most sensitive part, its purse. Cosimo II could not refuse the insistent demands for money from his uncle, Maximilian of Bavaria, the leader of the Catholic forces, and his brother-in-law, now Emperor. On Cosimo's death his mother, the devout Maria Maddalena, became regent. A Florentine memorialist of the day, Solerti, recorded the change of atmosphere at the court after the death of the grand duke:

> The death of the grand duke wiped out the brilliance of the Court. Under the regency of the austere and bigoted Grand Duchess Maria Maddalena one spoke only of masses, vespers, and sermons. The Jesuits were now the masters; popular festivities no longer had their former importance.

An economy drive started well before the burial of Cosimo II. Dozens of court officials and employees were dismissed. The records show that Callot was still on the payroll as late as 22 March 1621, but he had clearly made up his mind to return to Nancy after the death of his master.

Callot arrived back at his old home in Nancy toward the end of July or early in August, 1621. According to Félibien he had been promised fine appointments and commissions at the Lorraine court, but his homecoming was a disappointment. Notwithstanding the influence of his family, he found he had to break into a closed preserve largely dominated by his old friend and fellow artist, Deruet. The number of commissions from the court was limited and the prospects for the future not encouraging. This was a reflection of the deterioration of the economic situation of Lorraine. The Lorraine silver mines were exhausted. The first skirmishing and fighting of the Thirty Years' War interrupted the once profitable salt trade which had extended from the Alps to the North Sea, where it was important in the Dutch herring industry. Duke Henri II, a man of mediocre abilities, joined the legion of born losers and frantically urged on his court alchemists to find the philosopher's stone (his subsequent burning of those unsuccessful unfortunates demonstrated only too graphically the peculiar hazards of that profession). Callot's immediate disillusionment with Nancy is reflected in a letter he wrote shortly after his arrival in Nancy to Pandolfini, his former protector at the Medici court: "If I did not believe that one day I would return there [Florence], I would die."

During the several years it took Callot to establish himself in Nancy, he kept himself fully busy by remaking some of the great plates he had planned or executed in Florence: the "Impruneta," *The Caprices*, "The Massacre of the Innocents," etc. In Nancy he also made plates from the drawings he had brought with him from Florence: the *Gobbi*, the *Balli di Sfessania*, the *Great Passion*. From the first years of his return to Nancy we have *The Beggars* (Nos. 153–177), *The Nobility* (Nos. 191–194), and "The Fair at Gondreville" (No. 195).

He had plenty of time on his hands to carry out the works just referred to as, in fact, he was never able to break far into Deruet's preserve. From time to time he received a minor commission from the court or some other insignificant mark of respect. Later (in 1624) when Charles de Vaudémont became duke as Charles IV, the official fortunes of Callot improved somewhat. Some writers believe that Callot had known the future Charles IV in Florence and had actually traveled with him to Nancy in 1621 when the artist returned to his native city after his long absence in Italy. We do know that later Callot was permitted to dedicate his "Parterre de Nancy" (No. 196) and his "Carrière de Nancy" (Nos. 210 & 211) to Charles' wife, the Duchess Nicole.

In the meantime his fortunes outside the court improved. On 8 November 1623 he signed a contract of marriage with Catherine Kuttinger, the daughter of an able, driving family not unlike the Callots who had made money and got themselves ennobled. It is thought that the marriage was arranged by Callot's protectors, Henri Humbert, an adviser in the Lorraine court, and the bishop of Toul. For the latter he made his "St. Mansuy," in which the first martyred bishop of the nearby town of Toul is shown performing a miracle. The figure of the saint is thought to be a portrait of Callot's protector. The fortune which came with Catherine Kuttinger gave Callot independence. He was no longer dependent on court commissions and could devote himself to the production and sale of his own prints. The court must have become aware that their most distinguished artist could exist without their aid. Whether Callot let this be known overtly or not, we do not know. Probably through his friend and protector Humbert the message must certainly have got through to the highest circles. In 1626, almost as if out of the blue, Callot received a special allocation from the court treasury of the then considerable sum of two thousand francs "to give him the means to remain in his own country." From then on the official affairs of Callot looked up. The following year he worked with Deruet—whose portrait (No. 240) he later etched—on a court celebration for the Duchess of Chevreuse, who had been given refuge in Nancy after a series of treasonable and botched intrigues at the French court. Callot's part in the design of this festivity is witnessed by his remarkable series, *The Combat at the Barrier* (Nos. 200–209).

The first years back in Nancy must have been a shock for Callot. Apart from the smallness and lack of brilliance of everything at the provincial court, and the lack of patronage and recognition, the times were tragic and brutal. The political wisdom of the house of Lorraine seems to have been interred with the remains of Charles III. His inept successors involved themselves more and more in the great power struggle between the Bourbons and the Hapsburgs, as allies of the latter. In 1621 the German Protestant mercenary leader Count Mansfeld was in Lorraine helping the Bourbon Catholic cause. The following year he devastated Lorraine in the interests of Louis XIII. The rape, pillage, and wanton destruction committed by his unpaid soldiers gave the unfortunate country people a terrible reply to his oft-quoted question, "Do you believe my men can live on air?" Let the journal of one of Callot's contemporaries, Pierre Vuarin, bear witness to the horror of the times:

> In transit they [Mansfeld and his mercenaries] killed everyone they encountered as if it were open warfare. They burnt villages, raped girls and women, pillaged and damaged churches and altars, carried away everything of value and did unheard of damage even though His Highness [Duke Henri II] provisioned them. Further, they cut growing corn as feed for their horses which they stabled in churches. Everywhere they did infinite damage, stealing furniture and livestock, which they managed to discover even when hidden in the remoteness of woods.

To gain time for a counteroffensive against Mansfeld, and to keep him out of the Lorraine towns, Duke Henri II permitted the devastation of the countryside. The eventual counteroffensive by his young relative, the Prince of Phalsbourg, only worsened the condition of the country folk. Vuarin continues his grim chronicle:

> For five whole days they [Phalsbourg and his men] lived off the country, pillaging and extorting money like the enemy forces. . . . The poor villagers returning to their villages after the passing of the soldiery picked up infections from human and animal carcasses left behind by the marauders. A third died from dysentery and other infectious diseases in the villages through which the soldiers had passed.

Vuarin's "infectious diseases" meant not only syphilis and gonorrhoea, but the even more lethal plague, which continued to take its toll in Lorraine well after the death of Callot.

The contrast between the peace, quiet, and orderliness of his life in Florence and the close-at-hand horrors of his first years back in his native Lorraine must have weighed heavily on Callot. Out of this experience came *The Beggars*, both series of *Miseries of War* (Nos. 259–282), and *The Gypsies* (*Les Bohémiens*; Nos. 149–152). Sadoul has shown convincingly that these latter were unlikely to have been Gypsies. It is true that these wandering tribes of Indian origin began to appear in Europe as early as the fifteenth century, but the Lorraine archives show that such was the xenophobia just prior to the Thirty Years' War that they were persecuted and often killed. They would certainly never have been permitted to carry arms. The "Bohemians" might well have been Hungarian or Croatian mercenary marauders and camp followers, fellow travelers of Grimmelshausen's and Brecht's famous Mother Courage.

After the passing of Mansfeld the rich lands of Lorraine were able to make a relatively fast recovery in spite of the continued suffering of the peasants. For the next three years before his departure for the Lowlands the affairs of Callot must have thrived. The archives of Nancy show that early in 1624 he bought a fine house in the handsome Place de la Carrière. The records also show that he lent substantial sums of money on the security of land. During this period he was busy with his art, cultivating his connections with the religious orders, for whom he made several large and highly involved works. In these works he was a sort of graphic Góngora. Artistically they have been called Jesuit opera. But at the same time he produced a series of other works in which he could express himself spontaneously and without playacting.

In the spring of 1624 he produced what might be considered a northern version of his famous "Impruneta" plate. This was his equally famous "Fair at Gondreville" (No. 195). Less of a *tour de force* than the crowded "Impruneta," the smaller work with its greater economy of means is a masterpiece pointing the way toward Rembrandt's superlative works later in the century. The perceptive French critic Sadoul, noting that the plate was etched shortly after the Mansfeld horrors, suggests that it might well be called "The Pleasures of Peace." The Nancy scholar Marot has shown that the place depicted was in fact not Gondreville but the small village of Xeuilley, close to Bainville-sur-Madon where Callot was a property owner.

From this same period of peace we have Callot's *Lorraine Nobility* (Nos. 191–194), in which some scholars claim to recognize members of the Callot family. The dress, mien, and bearing of his figures suggest that they are ennobled bourgeoisie whose pleasures and values come from peace and not war. Two other works illustrating the arts of peace are his "Two Ladies Standing" and "The Winder and the Spinner" (No. 178). During this same period he also produced one of his finest religious works, *The Small Passion* (Nos. 179–190).

The year 1624 had its share of events for Callot. Duke Henri II died. The troubles which might have ensued because his successor was his sixteen-year-old daughter Nicole were dramatically resolved the following year when her husband (and cousin) Charles assumed all power as Charles IV with the backing of the Hapsburgs. As we shall see, this spoilt prince brought nothing but disaster to Lorraine. His judgment had been warped by the prestige acquired through his almost fortuitous connection with the Catholic victory at the Battle of the White Mountain outside Prague. The cast of his mind as civilian ruler is shown by his first edicts, which were directed against blasphemy, prostitution, concubinage, dying without taking the sacraments, the holding of markets on holy days, and the bringing up of children outside the established religion. Much more serious for Callot was the death of his protector, the bishop of Toul. These events seem to have had little effect on Callot's art. At the time of Henri II's death and during the somewhat comic-opera activities to resolve the problem of the succession, Callot was busy on one of his great plates, " The Parterre (or Garden) of Nancy" (No. 196). At about the same time he produced his charming small work "Pandora" (No. 198). Some critics believe he was also busy at this time on his "Great Hunt" (No. 90), a work which seems to owe some formal debt to his fellow Lorraine artist, Bellange, and to his former master Tempesta. One scene which owes nothing to any other artist but much to a wit which admired the *commedia dell'arte* is the group of peasants laughing at the discomfited noble who has just been thrown from his mount.

The economic independence of Callot coinciding with the dearth of interesting and profitable court commissions and the dynastic uncertainties were probably instrumental in persuading him to accept the invitation of the Infanta Isabella, Spanish regent of the Lowlands, to commemorate the capture of Breda. This important Dutch fortress in what is now southern Holland was defended by Maurice of Nassau against a Spanish besieging force of mixed nationality led by the Genoese banker-general Spinola. The Spanish Hapsburgs, cut off from reality for many years, believed that their capture of Breda was the beginning of the end of their troubles. It was in fact the actual reverse. Had it not been for the commemoration of the event in Velázquez's magnificent painting *The Lancers* and Callot's enormous panoramic etching *The Siege of Breda* (Nos. 212–215), it would have sunk into the oblivion of other futile military acts. Callot is thought to have visited the Lowlands in the autumn of 1625 not long after Breda capitulated and to have returned to Nancy in the early summer of 1626. He worked on the six great plates of *The Siege of Breda* for several years. The great work appeared in 1628. Spinola had employed several Florentine military engineers who had been friends of Callot at the Medici court. He benefited from their technical advice. It is interesting to compare the work of Velázquez with that of Callot. The Spaniard produced a magnificent painting whose atmosphere is redolent of that nonexistent chivalry in which Spanish rulers were still imprisoned. Callot's work is a panorama of war as it really was: a little color, bravado, and panache, but a great deal of violence, terror, and suffering.

Callot's travels and work connected with *The Siege of Breda* brought him into contact with a world whose personalities were far richer and more powerful than those of Nancy. A man as intelligent as Callot was probably aware that his Nancy patrons were scarcely worthy of him. His travels abroad—he made several visits to the Lowlands between 1625 and 1627—and his meeting with artists who enjoyed the lavish patronage of the Brussels court, including in all possibility Van Dyck and Rubens, probably emphasized this awareness.

Such was the reputation of Callot during the latter part of 1627 when he was finishing his *Siege of Breda*—he signed a contract in Nancy on 29 October 1627 with the Paris dealer Pierre Chevalier giving him the right to handle sales—that his fame spread widely. During this period Louis XIII and Richelieu were undertaking the military and naval siege of the French Huguenot strongholds, the Isle of Ré and La Rochelle. Some courtiers carrying out their function of perpetuating the glory of their masters, must have drawn the attention of Louis XIII and his chief minister Richelieu to the—for them particularly interesting—talents of Callot. The Isle of Ré was reoccupied by the French in November 1627 and La Rochelle capitulated on 28 October 1628. In the middle of 1628 Callot's six great plates of *The Siege of Breda* appeared. The negotiations for the two French sieges dragged on for some time and involved Callot in many visits to France, particularly to Paris.

The wealth which came to Callot through his marriage and his artistic success enabled him to engage in a continuing series of profitable investments, mostly in real estate—farms and estates devastated by the war—in and around Nancy. For a man with capital and the acumen of the ennobled bourgeois, the opportunities were excellent. He must have been extremely busy. The great siege plates contain thousands of figures requiring thousands of hours of highly concentrated, painstaking work. While he was working on these plates he found time for other studies. Some of these were done for himself, others were commissioned. Among these works are the magnificent "Disembarking of Troops" (No. 220), "Crossing the Red Sea" (No. 221), the moving "St. Sebastian" (No. 233), and the portrait of Charles Delorme (No. 222). The latter was physician to the French court and had undoubtedly pushed the cause of Callot in the highest circles in Paris. It was during his many visits to Paris that Callot etched his two large views of Paris, "The Pont Neuf" (No. 232) and "The Louvre" (No. 231). About this time he executed a number of works for himself or for his friends and connections among the Franciscans, including "St. John on Patmos" (No. 197), "The Resurrection" (No. 234), "The Assumption of the Virgin Mary" (No. 235), *The Mysteries of the Passion* (No. 236), and the remarkable and quite unusual "Benediction" (No. 216). This work of *ténébrisme* and its companion piece "Le Brelan," or gambling den (No. 217), are strikingly similar to the art of Callot's compatriot de La Tour and his Mannerist predecessors. These two works and the 27 plates of the *Lux Claustri* (Nos. 218 & 219) show how truly Callot was a man of his times. "The Benediction" reflects the simple piety of a man who clearly admired the practical, down-to-earth decency of the Franciscans. The "Brelan" shows Callot as a man of the world, the slightly shabby world of the fringe nobility and adventurers who lived by their wits off cards and women. And the *Lux Claustri* illustrated the obscurantist and semi-mystical symbology of a world which could truly believe in the existence of a "philosopher's stone." This work was commissioned by the Franciscans with whom, as we know, Callot had close links.

These last works must have taken up very little of the time he chiefly devoted to the enormous labors which produced the two great French sieges, *The Siege of the Isle of Ré* and *The Siege of*

La Rochelle (Nos. 223–230). These etchings are the highly competent productions of a skilled professional, but they are not nearly as interesting as the Breda work, one of the greatest anti-war works ever conceived by an artist.

It is interesting to note that during the years when Callot was busy with his enormous plates covering the three sieges, Nancy was a center of intense anti-French intrigues. High-ranking courtiers contested the increasingly successful efforts of Louis XIII, aided by Richelieu, to establish uncontested, absolutist power. The intrigues and conspiracies were led by Gaston of Orleans, the brother of Louis XIII, and the beautiful and talented Duchess of Chevreuse. Their intrigues involved them in treasonable contacts with the English, their resistance to the royal French encroachment on their feudal power overriding such—to them—minor matters as national loyalty. The conspirators were blatant in their contestation of royal power. The Duchess became the mistress of the Duke of Buckingham, the chief minister of Charles I. Overplaying their hands and underestimating the ability of Richelieu, Gaston and Mme. de Chevreuse had to flee from France. As we have seen, they sought refuge at the court of Charles IV in Nancy. Their intrigues were theatrical but more the theater of terror than of tragicomedy, for they had planned the murder of Richelieu.

Duke Charles IV fell in love with Mme. de Chevreuse and, as already mentioned, organized a series of fêtes and festivals for her and for Gaston of Orleans. While Callot was on good terms with these noble visitors of his master—he engraved a number of plates of European coins for Gaston (No. 237)—he was aloof from their political activities. It was just as well. Gaston of Orleans and his followers and friends such as Charles IV openly joined with the Hapsburgs against France. These intrigues finally brought the French into Lorraine, drove Gaston to seek refuge in Brussels, and finally, after the capture of Nancy by Louis XIII and Richelieu, forced Charles IV to abdicate in favor of his brother, the young Cardinal Nicolas-François. According to Félibien, shortly after their entry into Nancy on 25 September 1633, Louis XIII and Richelieu asked Callot to commemorate their capture of his city by executing a large work in the manner of his three other sieges. Callot is reported to have replied that he would cut off his right thumb before doing such a shameful thing. So impressed was Louis XIII by this forthrightness that he offered the artist a handsome allowance if he would enter his service in Paris. This, too, Callot was able to refuse, his local patriotism greatly fortified by economic independence.

The affluence which came to Callot through his marriage and which increased when he received the lucrative commission to commemorate the siege of Breda seems not only to have spurred him on to greater efforts but to have sharpened his sensibility. His last years of great prosperity made him the reverse of complacent. Indeed the wealth which came to him in what were to be the last years of his life made him only too self-conscious of the pleasures of peace. It might well be said that he never recovered from *The Siege of Breda*. As he did his research for this great work and studied the terrible phenomenon of war at first hand in Lorraine, the Lowlands, and elsewhere, the whole frightful institution was fermenting in his mind. Out of this deep and shattering experience came one of the first and clearest indictments of war as the most pointless and destructive of all human activities. The two series of etchings on this all-consuming subject, *The Miseries of War*, were both probably produced in 1632–1633. The small series of six plates Nos. 259–264)—technically an incomparably finished rehearsal—were etched first but did not appear until 1635. The large series of eighteen plates (Nos. 265–282) were published in 1633. From approximately the same period, when Callot's sensitive personality must have been seething from his contemplation of that ghastly institution which imposed an order on mankind solely for destructive purposes, came a series of other brilliant works: the *Cavalry Combats* (Nos.

244 & 245), *Military Exercises* (Nos. 246–258), and "The Tortures" (No. 315).

The culmination of these studies of utter irrationality was Callot's second version of "The Temptation of St. Anthony" (No. 327). It is interesting to compare the two large plates devoted to this subject for the light they shed on his intellectual and human development. The first plate appears to be a design for a Medici court entertainment, but its connection with the actual world is real. It is witty, satirical, and graceful. Some scholars are certain that it was never reproduced while Callot was in Florence for fear that its social criticism might have been recognized. The second is a bitter indictment of war, though its message is apt to be missed because Callot's precise, choreographed horrors, in the Baroque language of his time, can be mistaken for a gigantic and fantastic ballet.

After Callot's return to Nancy in the spring of 1631 he remained in the city until his death a few years later. His health deteriorated and he began to suffer from the ravages of a stomach ailment which Georges Sadoul diagnosed as cancer but which was more probably peptic ulcer. Premonitions of incipient death may well have directed his art toward religious subject matter. We know that on his return he resumed the normally close relationship he enjoyed with the Franciscans. Then, too, the terrible epidemic of plague which ravaged Nancy in 1630–1631 and which carried off his father, would have turned his thoughts to religious themes. In any case, in his last busy years he found time to produce a series of outstanding religious works. A number of them, such as *The Life of the Virgin* (Nos. 283 & 284), were commissioned by the Franciscans. In 1631 appeared his magnificent series of sixteen plates known as *The Great Apostles* (Nos. 241–243), followed shortly after by the set of *Small Apostles* including "The Death of Judas" (Nos. 299–314). The smaller version of this subject, as well as *The New Testament* (Nos. 328–337), *The Prodigal Son* (Nos. 316–326—perhaps autobiographical as the Callot arms appear on several buildings), and the *Images of All the Saints* (Nos. 238 & 239), were etched during his last years but not all of them were published while he was alive. These works were highly profitable for Callot and his successors, *The Saints* in particular. This work consisted of 123 plates covering 489 subjects, each print being sold separately. Such was their success that print dealers soon put counterfeit versions on the market. Another brilliant series of etchings which was done at this time but which appeared only after his death was the *Fantasies* (Nos. 285–298).

Félibien gives an interesting account of the orderly and dignified way in which Callot organized his life and work in his last years:

> He got up early every morning and went for a walk outside the city with his eldest brother. On his return he attended Mass and then worked until lunch time. Immediately afterward he made a number of visits in order to have a respite from work. He then worked until evening, generally having some of his friends present to chat with him as he worked.

As Callot's stomach disorder worsened he seems to have driven himself into harder and harder work as if aware that he was in a race with death. His productivity during his last years was formidable. This only worsened his condition, which called for absolute rest and mental peace. The latter was denied to him by the turn of history. During 1634 Louis XIII and Richelieu established their power in the whole of Lorraine. Every notable was forced to take an oath of loyalty to Louis XIII. This evidently weighed heavily on the Callots, who owed their position entirely to the generosity and patronage of the ducal house, although Jacques Callot himself had scarcely been a direct and noticeable beneficiary. But loyalty to this house was clearly bitten into their souls. They resisted for as long as it was possible. Richelieu's military governor Brassac threatened to expel from the duchy, and confiscate the property of, anyone not taking the oath of allegiance before the deadline of 17 December 1634. Jacques and his elder brother Jean finally took the oath of loyalty on 9 December 1634. Their names are almost the last on the list. The tensions of the events created an emotional climate which could not have been worse for Callot's illness. It may reasonably be assumed that Callot's ulcer followed the classic pattern of a flare-up in spring. In the spring of the following year the flare-up may have perforated the wall of his stomach. On 15 March he made his will. He died on 25 March 1635, in all likelihood from peritonitis caused by the haemorrhage from the blood vessels in his perforated stomach.

The work which Callot was engaged on and left unfinished when he died was "The Little Trellis" (No. 338). In what in reality is his brilliantly illuminating epitaph, the great artist states his philosophy in graceful pictorial terms. The plate he was working, etched after his death, reveals a peaceful summer scene in which some elegantly clad bourgeois enjoy an outdoor meal under a trellis while several members of the group dance to the measure of two musicians. It is essentially a happy scene of peace and security.

Those who seek in Jacques Callot a conscious revolutionary are searching for a person who did not exist, and who could not have existed, history being the stubborn thing it is. Although ennobled, Callot was essentially a member of the bourgeoisie, a class which one great philosopher noted was to play an eminently revolutionary role in the following century. But in Callot's time this role was embryonic. He was a notable member of a class which had become enmeshed in the productive characteristics of property in contrast to the feudal nobility, who were solely concerned with its consumption and status aspects. For a humanist bourgeois such as Callot the senseless and wanton destruction of property which he had seen at its height in the Thirty Years' War was the greatest of evils. The bourgeois message of "The Little Trellis" is that property is to be enjoyed in moderation and dignity but that this is only possible if there is peace. Like any intelligent, sensitive bourgeois, as much as he believed in the life hereafter, Callot was also completely in favor of enjoying the simple, orderly pleasures which ownership of property made possible in the here and now.

Howard Daniel

Bibliography

Baldinucci, Filippo. *Notizie de'professori del disegno.* Florence, 1681.

Bechtel, Edwin De T. *Jacques Callot.* New York, 1955.

Braudel, Fernand. *Civilisation matérielle et capitalisme (XVe–XVIIIe siècles).* Paris, 1967.

Bruwaert, Edmond. *Vie de Jacques Callot, graveur lorrain.* Paris, 1912.

Calmet, Dom Augustin. *Histoire ecclésiastique et civile de Lorraine.* Nancy, 1728.

———. *Bibliothèque lorraine, ou histoire des hommes illustres qui ont fleuri en Lorraine.* Nancy, 1751.

Choux, J., Taveneaux, R., and Vahl, A. *Études sur Jacques Callot.* Nancy, 1968.

Clark, George N. *The Seventeenth Century.* London, 1960.

BIBLIOGRAPHY

Daniel, Howard. *The World of Jacques Callot.* New York, 1950.

———. *The Commedia dell'Arte and Jacques Callot.* Sydney, 1965.

Duchartre, Pierre-Louis. *La Commedia dell'Arte.* Paris, 1955.

Elliott, John H. "The Decline of Spain," in *Crisis in Europe.* New York, 1967.

Félibien, A. *Entretiens sur les vies et sur les ouvrages des plus excellens peintres anciens et modernes.* Trévoux, 1727.

Focillon, Henri. *Jacques Callot ou le microcosme*, in *Maîtres de l'Estampe.* Paris, 1969.

Glikman, Aleksandr. *Jacques Callot.* Leningrad, 1959.

Hauser, Arnold. *The Social History of Art.* New York, 1951.

Hobsbawm, Eric J. "The Crisis of the Seventeenth Century," in *Crisis in Europe.* New York, 1967.

Le Roy Ladurie, E. *Climat et Récoltes. Annales.* Paris, 1960.

Levertin, Oscar. *Jacques Callot. Vision du microcosme.* Paris, 1935.

Lieure, Jules. *Jacques Callot.* Paris, 1924–1927.

Lubinskaya, Alexandra D. *French Absolutism: the crucial phase 1620–1629.* Cambridge, 1968.

Mannheimer, V. *Die Balli von Jacques Callot.* Potsdam, 1921.

Marot, Pierre, Philippe, A., Pariset, F.-G., and Weigert, Roger-Armand. *Jacques Callot et les peintres et graveurs lorrains du XVIIe siècle.* Nancy, 1935.

Marot, Pierre. *Jacques Callot d'après des documents inédits.* Paris, 1939.

Mayor, A. Hyatt. Article in *Encyclopaedia of World Art.* New York, 1960.

Meaume, Edouard. *Jacques Callot.* Paris, 1860.

Mousnier, Roland. *Les XVIe et XVIIe siècles.* Paris, 1954.

Nasse, Hermann. *Jacques Callot.* Leipzig, 1909.

Parisot, Robert. *Histoire de Lorraine.* Paris, 1922.

Plan, Pierre-Paul. *Jacques Callot, maître graveur.* Brussels and Paris. 1911.

Sadoul, Georges. *Jacques Callot, miroir de son temps.* Paris, 1969.

Singer, Hans W. Article in *Thieme-Becker.* Leipzig, 1911.

Steinberg, S. H. *The "Thirty Years War."* London, 1966.

Tapié, Victor-L. *La France de Louis XIII et Richelieu.* Paris, 1952.

Ternois, Daniel. *L'Art de Jacques Callot.* Paris, 1962.

Trevor-Roper, Hugh R. "The General Crisis of the Seventeenth Century," in *Crisis in Europe.* New York, 1967.

Watelet, C.-H. Article "Gravure" (section "Eau-forte") in the *Encyclopédie* of Diderot and D'Alembert. Paris, 1757–1767.

Weigert, Roger-Armand. *Jacques Callot.* Paris, 1935.

The indispensable works on Callot are: *Meaume*, *Lieure* (the standard catalogue), *Ternois* (the definitive art-historical study), and *Sadoul.*

List of Illustrations

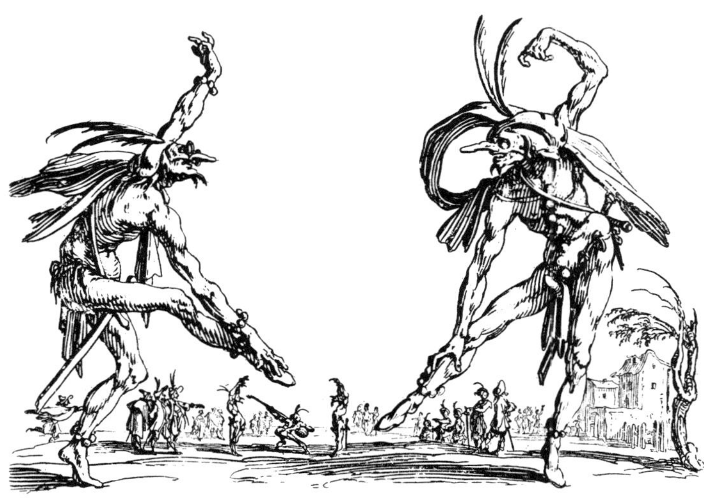

DIMENSIONS ARE EXPRESSED IN MILLIMETERS, HEIGHT BEFORE WIDTH.
THE L NUMBERS ARE THOSE ASSIGNED TO CALLOT'S PRINTS
IN THE CATALOGUE RAISONNÉ COMPILED BY LIEURE.

THE ILLUSTRATIONS

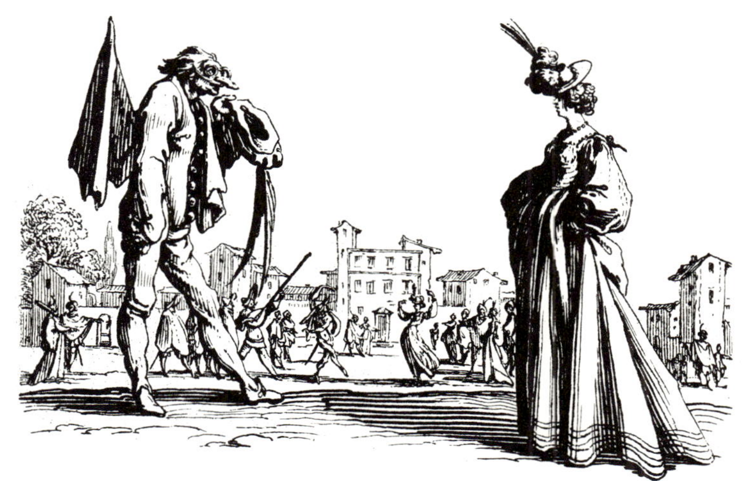

An attempt has been made to arrange the illustrations in chronological order, although the dates of numerous Callot prints are disputed. In general we have followed the sequence of the chronology-based Lieure catalogue of Callot's work, departing from this sequence only where later scholarship has fixed a firm date differing from Lieure's.

The Lieure numbers (L. 1, etc.) are given in the List of Illustrations, as are the dimensions of each print (expressed in millimeters, height preceding width).

Where no specific ownership credit is given, the illustration is from an original print in the Lessing J. Rosenwald Collection of the National Gallery in Washington.

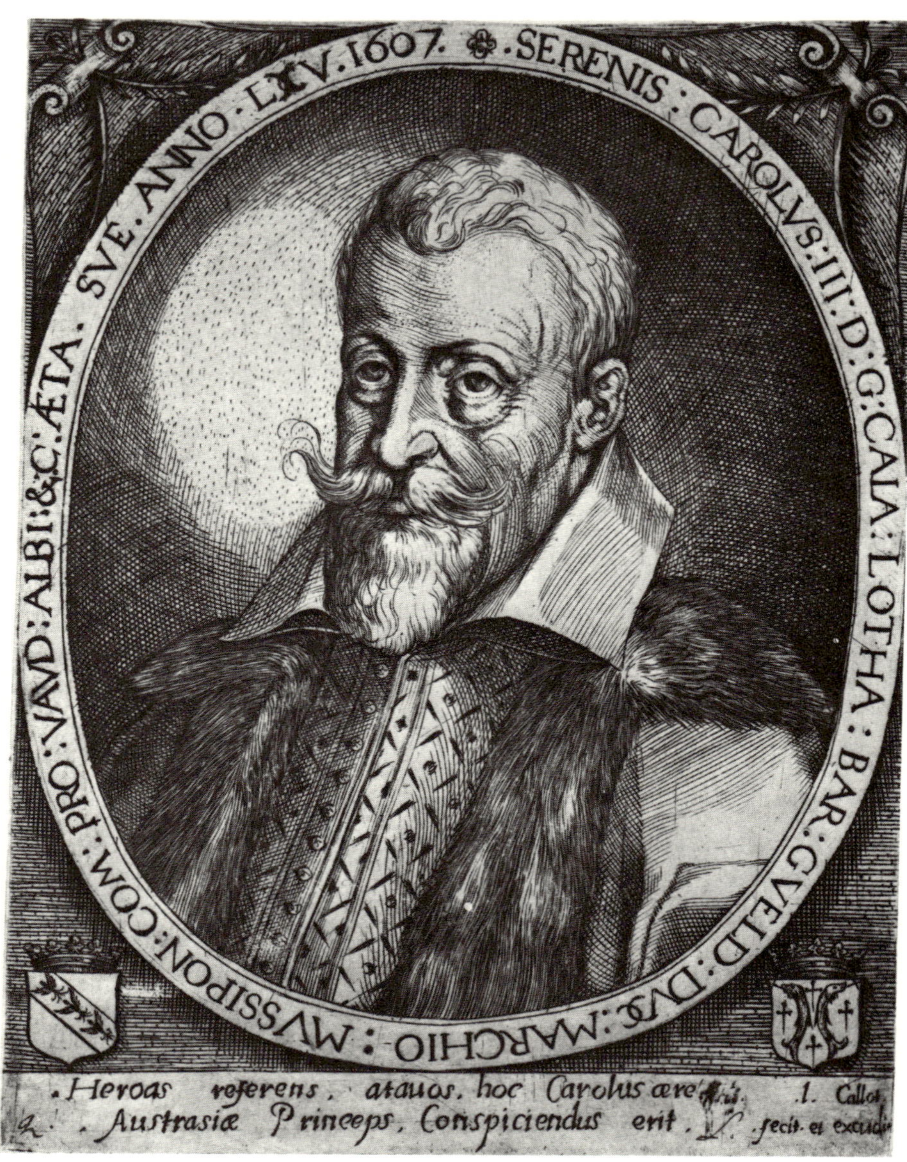

1 Portrait of Duke Charles III of Lorraine. Engraving, 1607. The Latin couplet reads: "Charles, ruler of Austrasia [name of northeastern France in Merovingian times], who boasts of heroic ancestors, will [always] be visible on this bronze [plate]." (Courtesy Trustees of the British Museum)

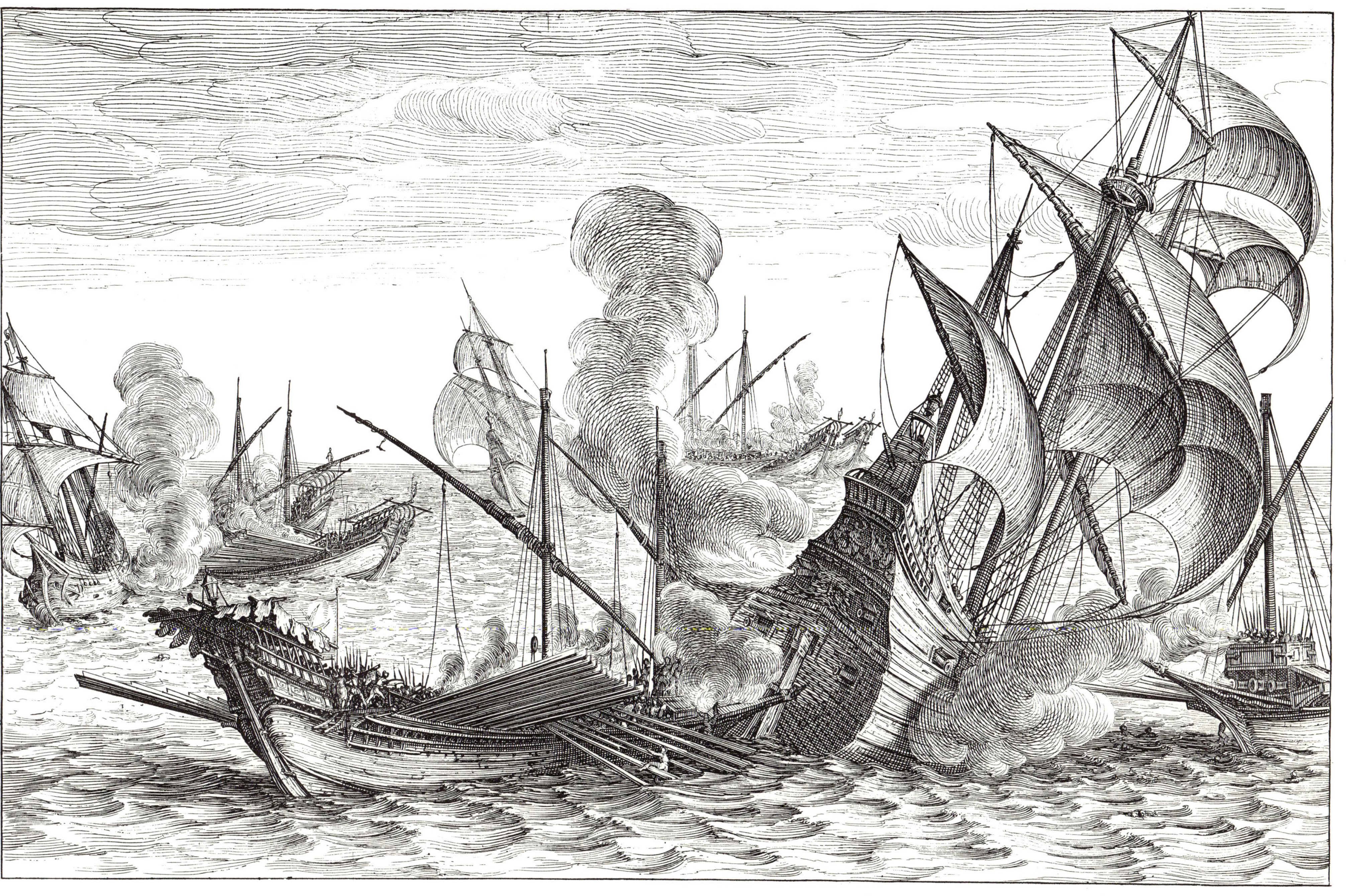

2 From *The Life of Ferdinand I de' Medici* (or, *The Medici Battles*), a series of 15 engravings and 1 etching, 1615–1619: Sea Battle in 1602. Etched (1617?). (National Gallery, Washington, R. L. Baumfeld Collection)

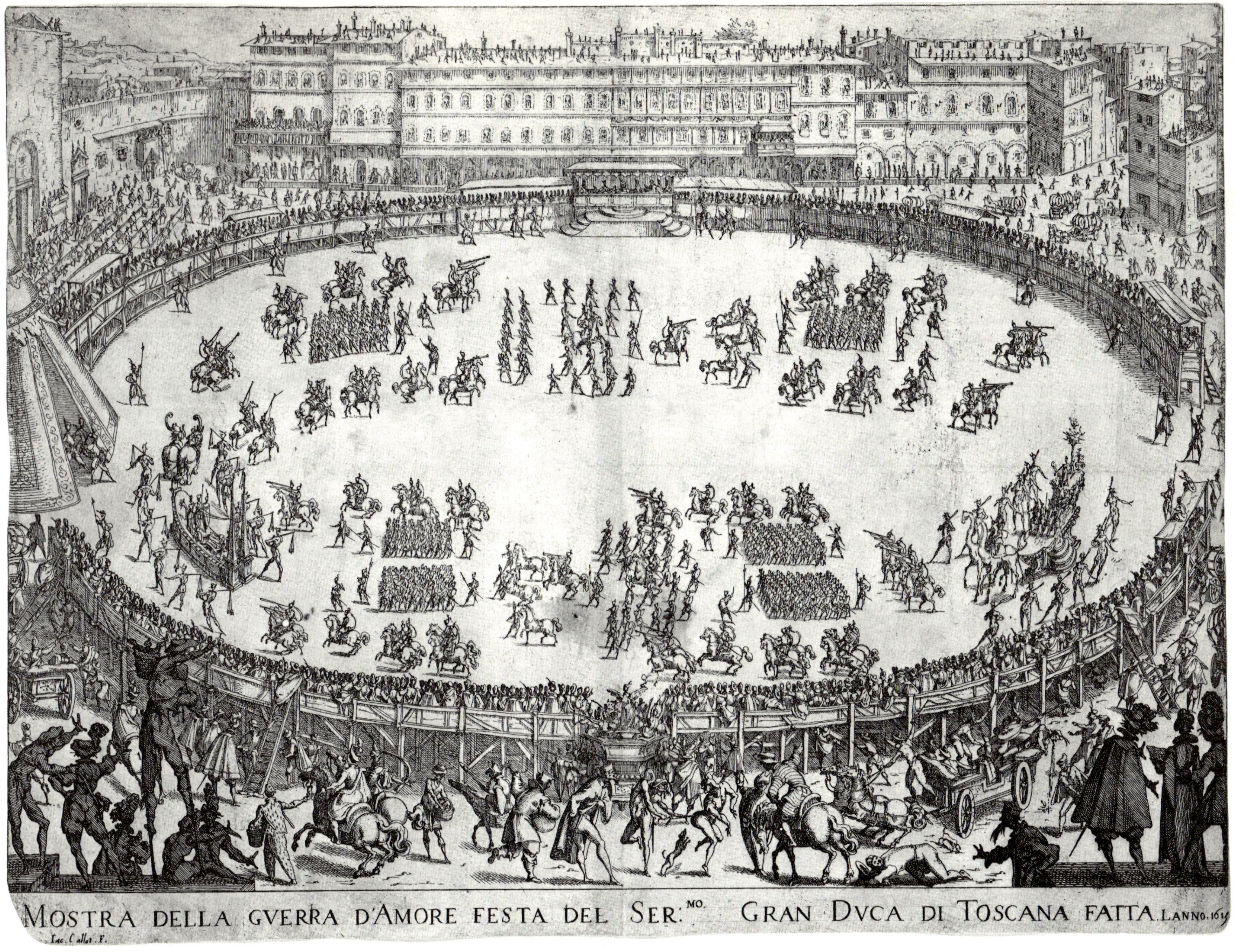

3 From *The War of Love* (*Guerra d'Amore*, a Carnival pageant of the Medici court), a series of 4 etchings, 1616 (1615 by earlier calendar): The Procession with the Floats of Africa and Asia.

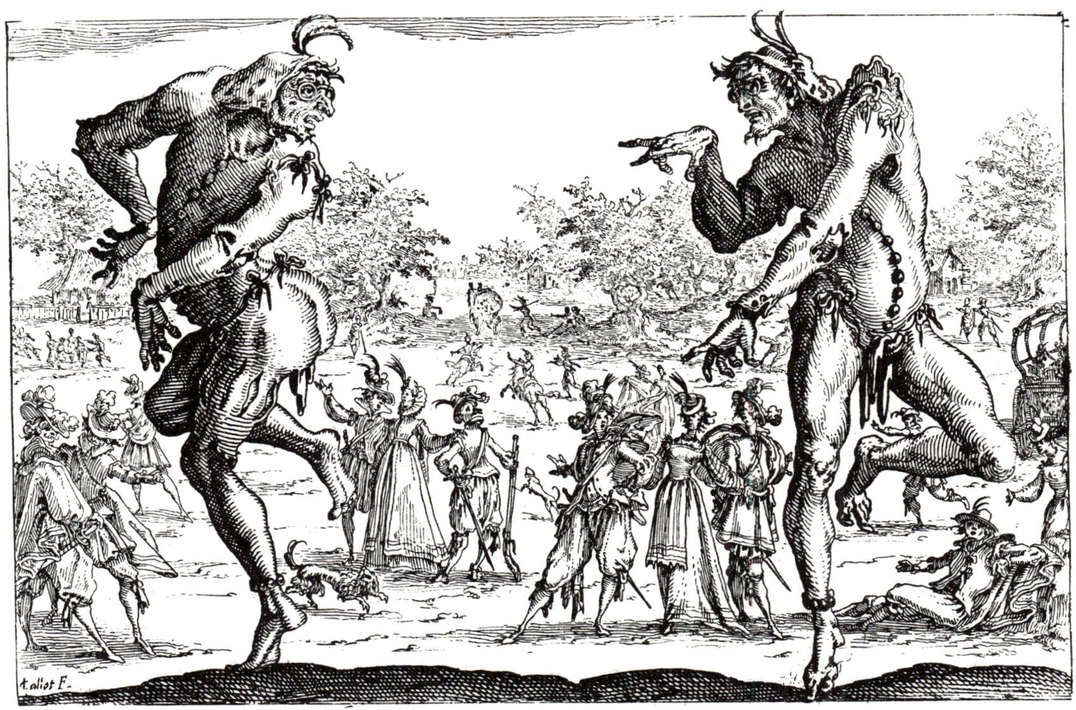

4 The Two Pantaloons. Etching, 1616.

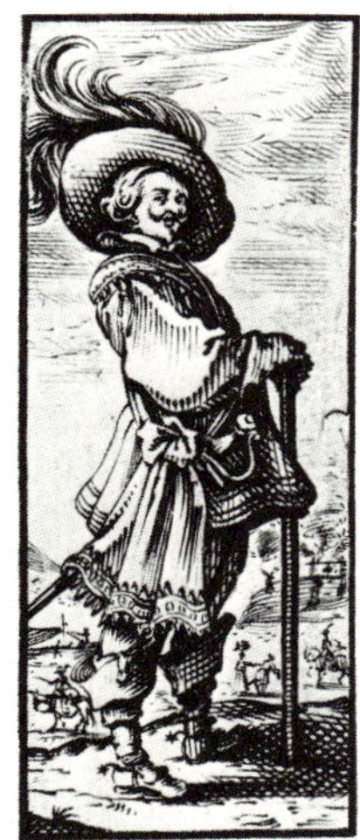

7 Small Self-Portrait (?). Engraving, 1616. (From the impression in the Musée des Beaux-Arts, Nancy)

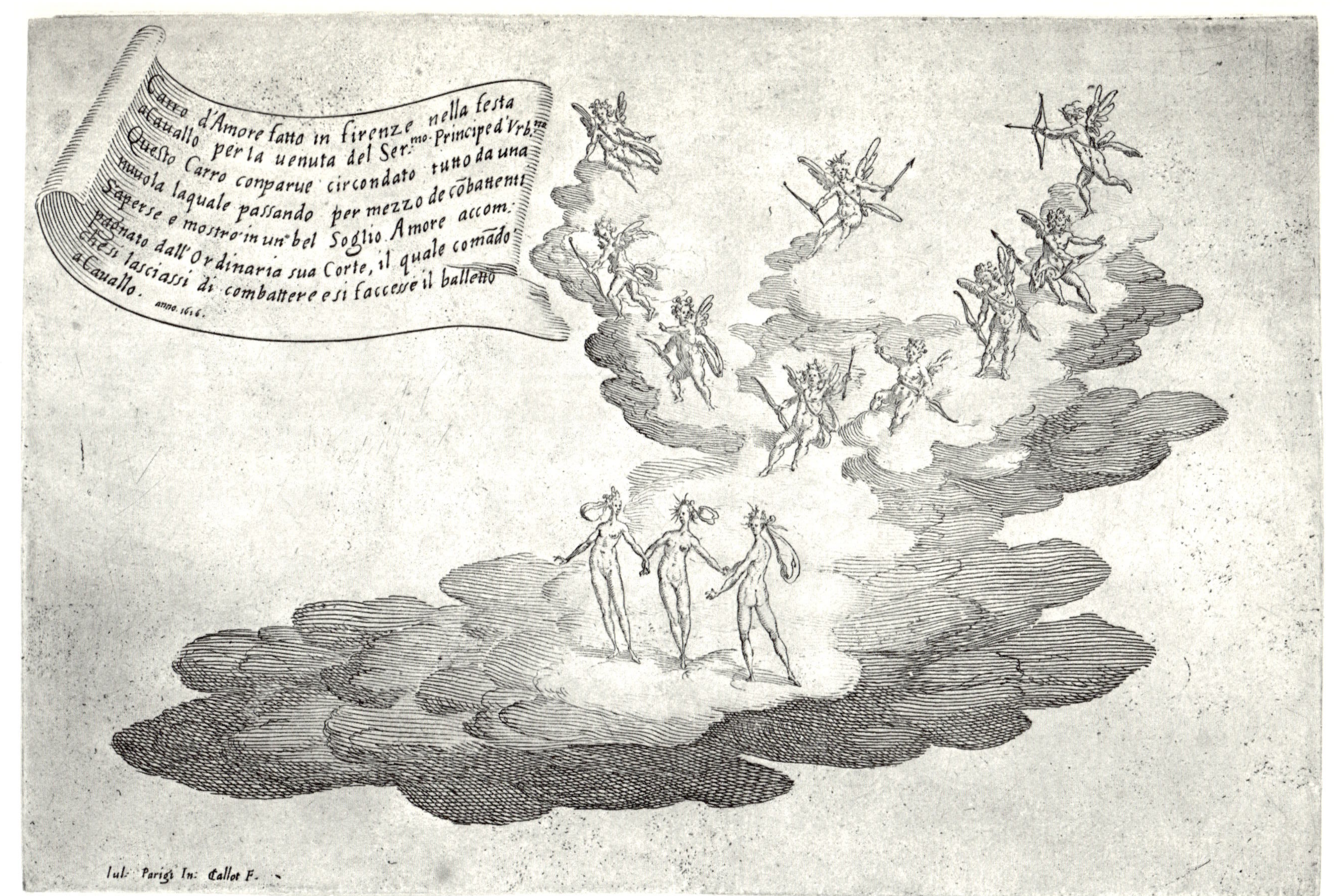

5 From *The War of Beauty* (*Guerra di Belezza*, Florentine pageant, October 1616), a series of 6 etchings, 1616: The Float of Love. The inscription reads: "The Float of Love, made in Florence in the equestrian pageant celebrating the visit of His Highness, the Prince of Urbino. This float made its appearance completely enveloped in a cloud, which, passing through the midst of the combatants, opened to reveal Love seated on a beautiful throne and accompanied by his customary courtiers. Love commanded the combat to cease and the equestrian ballet to begin."

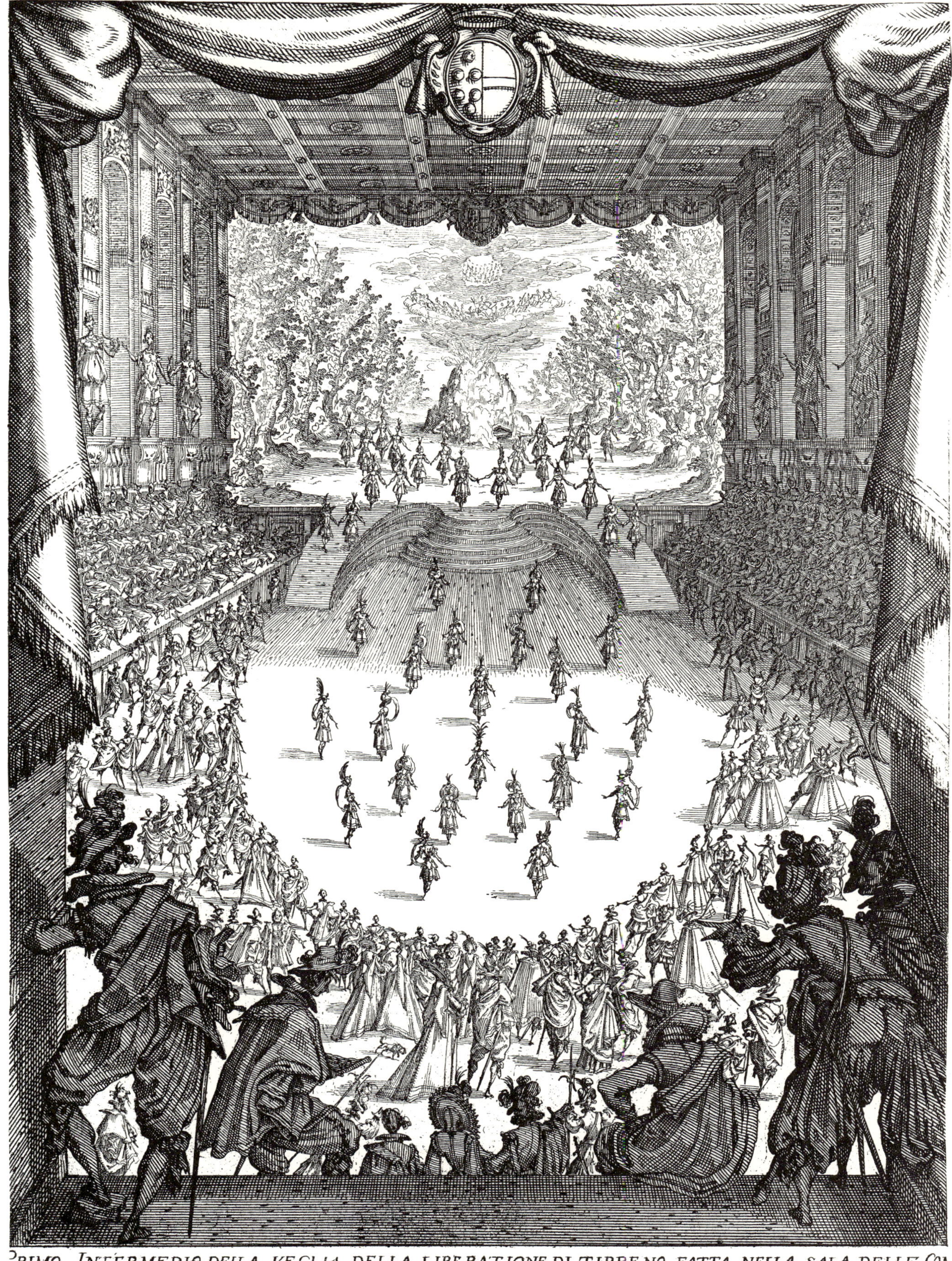

6 From *The Three Interludes* (or, *Les Trois Intermèdes*, scenes from a Carnival opera-ballet of the Medici court), a series of 3 etchings, 1617 (1616 by earlier calendar): Typhoeus Beneath the Mountains of Ischia. The inscription reads: "First interlude of the evening entertainment *The Liberation of Tyrrhenus*, performed in the theater of His Highness, the Grand Duke of Tuscany, at Carnival, 1616. In which is depicted the mountains of Ischia with the giant Typhoeus beneath them." (Howard Daniel Collection)

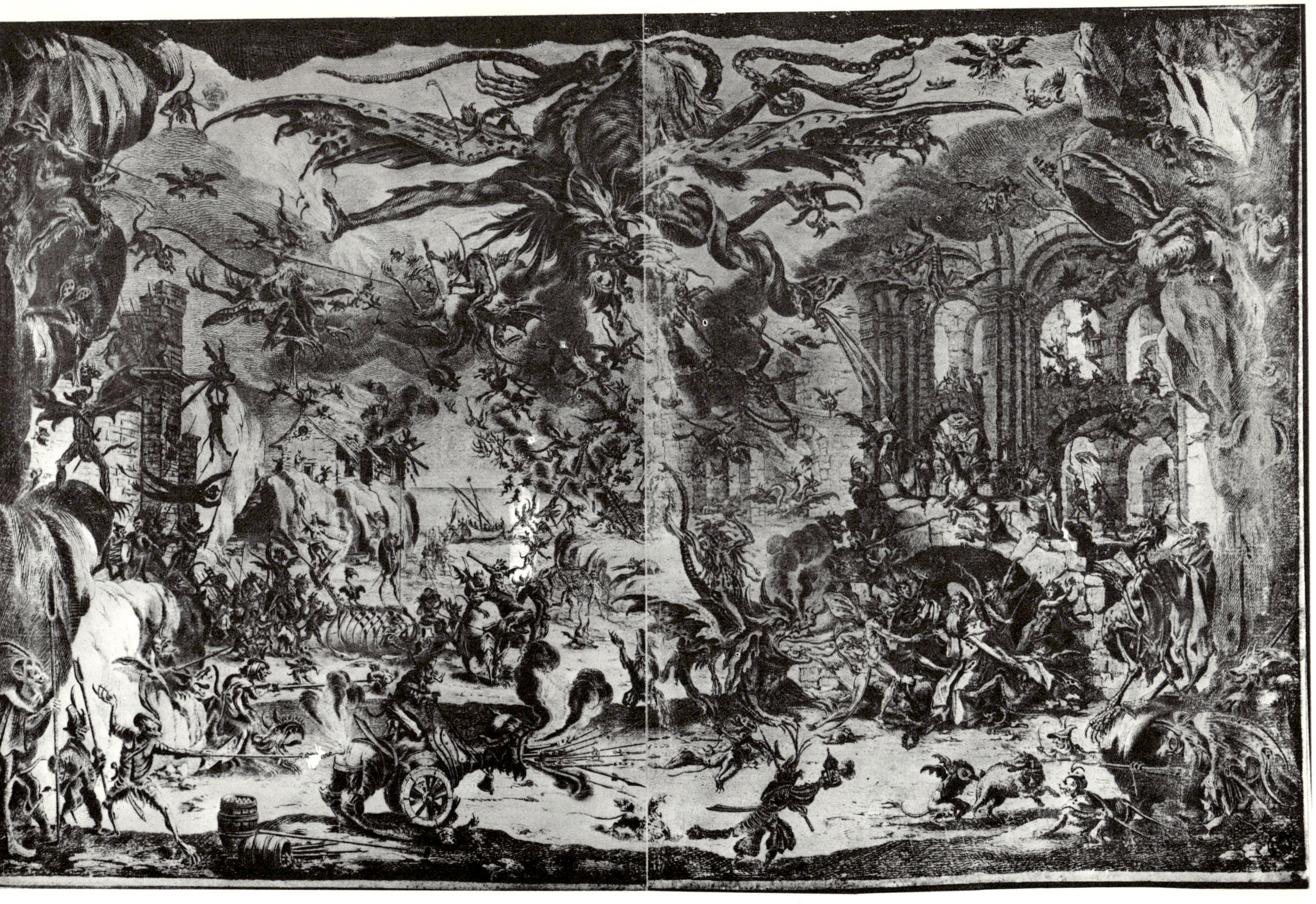

8 The Temptation of St. Anthony (first version). Etching, 1617. Impression pulled after plate was damaged and cut down. (Cabinet des Estampes, Bibliothèque Nationale)

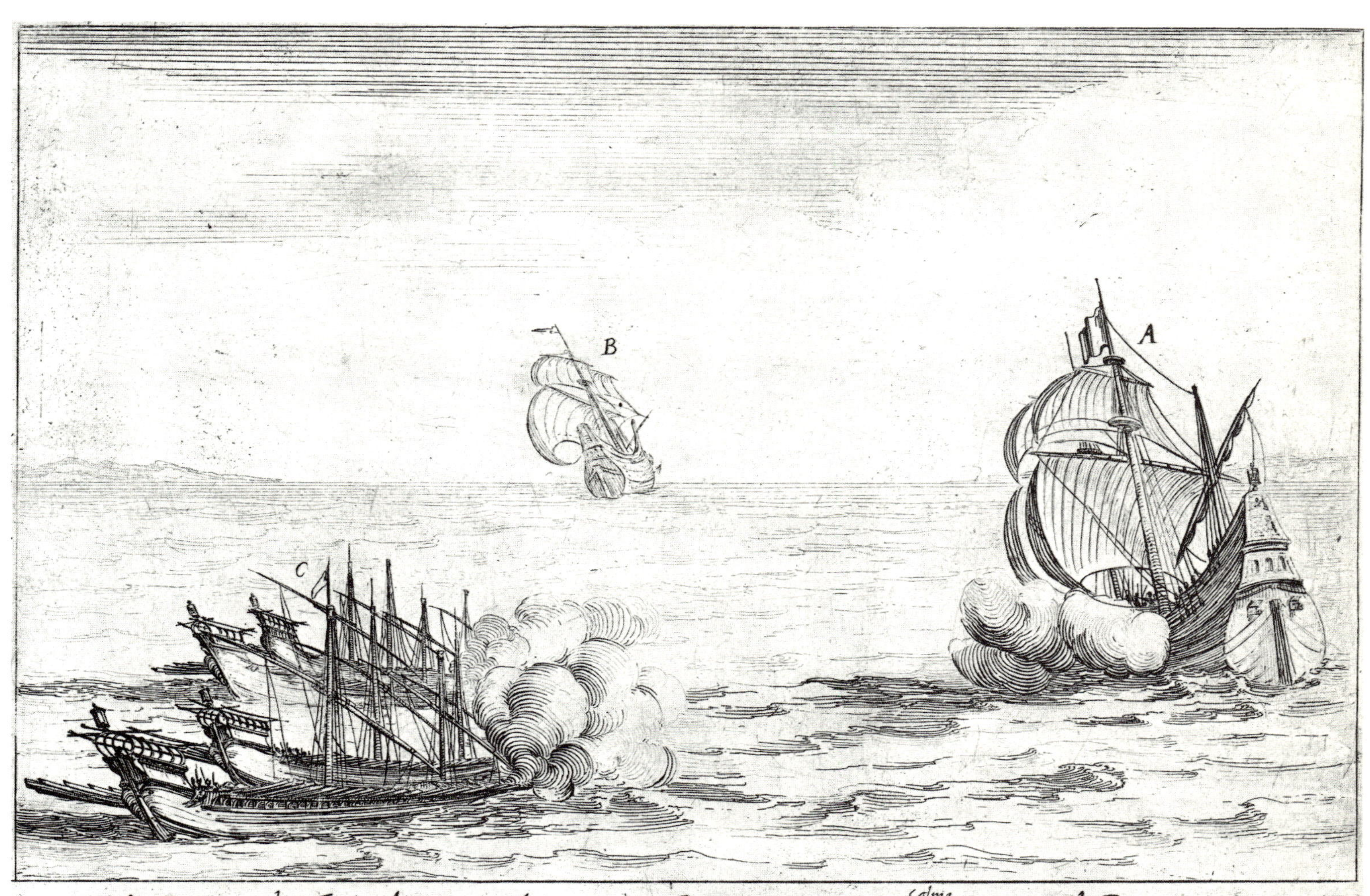

9 From *The Combat of Four Galleys* (Tuscan galleys vs. Tunisian pirates off Corsica, reportage of a current event), a series of 4 etchings, 1617: No. 1, The Attack. The inscription reads: "A. Tunisian *bertone* [type of ship] of 1500 *salme* [old unit of measure]. B. *Petaccio* [another type of ship] of 800, sailing as convoy to the *bertone*. C. Four galleys of His Royal Highness opening the attack on the *bertone*." (National Gallery, Washington, R. L. Baumfeld Collection)

10–25 The complete *Various Figures* (*Varie Figure*), a series of 16 etchings, sometime between 1617 and 1623.

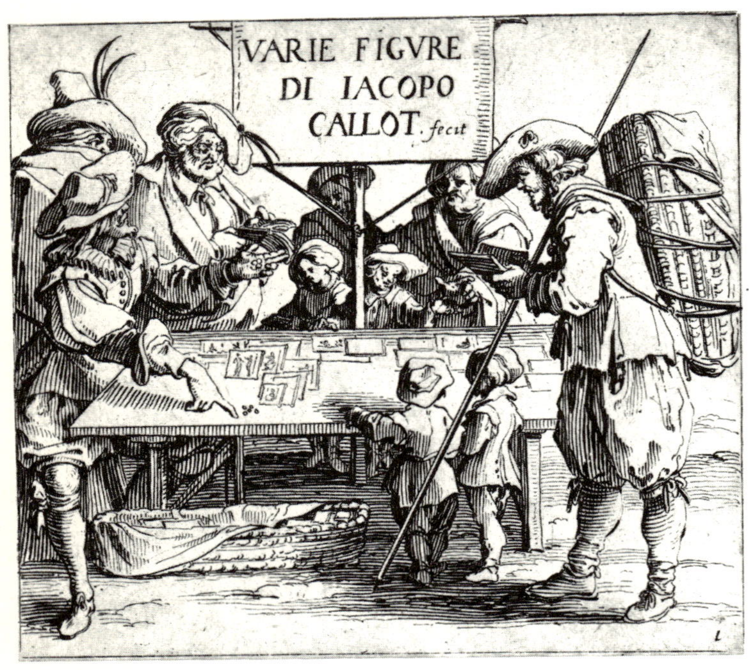

10 Title.

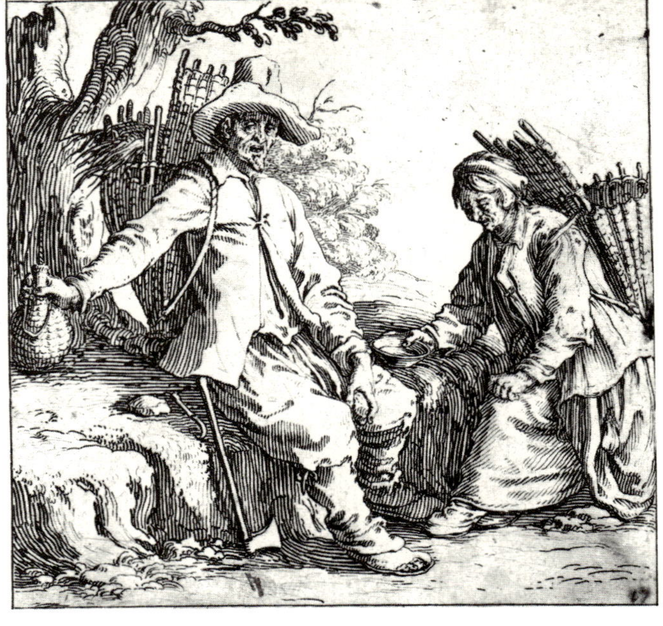

11 Peasant Couple at Rest.

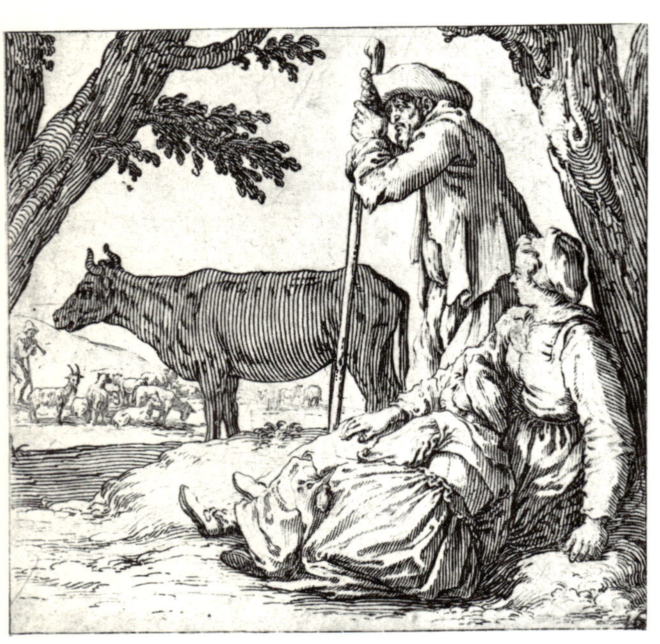

12 Peasant Couple with Cow.

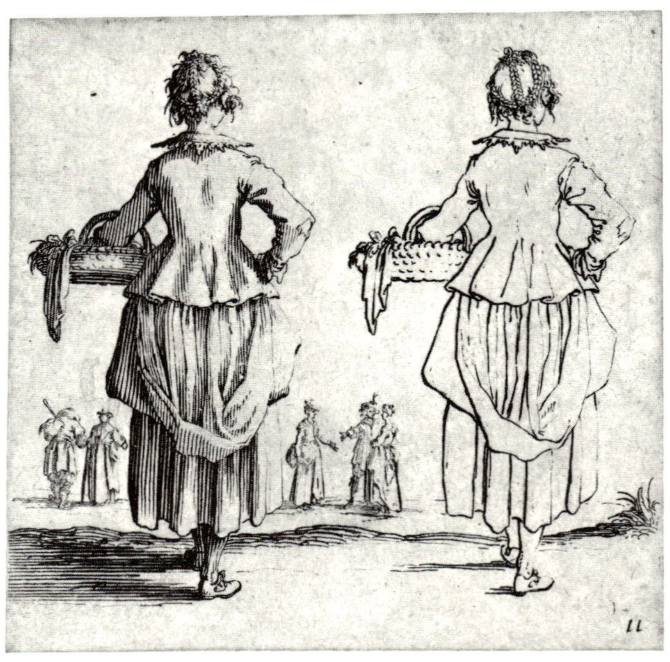

13 Peasant Woman with Basket, Seen from Behind.

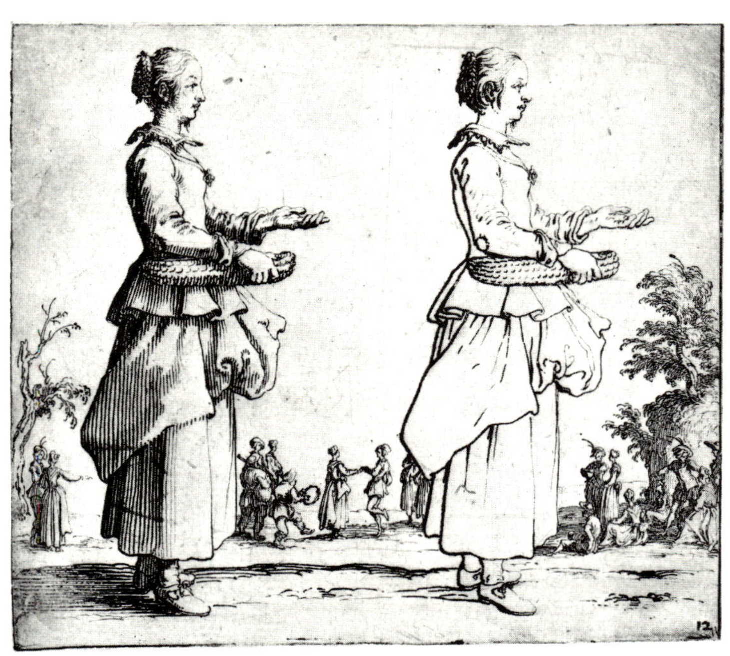

14 Peasant Woman with Basket, in Profile, Facing Right.

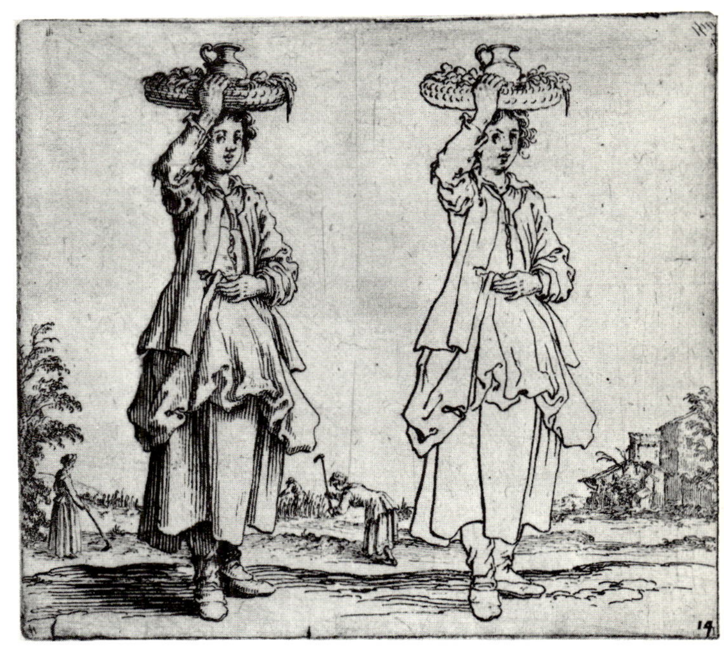

15 Peasant Woman with Basket on Head, Front View.

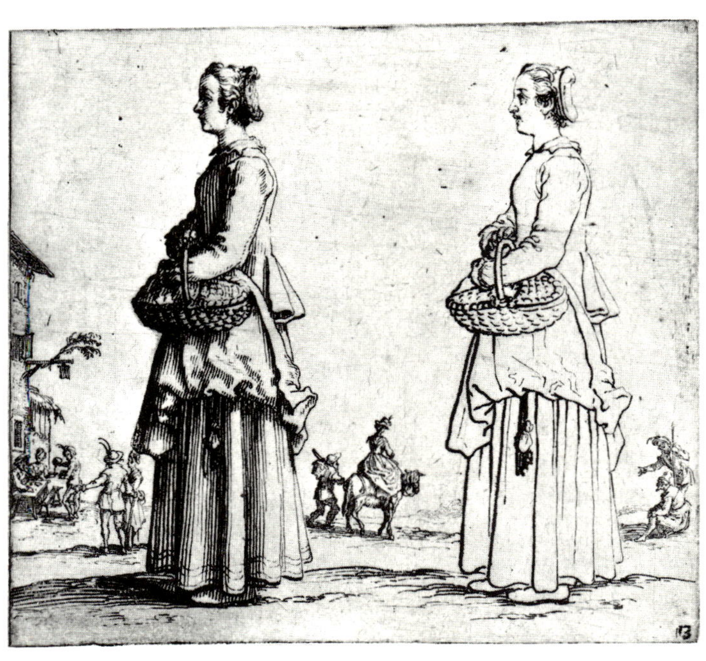

16 Peasant Woman with Basket, in Profile, Facing Left.

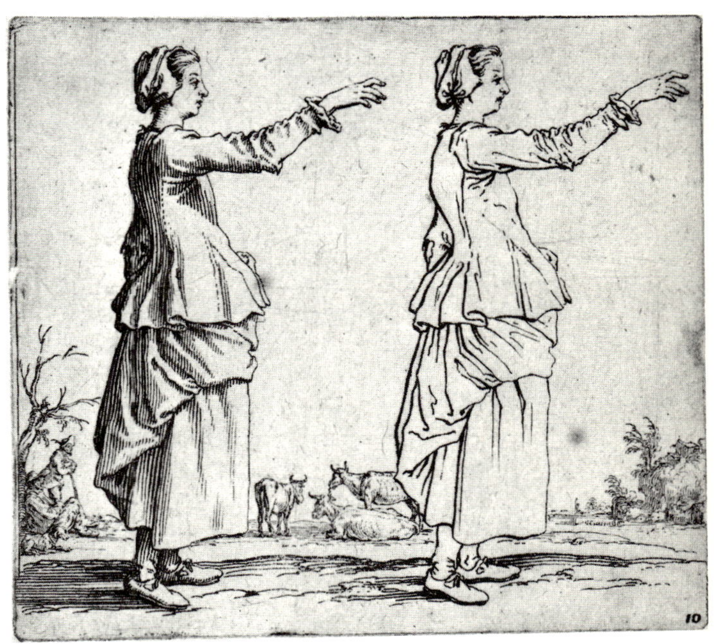

17 Peasant Woman, in Profile, Facing Right, with Arm Extended.

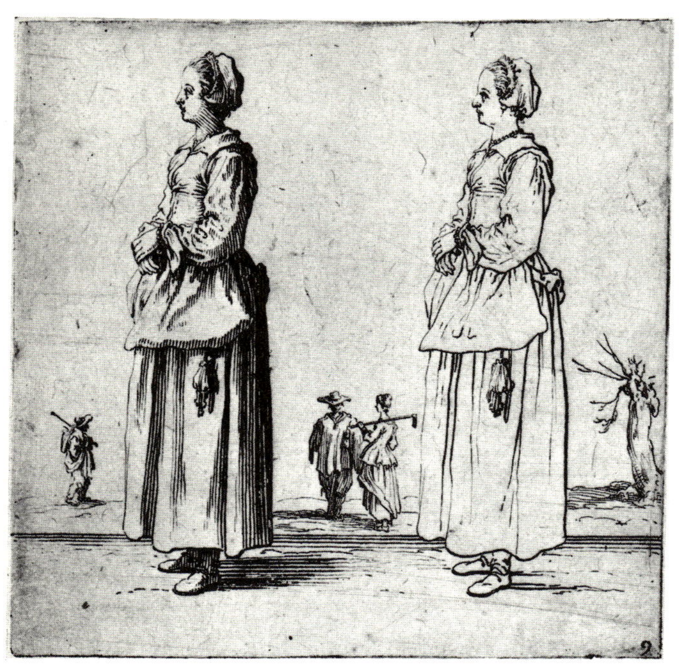

18 Peasant Woman, in Profile, Facing Left.

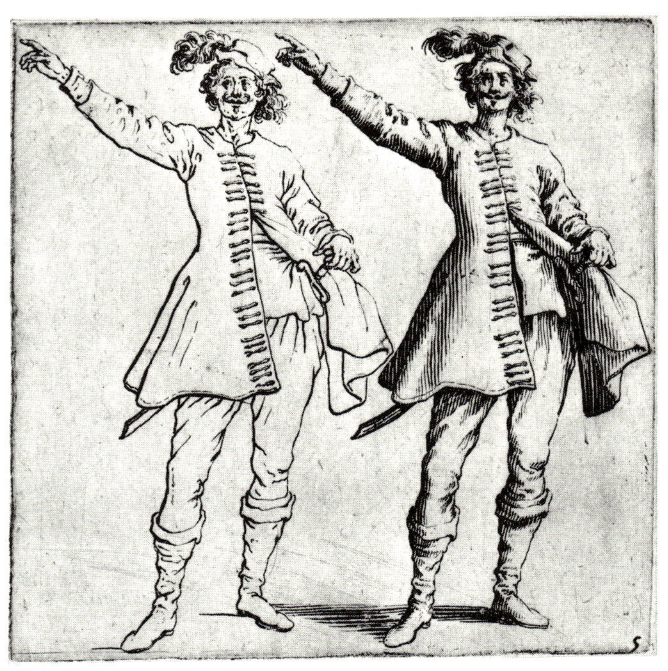

19 Officer, with Arm Extended, Front View.

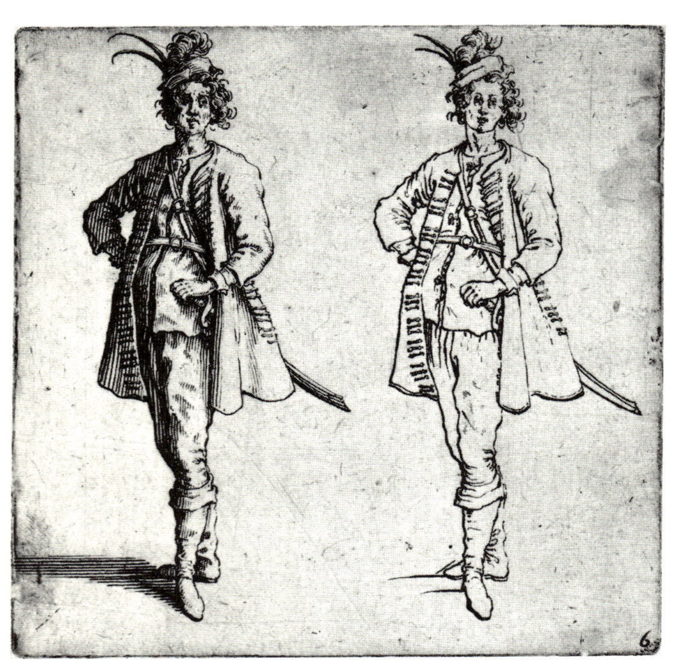

20 Officer, Front View.

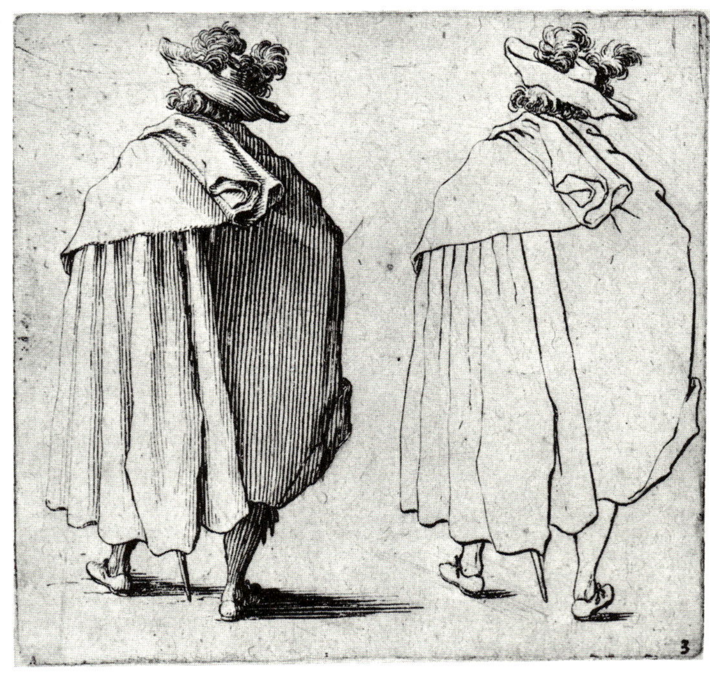

21 Man in Cloak, Seen from Behind.

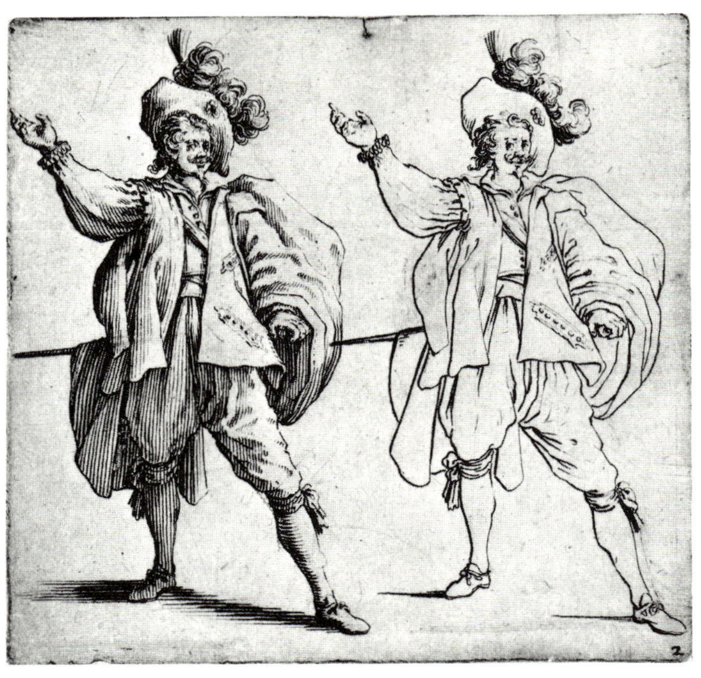

22 Officer with Large Plume, Front View.

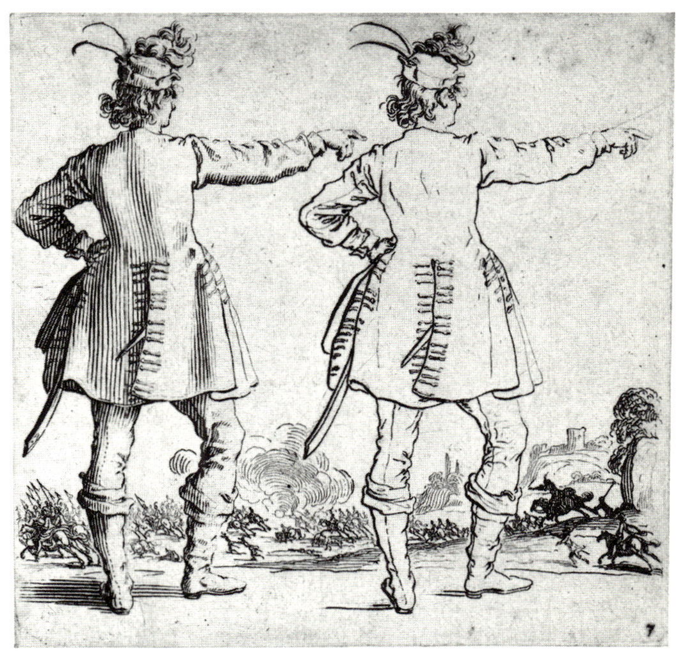

23 Officer with Feathers in Cap, Seen from Behind.

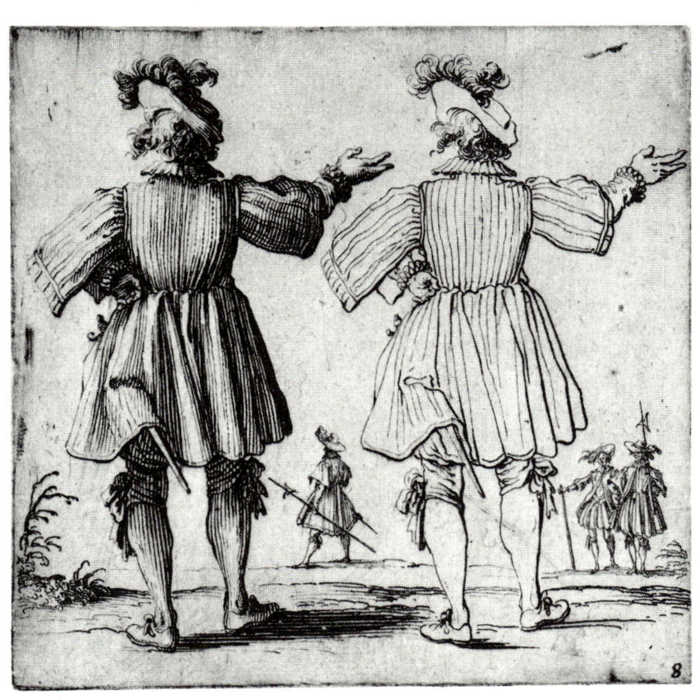

24 Officer with Plume, Seen from Behind.

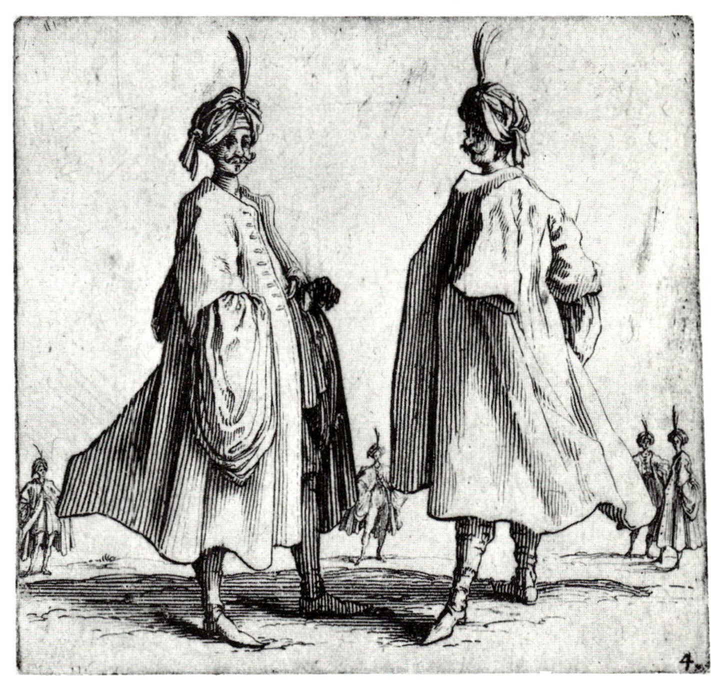

25 Two Turks.

26–75 The complete *Caprices* (*Capricci di Varie Figure*), a series of 50 etchings, first version 1617, second (very slightly altered) version 1621 or 1622 (the latter version is illustrated here). (Nos. 26–49 courtesy Trustees of the British Museum; No. 50 Cabinet des Estampes, Bibliothèque Nationale)

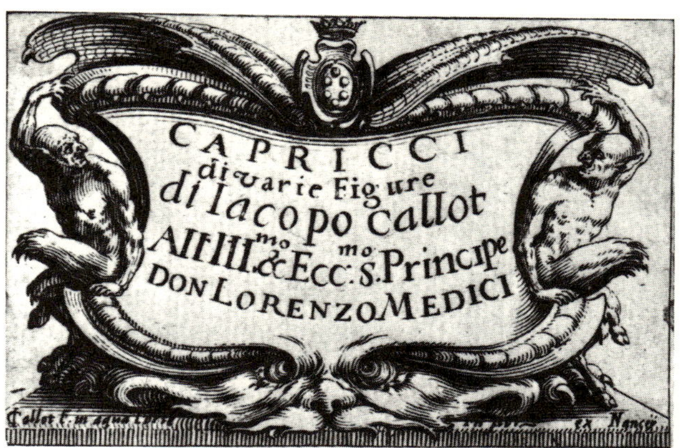

26 Title.

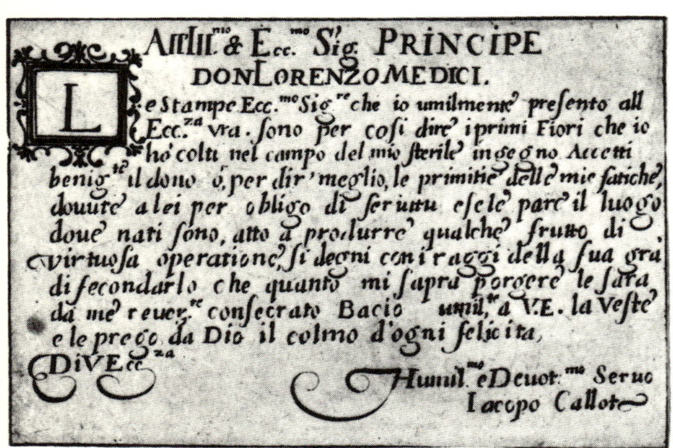

All'Ill.mo & Ecc.mo Sig. PRINCIPE
DON LORENZO MEDICI.
Le Stampe Ecc.mo Sig.re che io umilmente presento all Ecc.za vra. sono per cosi dire i primi Fiori che io hò colti nel campo del mio sterile ingegno Accetti benig.te il dono ò, per dir' meglio, le primitie delle mie fatiche, douute a lei per obligo di seruitu e se le pare il luogo doue nati sono, atto a produrre qualche frutto di virtuosa operatione, si degni con i raggi della sua gra di secondarlo che quanto mi sapra porgere le sara da me reuer.te consecrato Bacio umil.te a V.E. la Veste e le prego da Dio il colmo d'ogni felicita,
Di V.Ecc.za
Humil.mo e Deuot.mo Seruo
Iacopo Callot

27 Dedication. The text reads: "To Prince Lorenzo Medici. The prints I humbly offer to Your Highness are as it were the first flowers I have gathered in the field of my barren talent. Kindly accept the gift, or rather the first-fruits of my labors, due to you as my master; and if you find the place from which they sprang fit to produce some fruit of healthful properties, deign to fecundate it with the rays of your grace; for all it can bestow on me I shall reverently consecrate to you. I humbly kiss your robe and pray God to shower every happiness upon you. Your most humble and devoted servant, Jacques Callot."

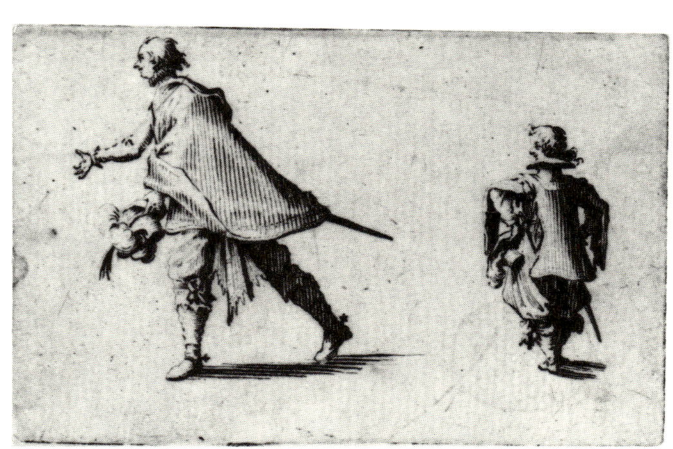

28 Nobleman and Page.

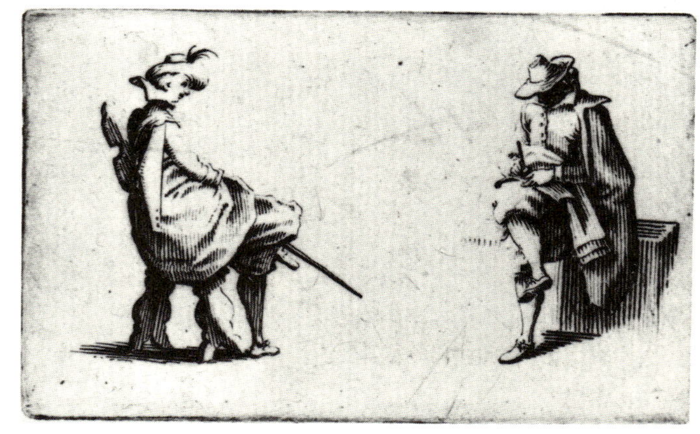

29 Two Seated Men.

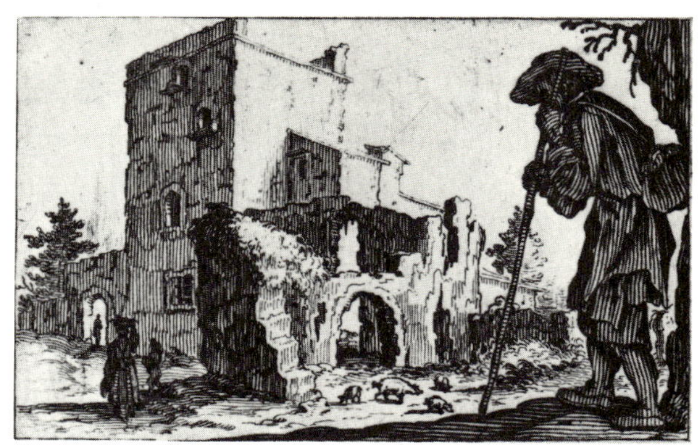

30 Shepherd and Landscape with Ruins.

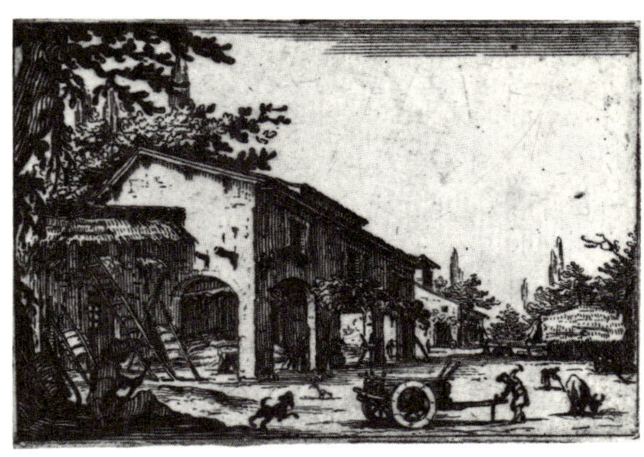

31 Italian Farmyard.

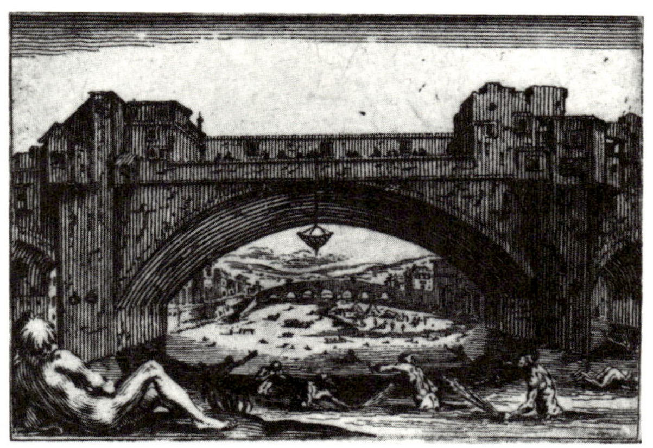

32 The Ponte Vecchio in Florence.

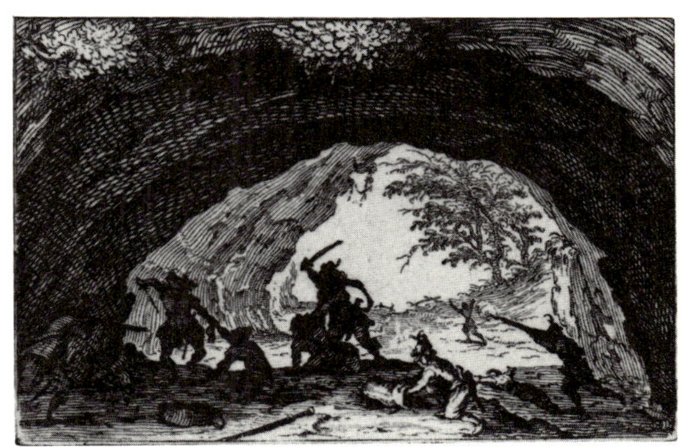

33 Bandits' Lair.

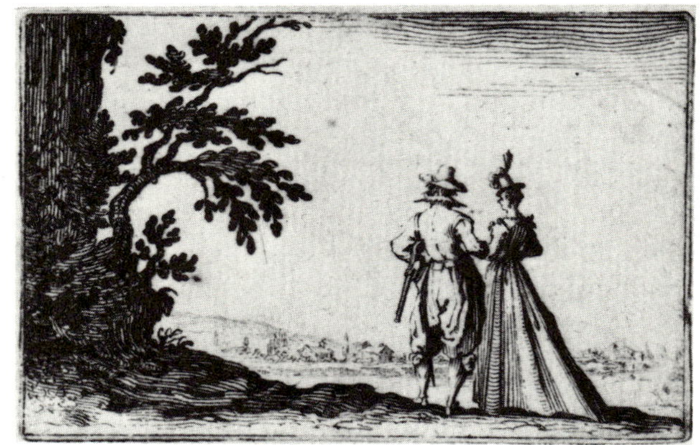

34 A Couple Promenading.

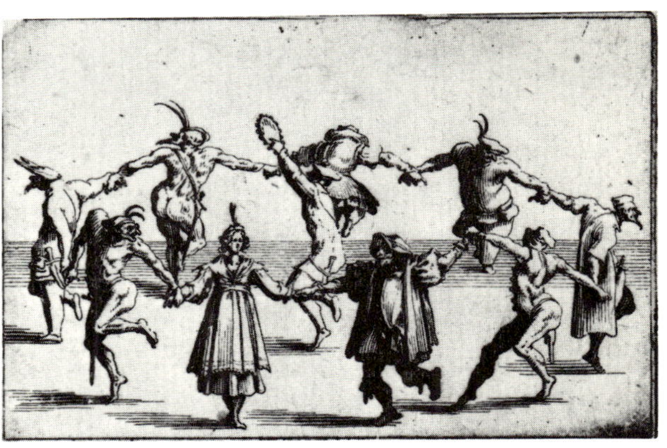

35 Round Dance.

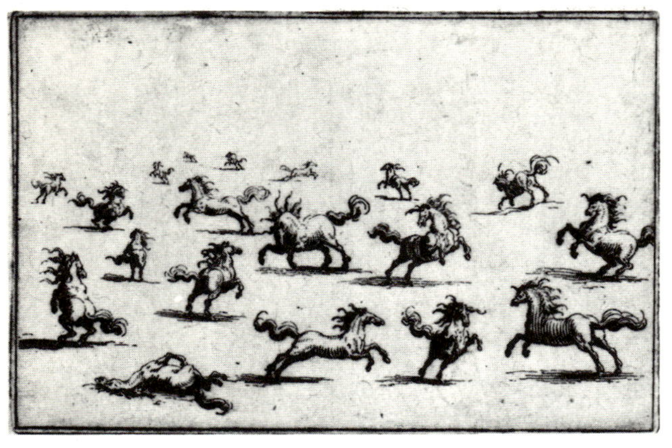

36 Study of Horses.

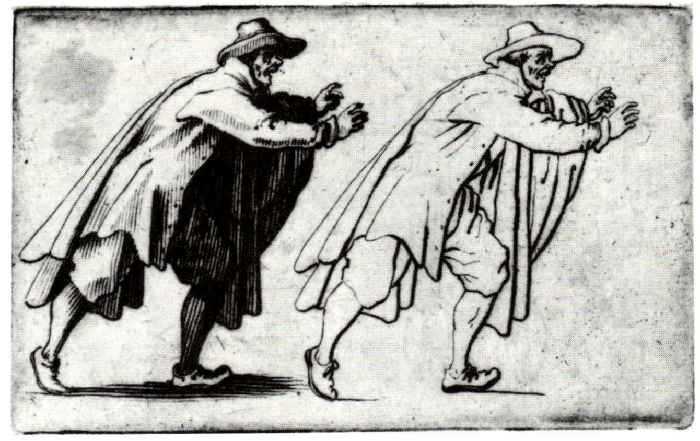

37 Man Moving Forward.

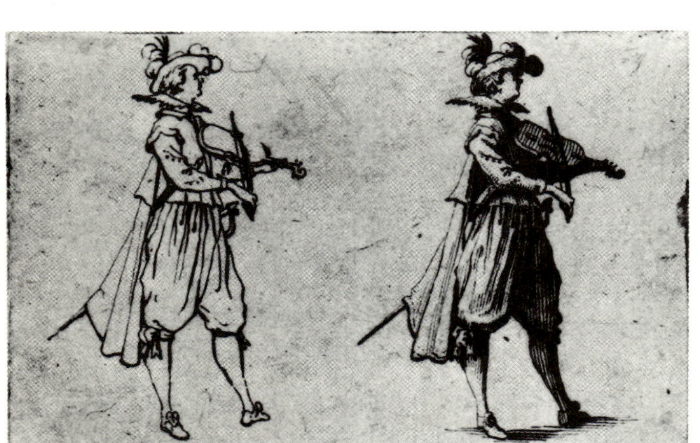

38 Violinist.

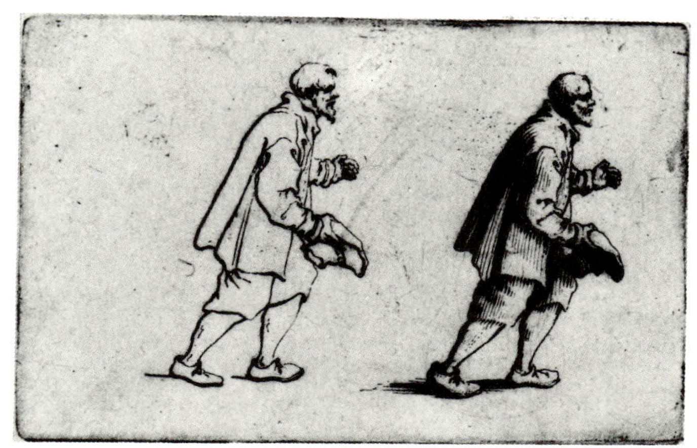

39 Peasant in Attitude of Greeting.

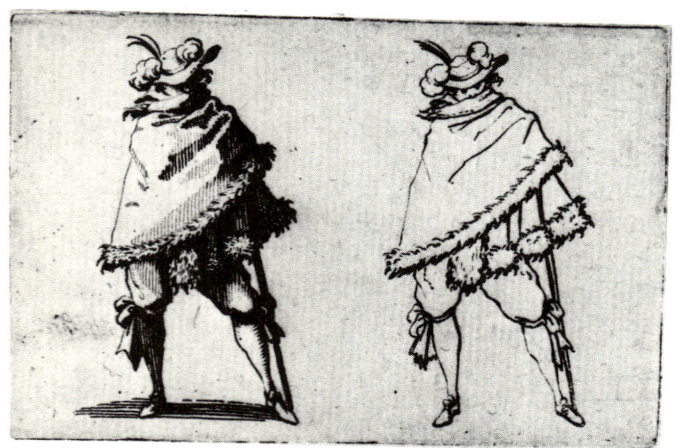

40 Nobleman with Muffled Face.

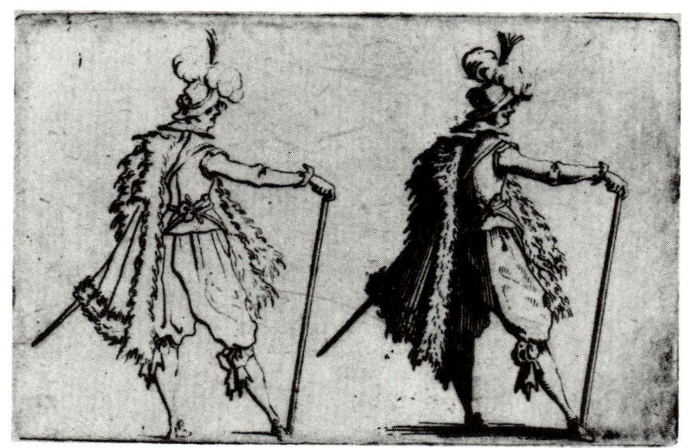

41 Nobleman with Long Walking Stick.

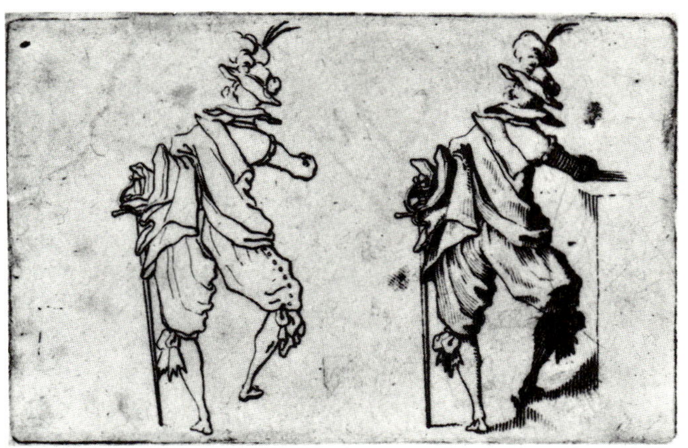

42 Nobleman Leaning, Seen from Behind.

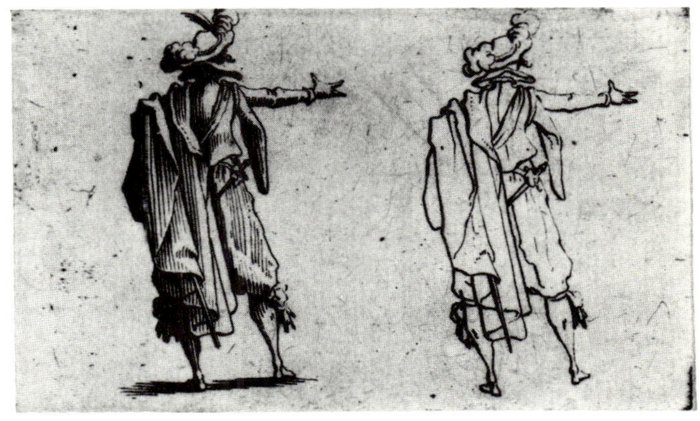

43 Nobleman with Arm Extended, Seen from Behind.

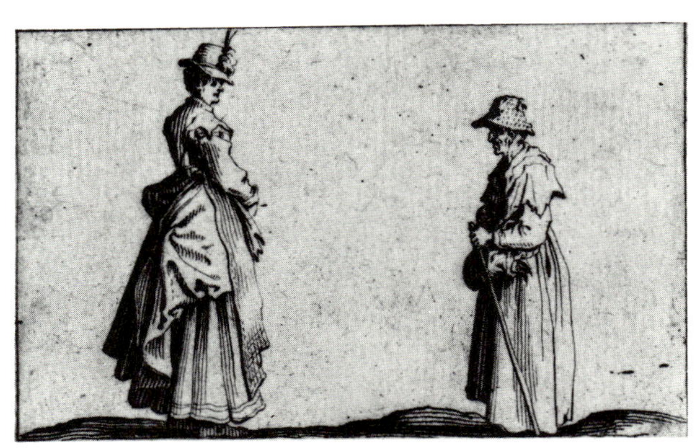

44 Two Women in Profile.

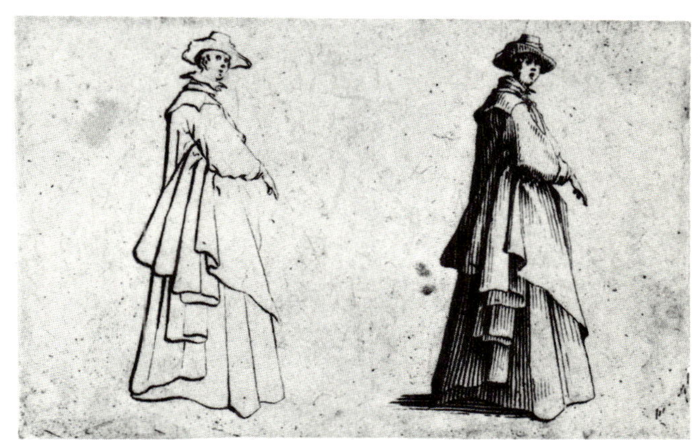

45 Lady in a Wide Dress.

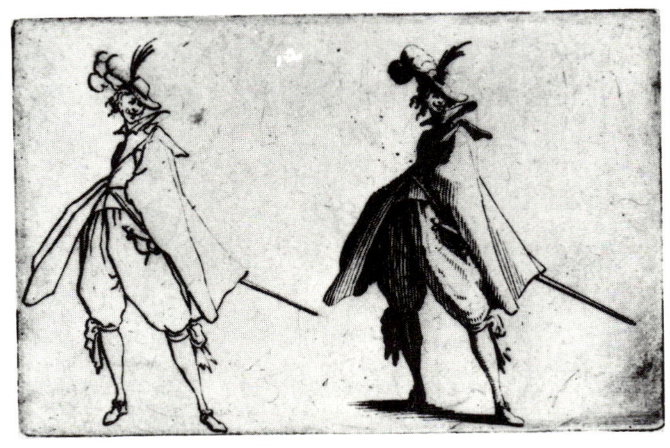

46 Nobleman in Broad Cloak, Front View.

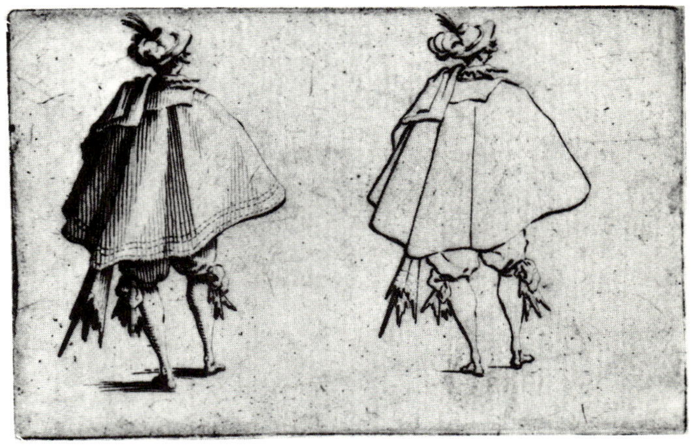

47 Nobleman in Broad Cloak, Seen from Behind.

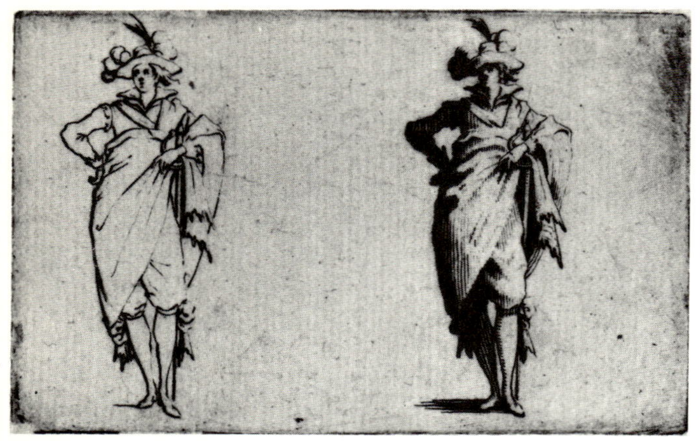

48 Nobleman, Front View.

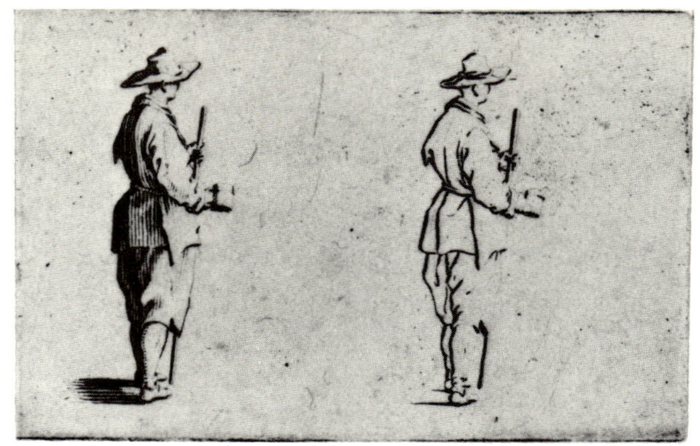

49 Peasant with Stick, Three Quarter Rear View.

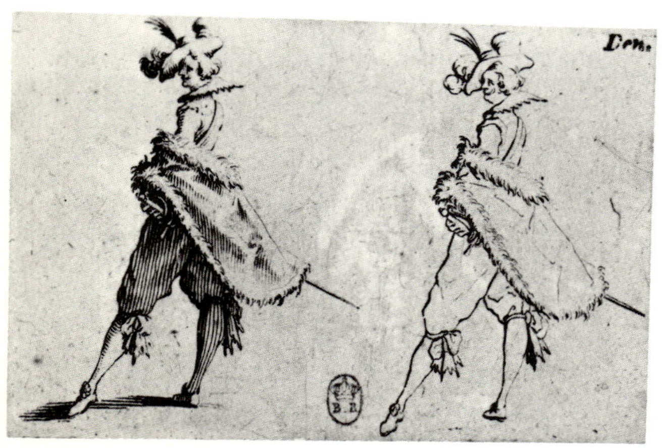

50 Nobleman in Profile.

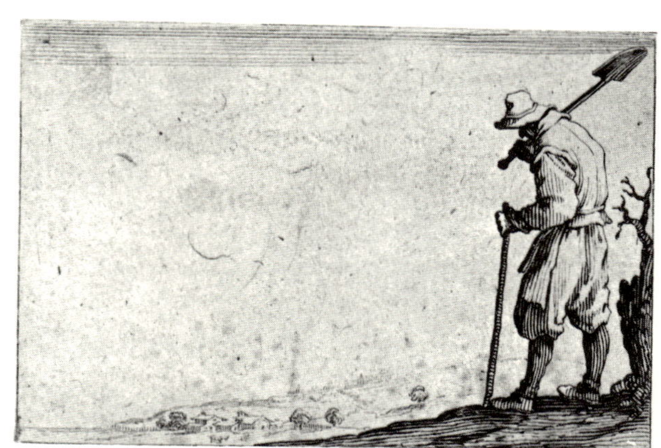

51 Peasant with Spade on Shoulder.

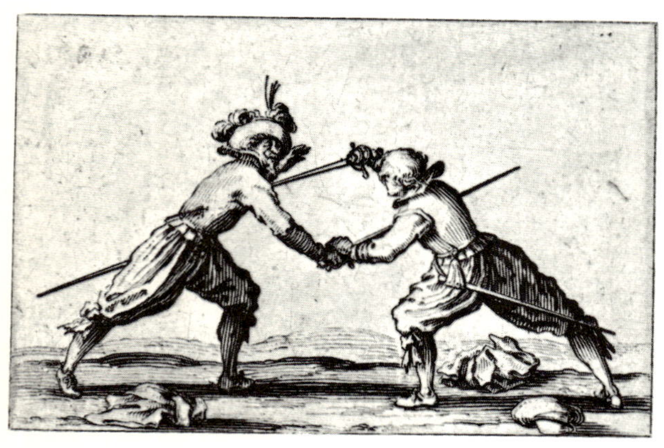

52 Duel, with Man Run Through.

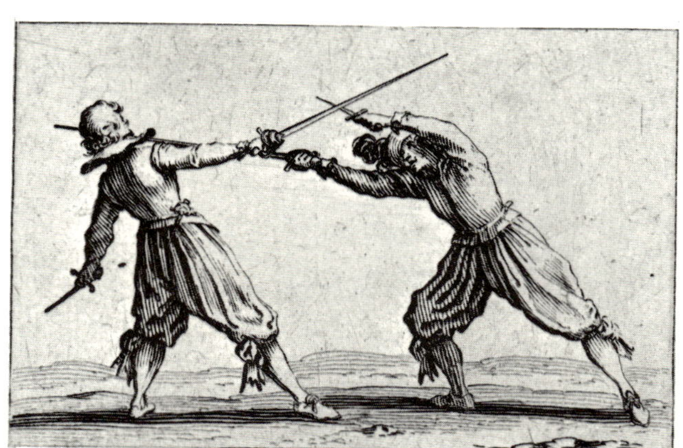

53 Duel with Swords and Daggers.

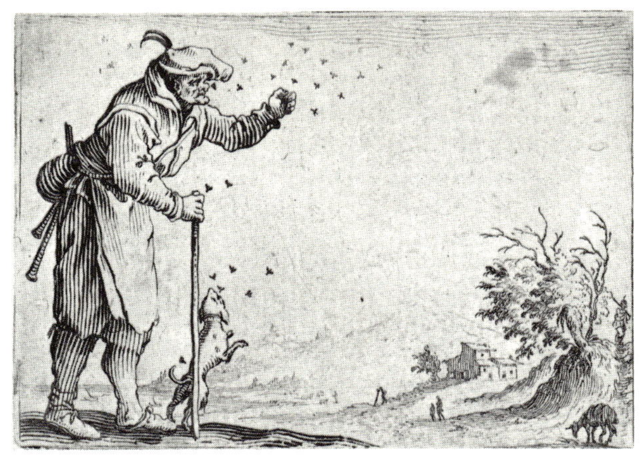

54 Peasant and Dog Attacked by Bees.

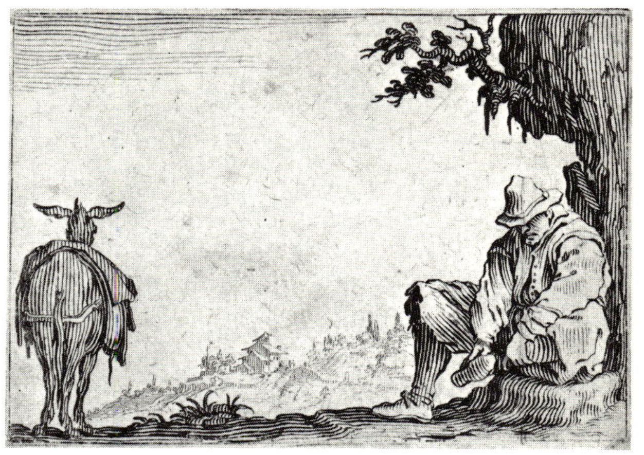

55 Seated Peasant with Donkey.

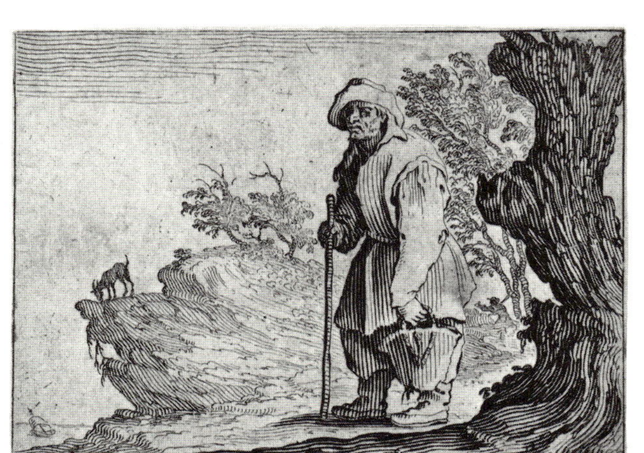

56 Peasant with Walking Stick and Basket.

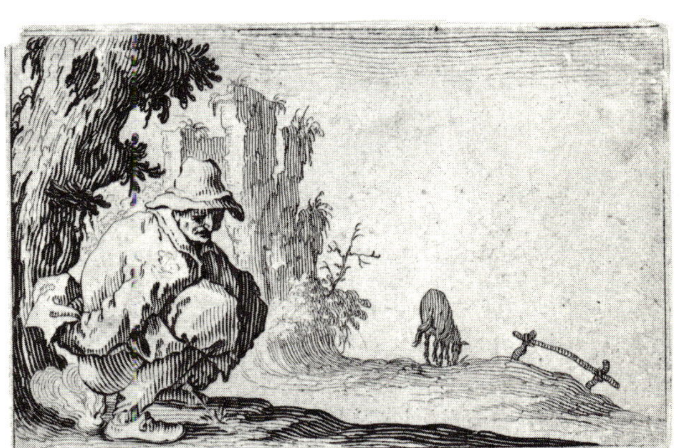

57 Peasant Squatting and Defecating.

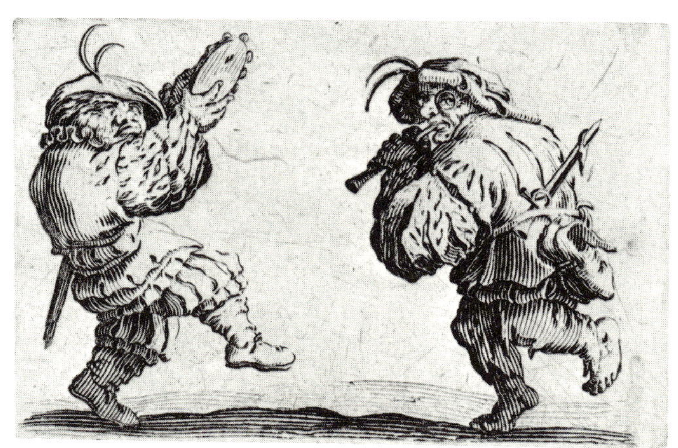

58 Two Grotesque Musicians Dancing.

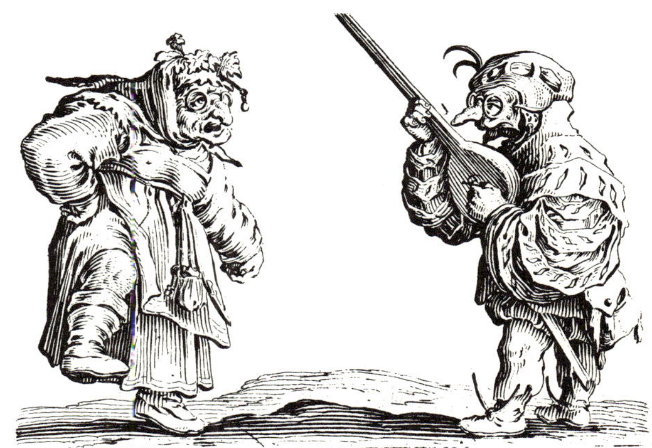

59 Grotesque Man and Woman Dancing.

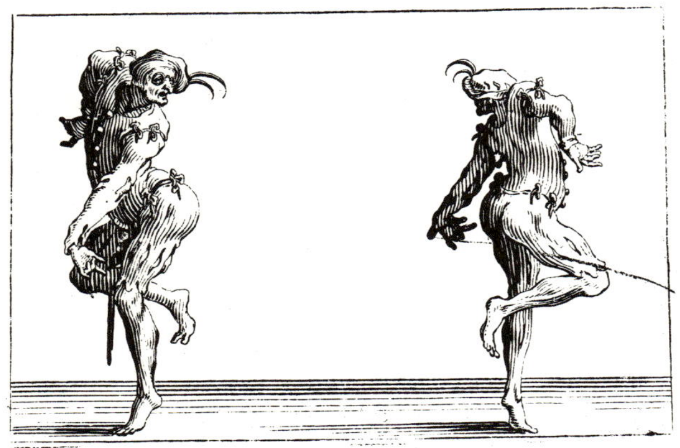

60 Two Pantaloons Dancing, Back to Back.

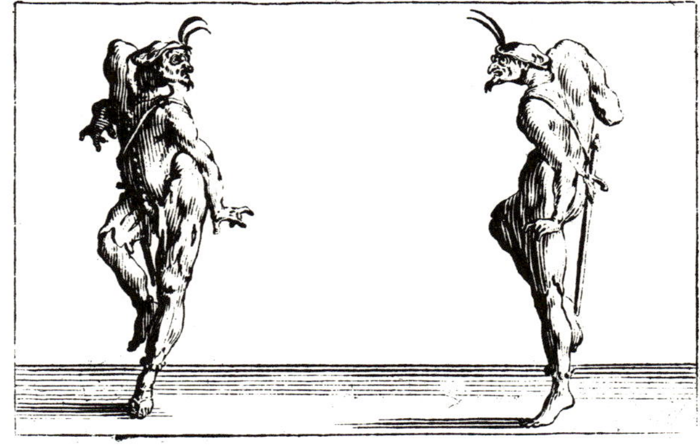

61 Two Pantaloons Dancing, Face to Face.

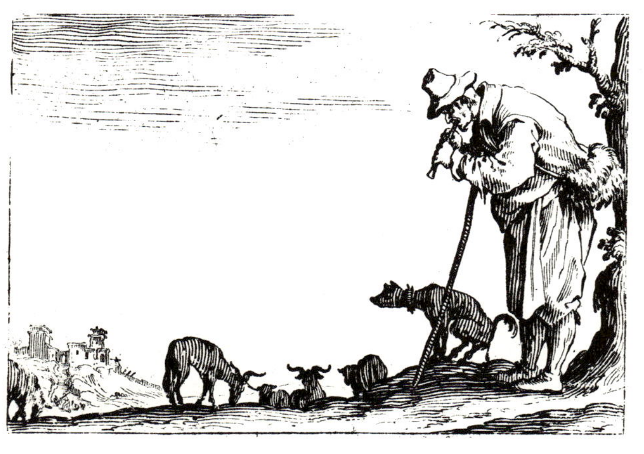

62 Old Shepherd Piping.

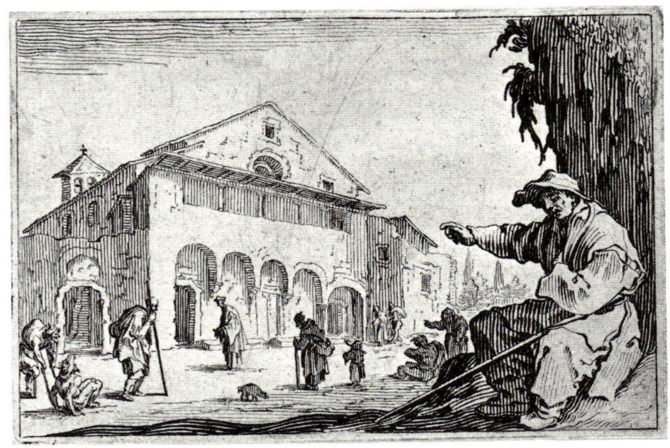

63 Hospital Scene.

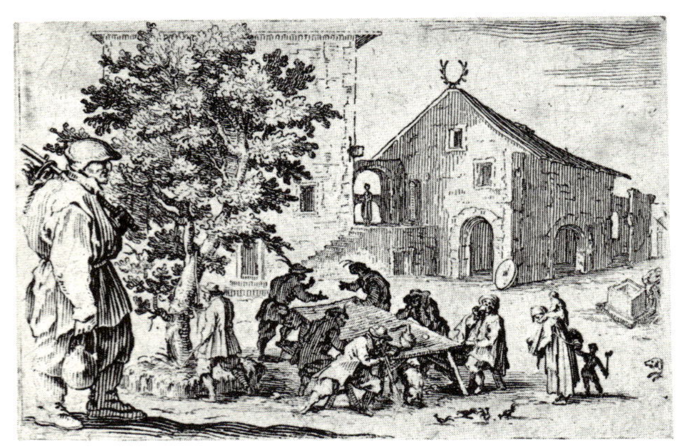

64 Inn Scene.

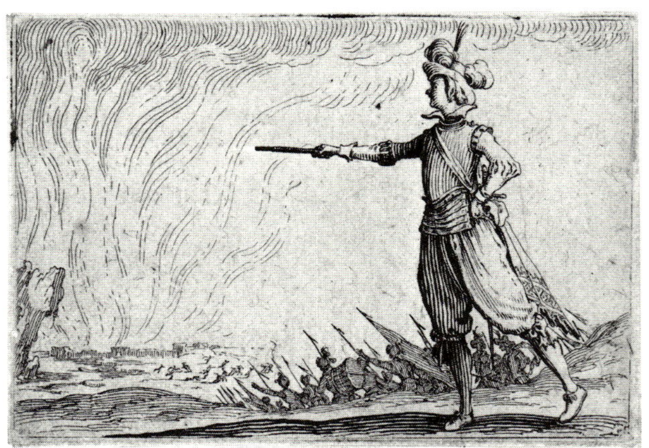

65 Officer on Foot, with Battle Scene.

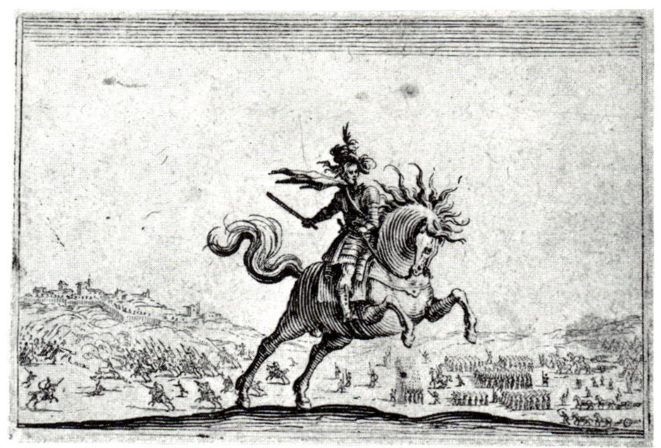

66 Officer on Horseback, with Battle Scene.

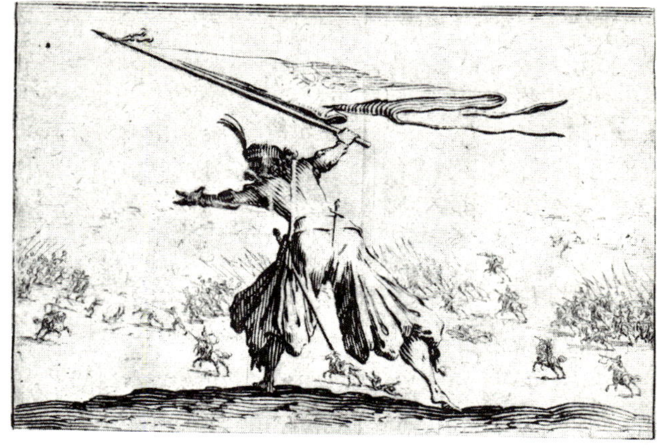

67 Standard Bearer.

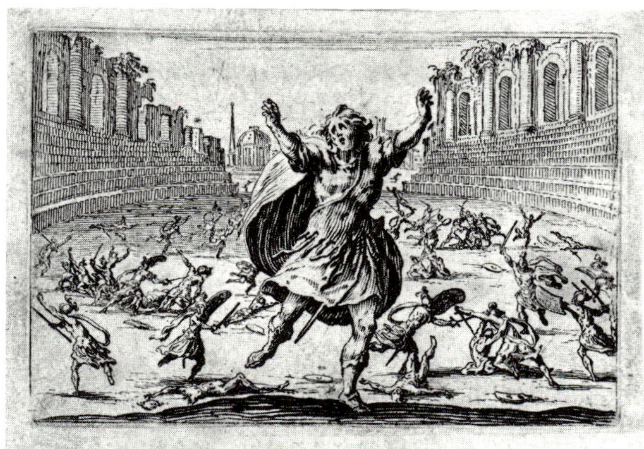

68 Combat of Gladiators in the Ruins of an Amphitheater.

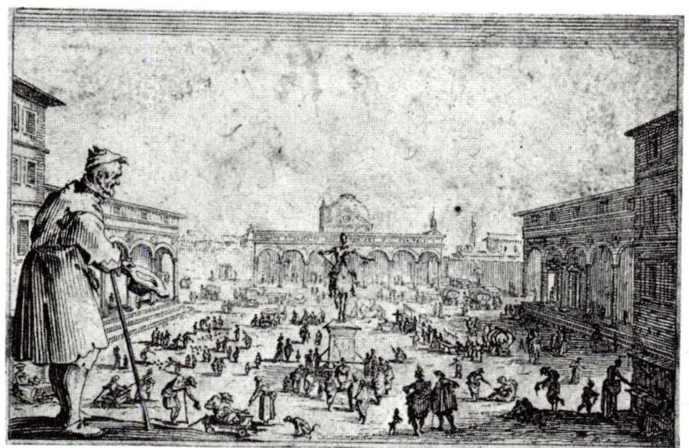

69 Market in the Piazza dell'Annunziata, Florence.

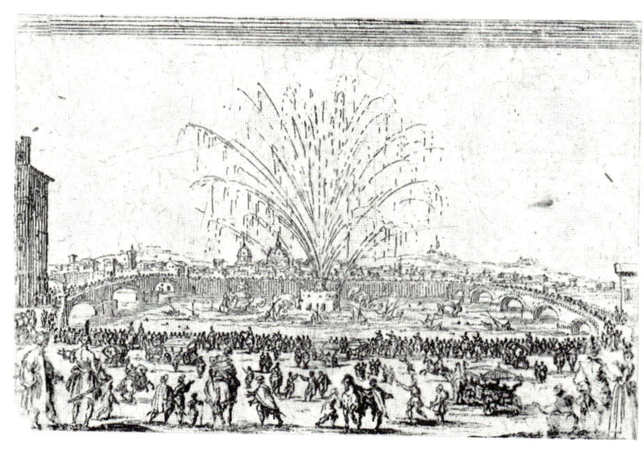

70 Fireworks Display over the Arno.

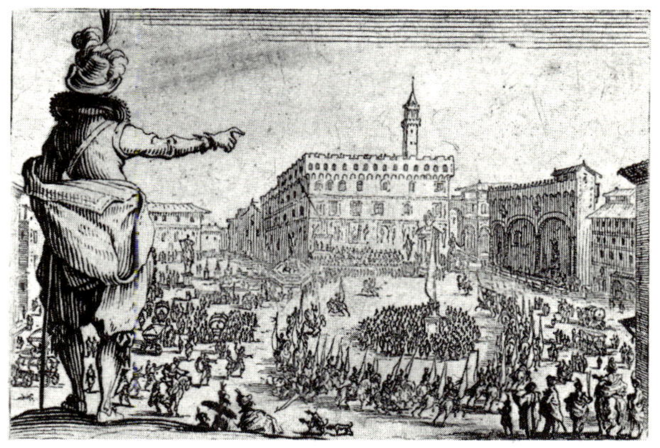

71 Pageant in the Piazza della Signoria, Florence.

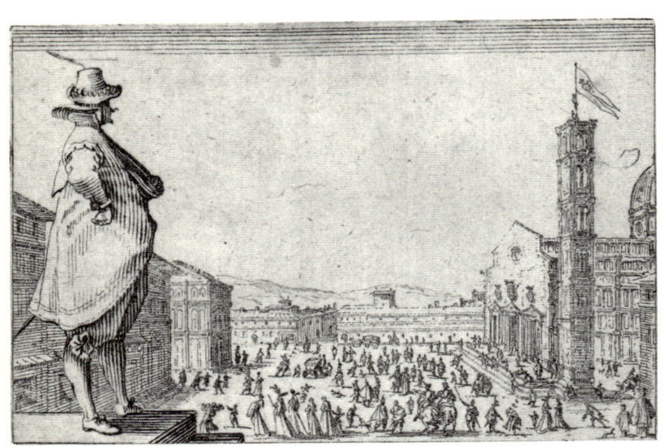

72 The Cathedral Square, Florence.

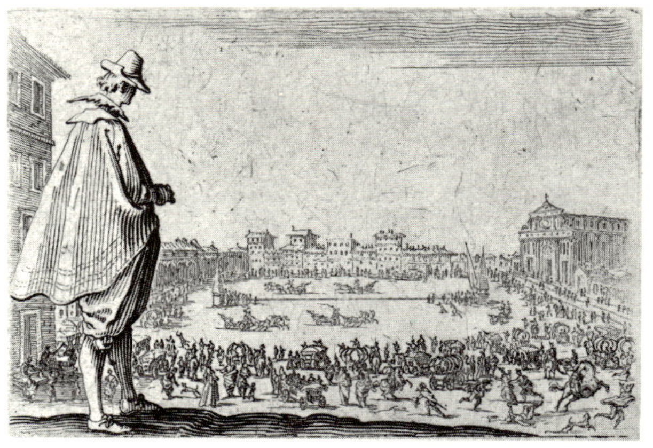

73 Chariot Race in the Piazza Santa Maria Novella, Florence.

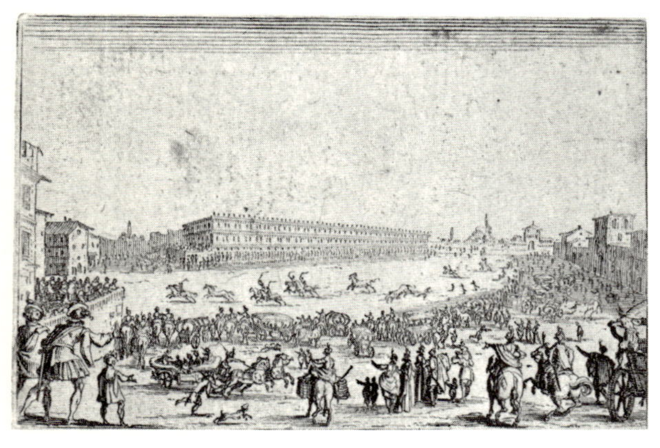

74 Chariot Race in Front of the Pitti Palace, Florence.

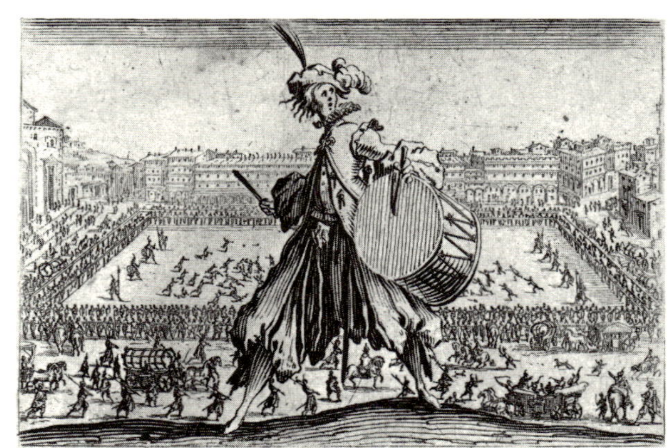

75 Handball on the Piazza Santa Croce, Florence.

76 & 77 From *The Four Landscapes*, a series of 4 etchings, 1617/18.

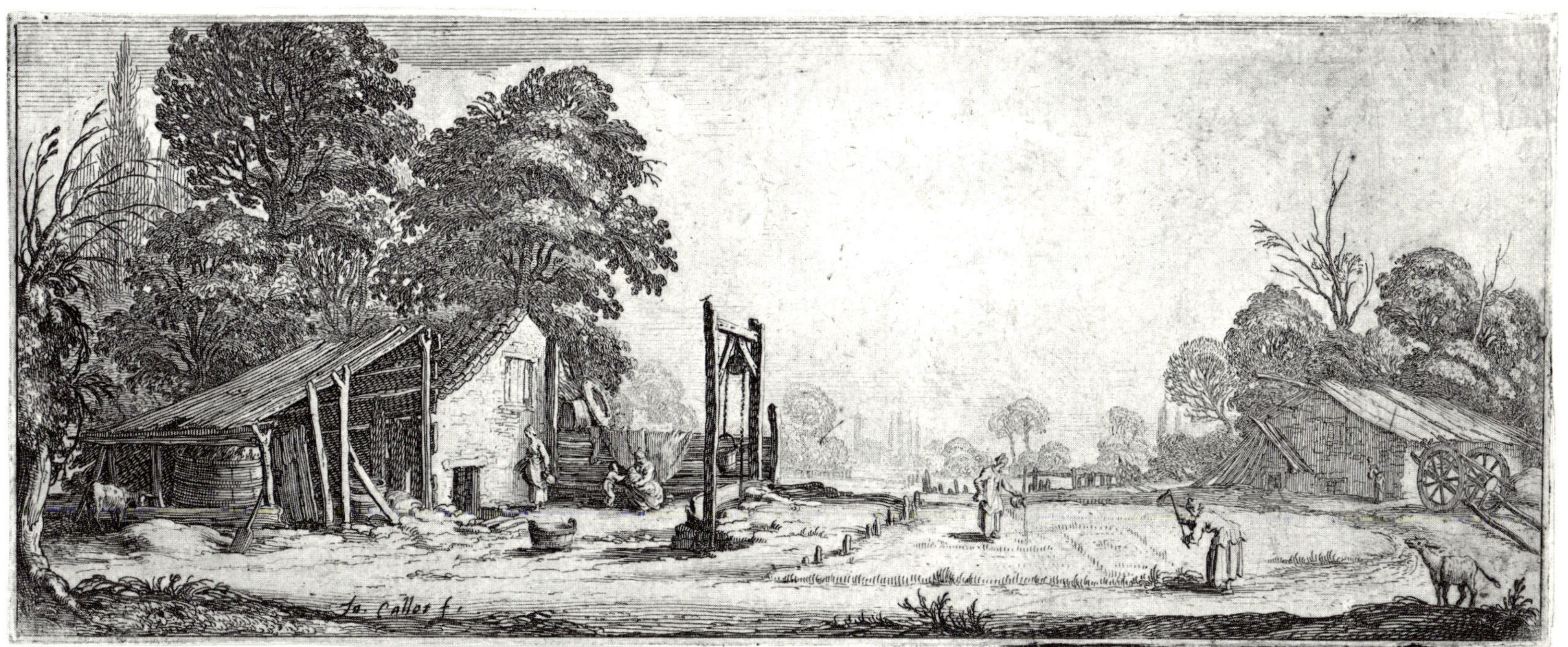

76 The Kitchen Garden.

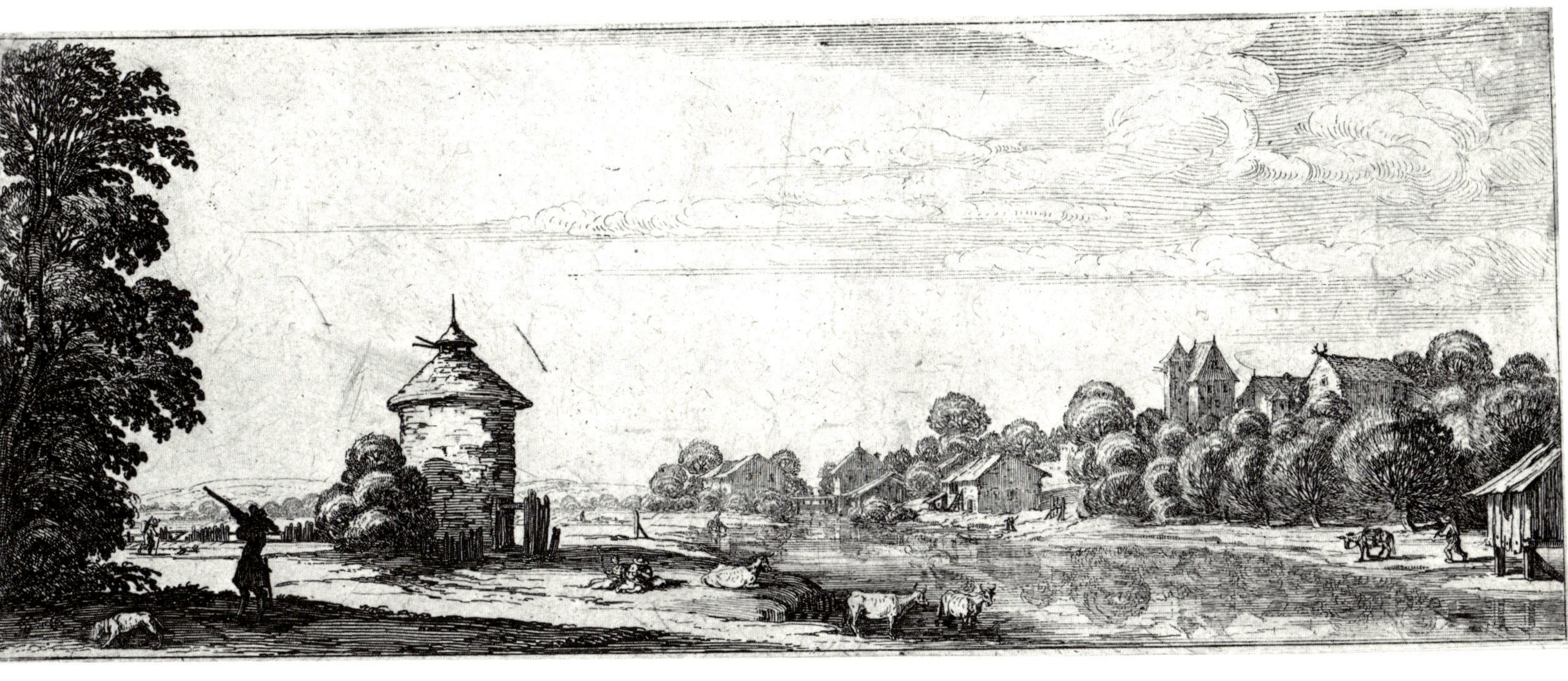

77 The Dovecote.

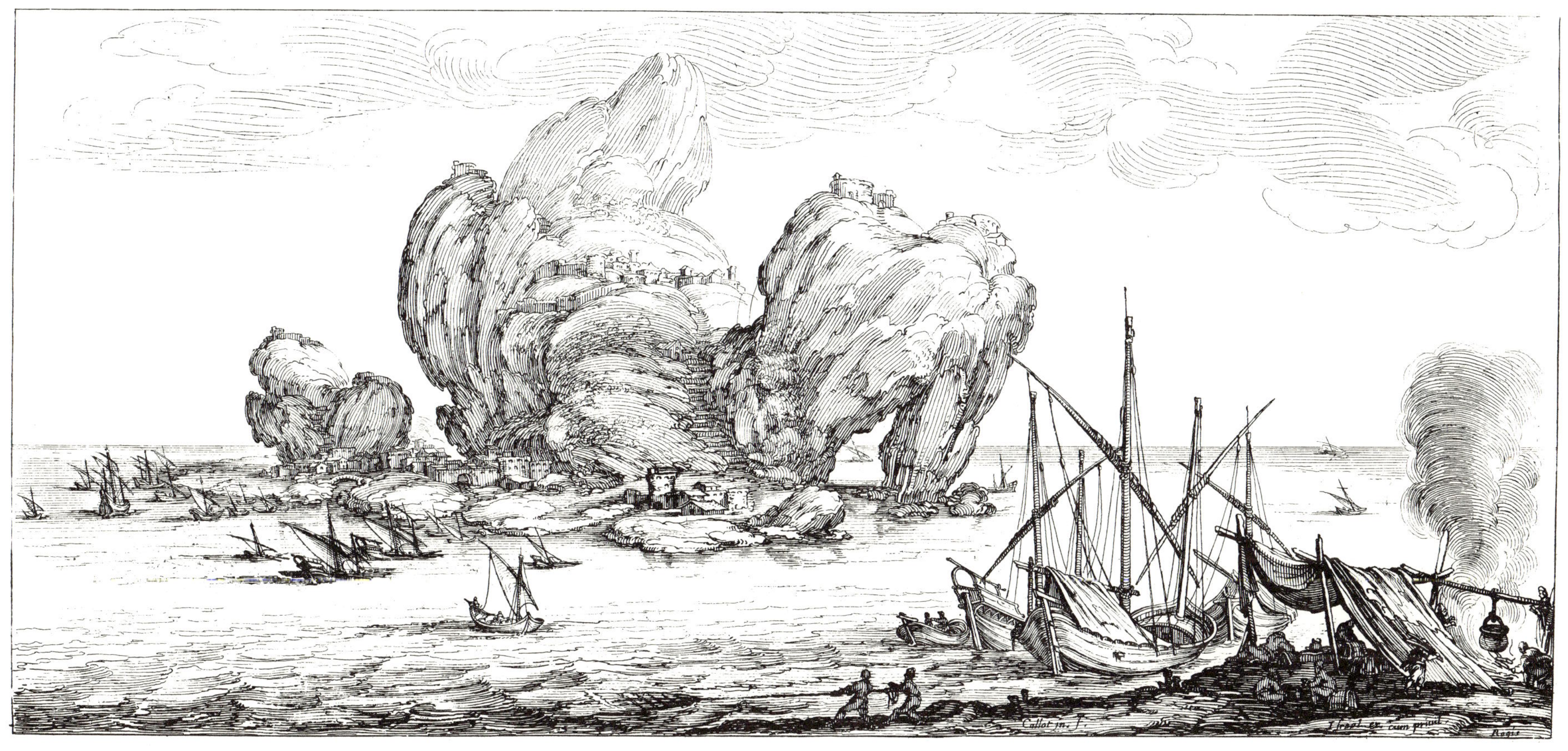

82 The Large Rock. (National Gallery, Washington, R. L. Baumfeld Collection)

83–85 From *The Great Passion*, a series of 7 etchings, sometime between 1618 and 1625.

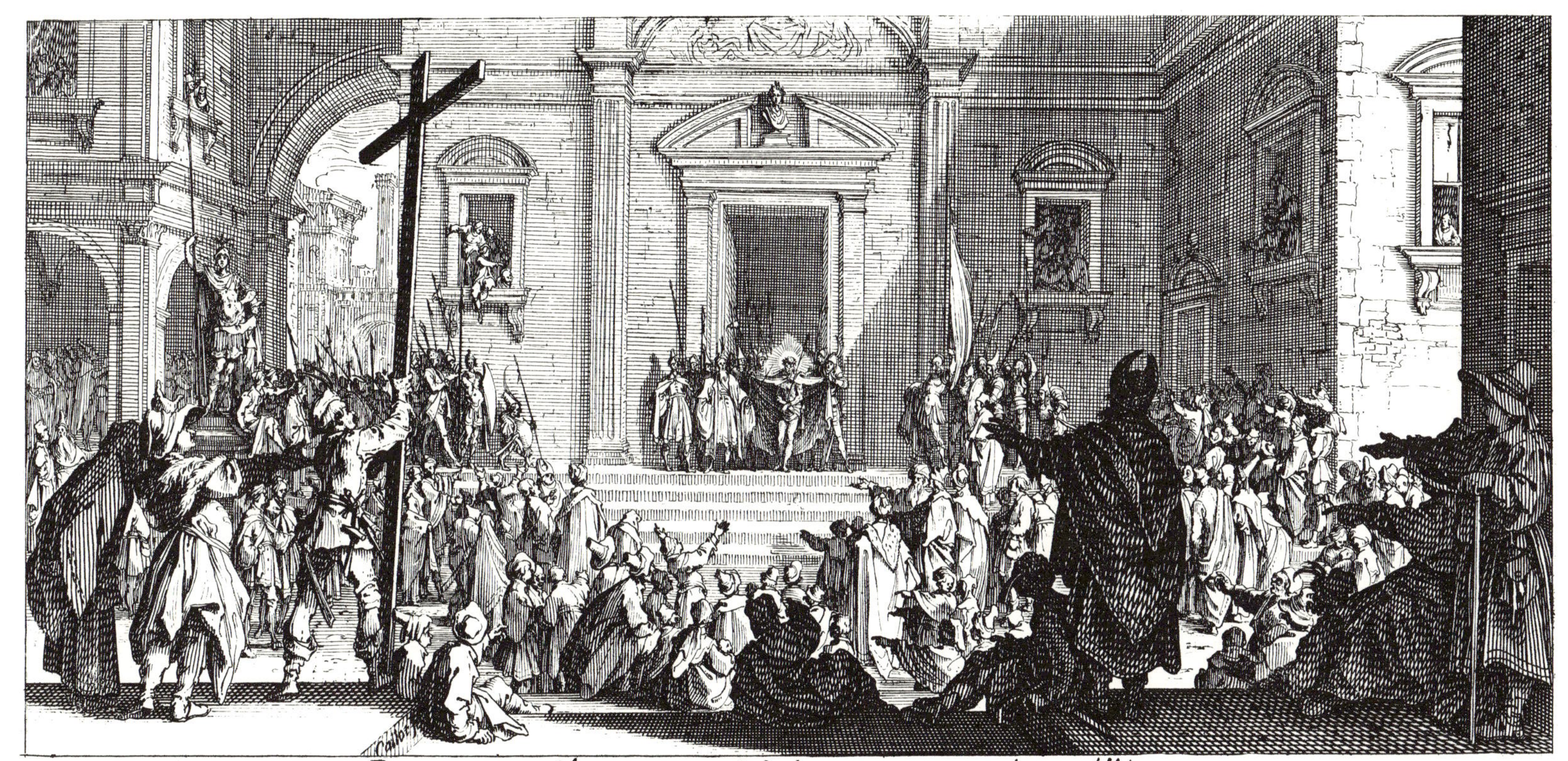

83 Christ Presented to the People. The Latin couplet reads: "What need of a purple robe? Alas! do you not see that all His limbs are flushed with purple blood?"

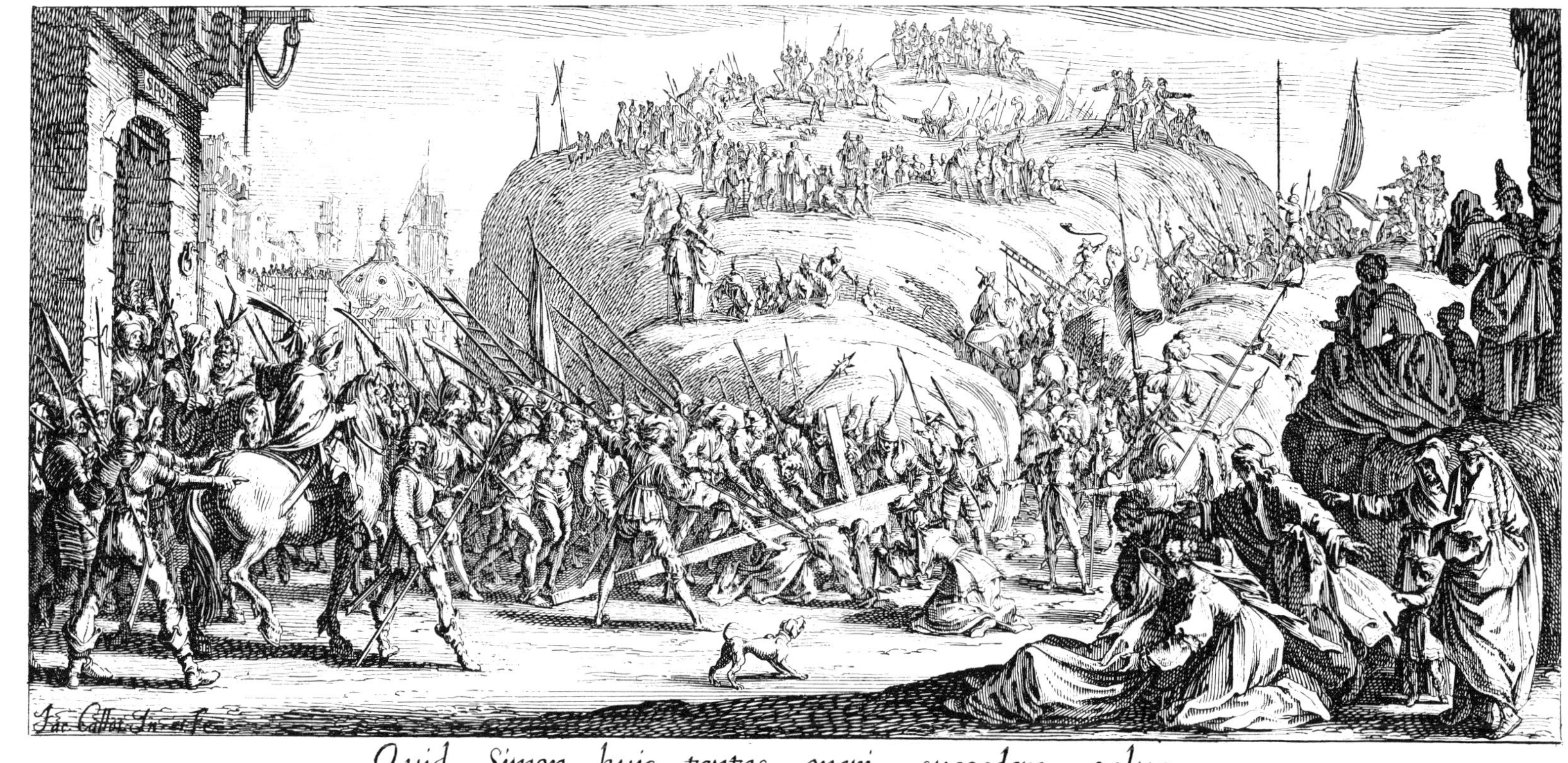

84 Christ Bearing the Cross. The inscription reads: "Simon, why do you try to take this burden upon yourself? Only He can bear the weight of so great a cross."

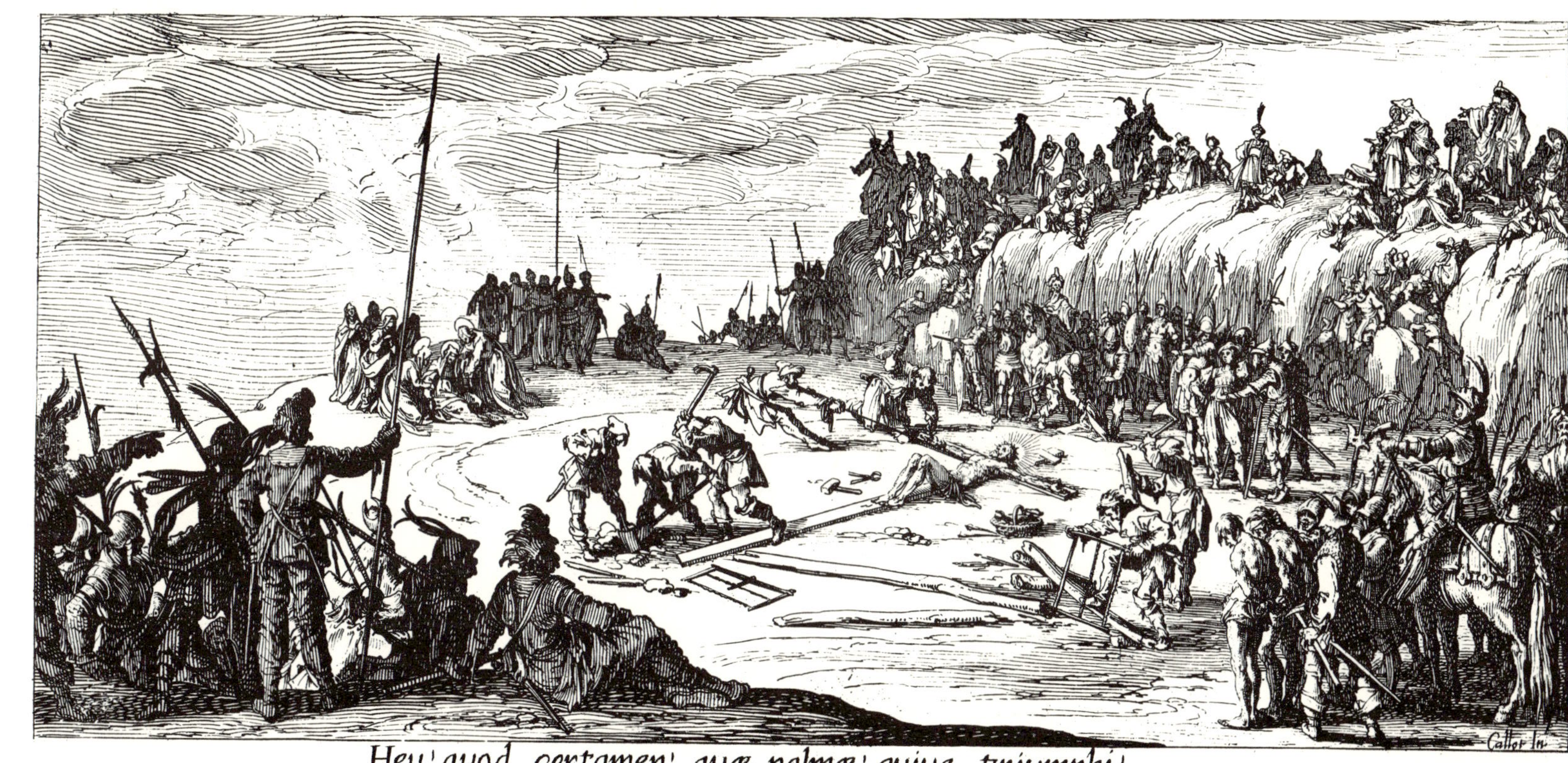

85 Christ Nailed to the Cross. "Alas! what a contest! what palms [of victory]! and what triumphs! And yet He tames death and the depths of Hell."

86–88 *Three Italian Comedy Performers* (*Three Actors*, *Three Pantaloons*), a series of 3 etchings, 1618/19.

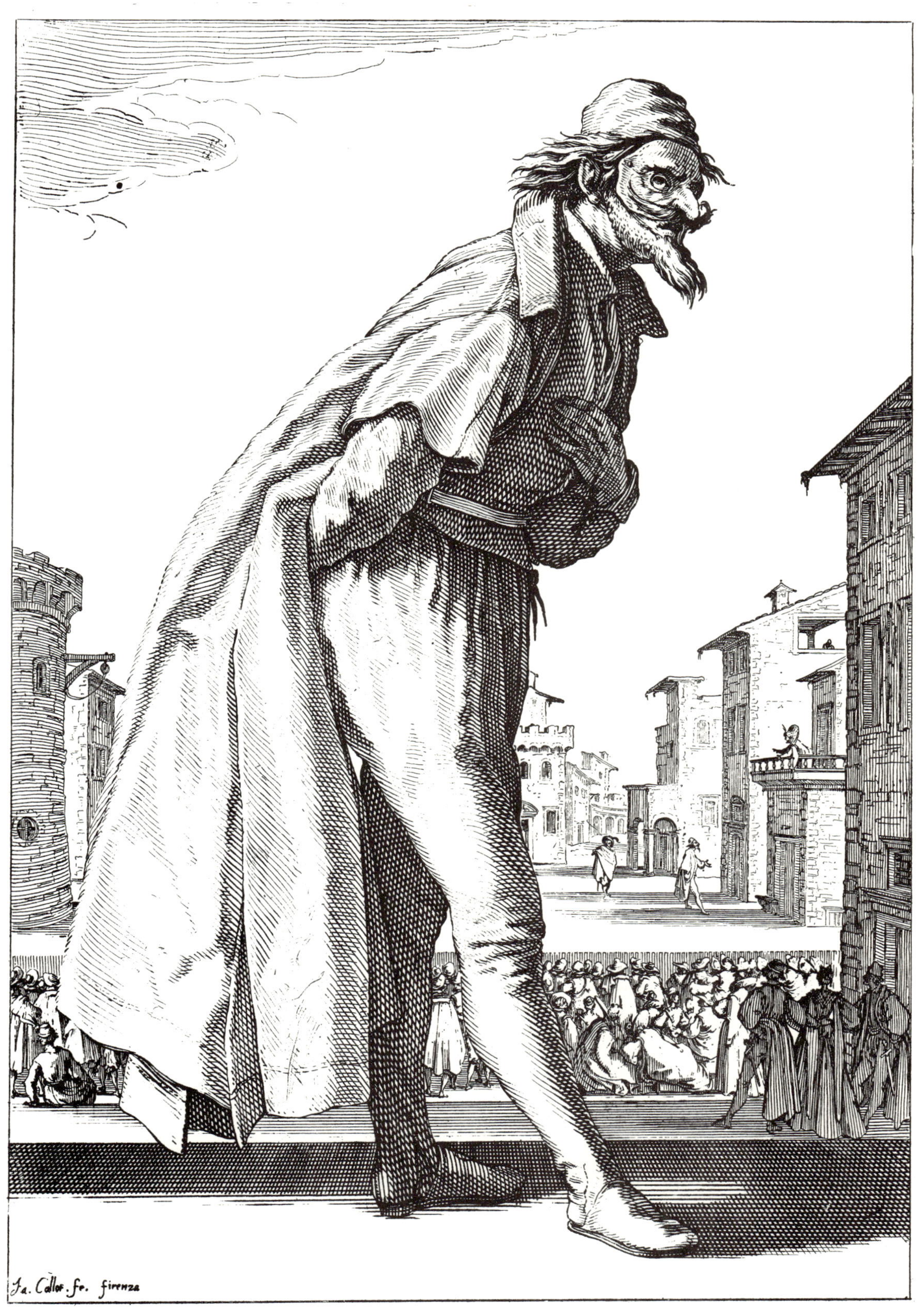

86 Pantalone, or Cassandre.

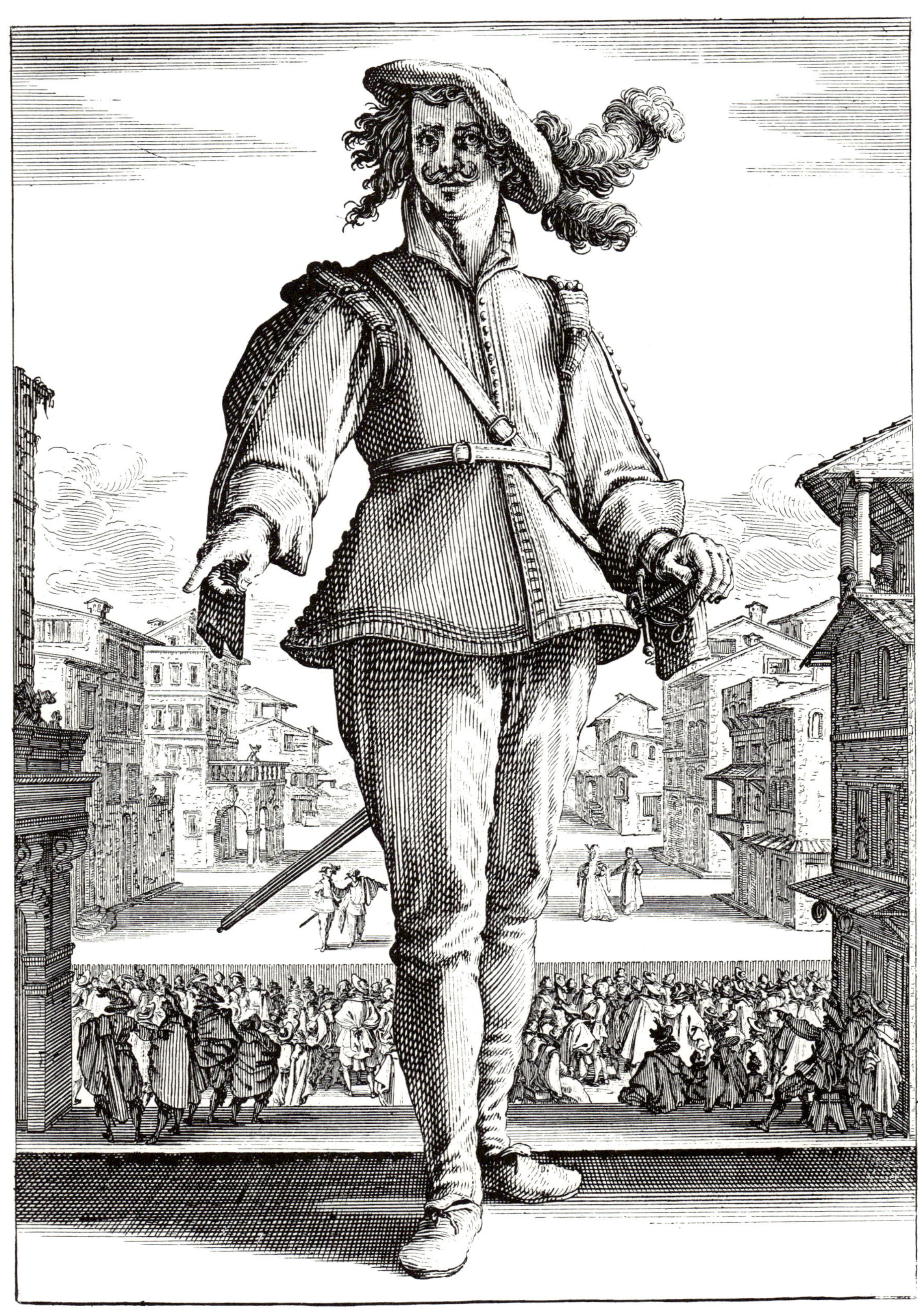

87 Il Capitano, or The Lover.

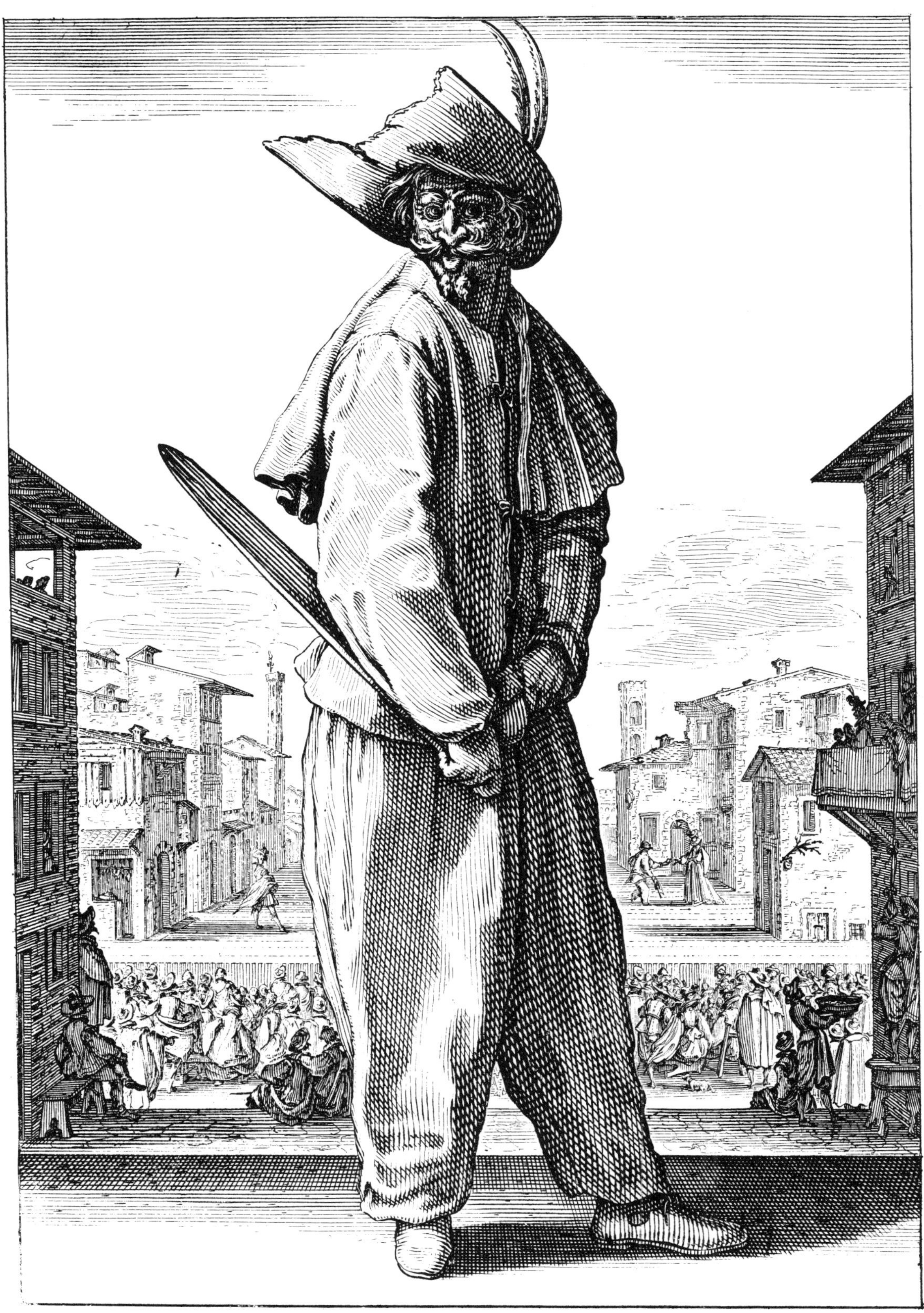

88 Zani, or Scapin.

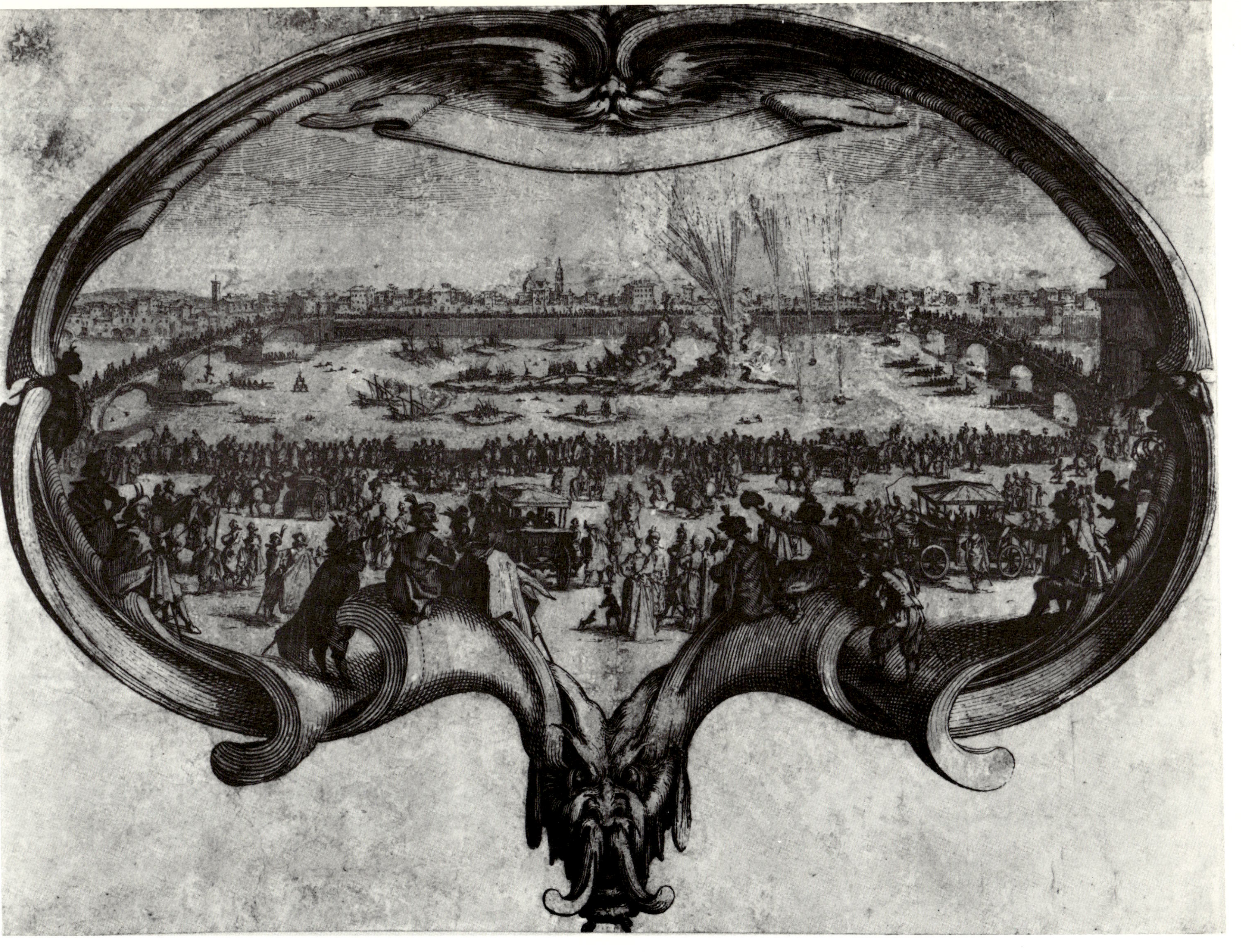

89 The Fan. Etching, 1619. Impression before lettering. In later impressions the banderole at the top bears an inscription in Italian: "Battle between the Weaver King and the Dyer King, pageant staged in Florence on the River Arno on July 25, 1619." (Courtesy Trustees of the British Museum)

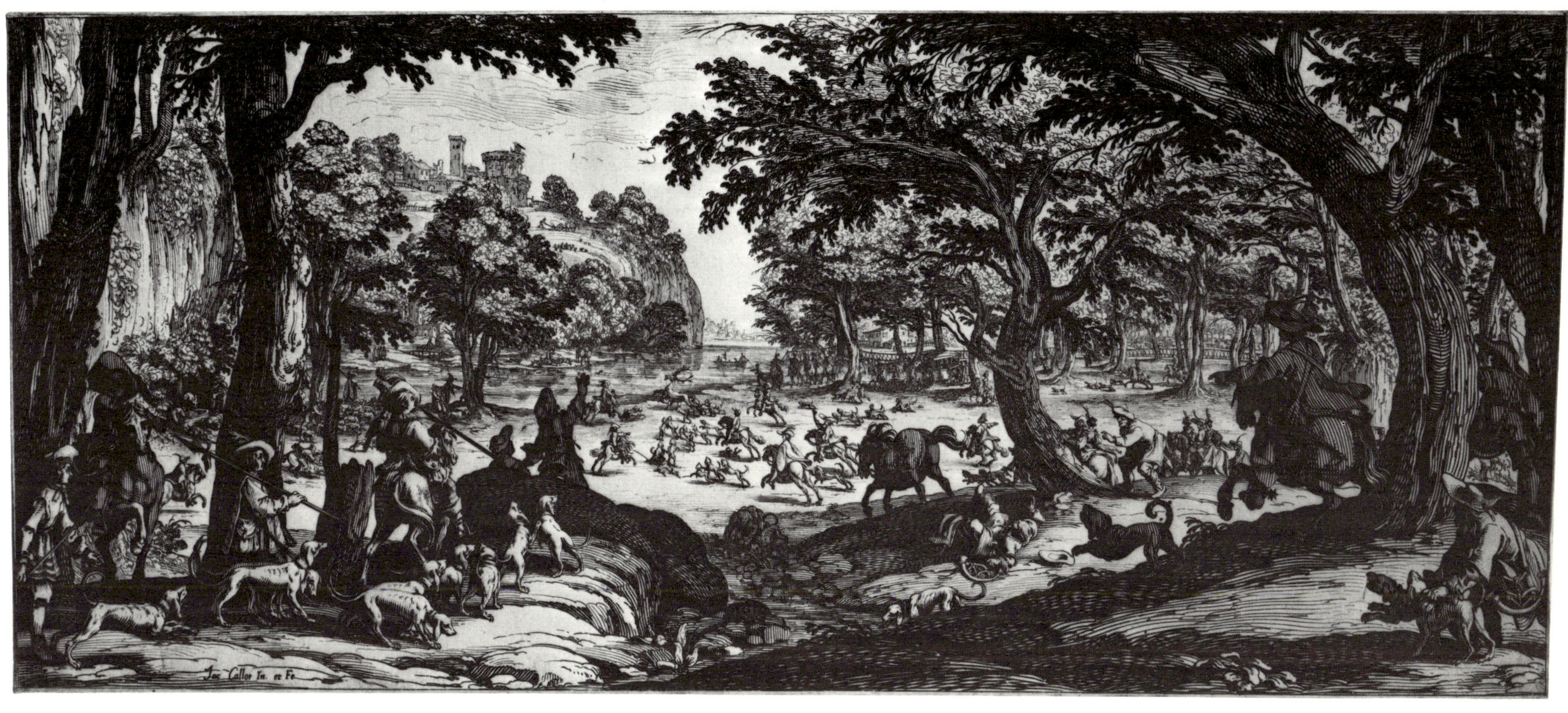

90 The Great Hunt. Etching, sometime between 1619 and 1629. (Courtesy Trustees of the British Museum)

91–97 *The Seven Deadly Sins*, a series of 7 etchings, sometime between 1618 and the early 1620's.

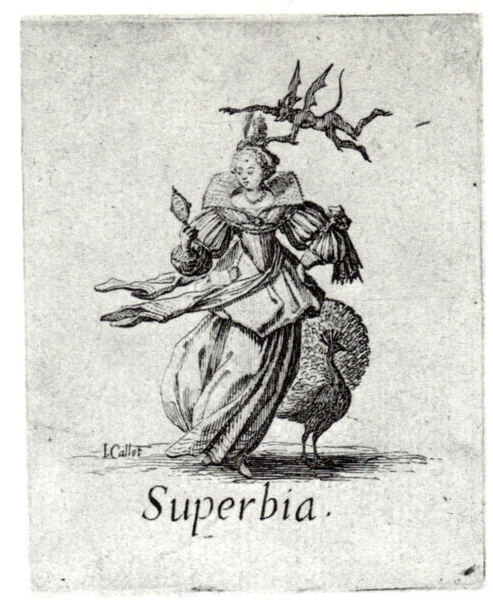

91 Pride.

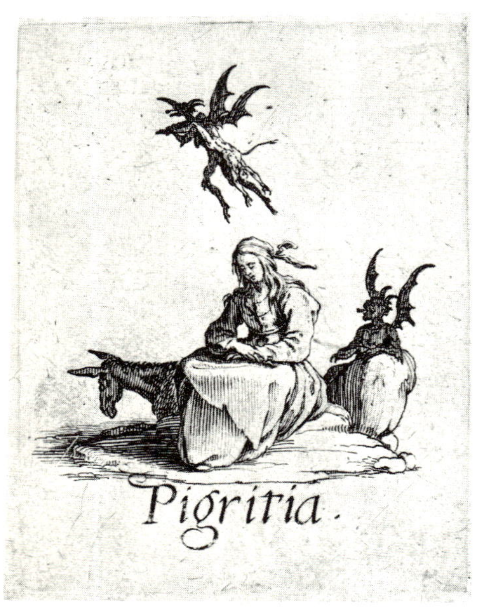

92 Sloth.

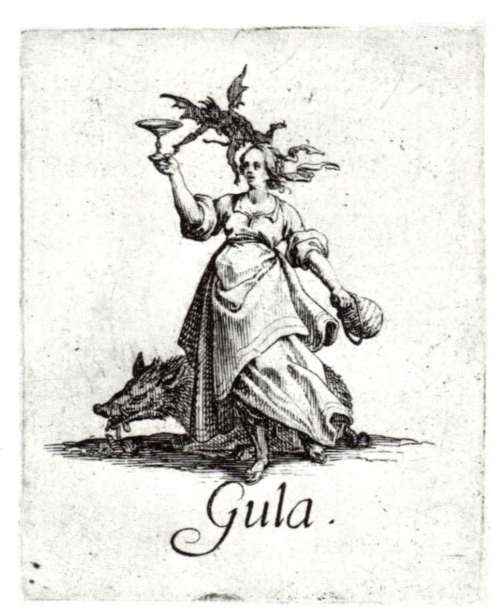

93 Gluttony.

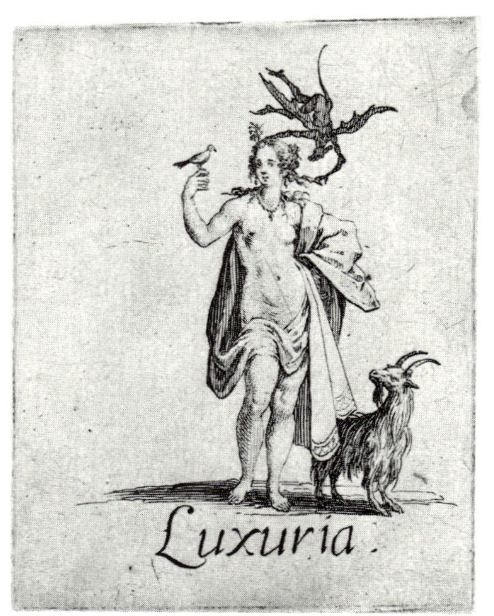

94 Lechery.

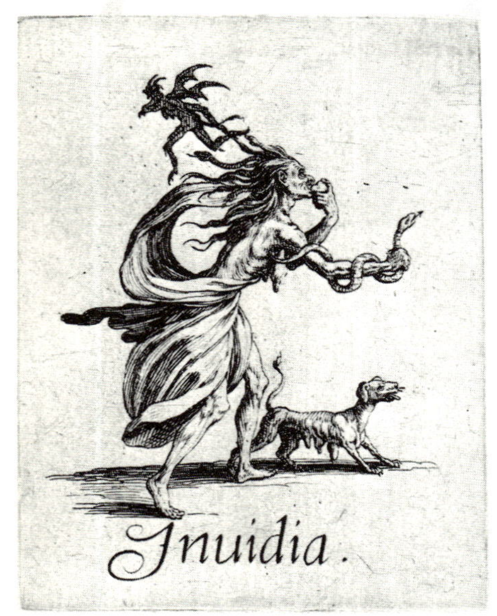

95 Envy.

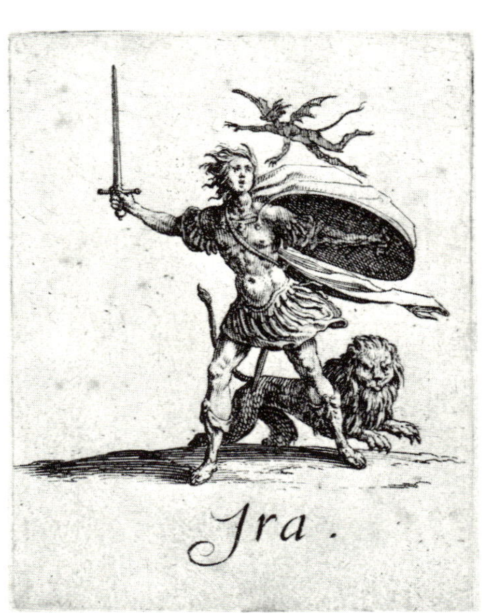

96 Anger.

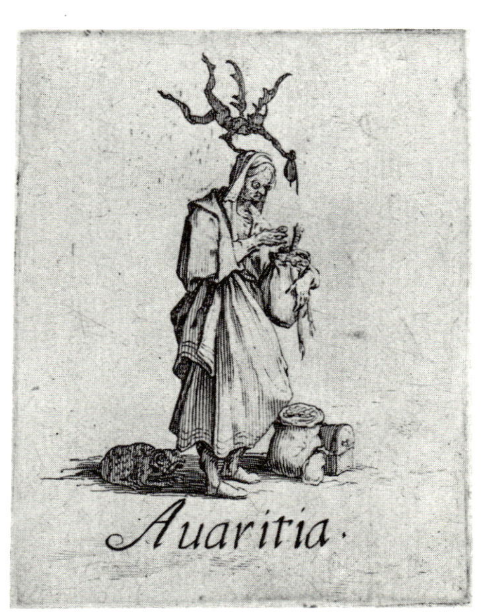

97 Avarice.

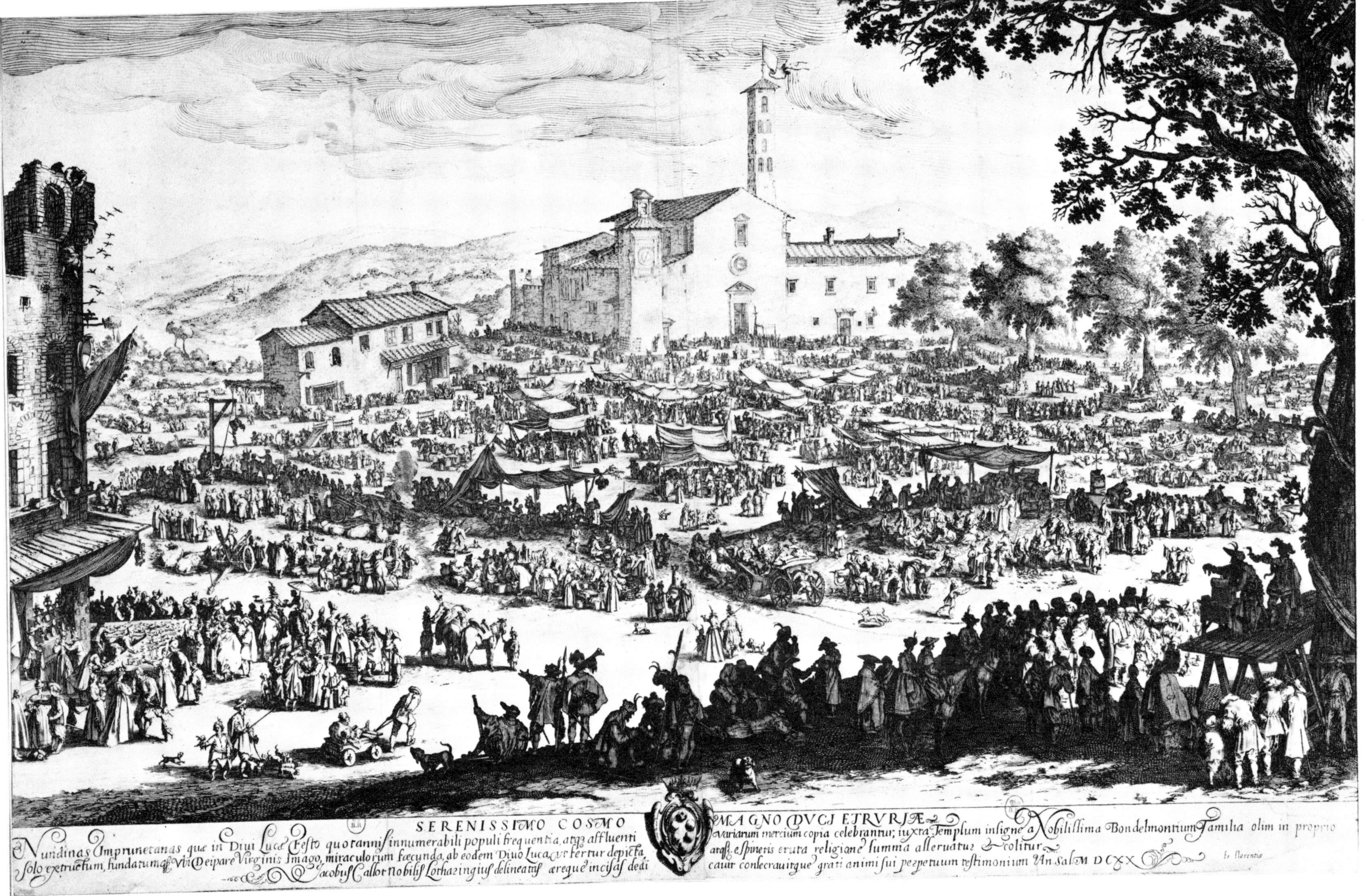

98 The Fair at Impruneta. Etching, first version 1620, second (somewhat smaller) version (reproduced here) ca. 1622. (Nos. 98–100 Cabinet des Estampes, Bibliothèque Nationale)

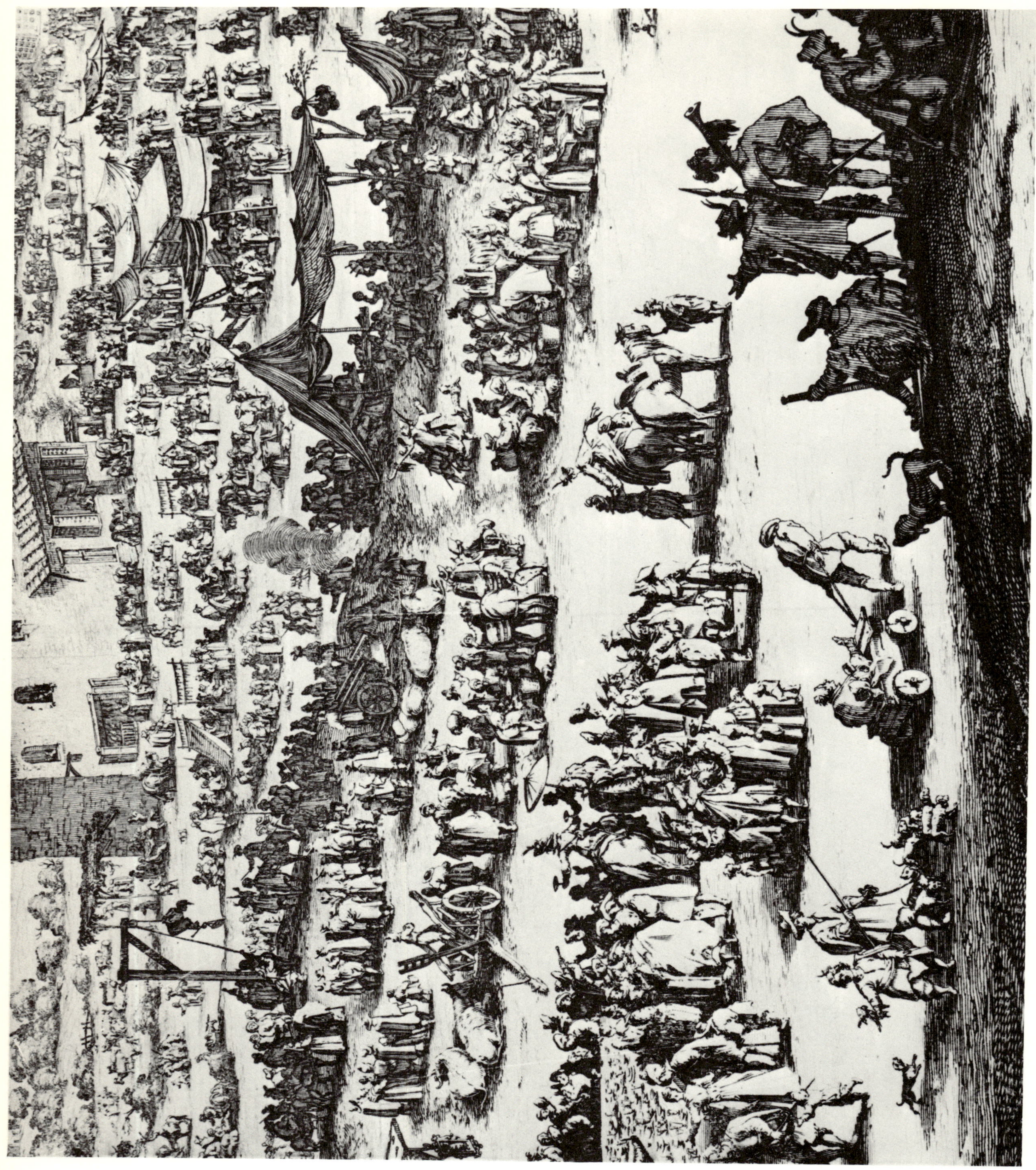

99 The Fair at Impruneta. Detail, actual size.

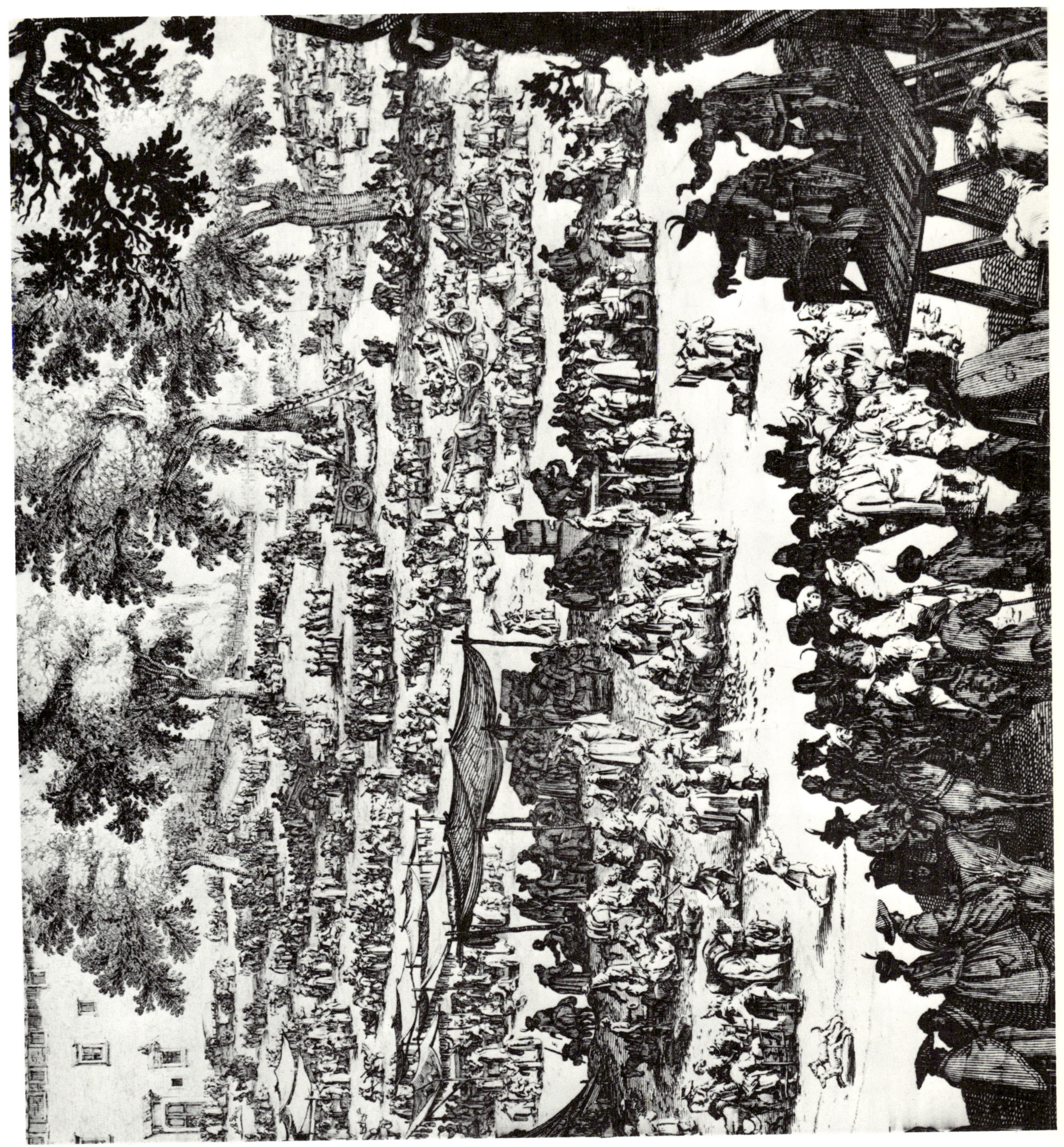

100 The Fair at Impruneta. Detail, actual size.

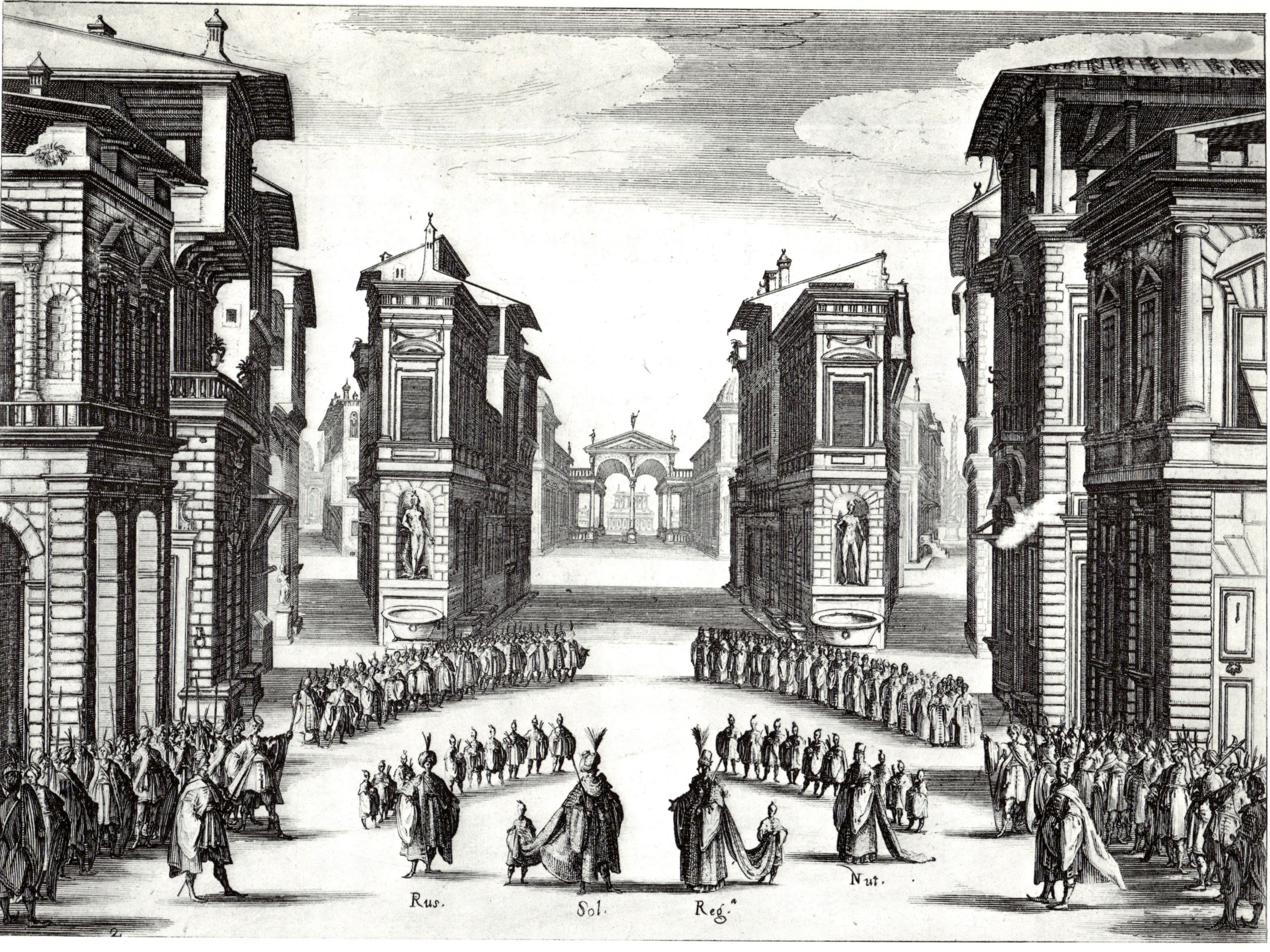

101 From *Soliman* (illustrations in a printed edition of Prospero Bonarelli's tragedy *Il Solimano*), a series of 3 etchings, 1619: Scene from Act II.

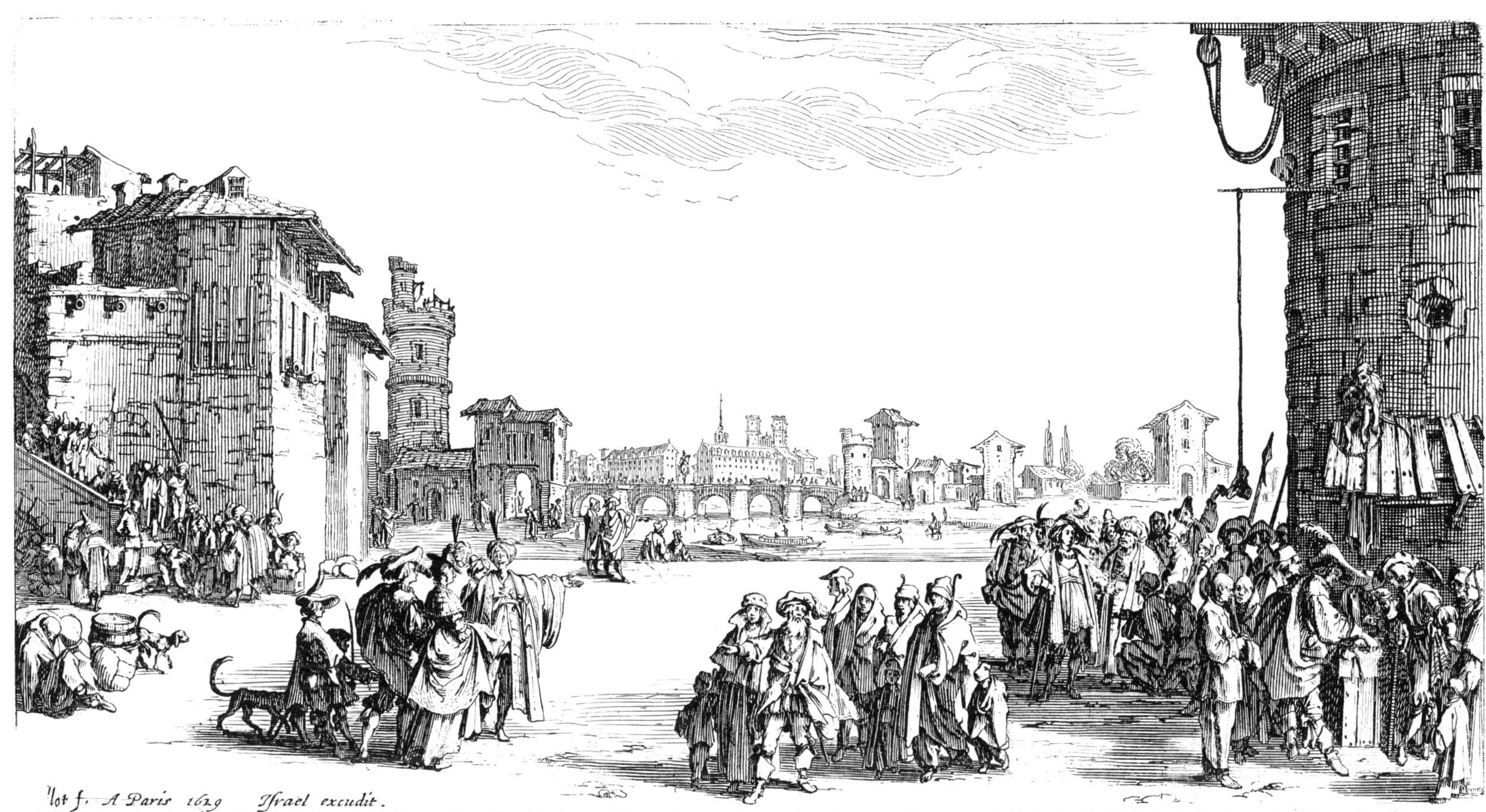

102 The Slave Market. Etching, first state ca. 1620, second state (with additions to background; reproduced here) 1629. (Howard Daniel Collection)

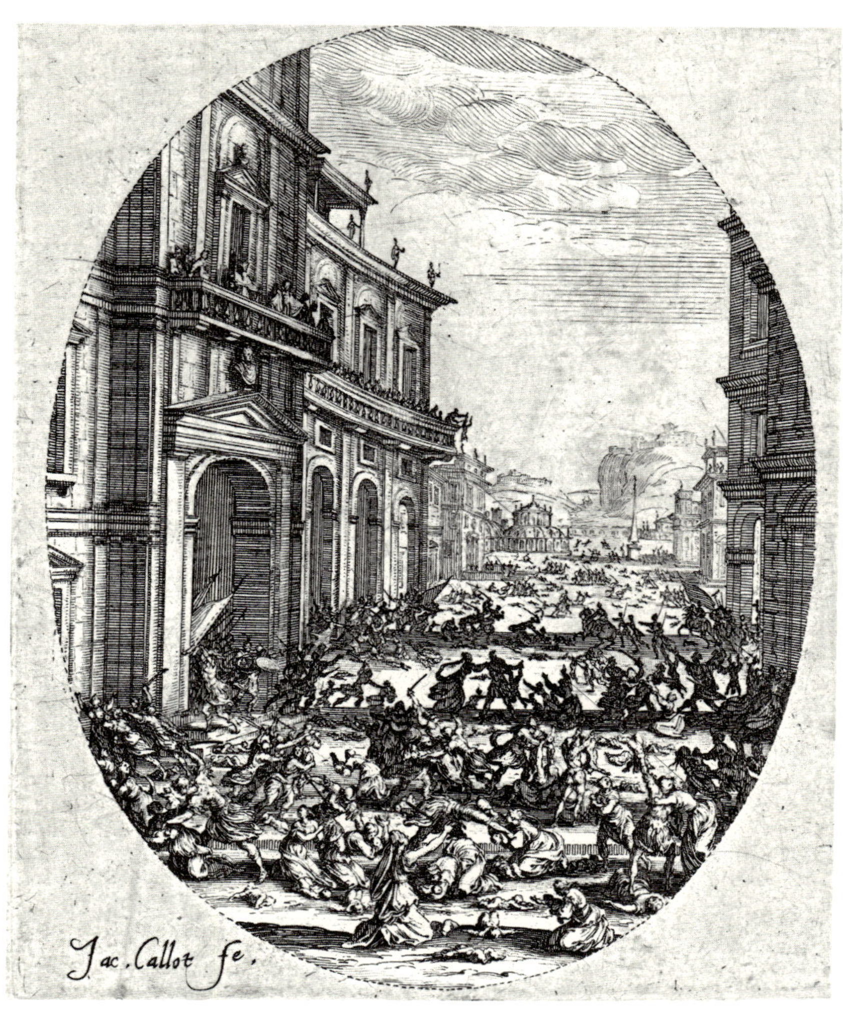

103 The Massacre of the Innocents. Etching, first version ca. 1617/18, second (slightly altered) version (reproduced here) 1622.

104–127 The complete *Balli di Sfessania*, a series of 24 etchings, ca. 1621/22.
(Nos. 107, 120–124 & 127 Howard Daniel Collection)

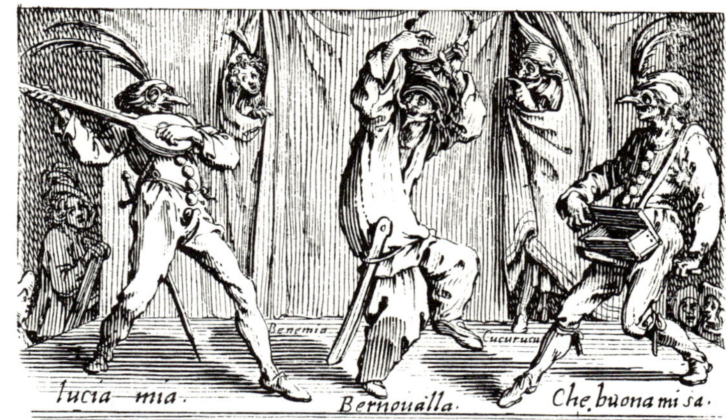

104 Title.

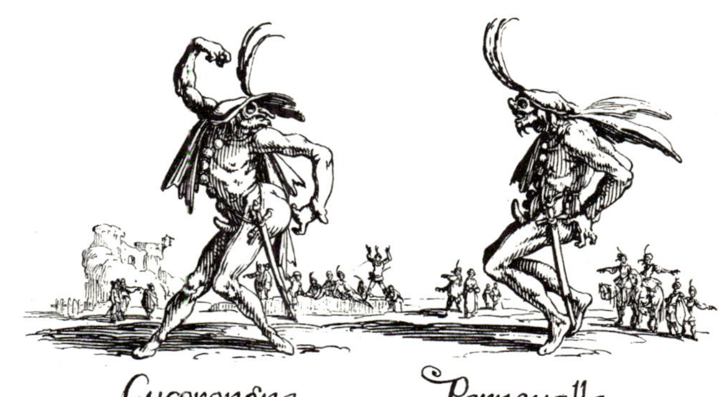

105

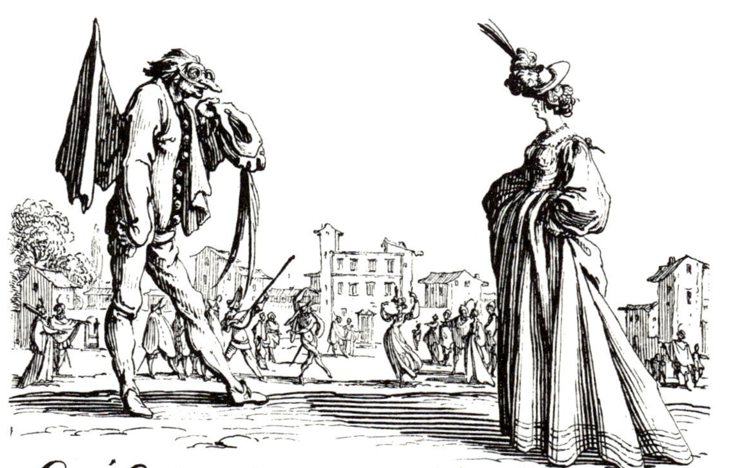

106

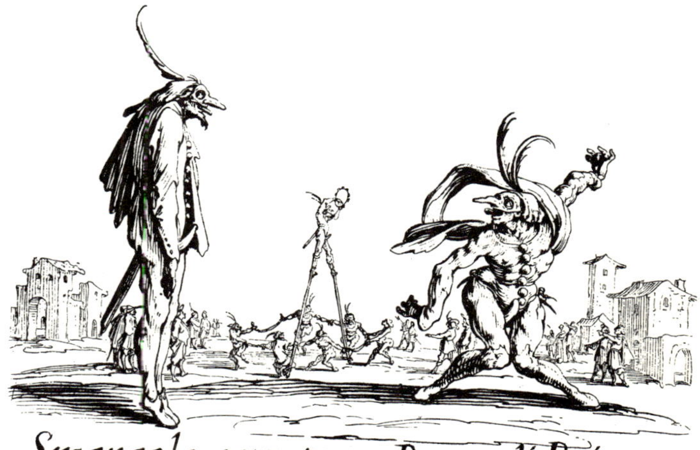

107

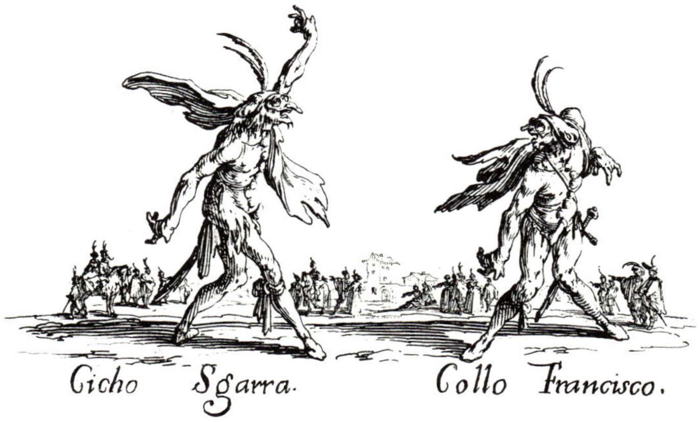

Cicho Sgarra. Collo Francisco.

108

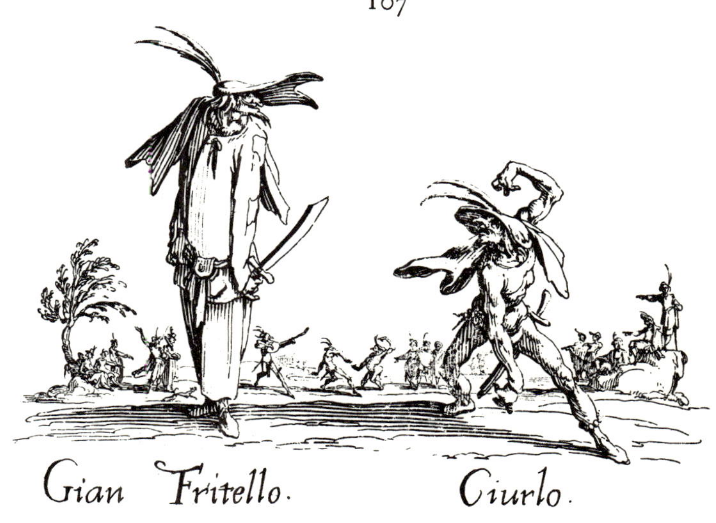

109

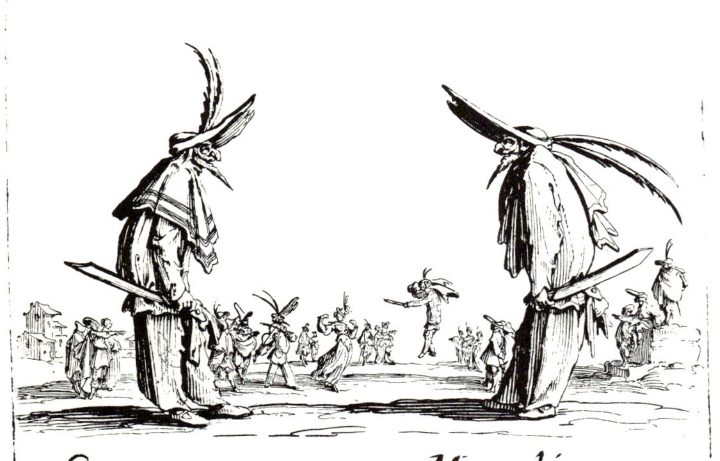

110

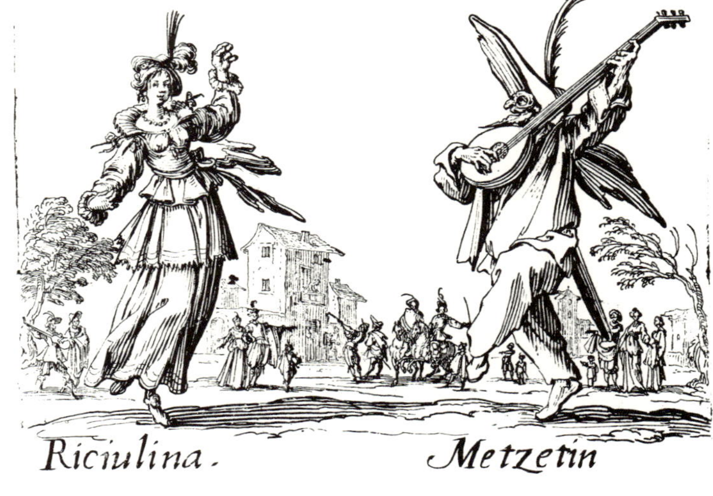

111

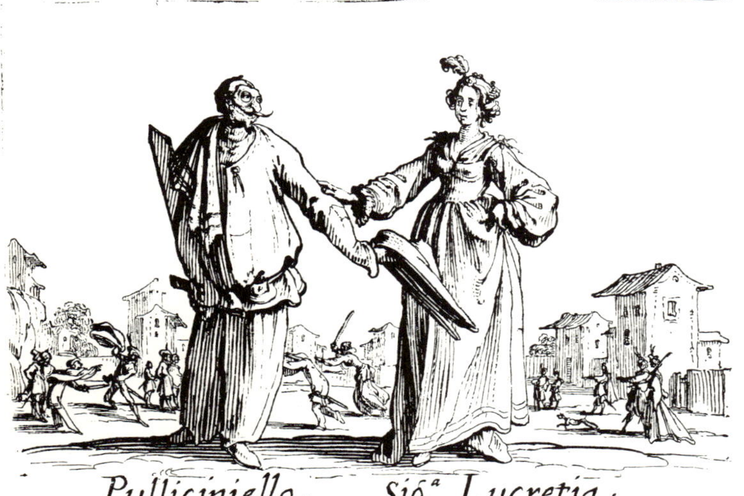

112

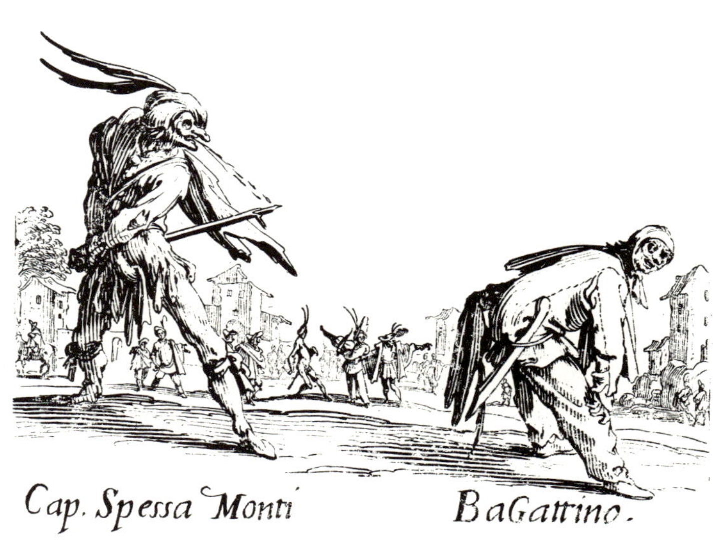

113

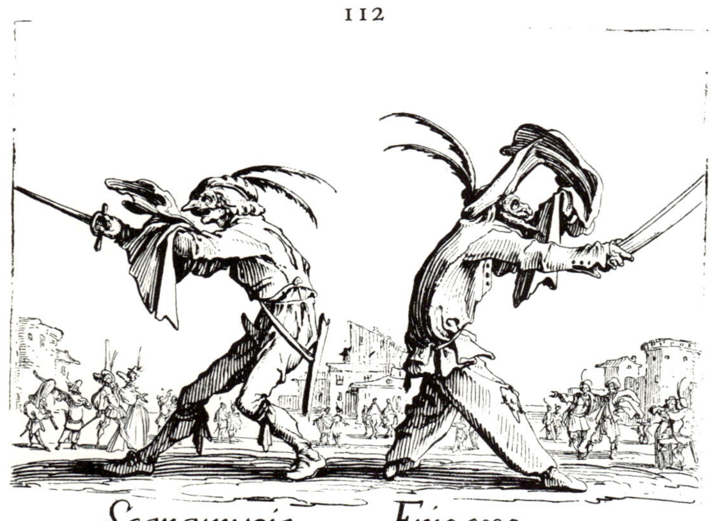

114

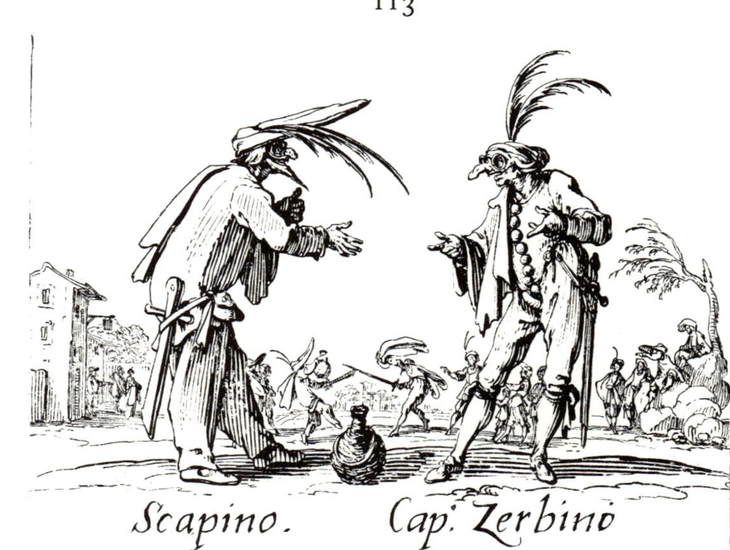

115

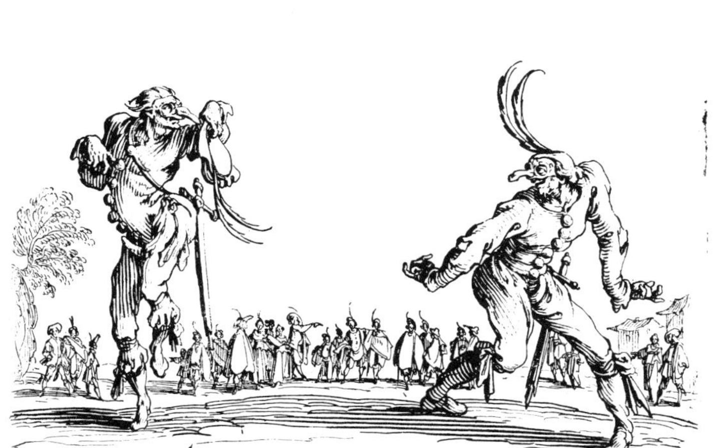

116

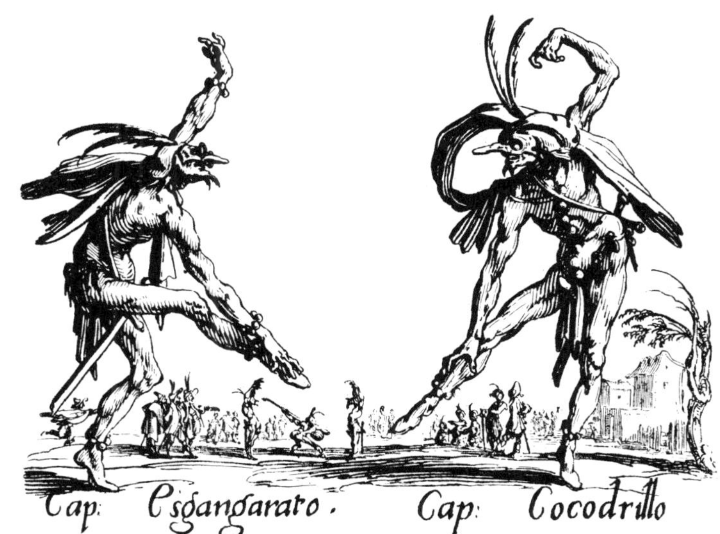

117

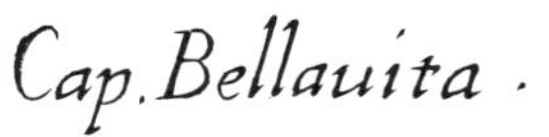

118

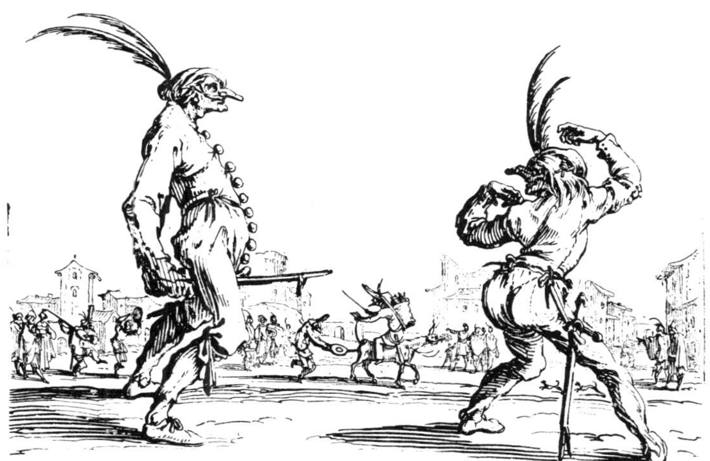

119

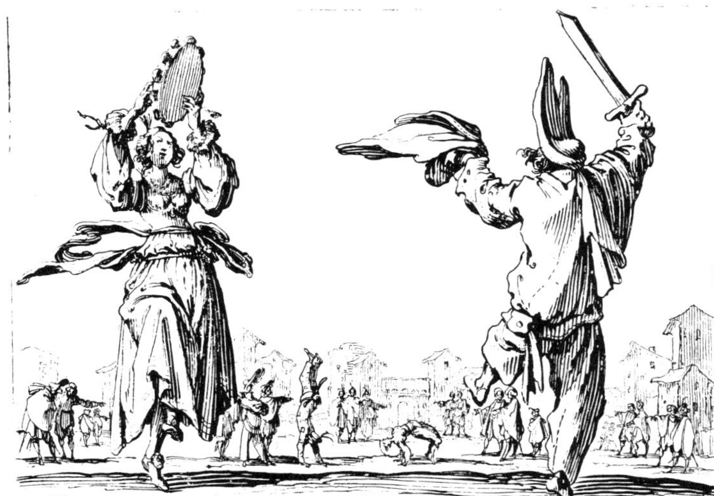

120

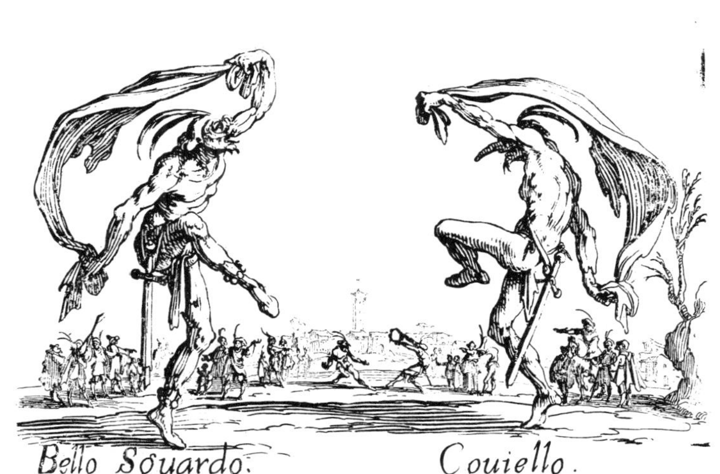

121

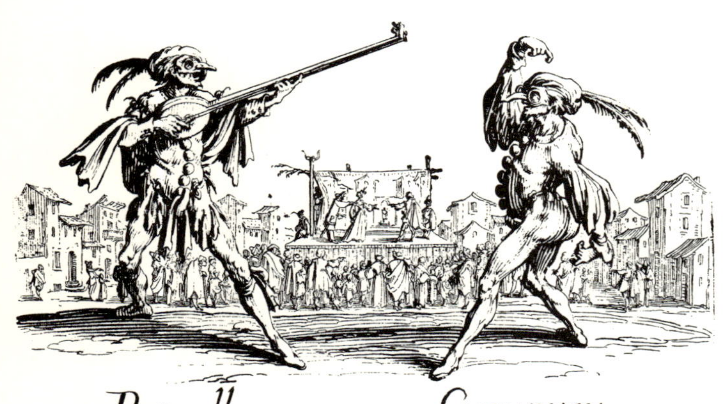

Razullo. Cucurucu.

122

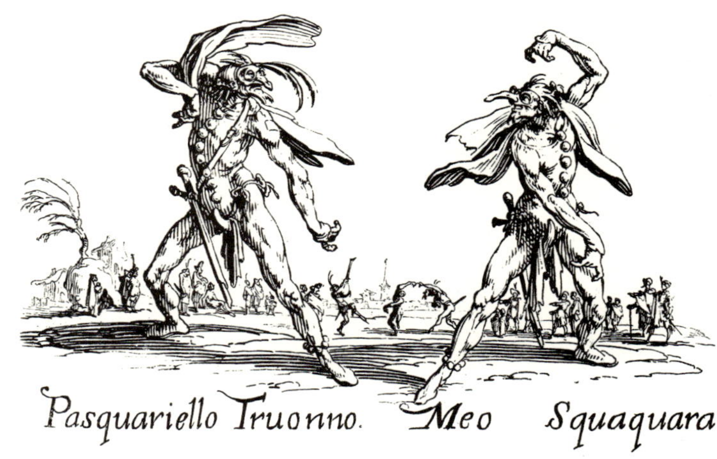

Pasquariello Truonno. Meo Squaquara

123

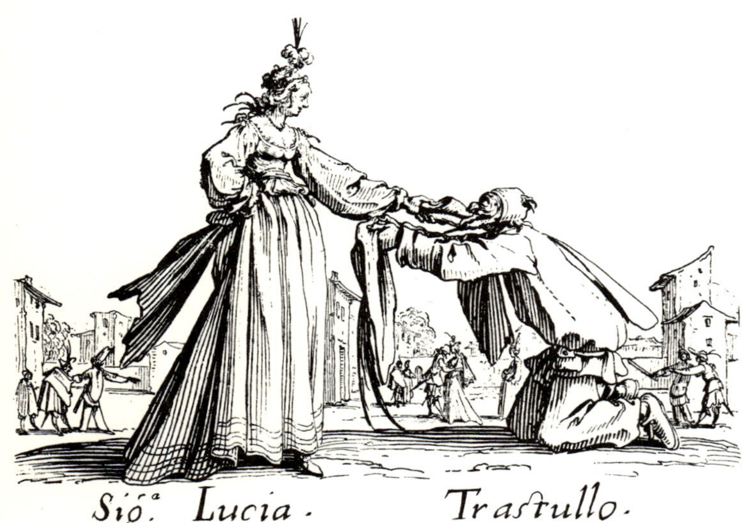

Sig.ª Lucia. Trastullo.

124

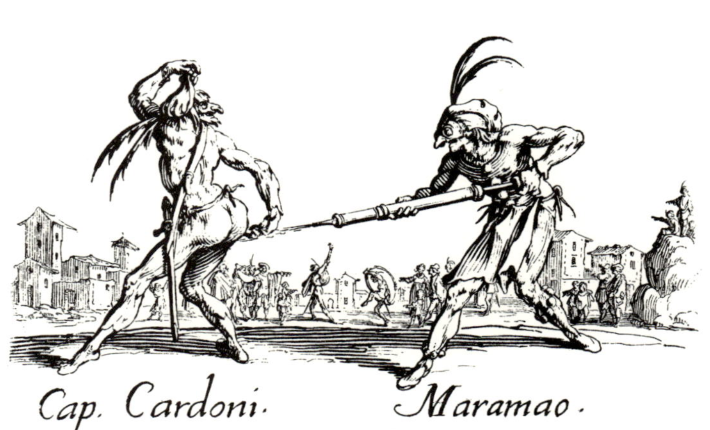

Cap. Cardoni. Maramao.

125

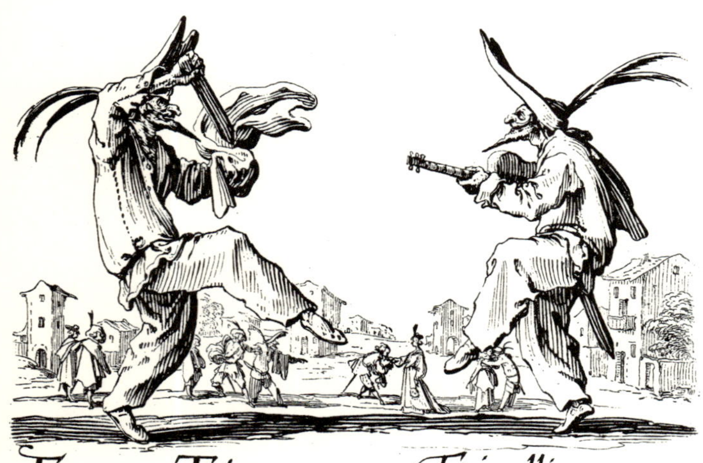

Franca Trippa. Fritellino.

126

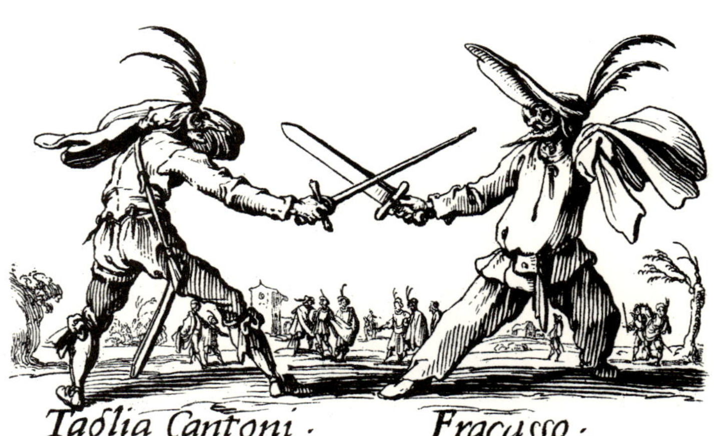

Taglia Cantoni. Fracasso.

127

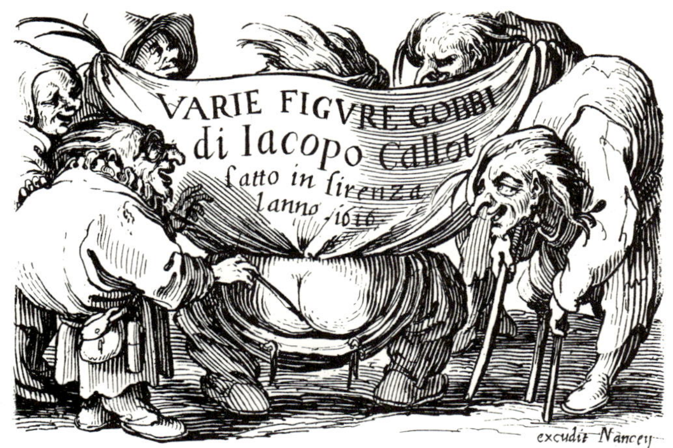

128 Title.

128–148 The complete *Gobbi* (*Grotesque Dwarfs*), a series of 21 etchings, ca. 1622 (title dated 1616).

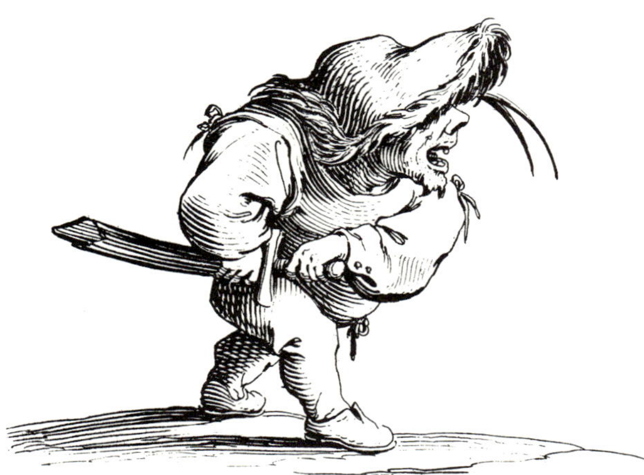

129 Dwarf with Slouch Hat and Sword.

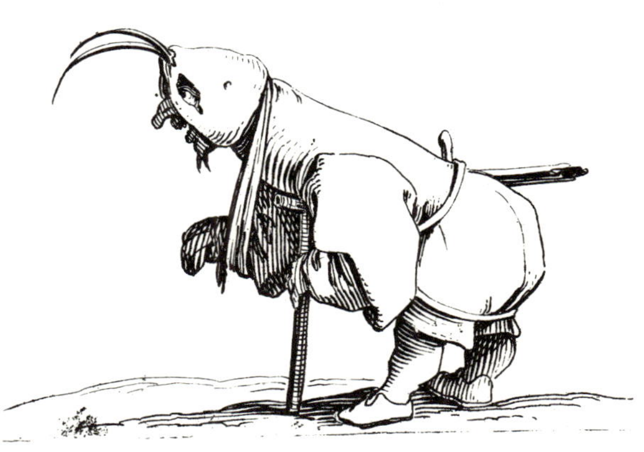

130 Crippled Dwarf with Hood.

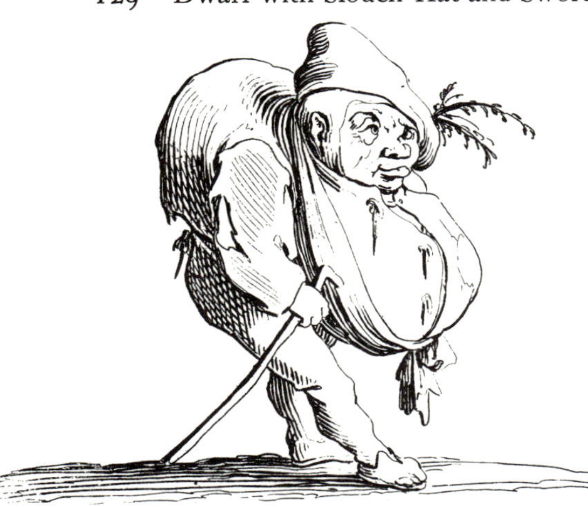

131 Hunchback with Walking Stick.

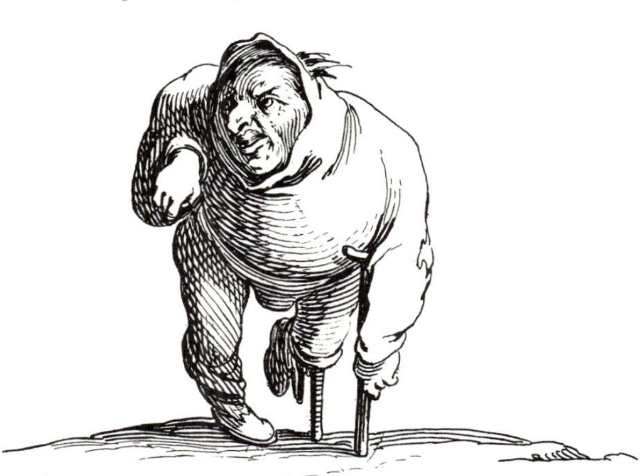

132 Cripple with Wooden Leg and Crutch.

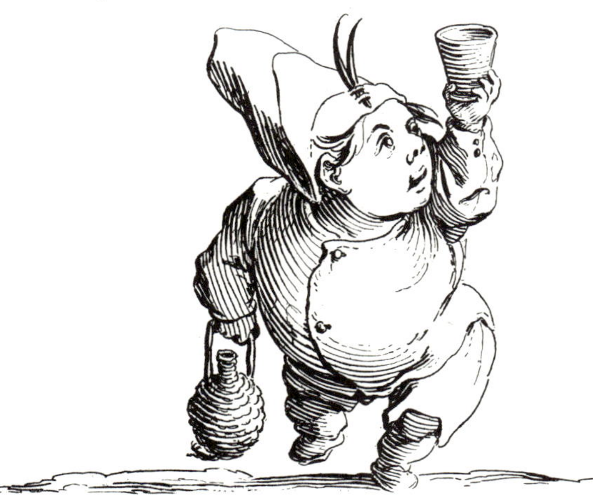

133 Dwarf with Wine Bottle and Glass, Front View.

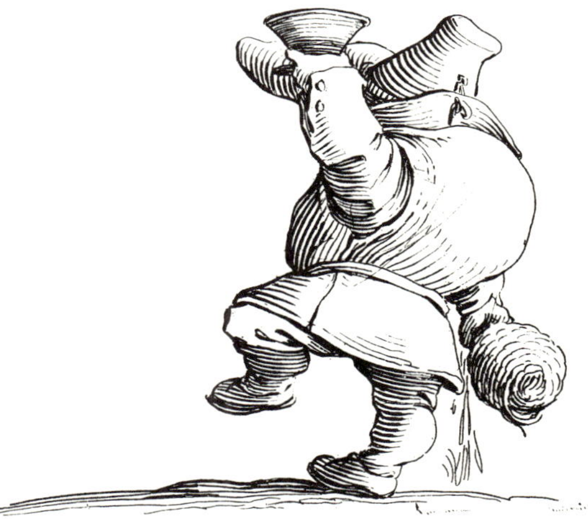

134 Another Dwarf with Wine Bottle and Glass, Seen from Behind.

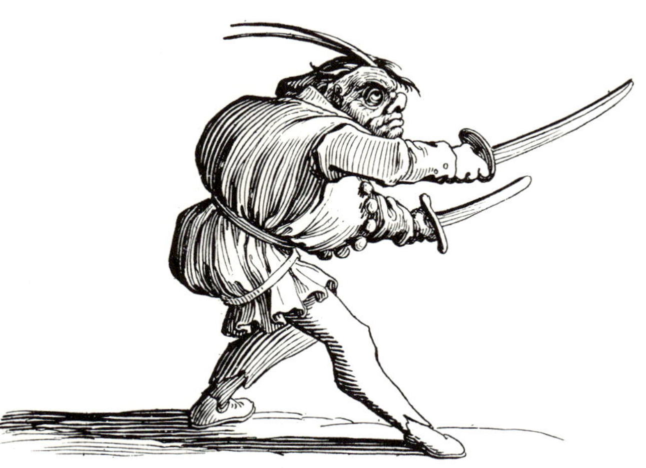

135 Dwarf with Two Sabers.

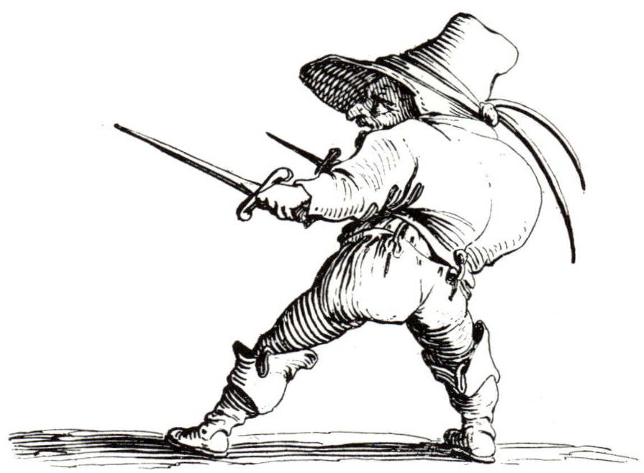

136 Dwarf with Sword and Dagger.

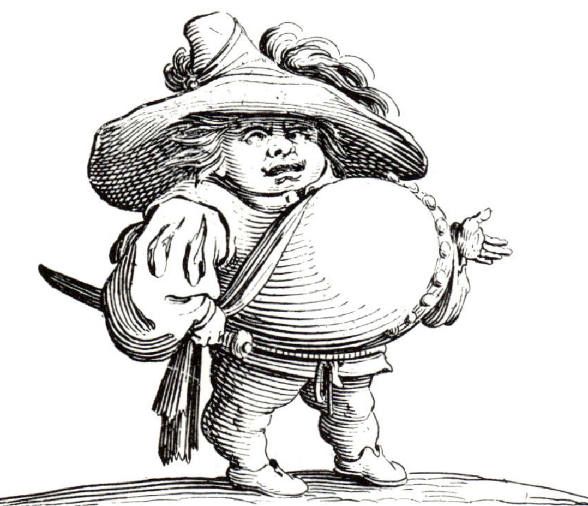

137 Dwarf with Big Belly.

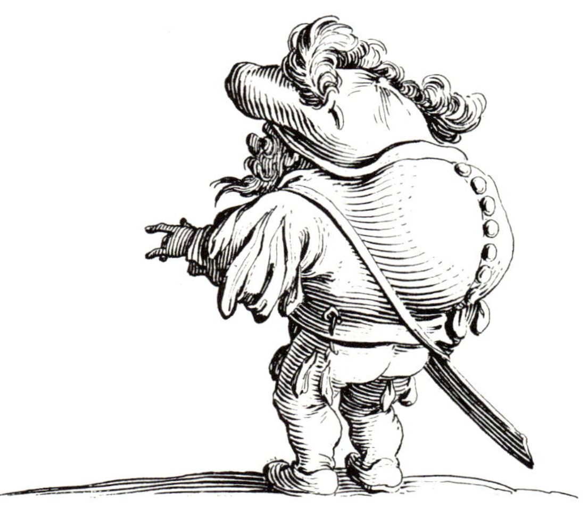

138 Hunchback, Seen from Behind.

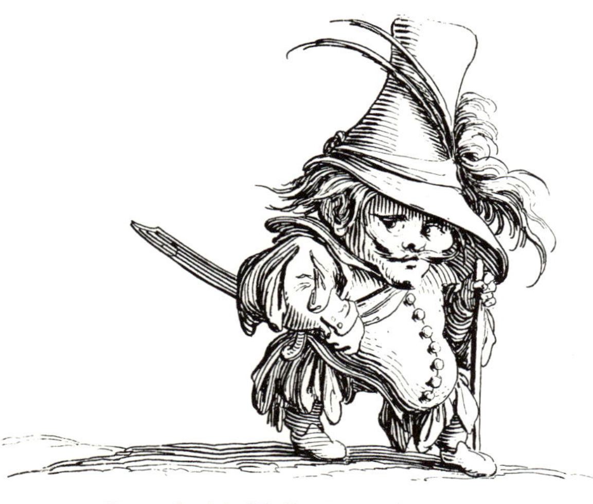

139 Dwarf with Tall Hat and Drooping Belly.

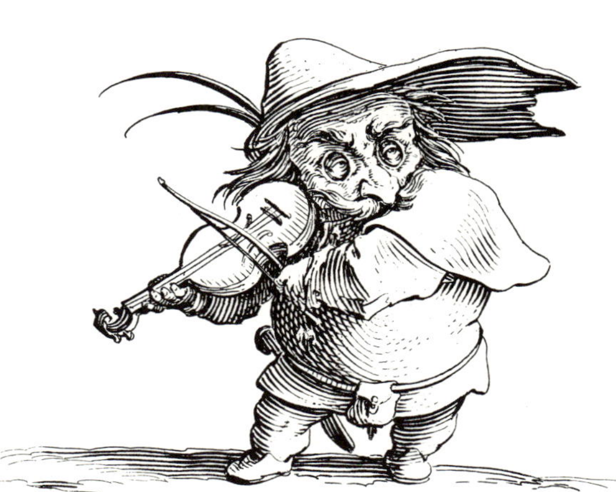

140 Dwarf Fiddling.

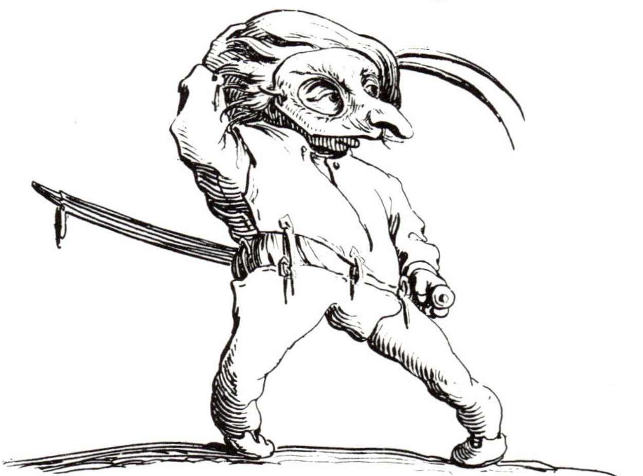

141 Masked Dwarf with Saber.

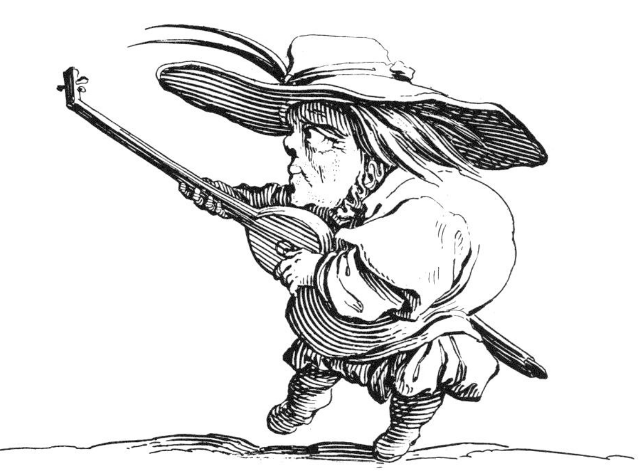

142 Dwarf Playing String Instrument.

143 Hurdygurdy Player.

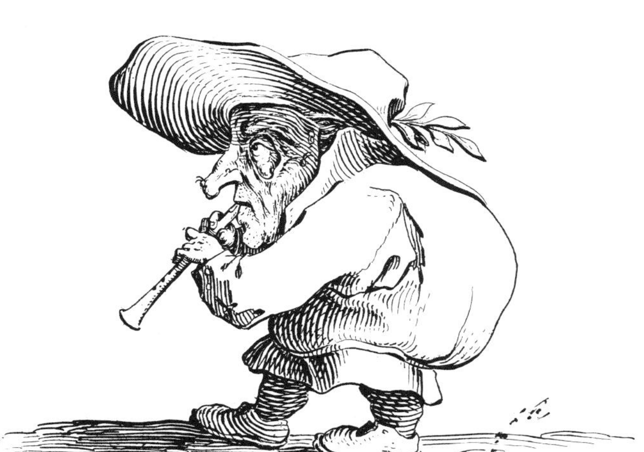

144 Dwarf Playing Wind Instrument.

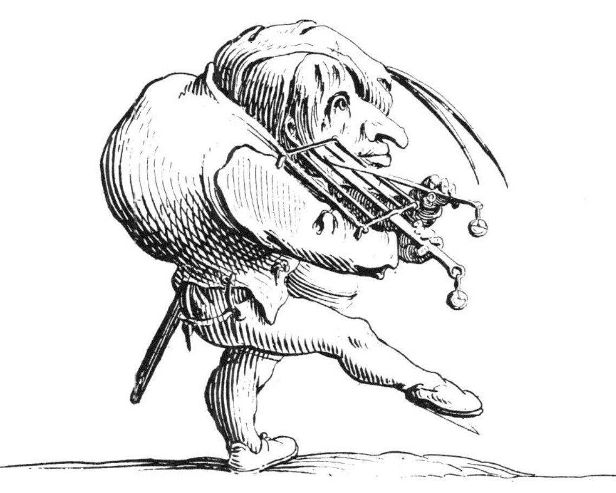

145 Dwarf Bowing a Grill.

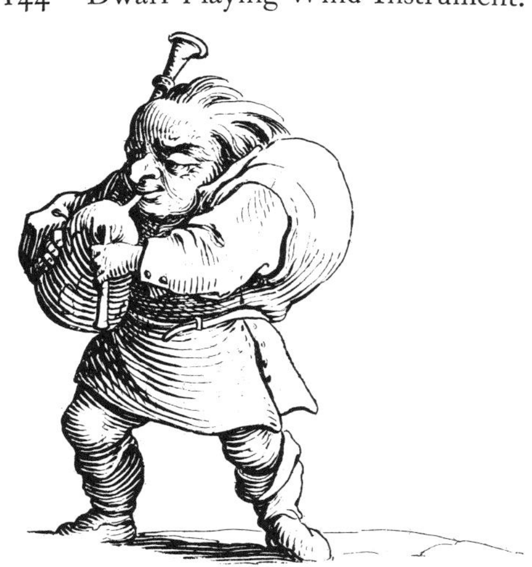

146 Dwarf Playing Bagpipe.

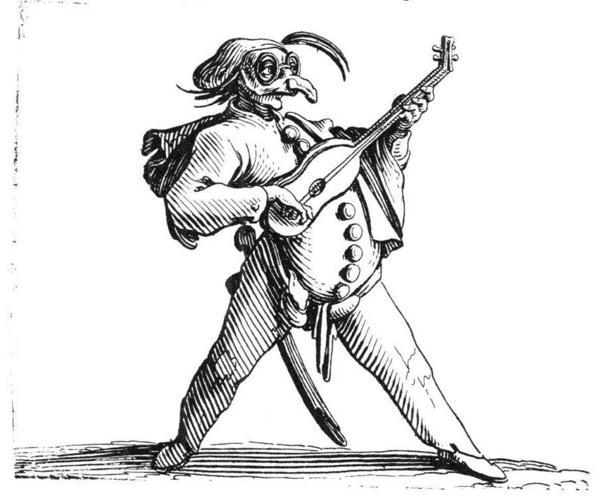

147 Masked Guitar Player.

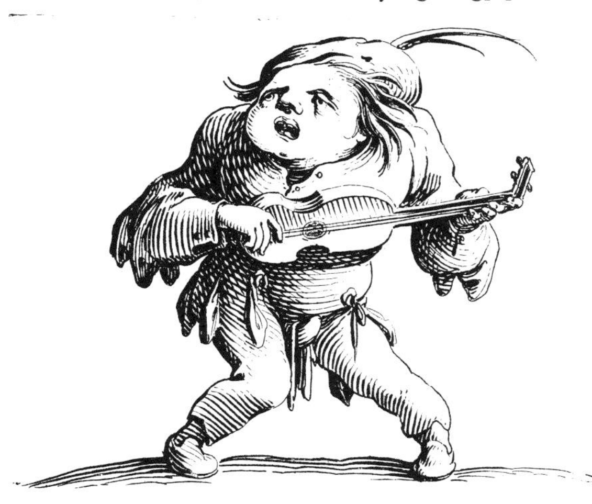

148 Guitar Player with Crooked Legs.

149–152 *The Gypsies* (*Les Bohémiens*), a series of 4 etchings, ca. 1621.

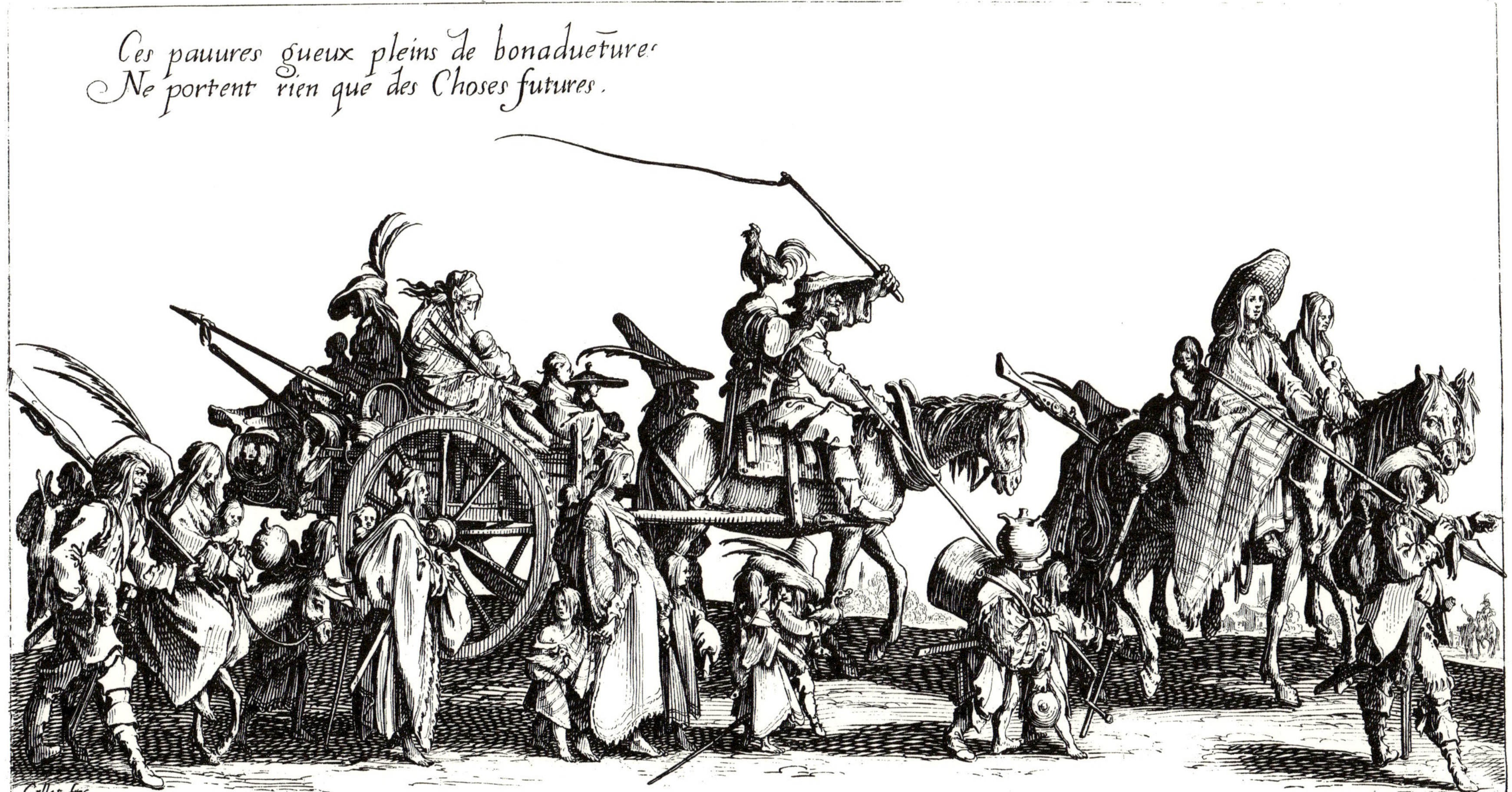

149 Journeying. The French couplet reads: "The only things these poor fortune-telling beggars carry with them are things yet to come." (Instead of "fortune-telling," *bonadve*[*n*]*tures* may refer to "living from hand to mouth.")

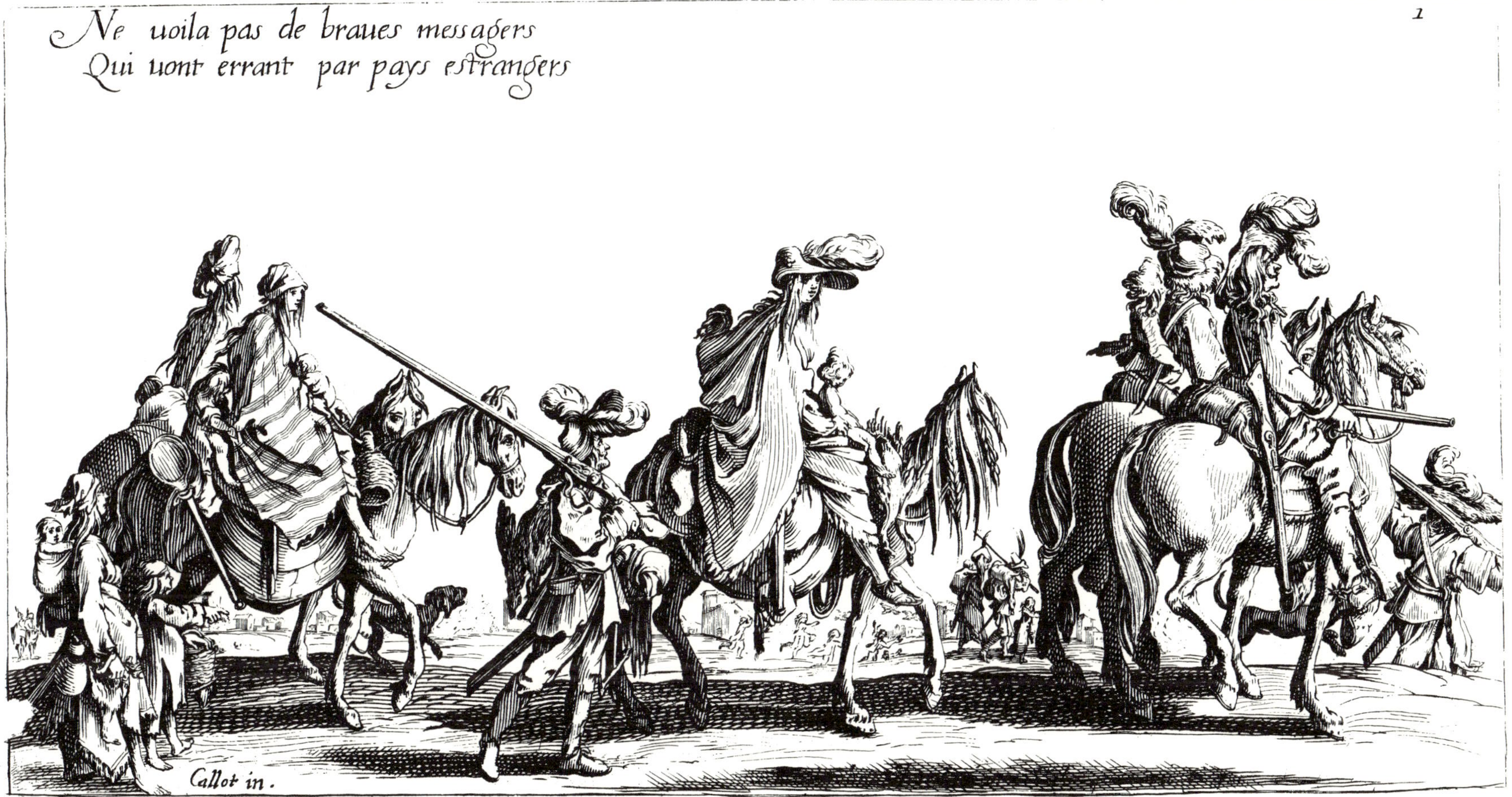

150 Journeying. The inscription reads: "Are these not fine messengers, straying through foreign lands?"

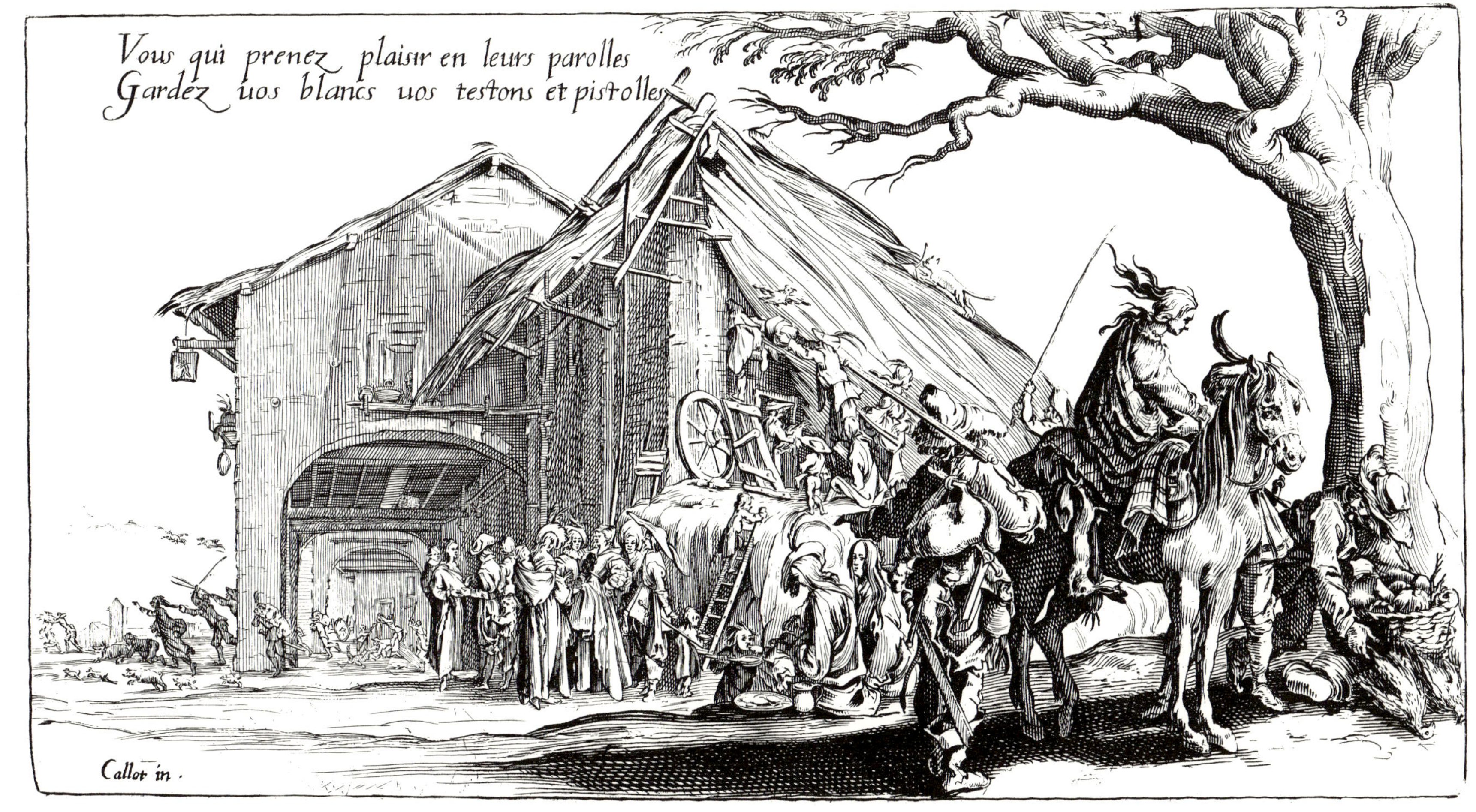

151 At a Resting Place. The inscription reads: "You who take pleasure in their words, watch out for your *blancs*, *testons* and *pistolles* [all of these were types of coins]."

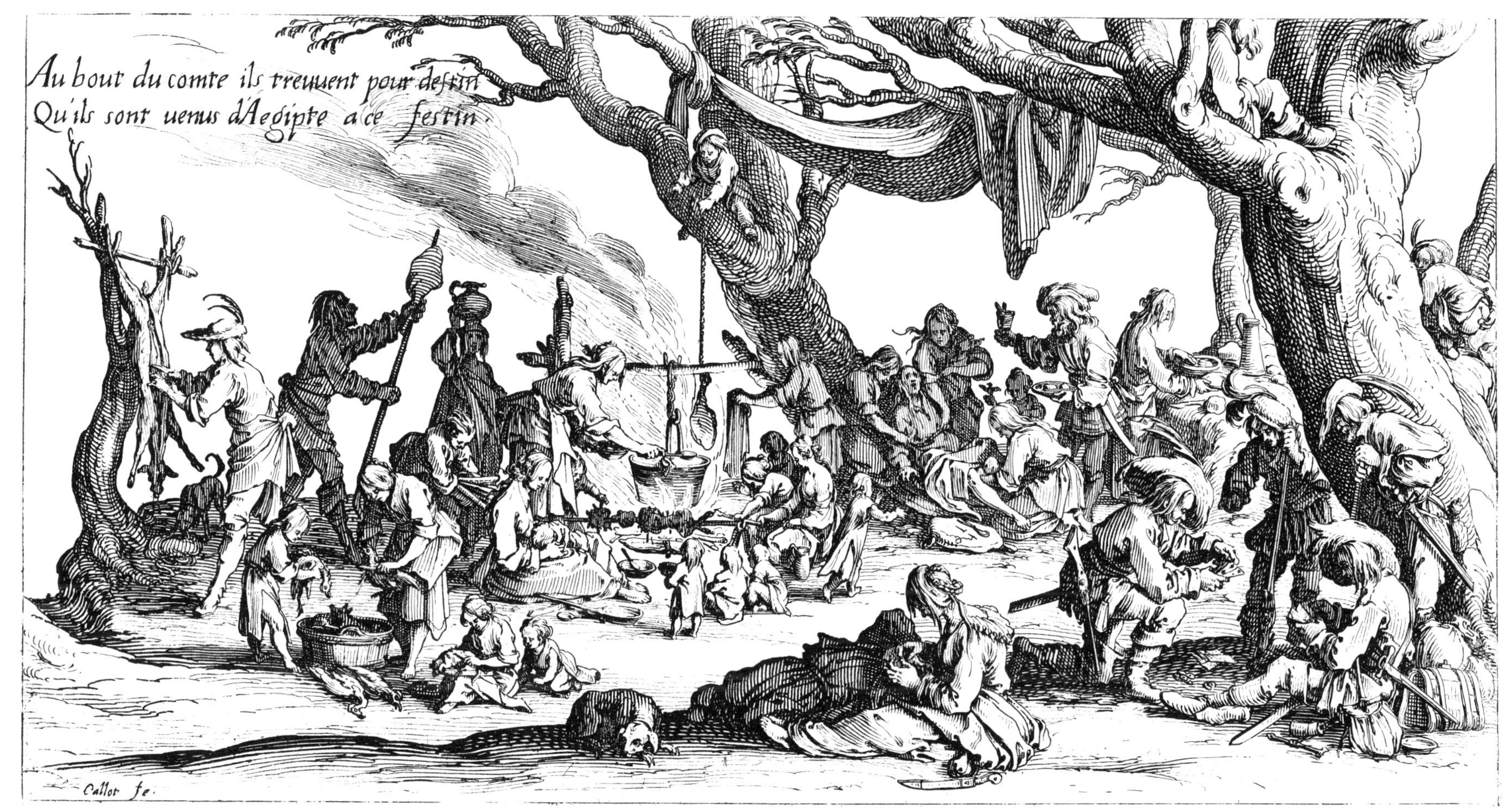

152 In Camp. The inscription reads: "When all is said and done, they find that their fate is to have come from Egypt to this feast."

153–177 The complete *Beggars* (*Les Gueux*), a series of 25 etchings, ca. 1622/23.

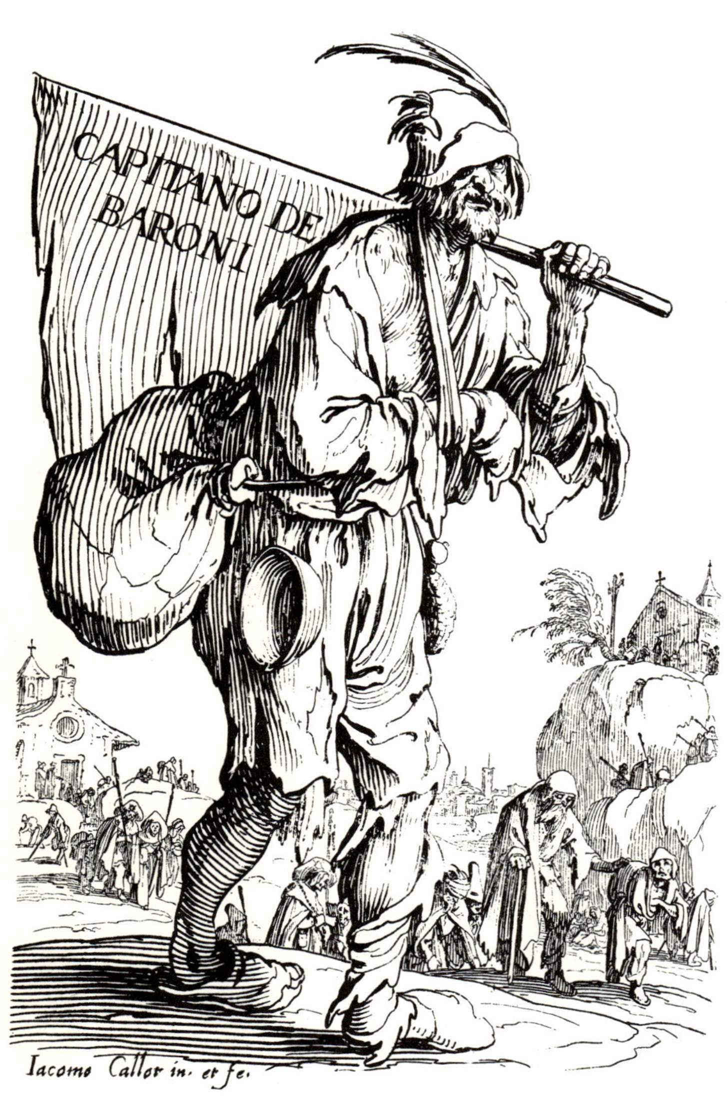

153 Title. The inscription reads: "Captain of the Scoundrels."

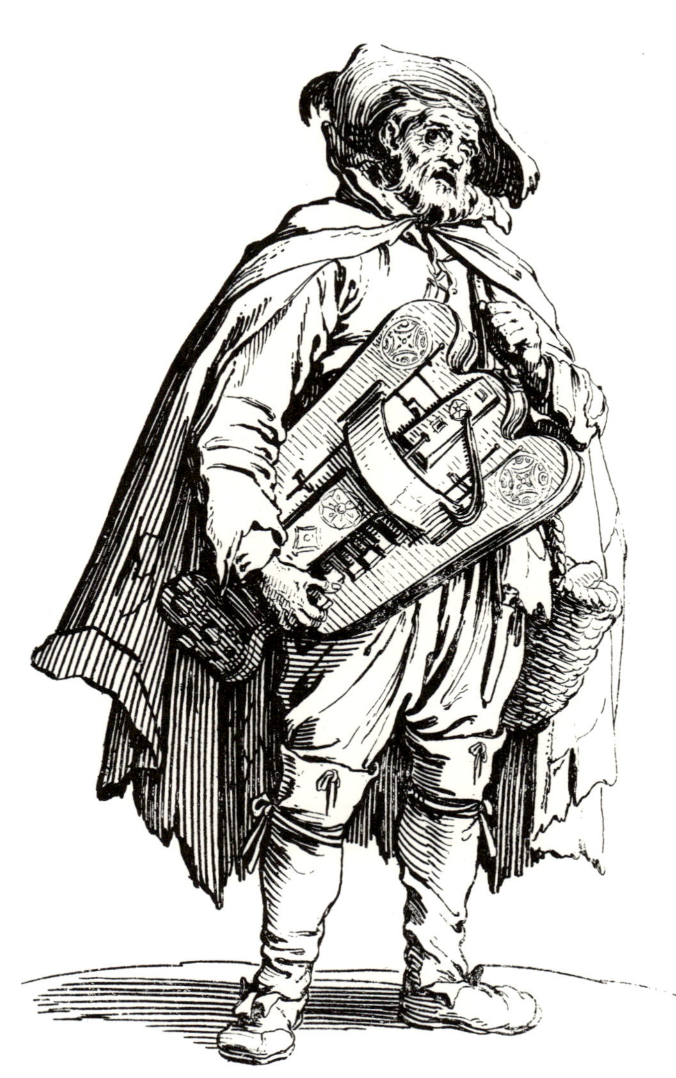

154 Beggar with Hurdygurdy.

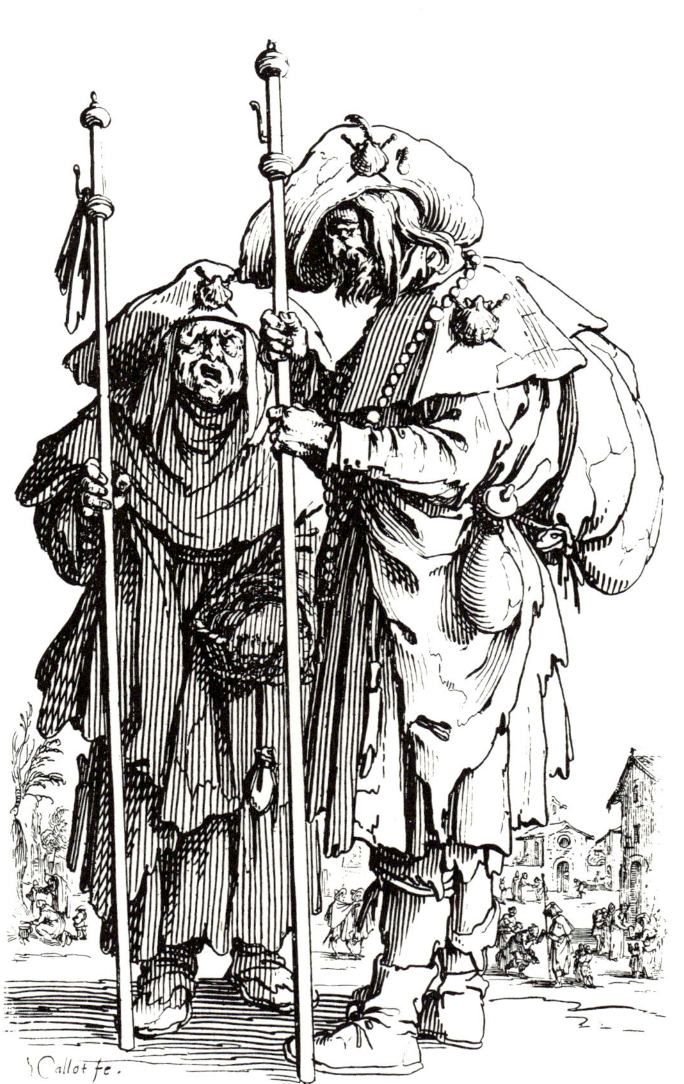

155 Two Pilgrims.

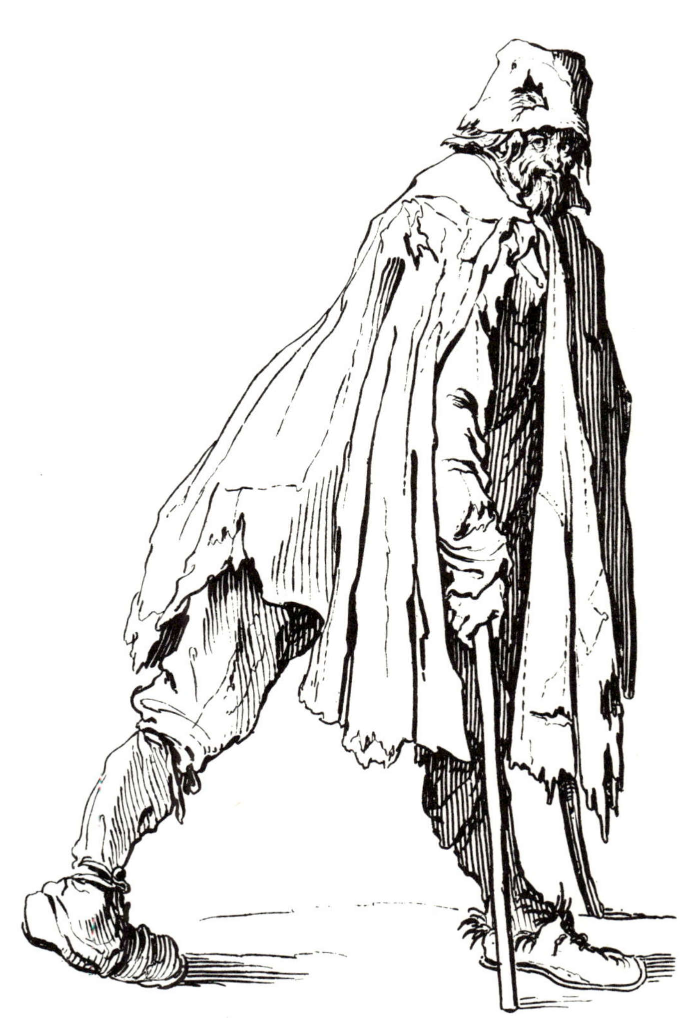

156 Beggar with Crutches, in Profile.

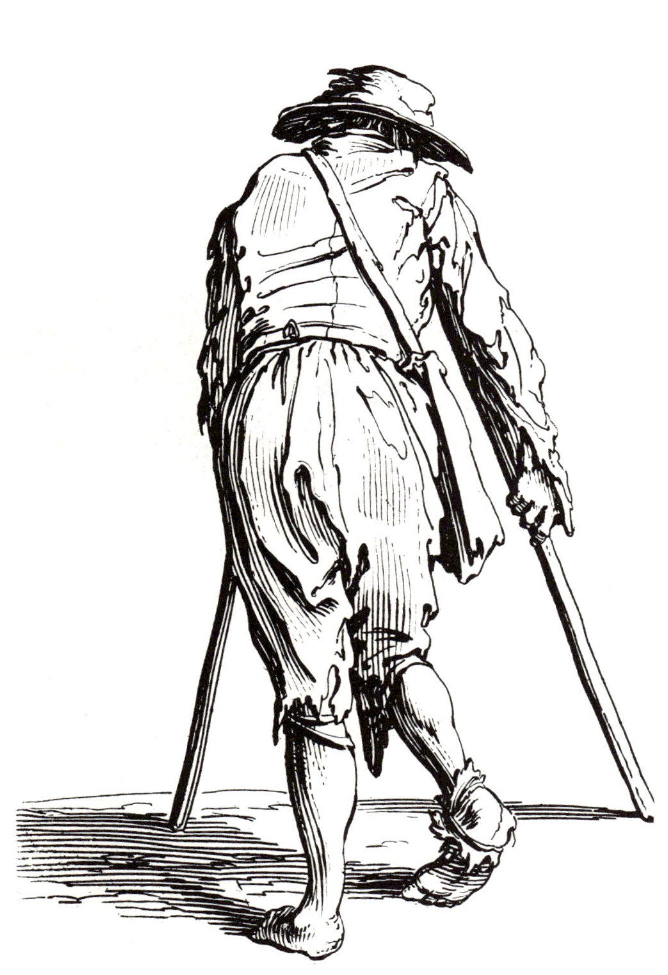

157 Another Beggar with Crutches, Seen from Behind.

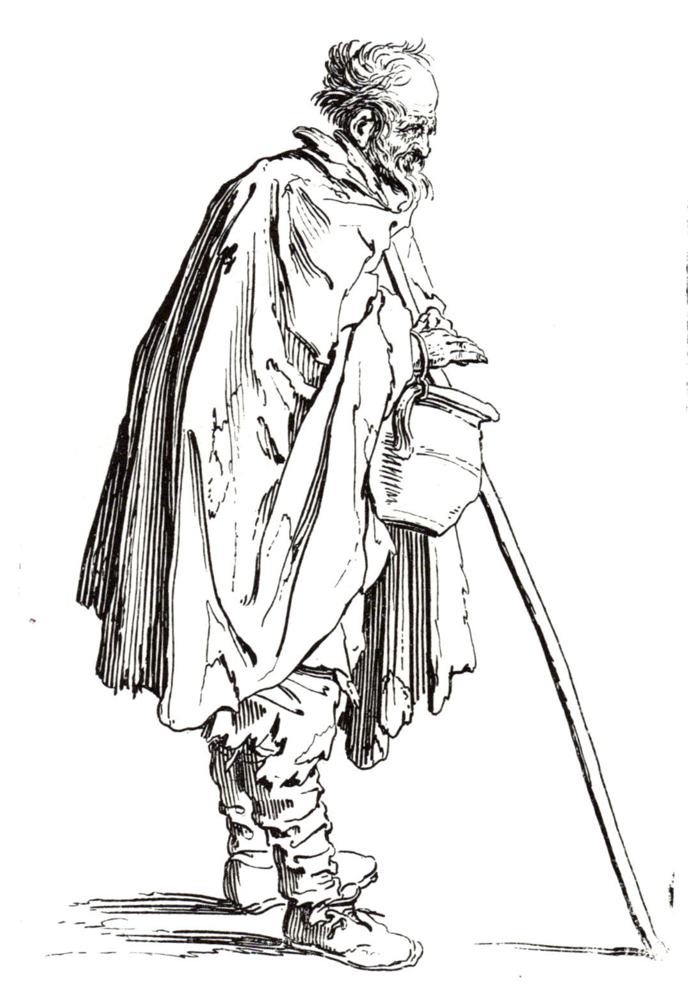

158 Beggar with Pot or Foot Warmer.

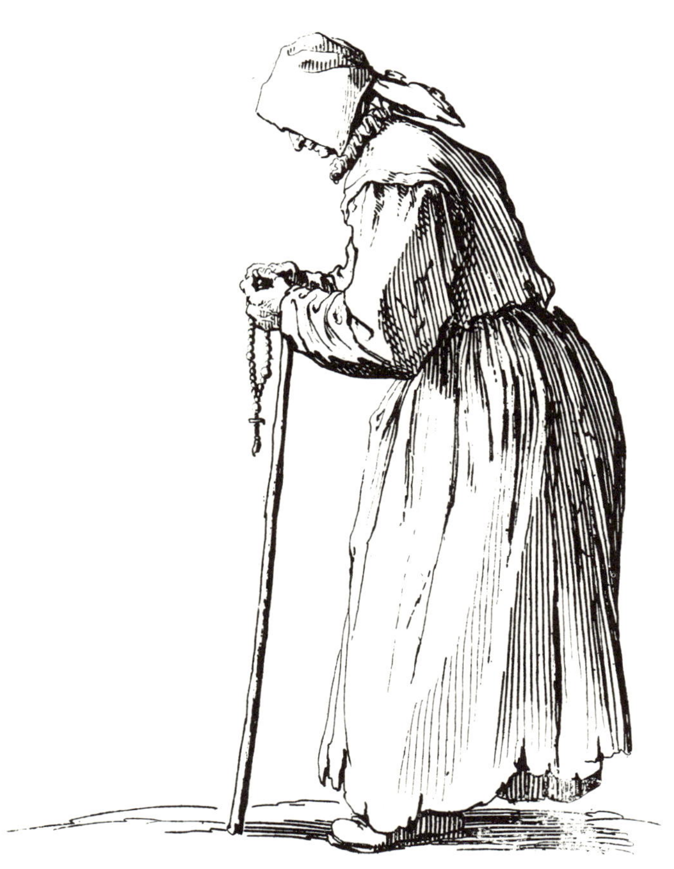

159 Beggar Woman with Rosary.

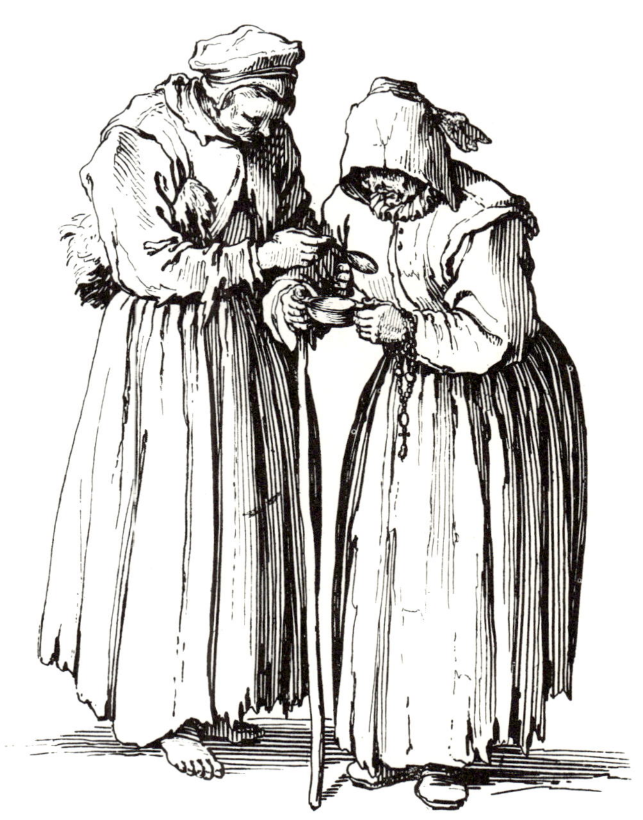

160 Beggar Women with Cup and Spoon.

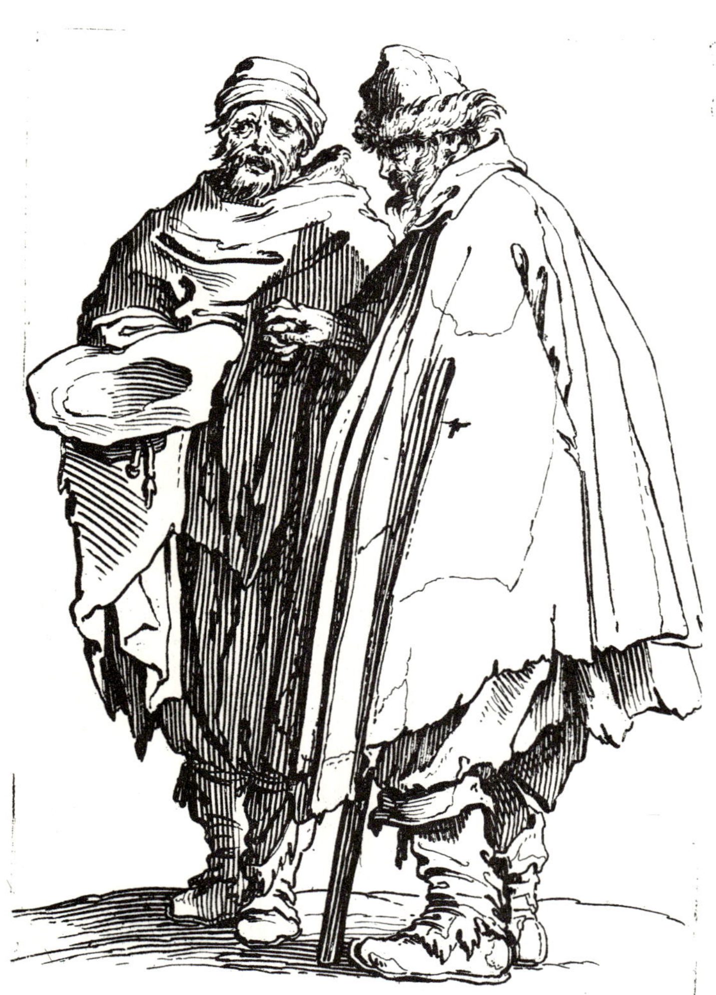

161 Blind Beggar and Companion. (Howard Daniel Collection)

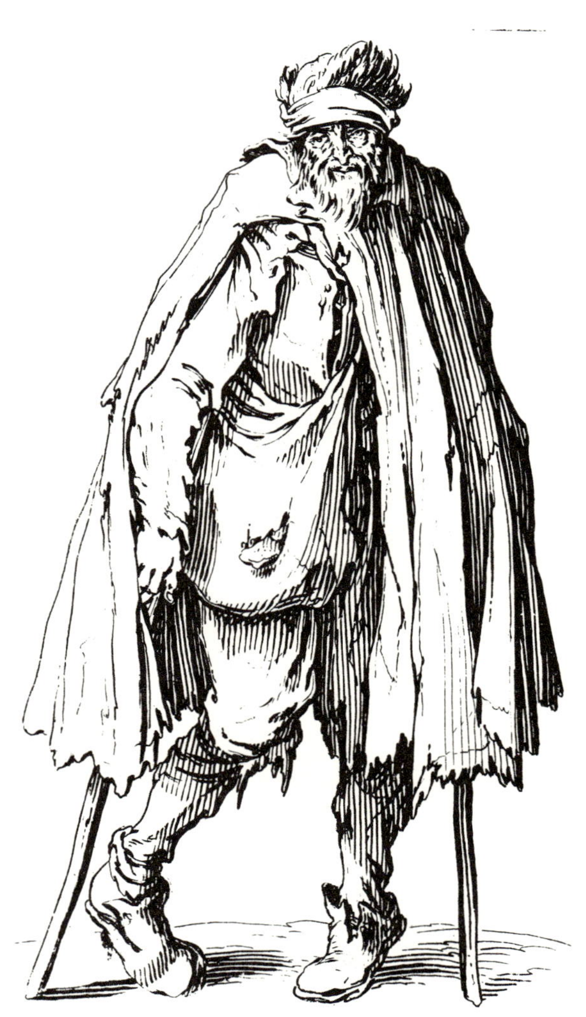

162 Crippled Beggar.

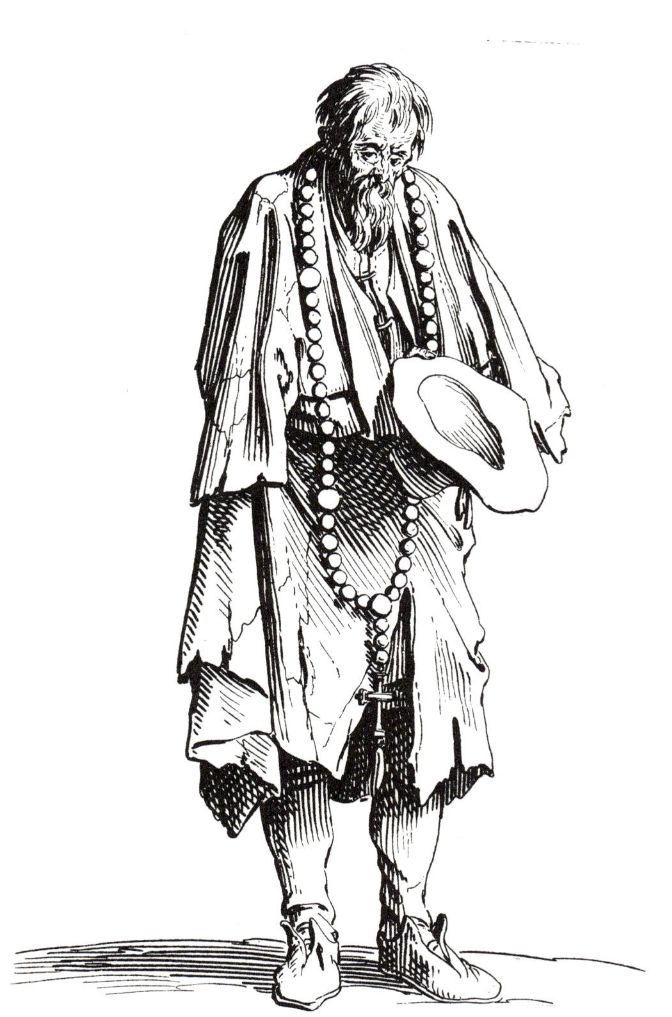

163 Beggar with Large Rosary.

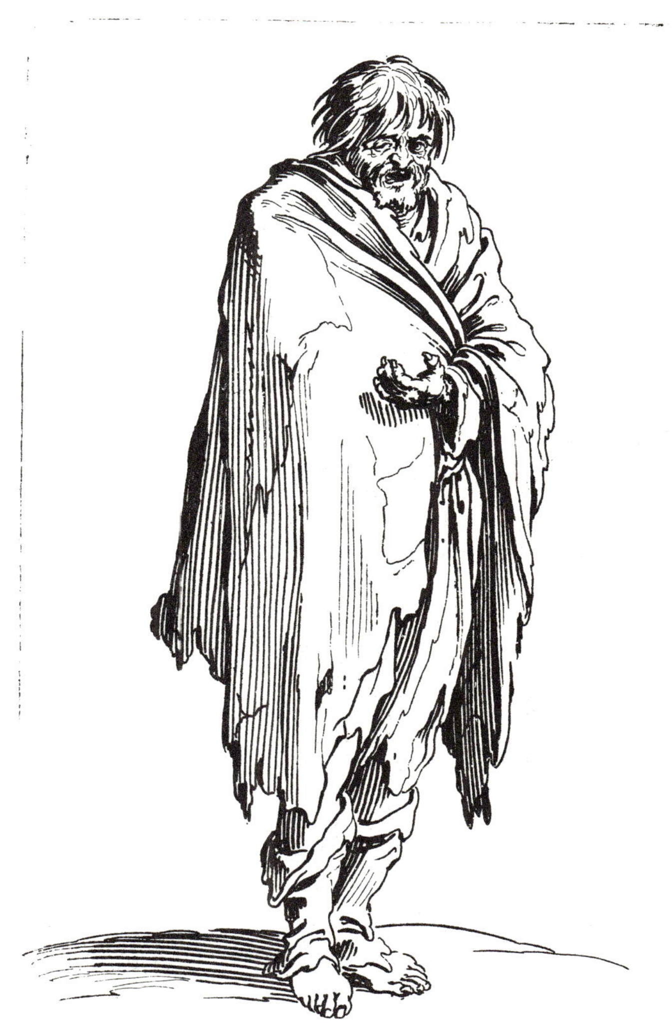

164 Barefoot Beggar.

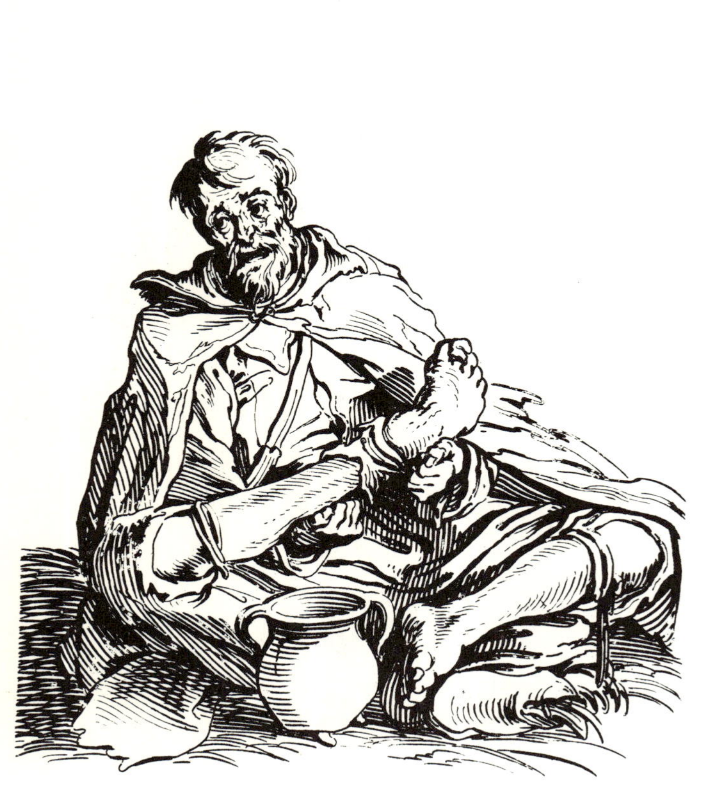

165 Sickly Beggar, Seated.

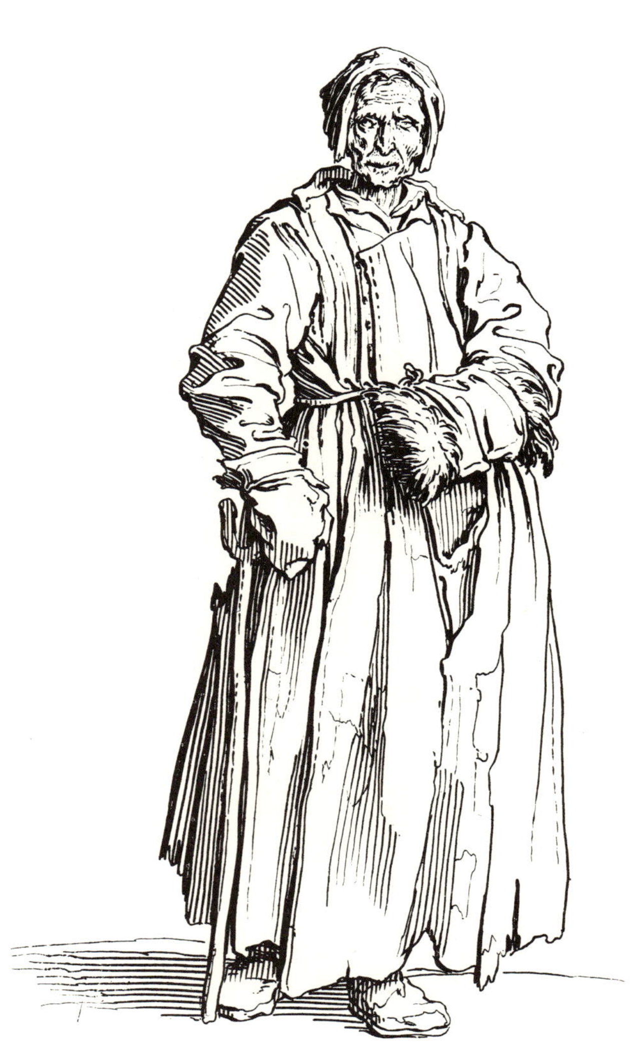

166 One-Eyed Beggar Woman.

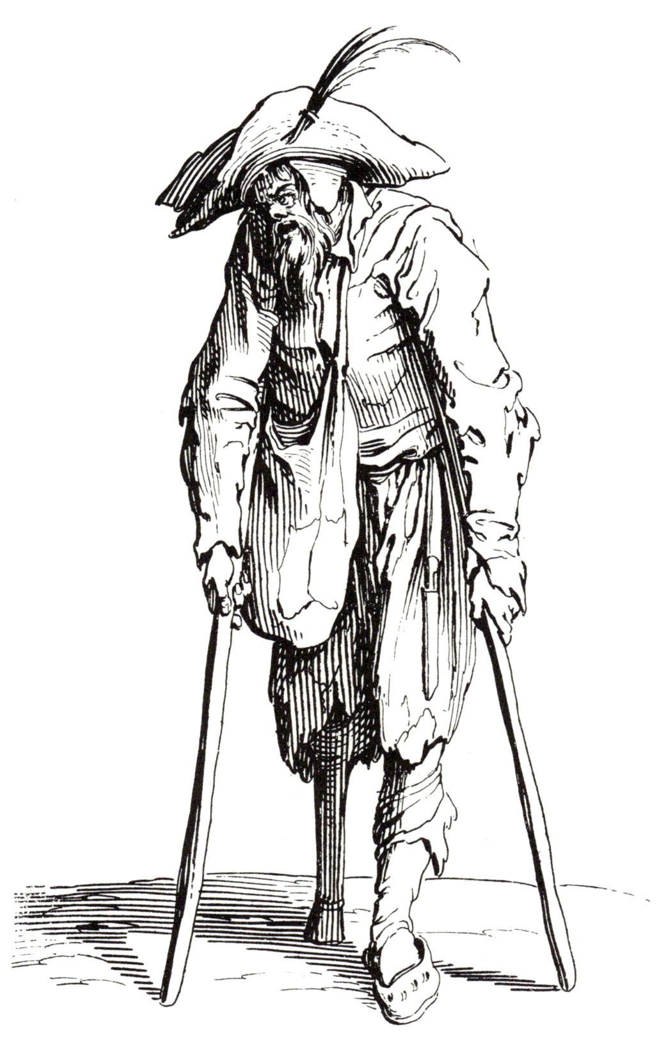

167 Beggar with Wooden Leg.

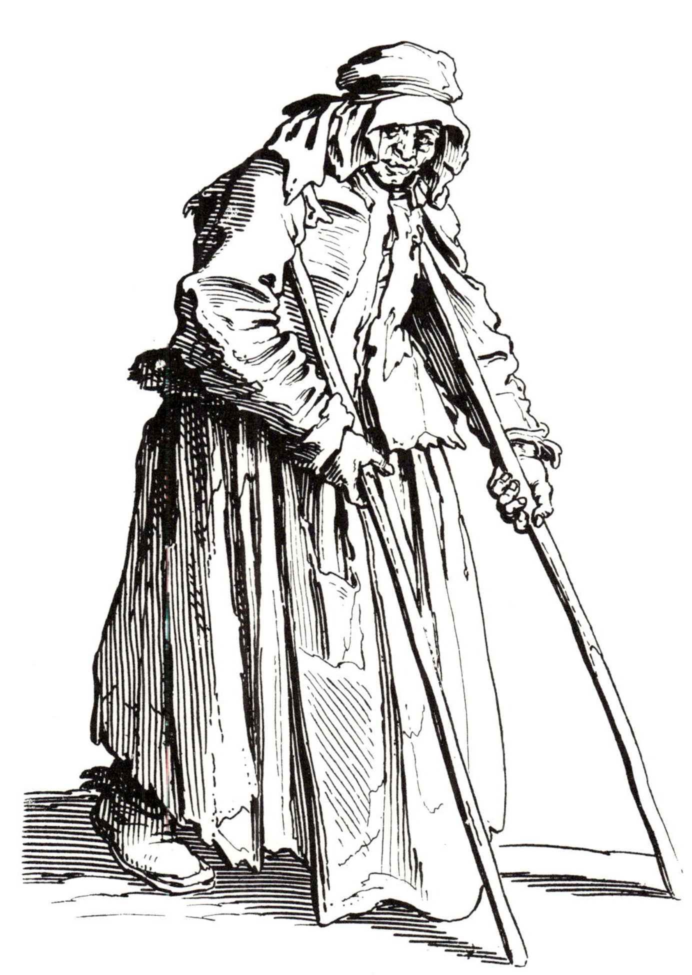

168 Beggar Woman with Crutches.

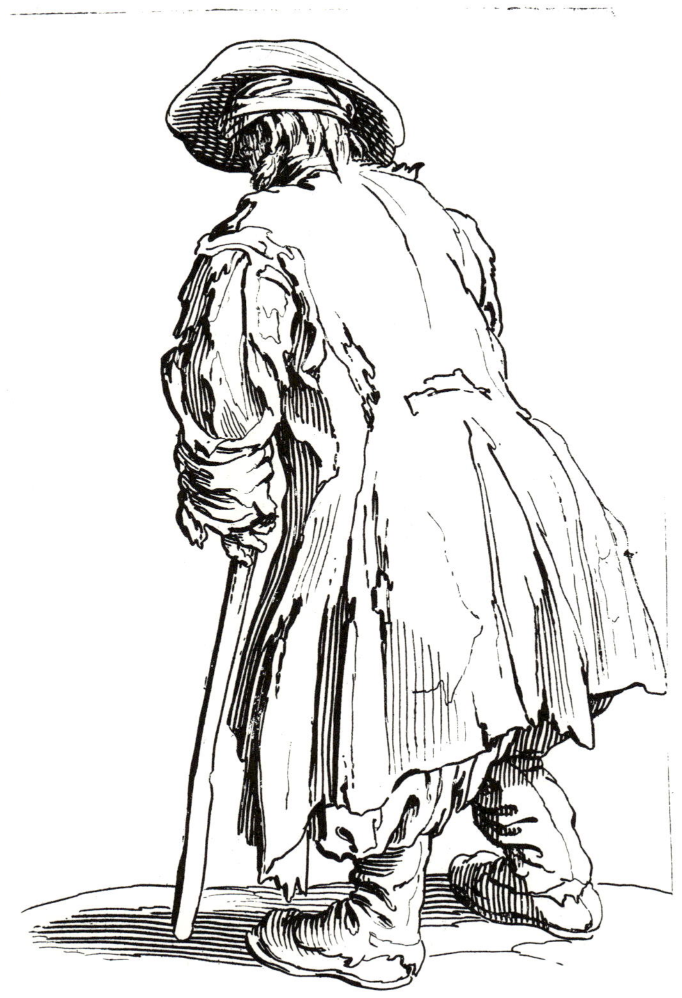

169 Beggar with One Crutch, Seen from Behind.

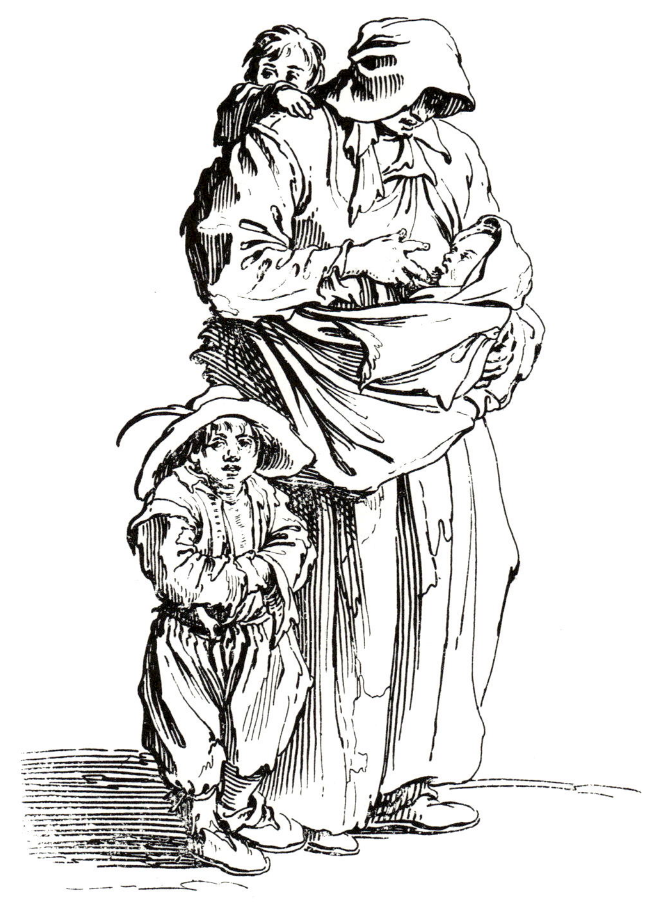

170 Beggar Woman with Three Children.

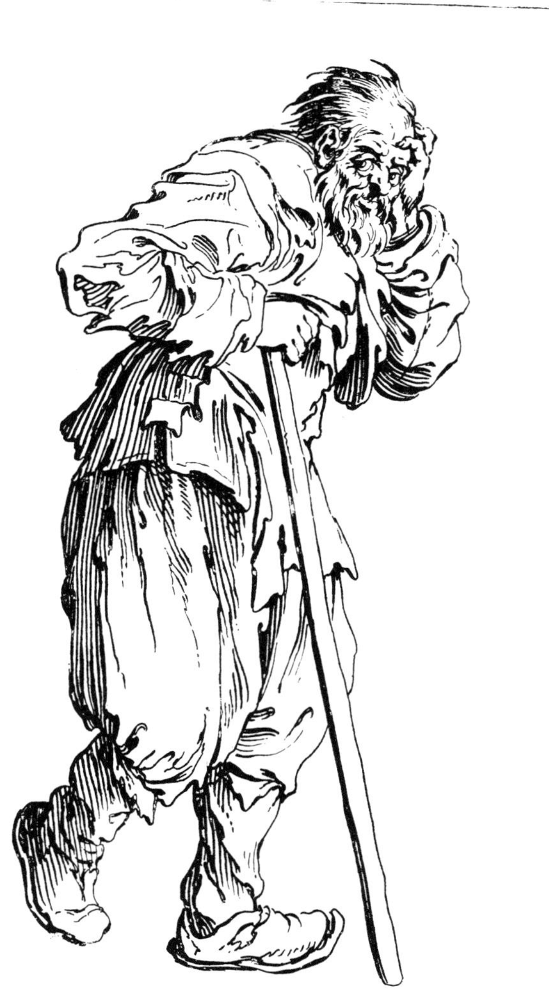

171 Beggar with Long Walking Stick.

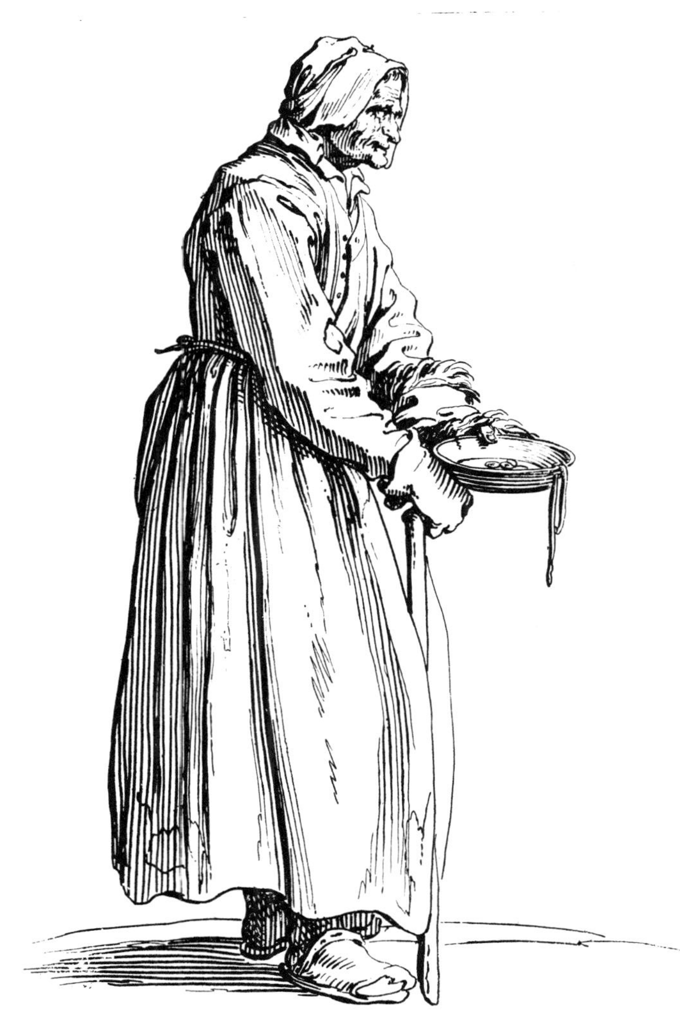

172 Beggar Woman with Bowl.

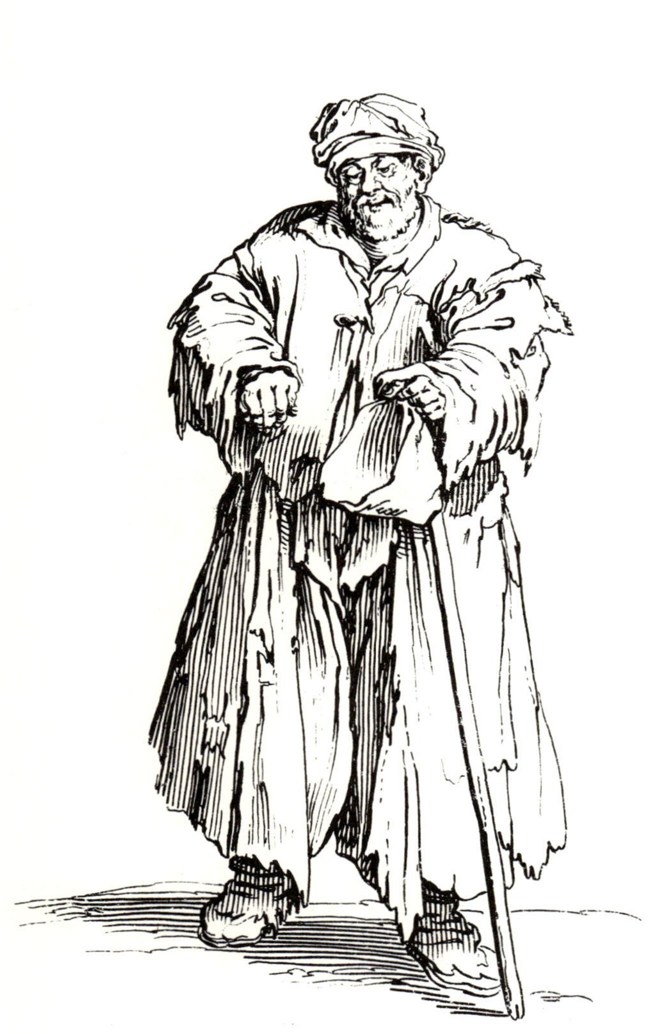

173 Corpulent Beggar with Empty Cap.

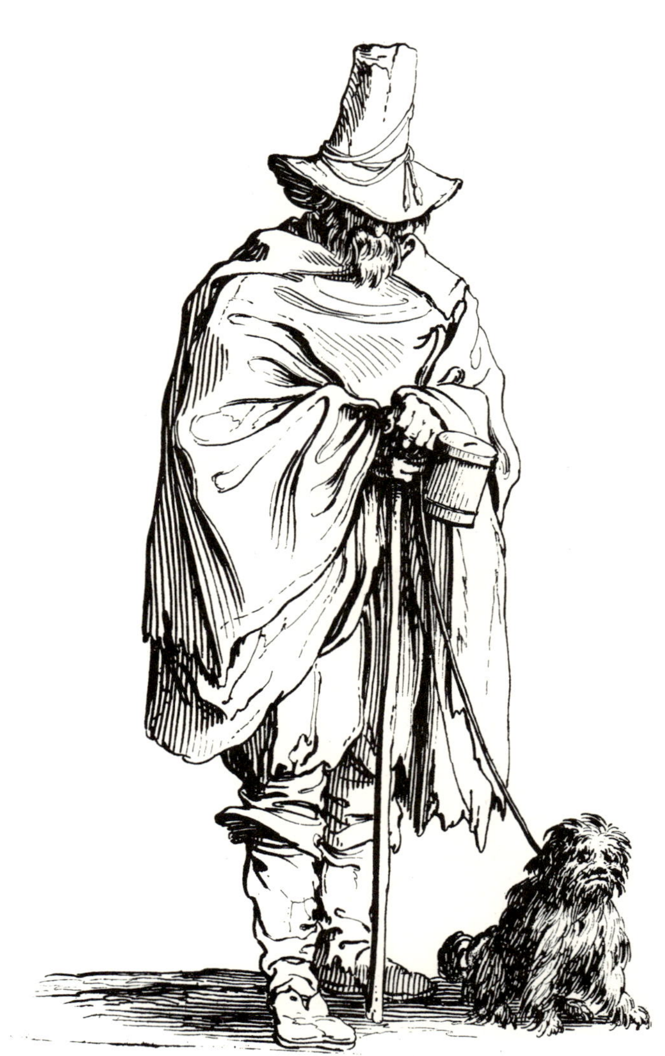

174 Beggar with Dog.

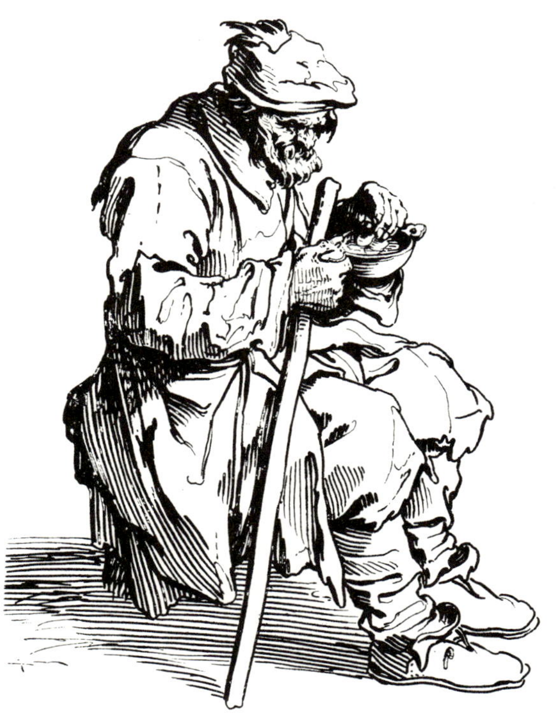

176 Seated Beggar Eating.

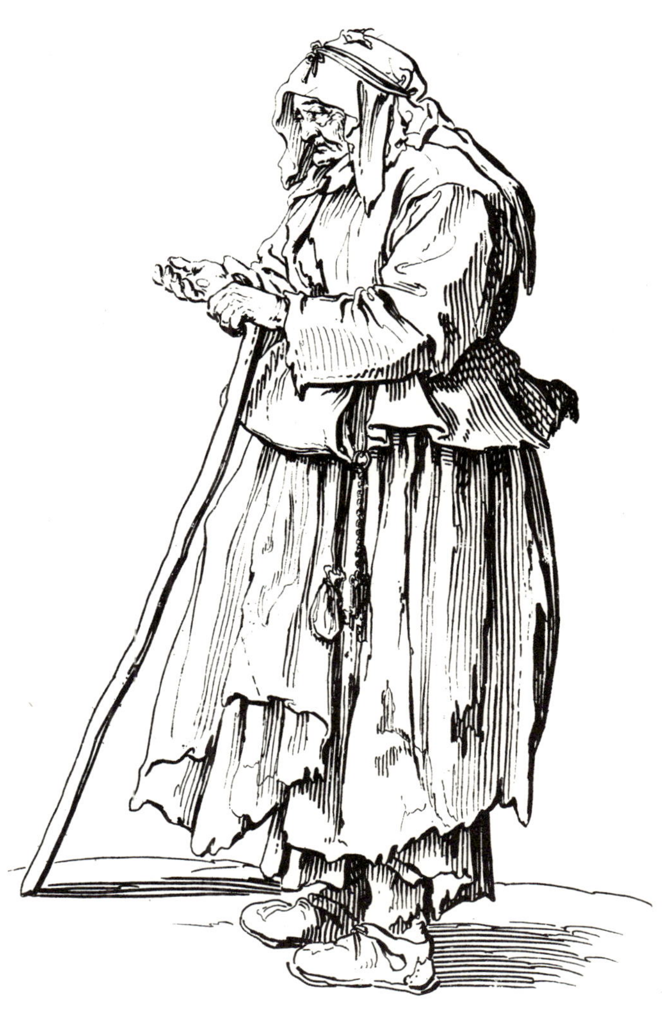

175 Beggar Woman Holding Coins.

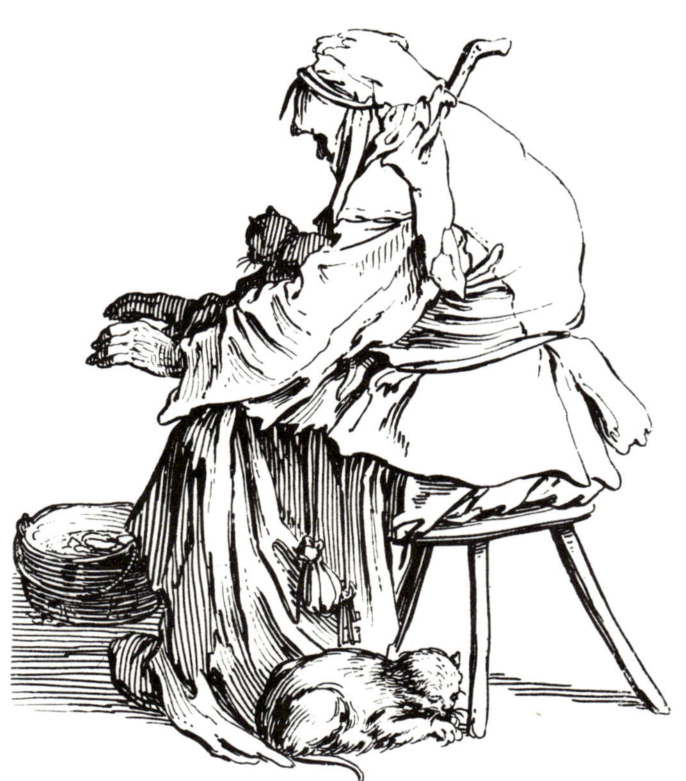

177 Beggar Woman with Cats.

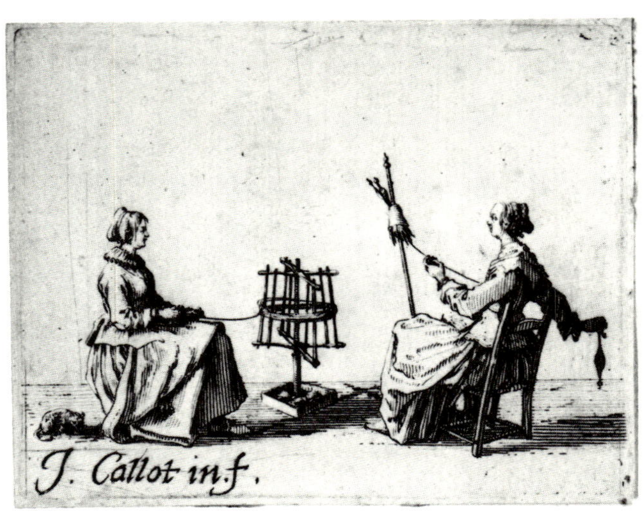

178 The Winder and the Spinner, ca. 1623. (Courtesy Trustees of the British Museum)

179–190 The complete *Small Passion*, a series of 12 etchings, ca. 1623.

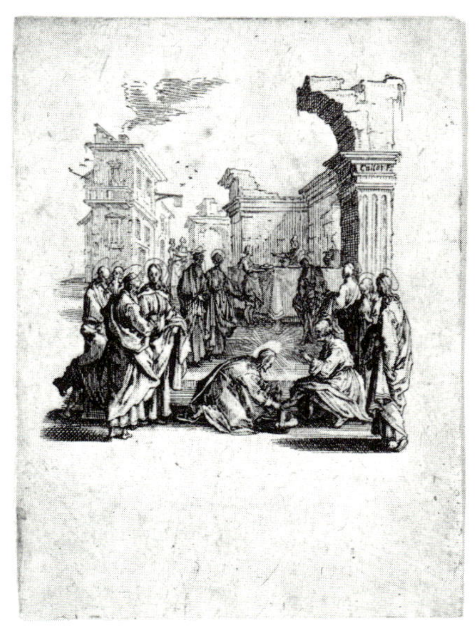

179 Christ Washing the Feet of the Apostles.

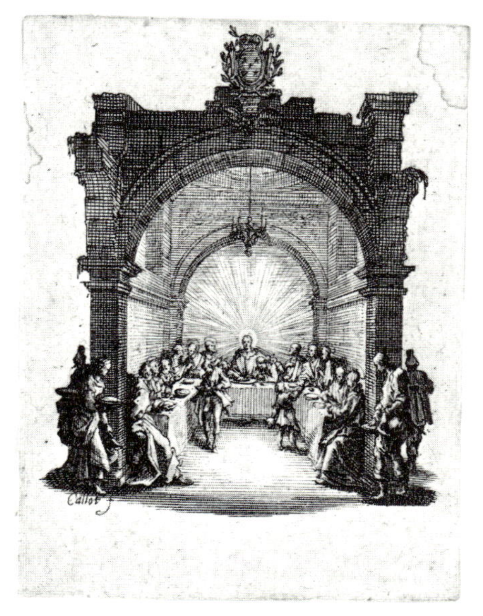

180 The Last Supper.

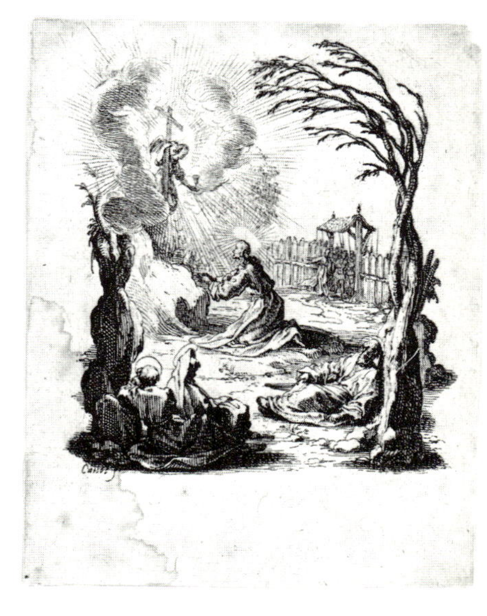

181 The Agony in the Garden.

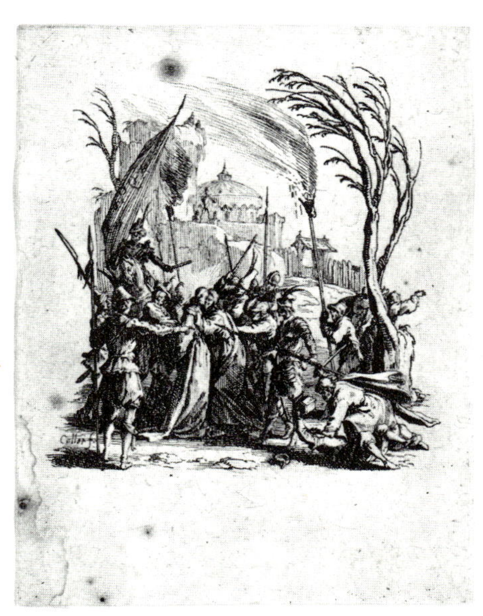

182 The Betrayal of Christ.

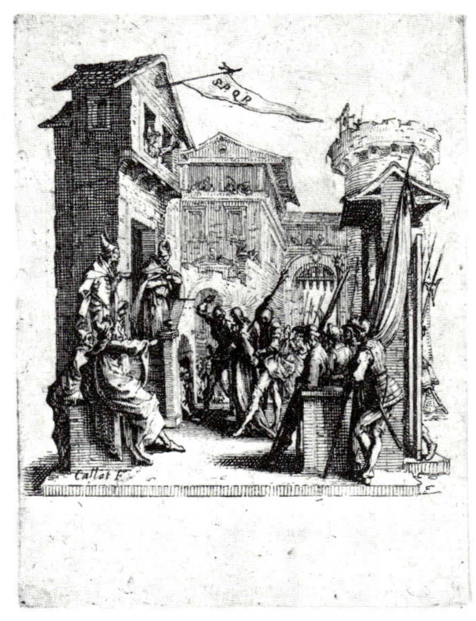

183 Christ Before Caiaphas.

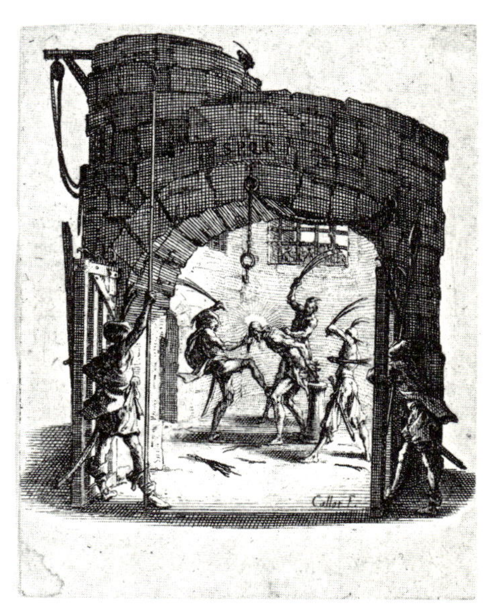

184 The Flagellation.

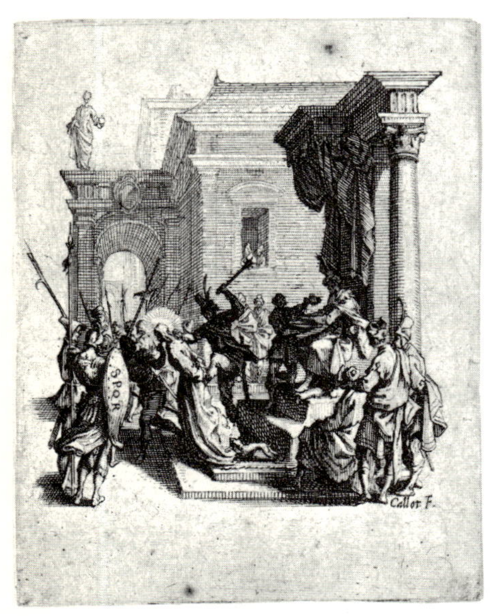

185 Christ Condemned to Death.

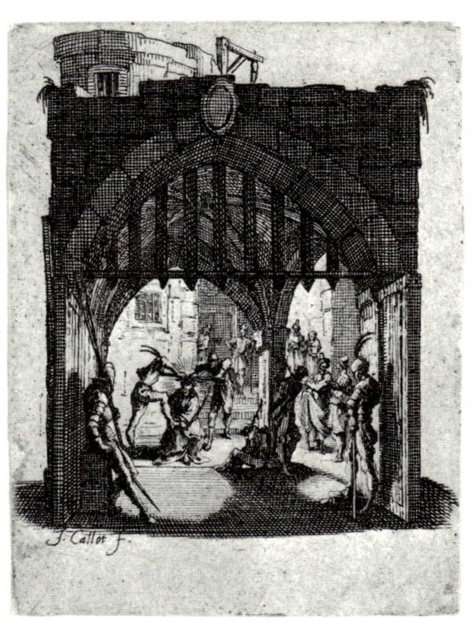

186 The Crowning with Thorns.

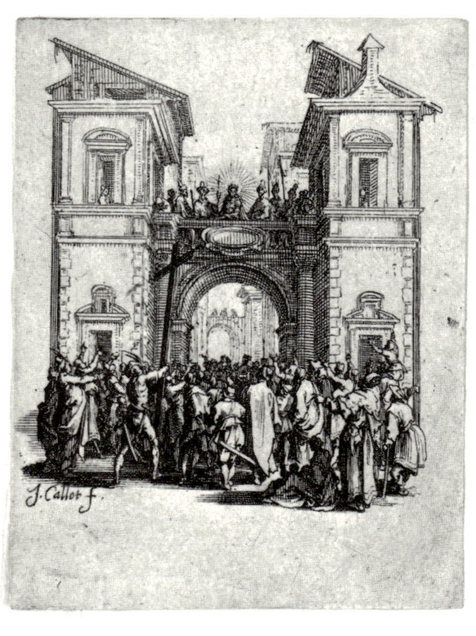

187 Christ Presented to the People.

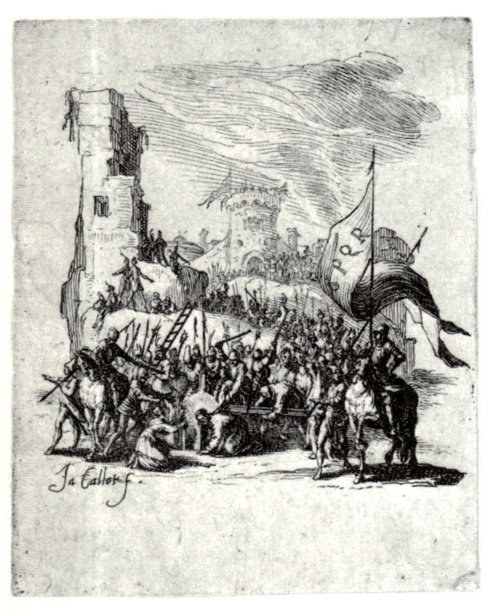

188 Christ Bearing the Cross.

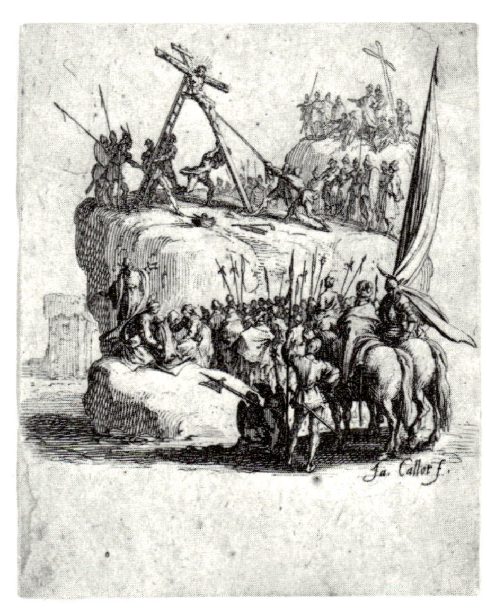

189 Christ Raised on the Cross.

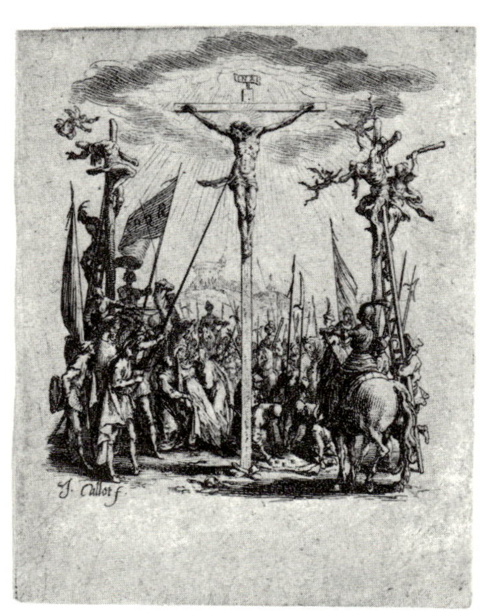

190 Christ Pierced by the Lance.

191–194 From the *Lorraine Nobility* (*La Noblesse lorraine*), a series of 12 etchings, 1624.

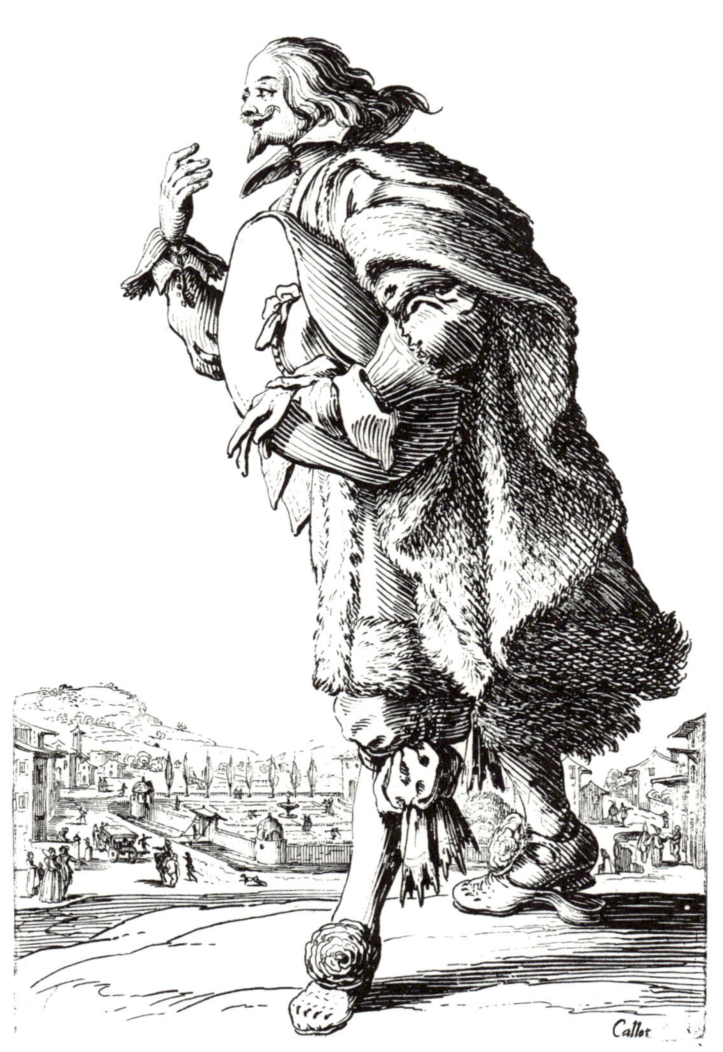

191 Nobleman in an Attitude of Greeting.

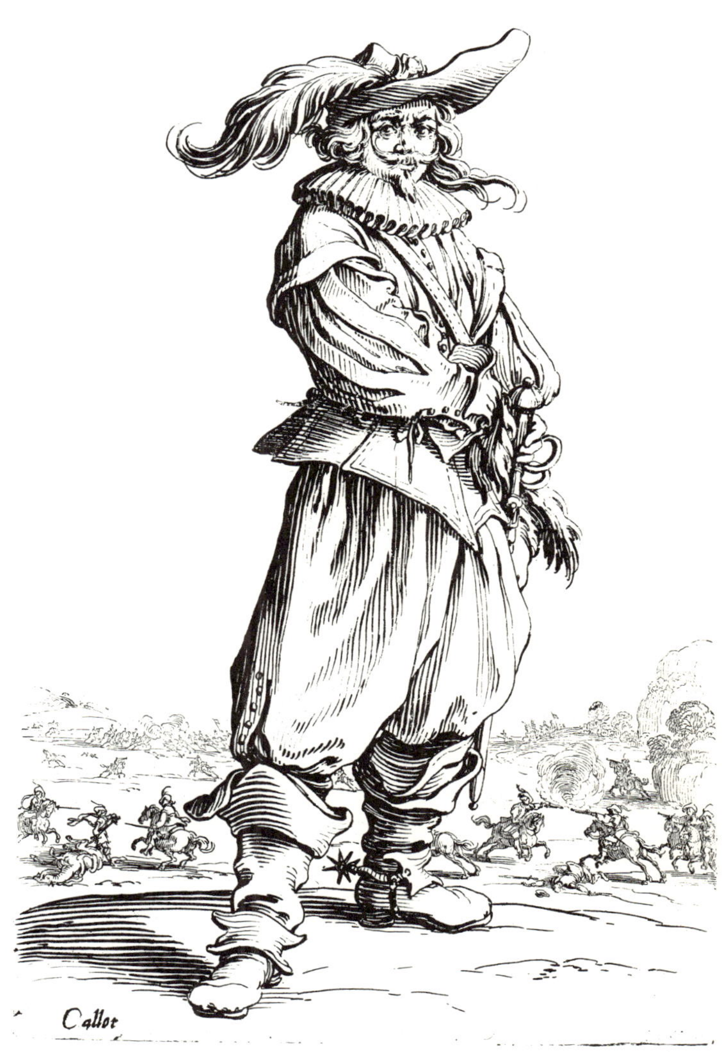

192 Man in Military Costume.

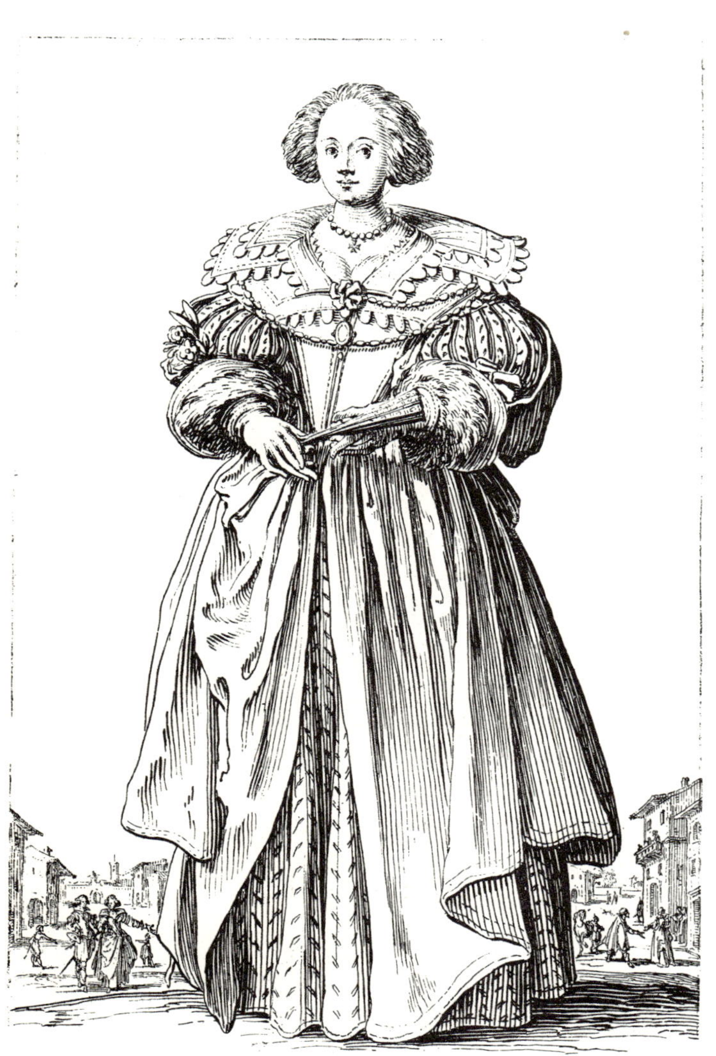

193 Noblewoman with Fan.

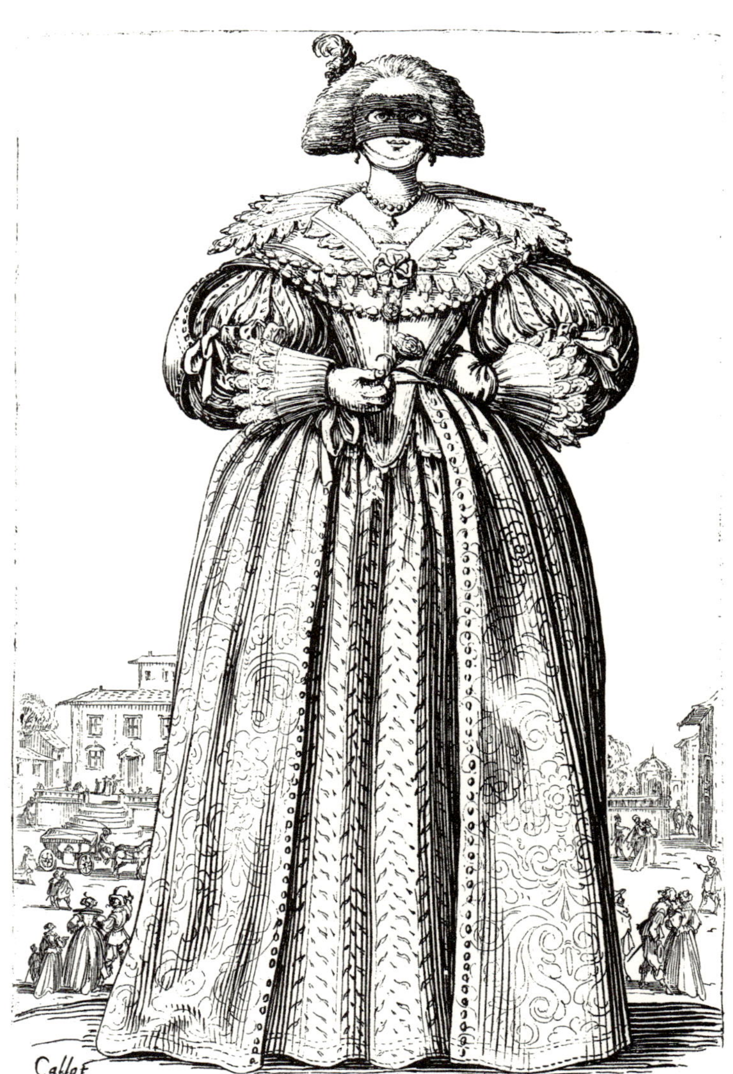

194 Lady in a Mask.

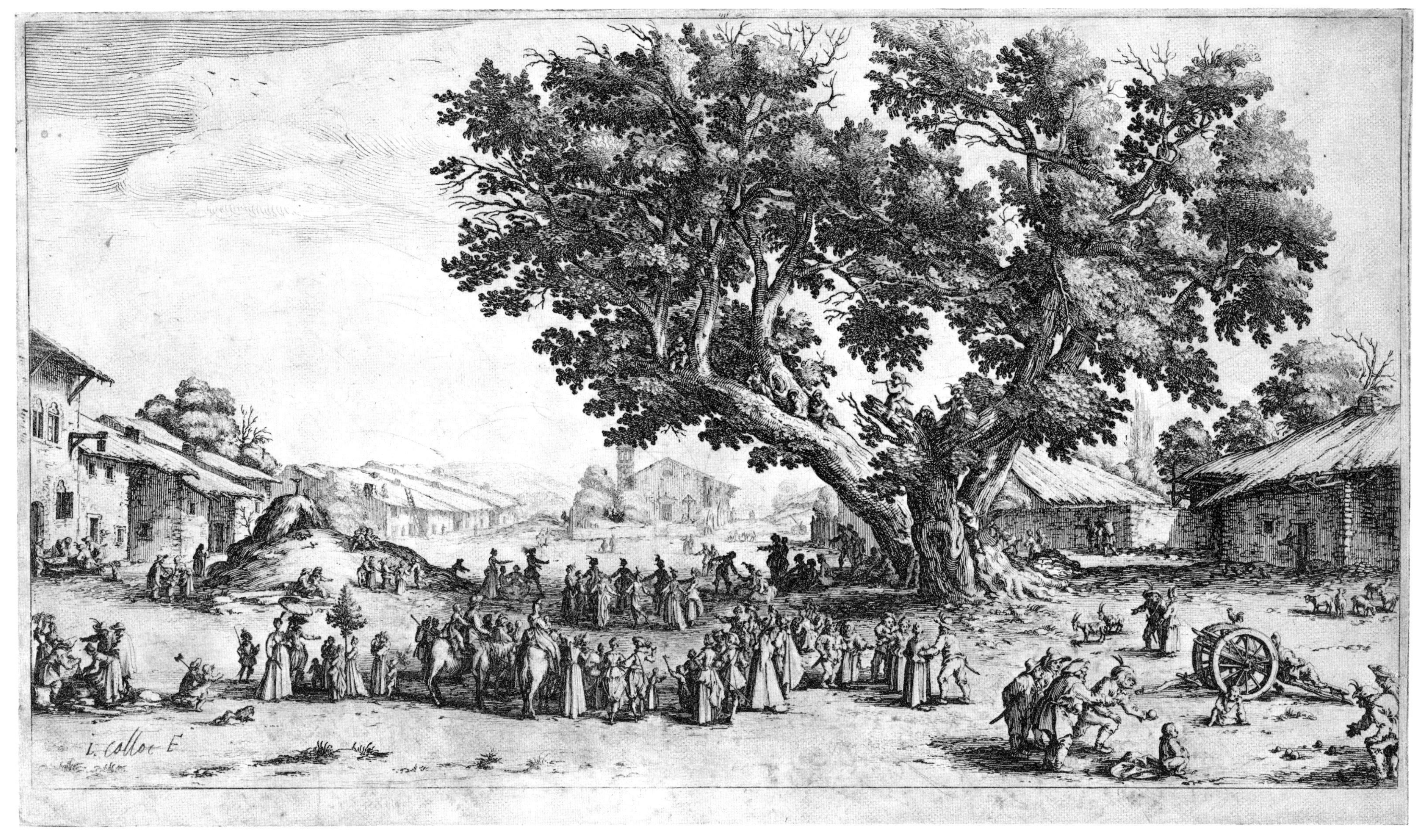

195 The Fair at Gondreville (or, The Holiday at Xeuilley). Etching, ca. 1624/25. (National Gallery, Washington, R. L. Baumfeld Collection)

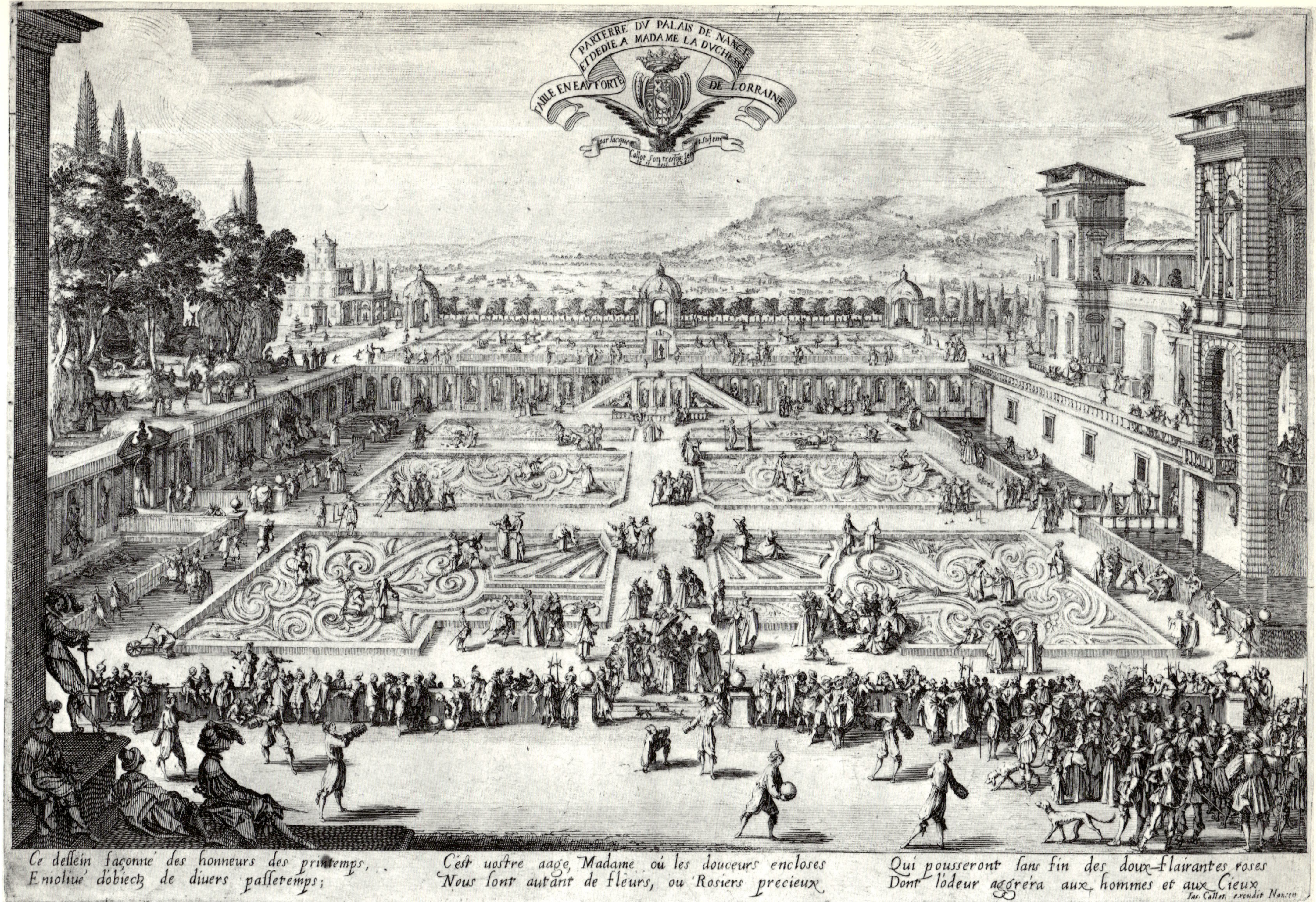

196 The Parterre (or, Garden) of Nancy. Etching, 1625. The inscription at the top reads: "Gardens of the Palace of Nancy. Etched and dedicated to the Duchess of Lorraine by Jacques Callot, her most humble servant and subject. Oct. 15, 1625." The poem at the bottom reads: "This drawing, fashioned with the honors of springtime, beautified with objects of various pastimes, represents your time of life, Milady, during which each sweetness there enclosed is like another flower or precious rosebush which will unceasingly produce sweet-smelling roses whose fragrance will please mankind and Heaven." (National Gallery, Washington, R. L. Baumfeld Collection)

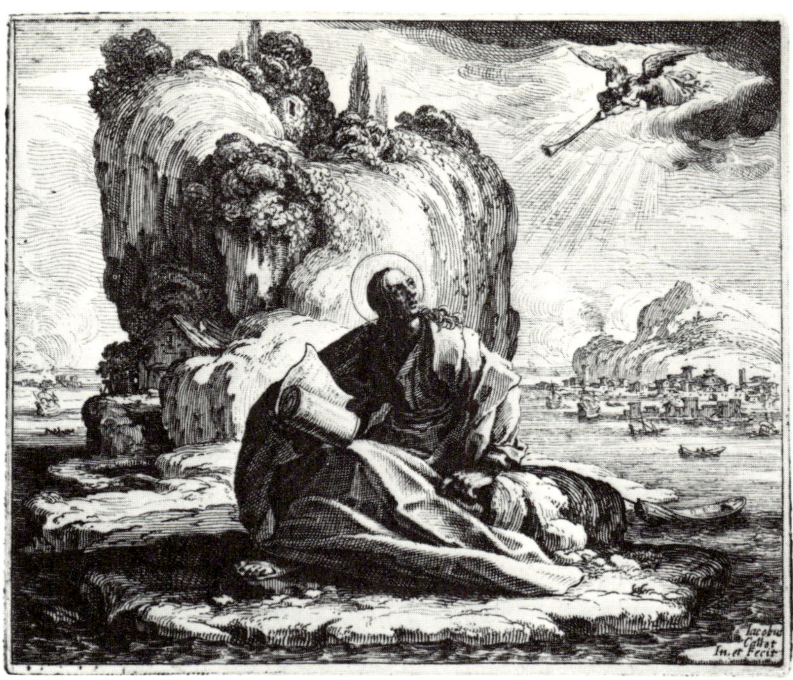

197 St. John on Patmos. Etching, 1625. (Courtesy Trustees of the British Museum)

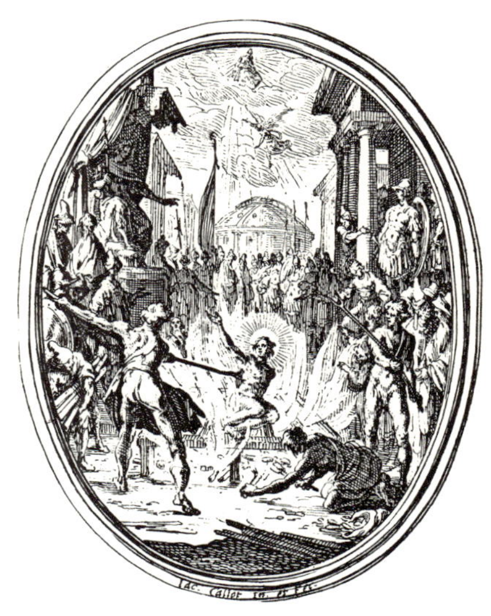

199 The Martyrdom of St. Lawrence (sometimes considered as part of a series of 5 etchings, *The Sacrifices*). Etching, ca. 1627 (?).

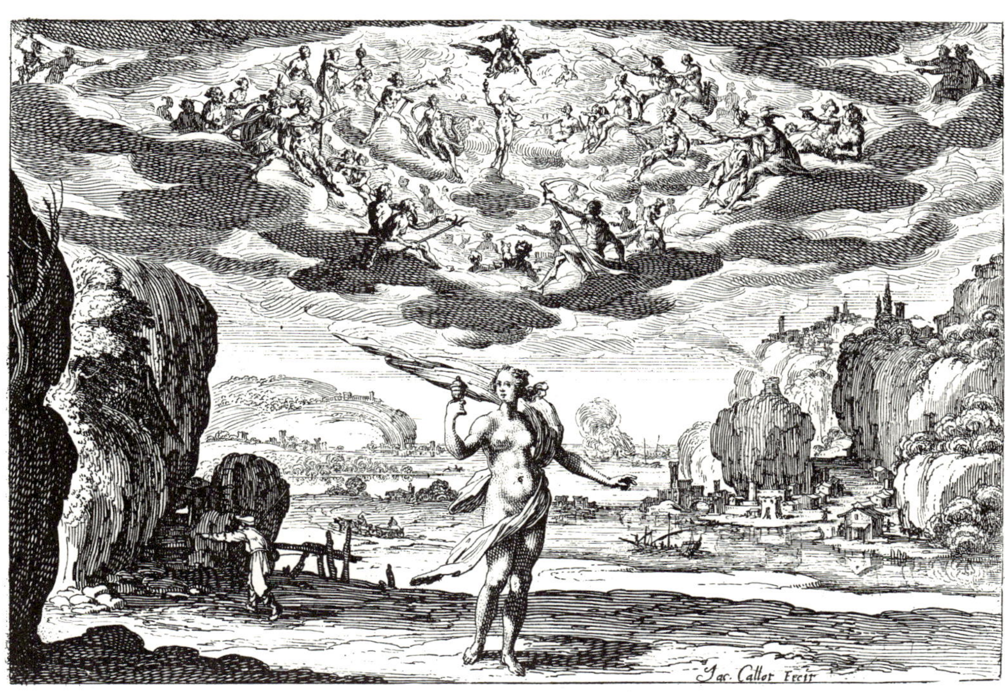

198 Pandora. Etching, ca. 1625. (National Gallery, Washington, R. L. Baumfeld Collection)

200–209 From *The Combat at the Barrier* (*Combat à la Barrière*, illustrating a printed account of a Lorraine court pageant and tourney in February 1627), a series of 14 etchings, 1627.

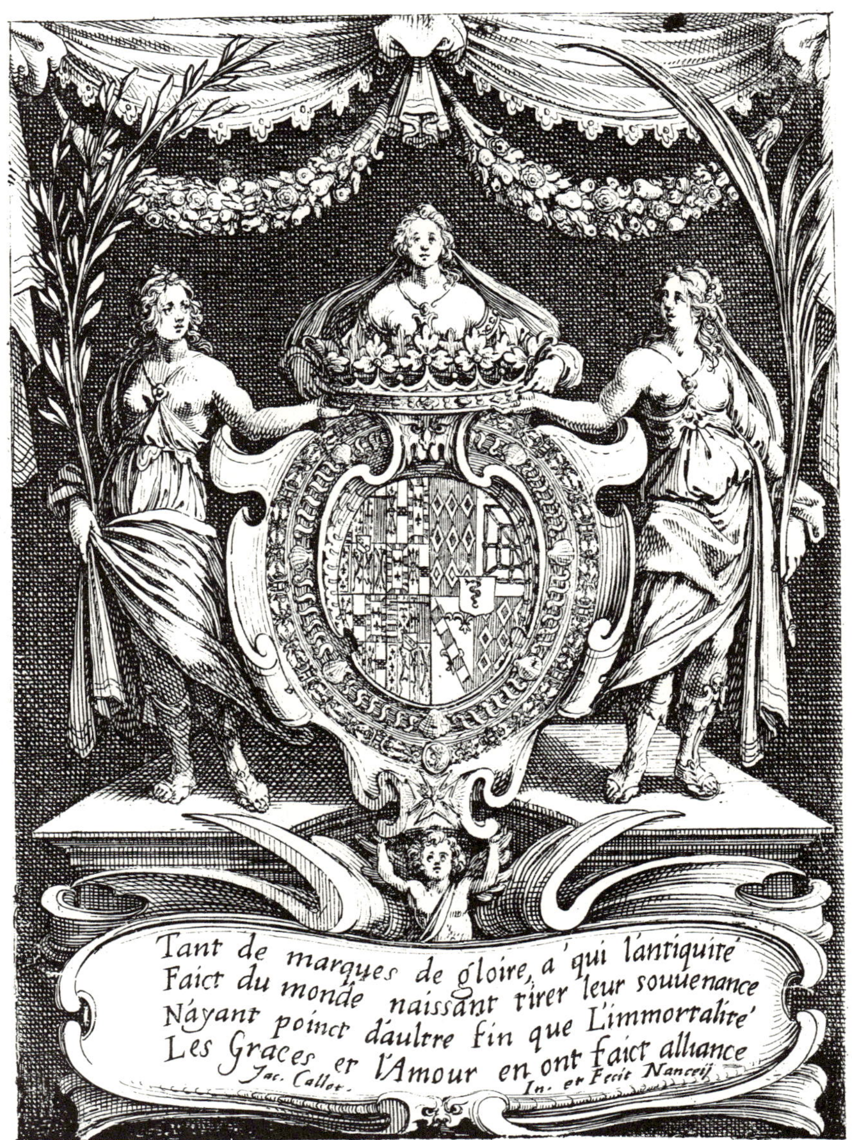

200 Title. The (slightly garbled) poem reads: "So many marks of glory to those whom antiquity causes to draw their remembrance from the early days of the world, having no other goal than immortality. The Graces and Love have made an alliance among them."

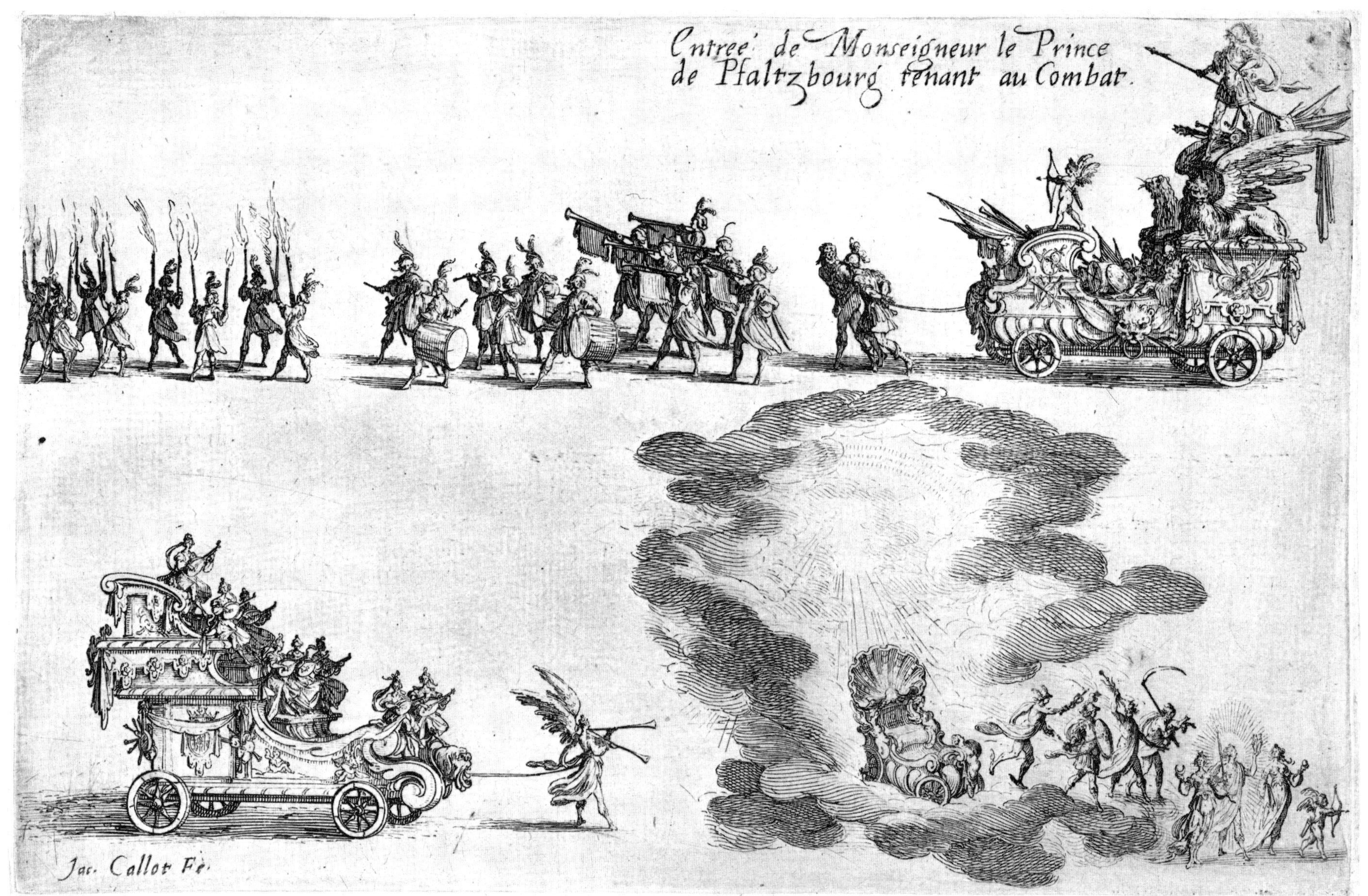

201 "The entrance of the Prince of Phalsbourg ready for combat."

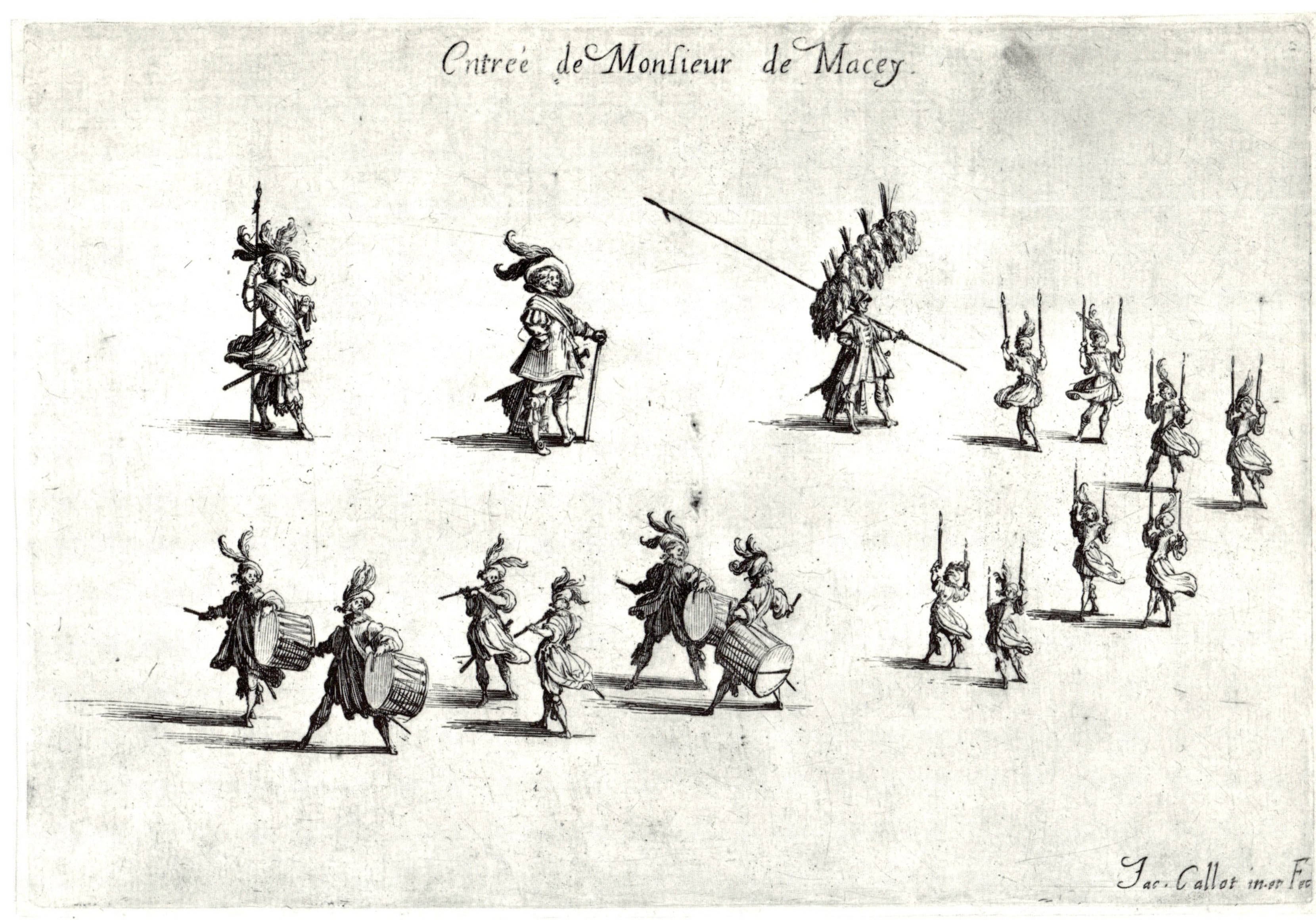

202 "The entrance of Monsieur de Macey."

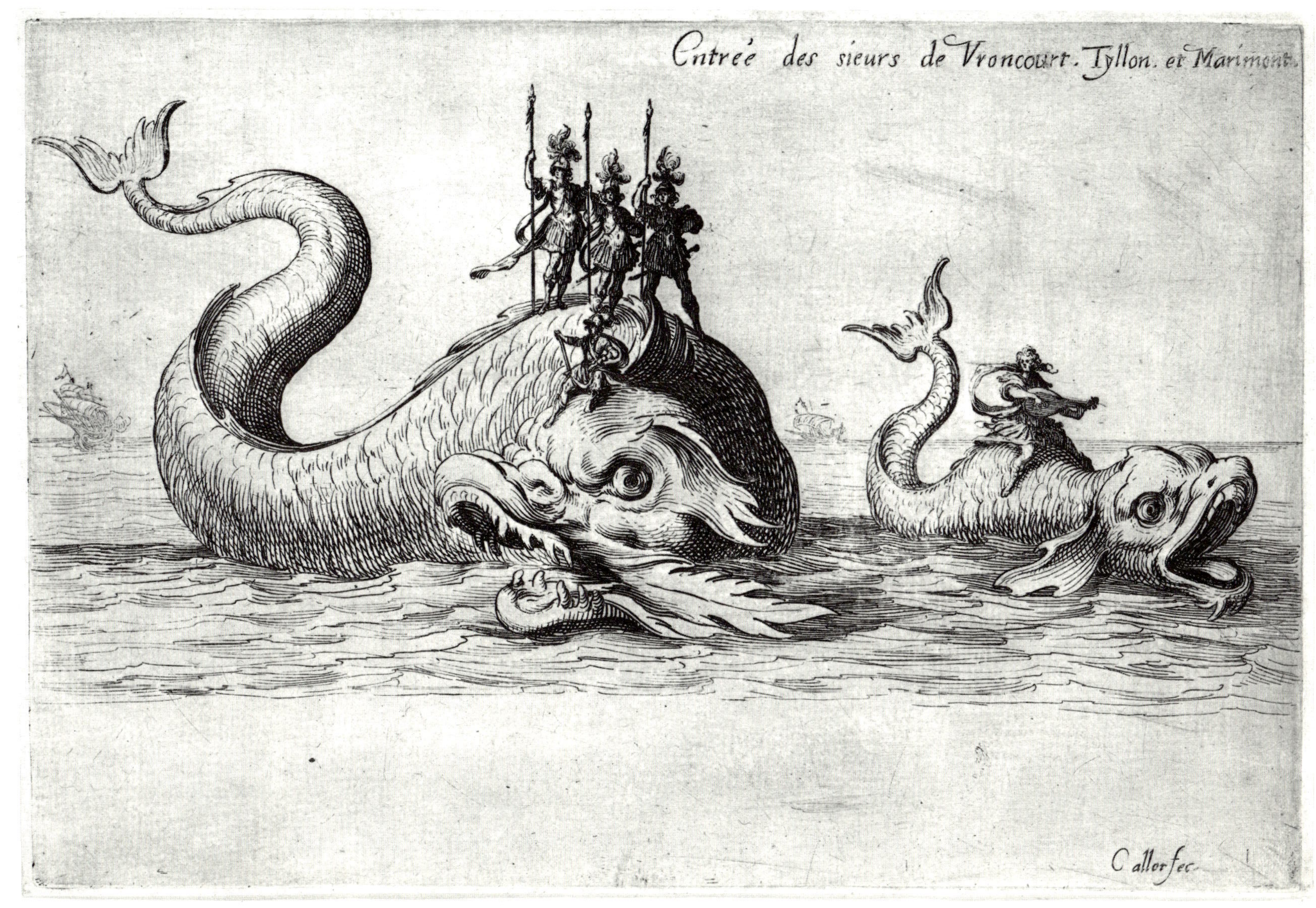

203 "The entrance of Messieurs de Vroncourt, Tyllon and Marimont."

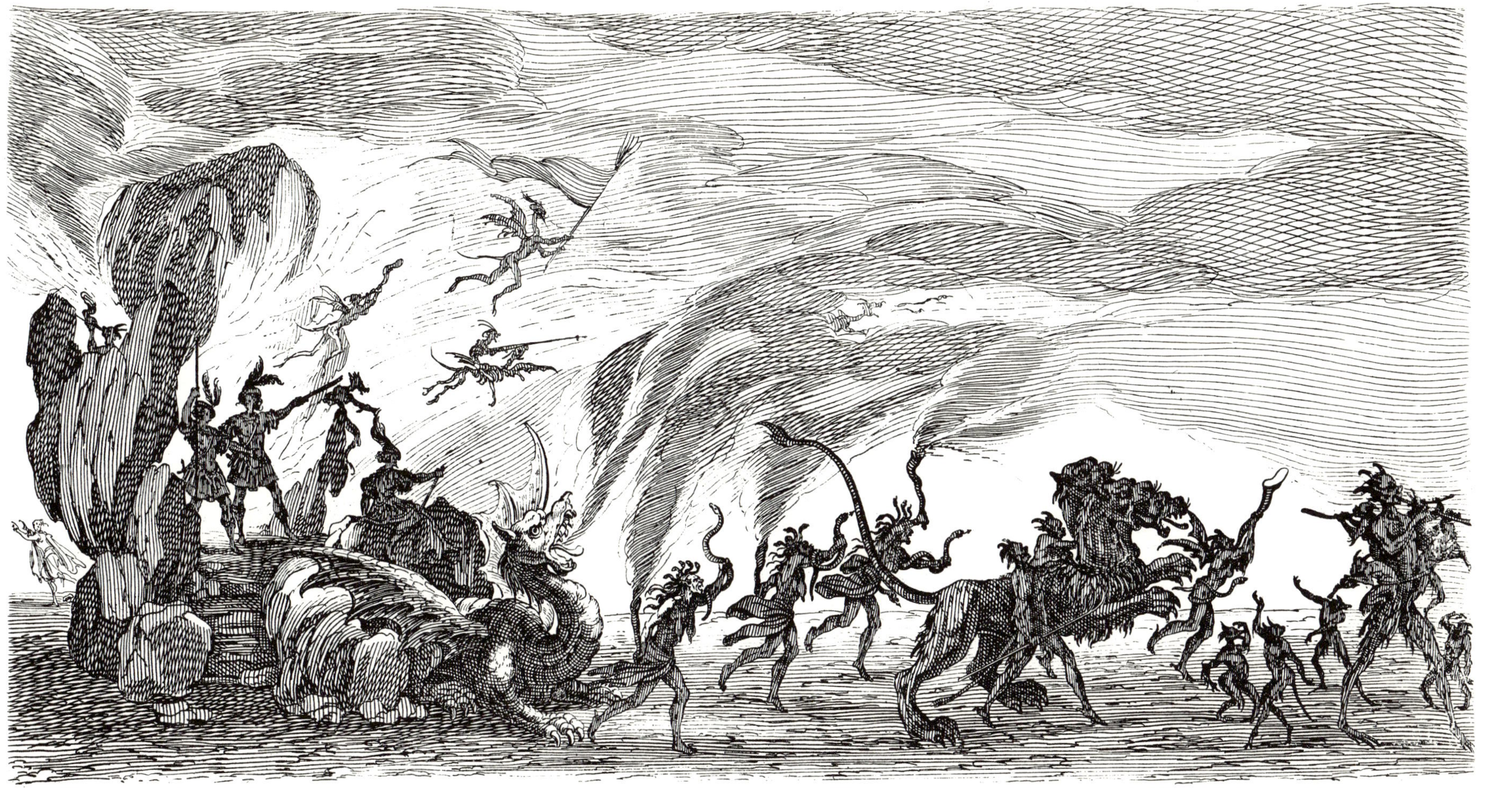

Entrée de Monſieur de Couuonge . et de Monsieur de Chalabre.

Jac. Callot In. et F.

204 "The entrance of Monsieur de Couvonge and Monsieur de Chalabre."

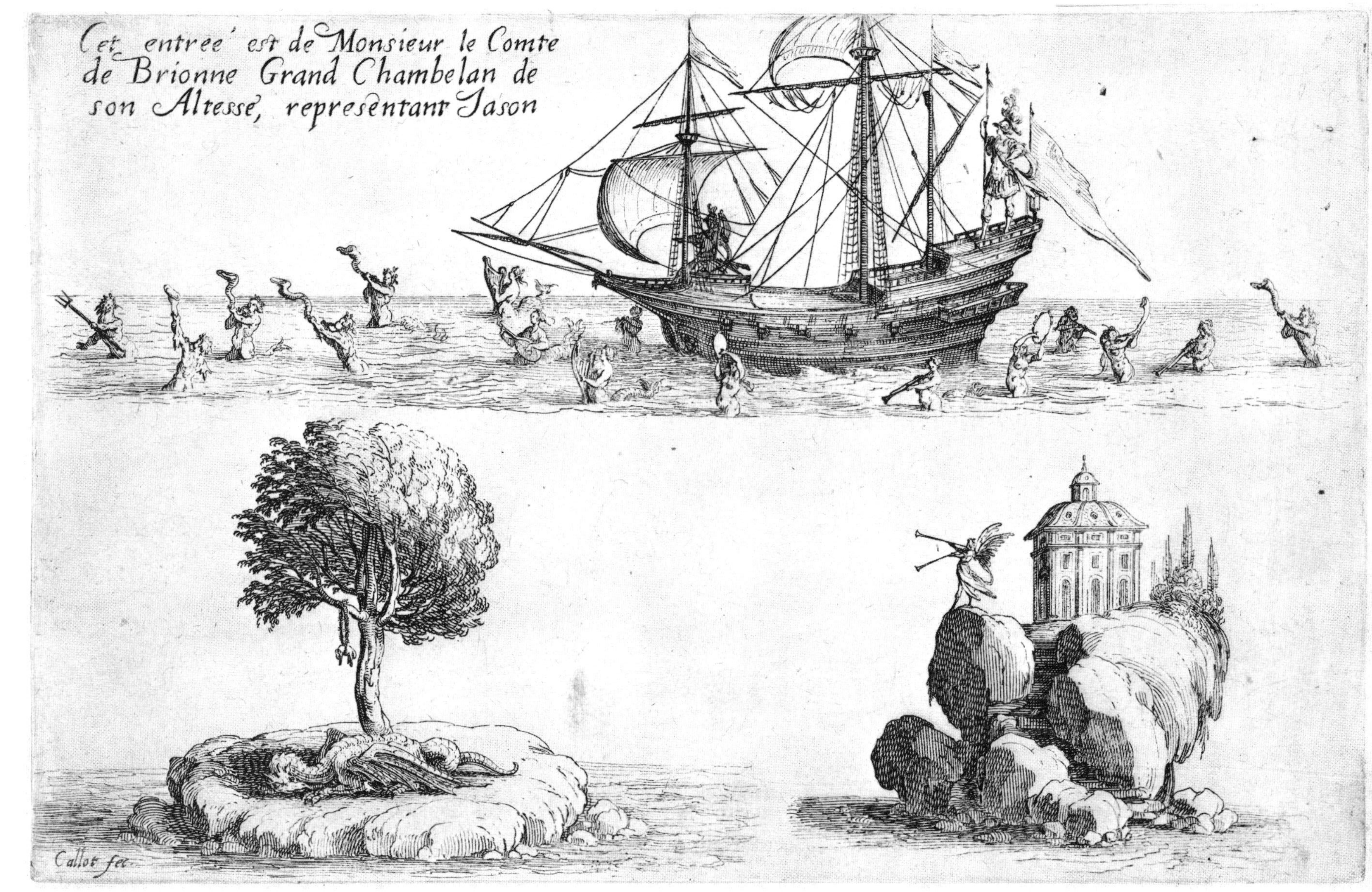

205 "This entrance is that of the Count of Brionne, Grand Chamberlain of His Highness, representing Jason." (Thus, the ship represents the *Argo*, and the picture at the lower left shows the dragon guarding the golden fleece in Colchis.)

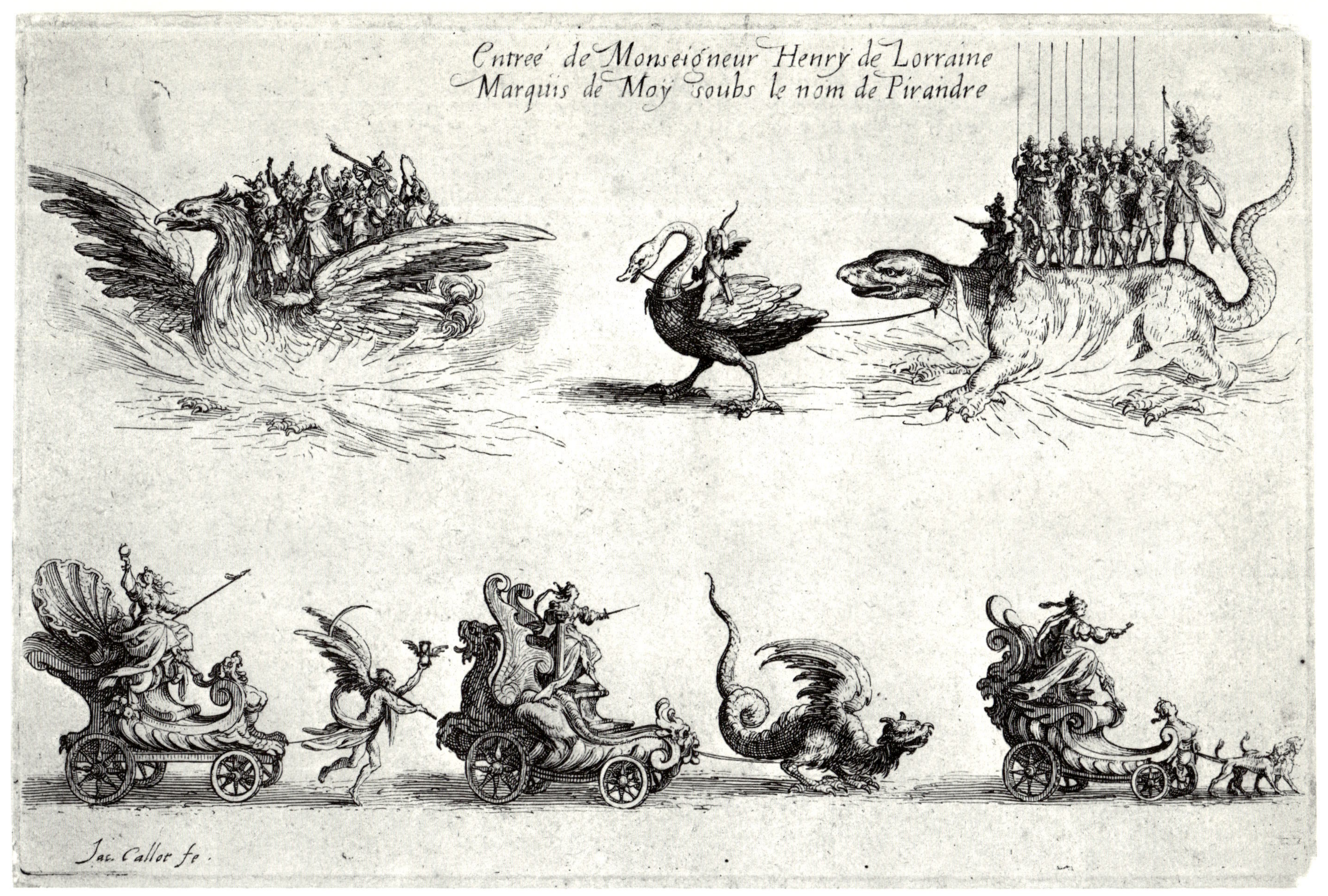

206 "The entrance of Henry of Lorraine, Marquess of Moy, under the name of Pirandre."

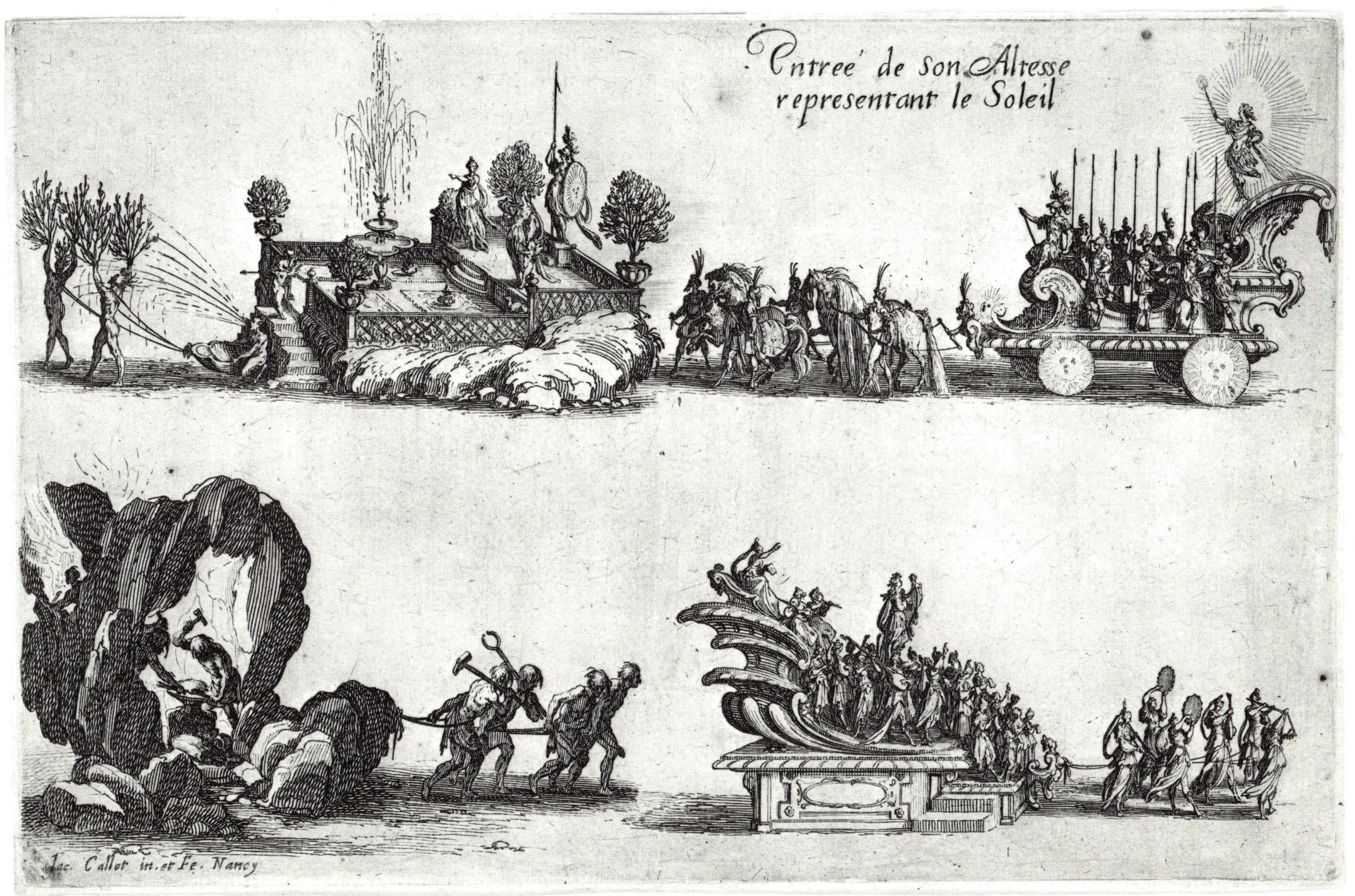

207 "Entrance of His Highness [Duke Charles IV] representing the Sun."

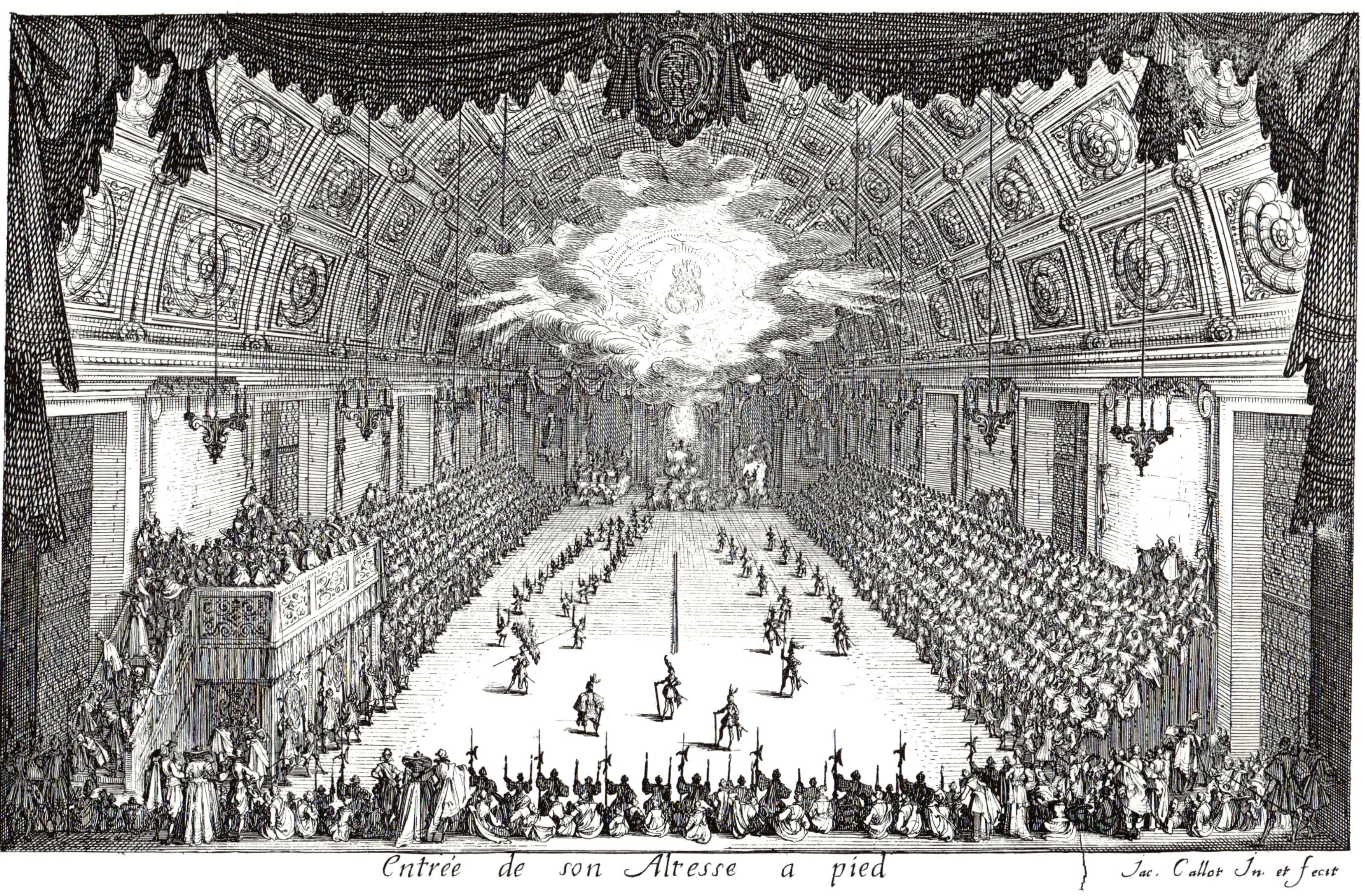

208 "Entrance of His Highness on foot."

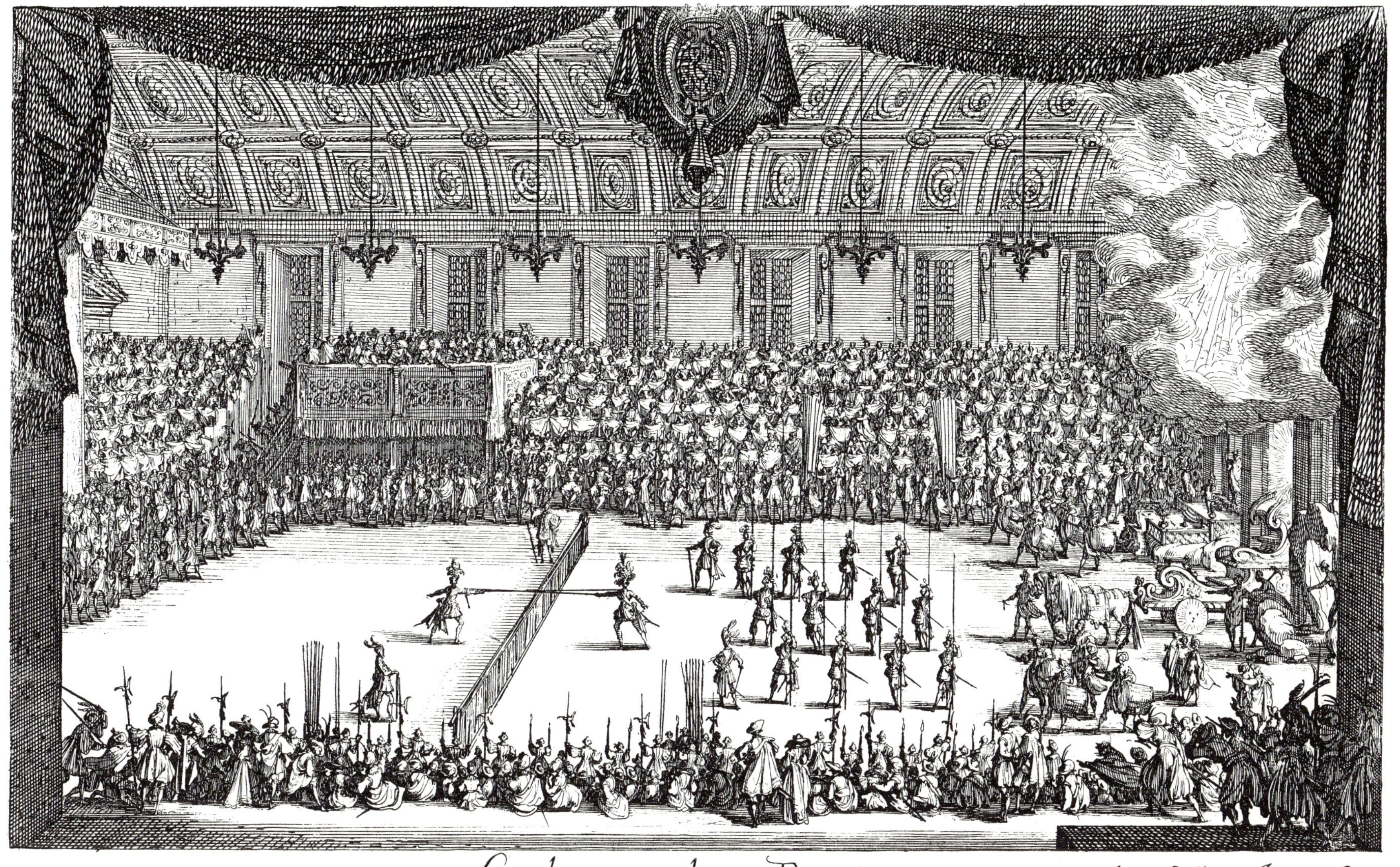

Combat a la Barriere   Iac. Callot In. et fec.

209 The Tourney.

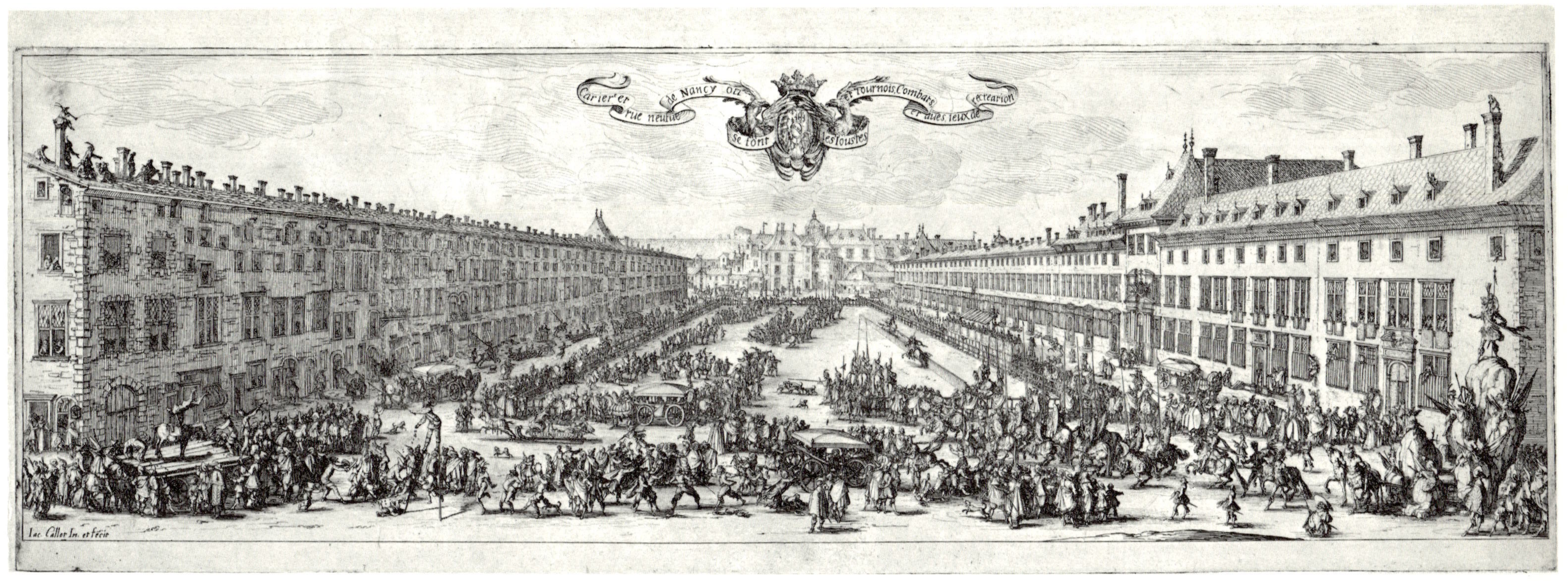

210 The Place de la Carrière in Nancy (La Carrière [jousting ground] de Nancy). Etching, ca. 1627/28. The inscription reads: "Jousting ground and new street in Nancy where the jousts, tourneys, combats and other sports take place." (National Gallery, Washington, R. L. Baumfeld Collection)

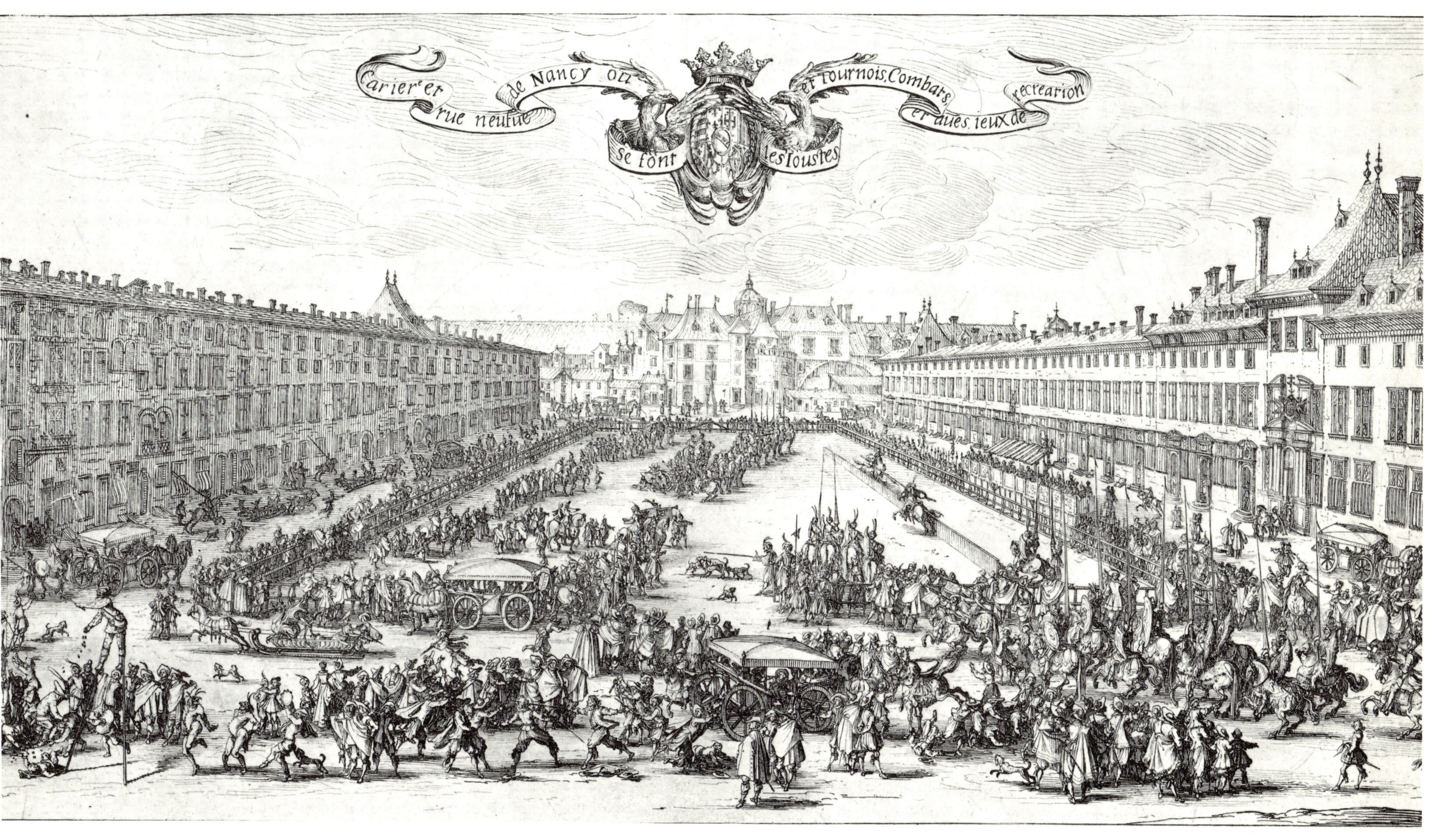

211 The Place de la Carrière in Nancy. Detail, actual size.

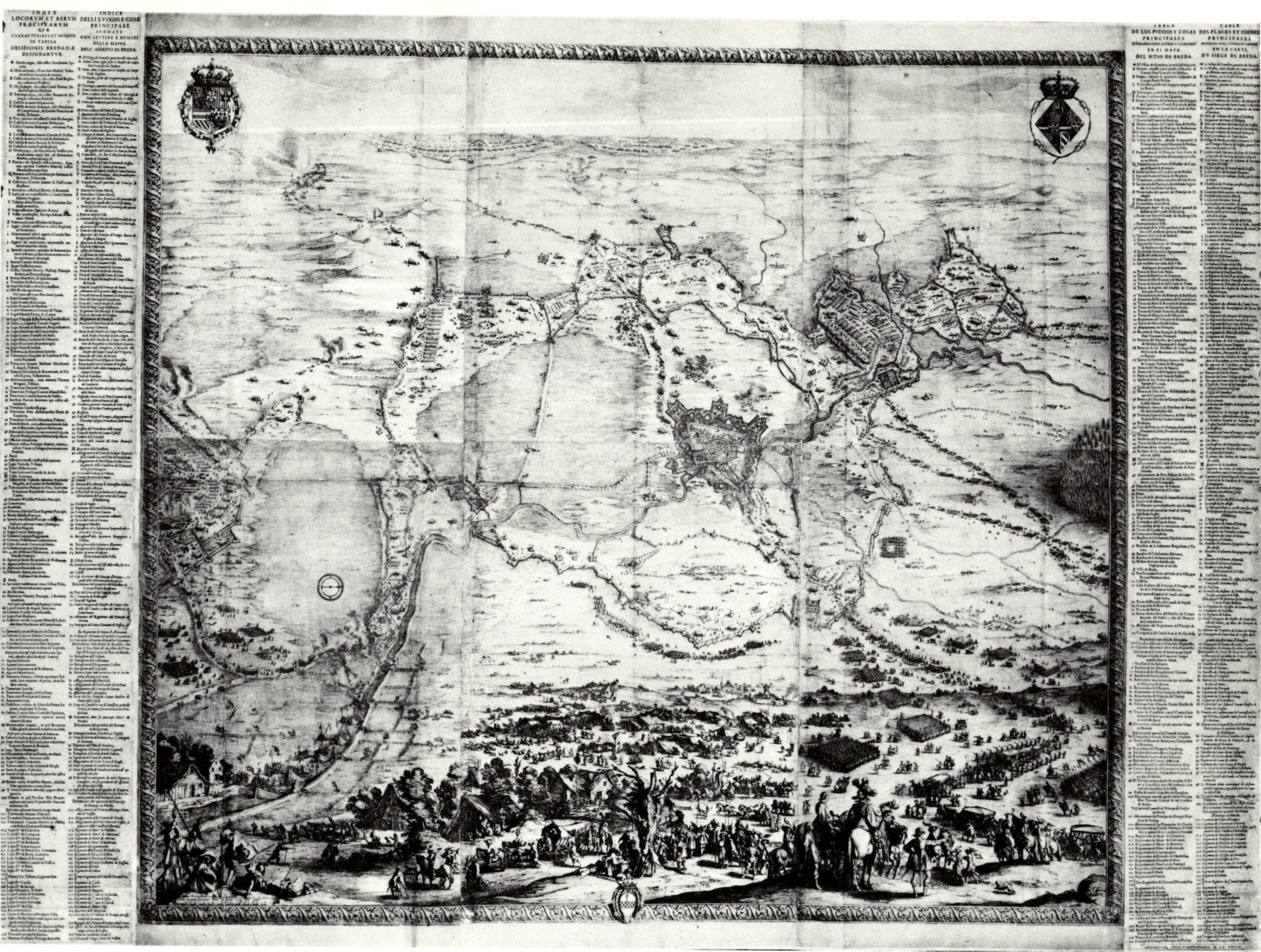

212 *The Siege of Breda.* Consists of 6 etchings, plus explanatory text, 1628. Illustrations show details of 3 of the 6 parts at 56% of original size. (Complete view courtesy Trustees of the British Museum)

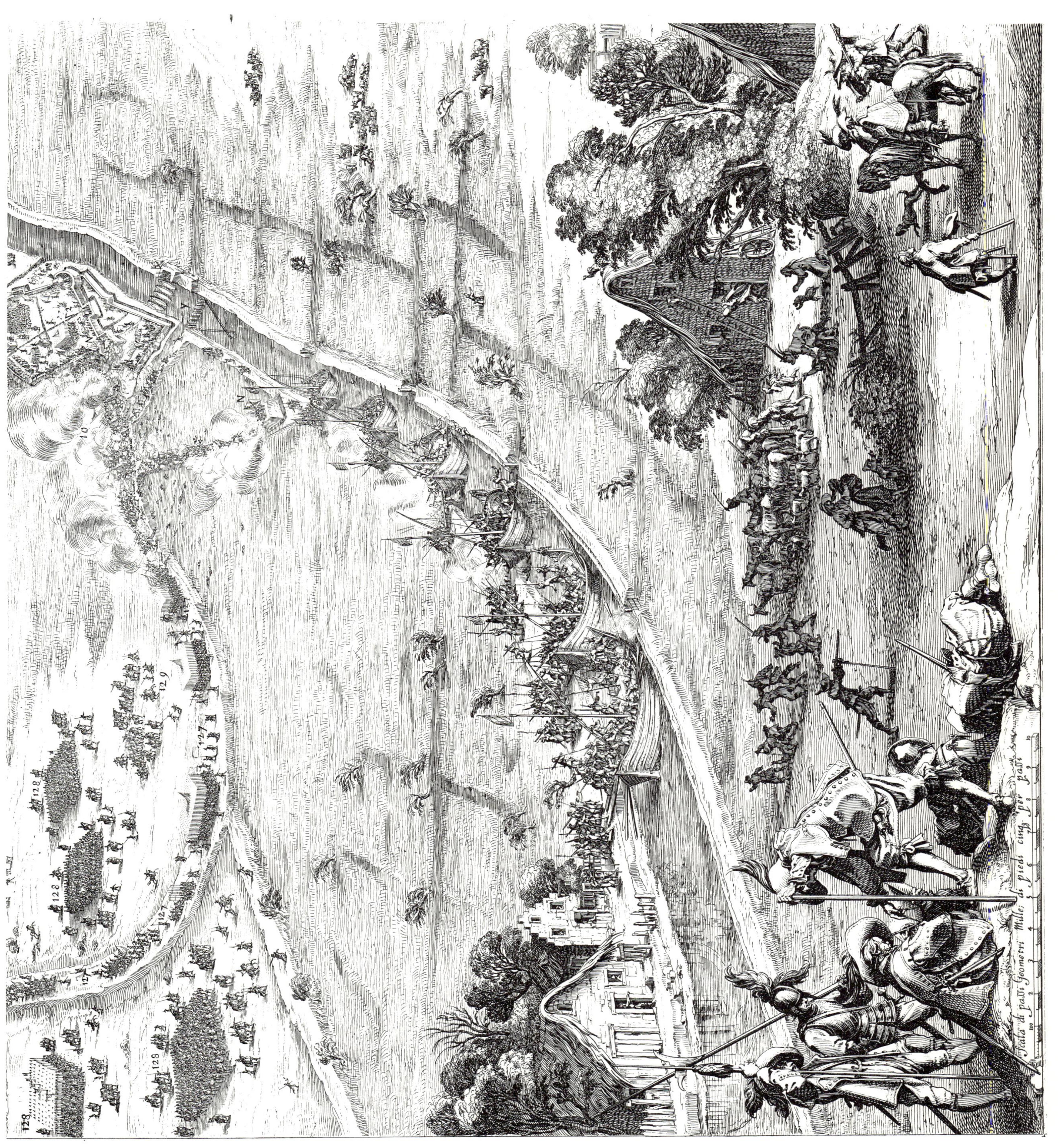

213 From *The Siege of Breda*: detail from the lower left plate.

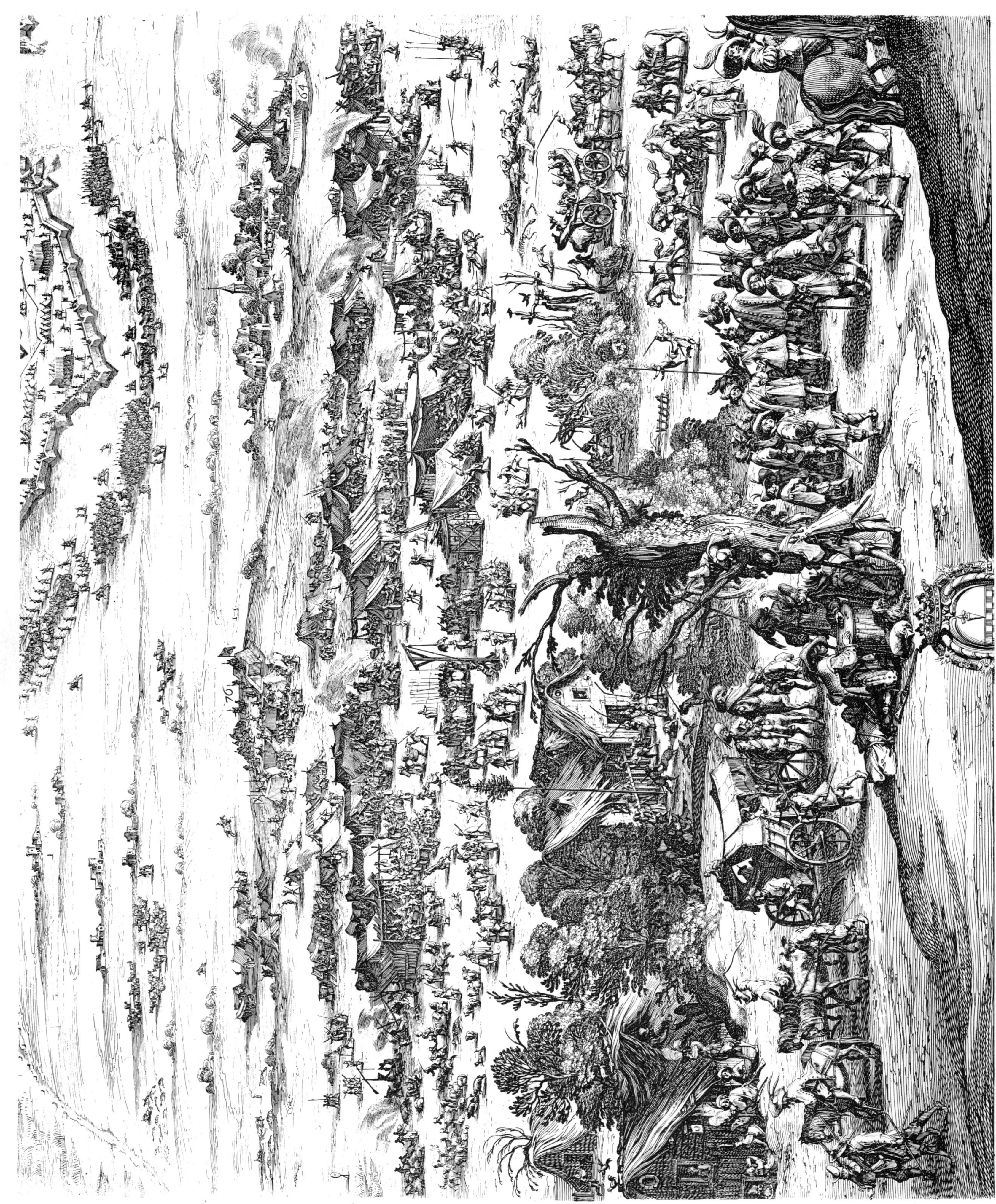

214 From *The Siege of Breda*: detail from the lower middle plate.

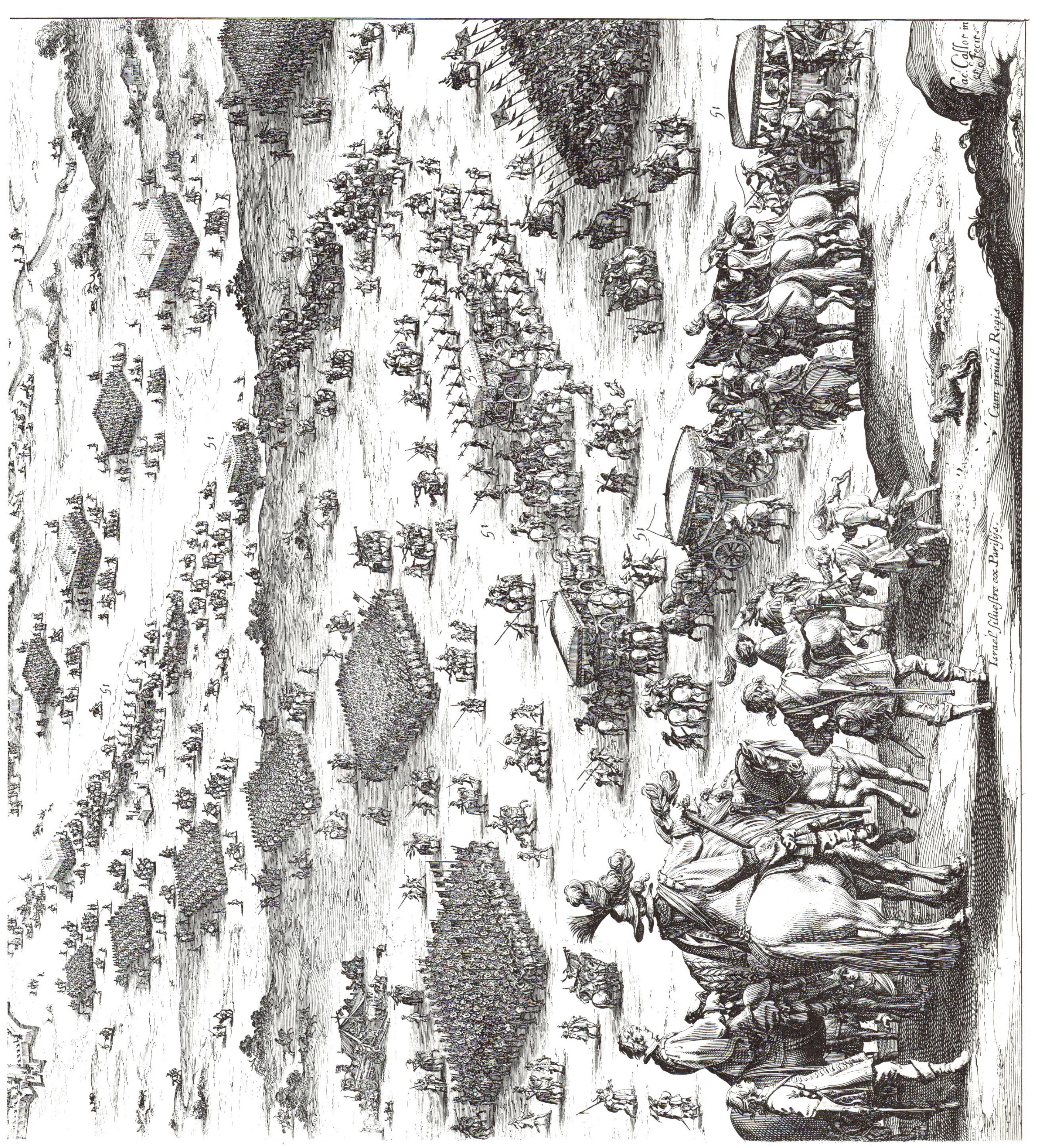

215 From *The Siege of Breda*: detail from the lower right plate.

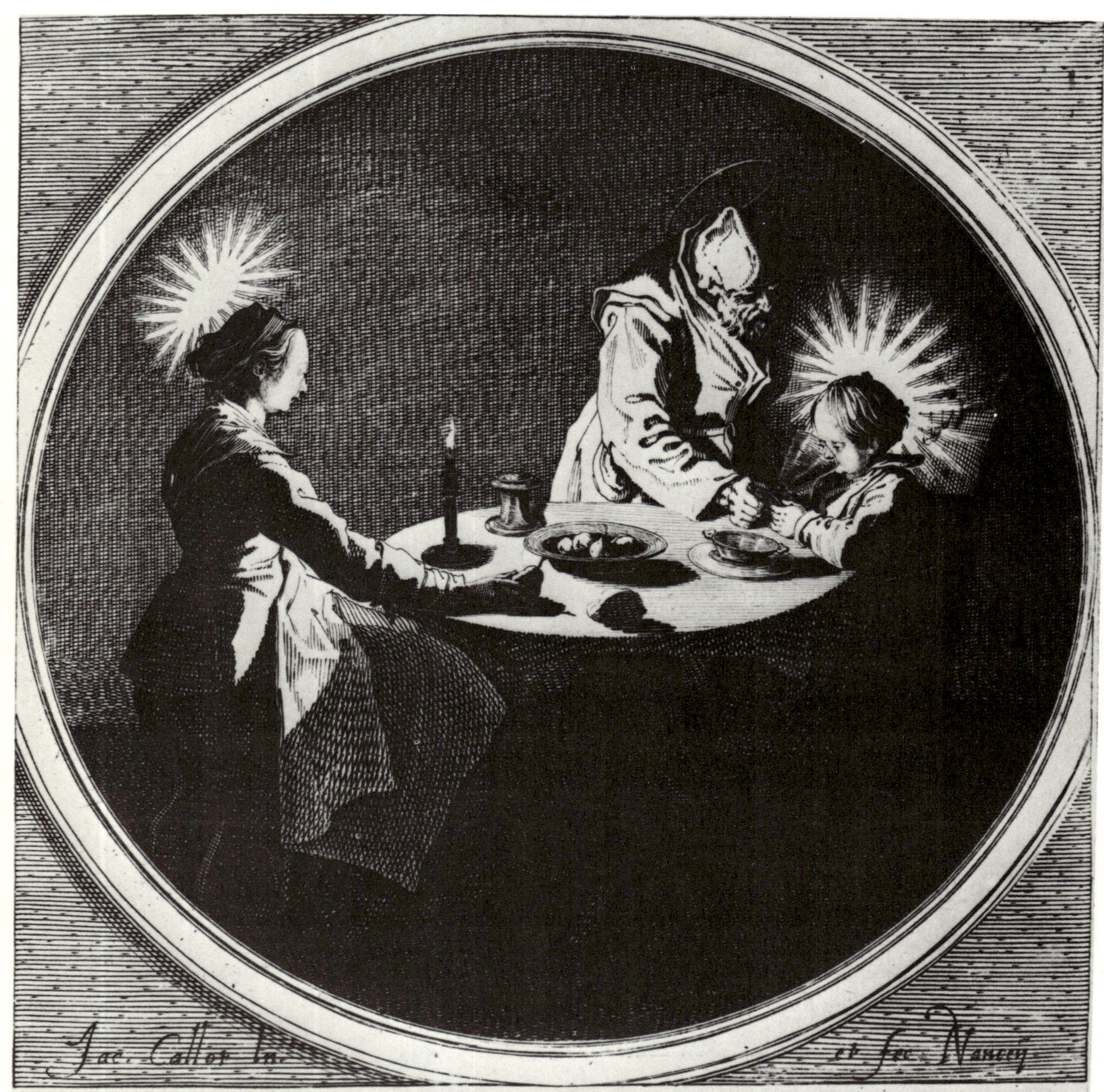

216 The Benediction. Etching, ca. 1627–1629. The Latin couplet reads: "Come, dear Child, drain the cup; another awaits you which only death will release from Your straining hands." (Courtesy Trustees of the British Museum)

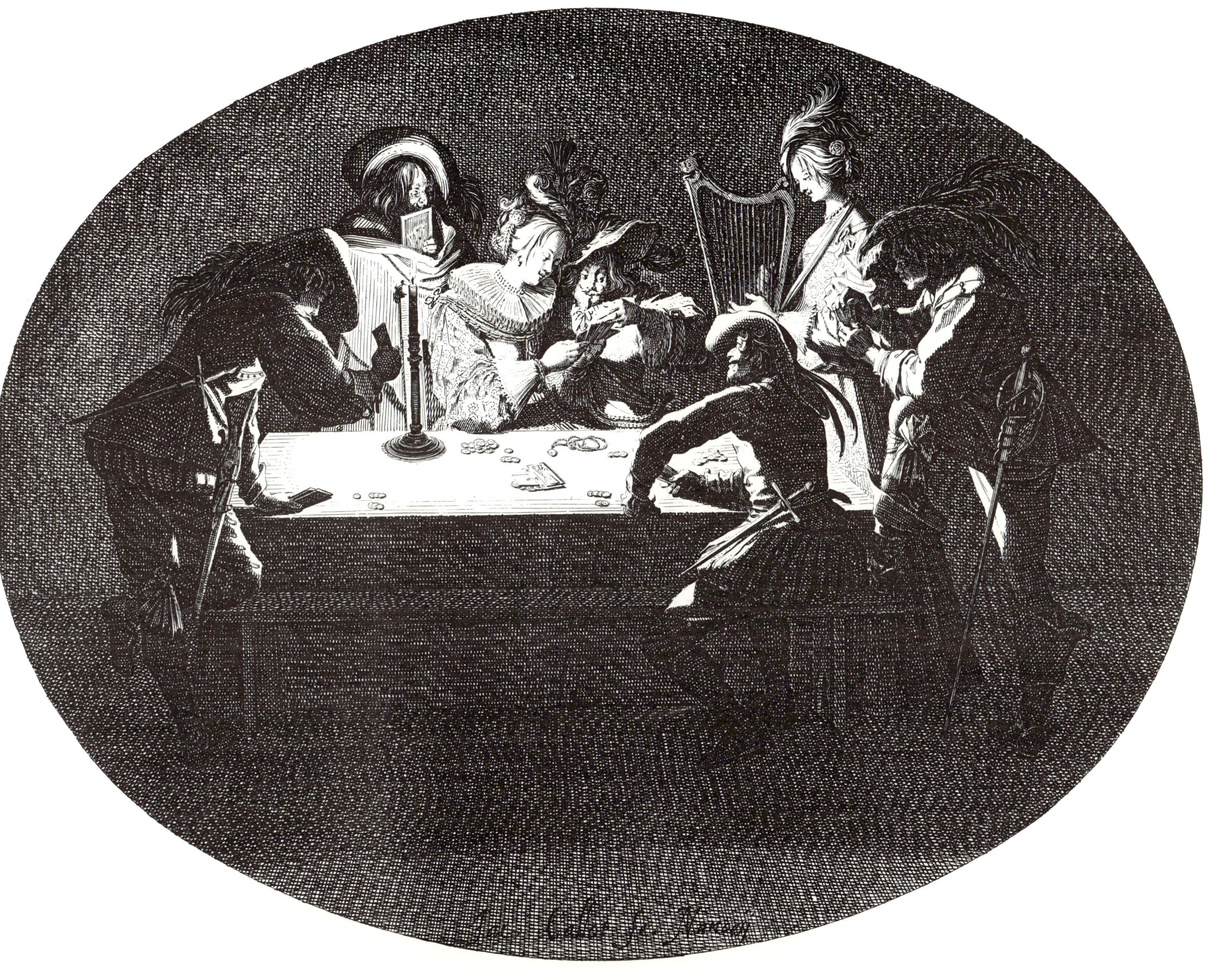

217 The Gambling Den (Le Brelan). Etching, sometime between 1628 and 1632. In another state of the etching, a Latin poem frames the entire picture; this text states that a young man (the Prodigal Son?) is being fleeced by sharpers and is losing his inherited wealth and honor. (Howard Daniel Collection)

218 & 219 From *Lux Claustri* (*Light of the Cloister*, emblems of monastic life), a series of 27 etchings, 1628.

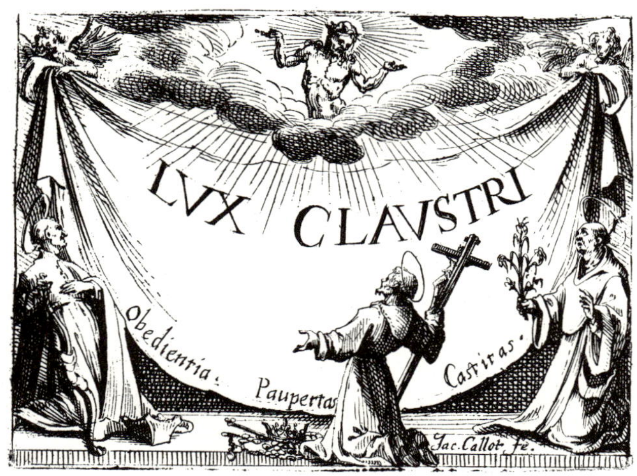

218 Title. The figures at the bottom, alongside the words "Obedience," "Poverty" and "Chastity," represent St. Bruno, St. Francis of Assisi and St. Bernard of Clairvaux.

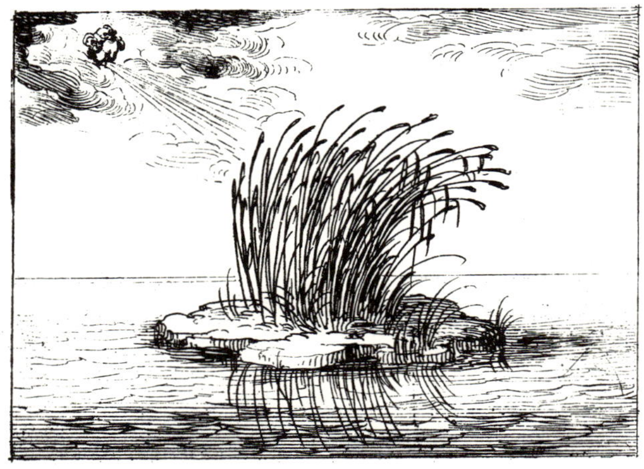

219 The Reeds and the Wind (last of the series).

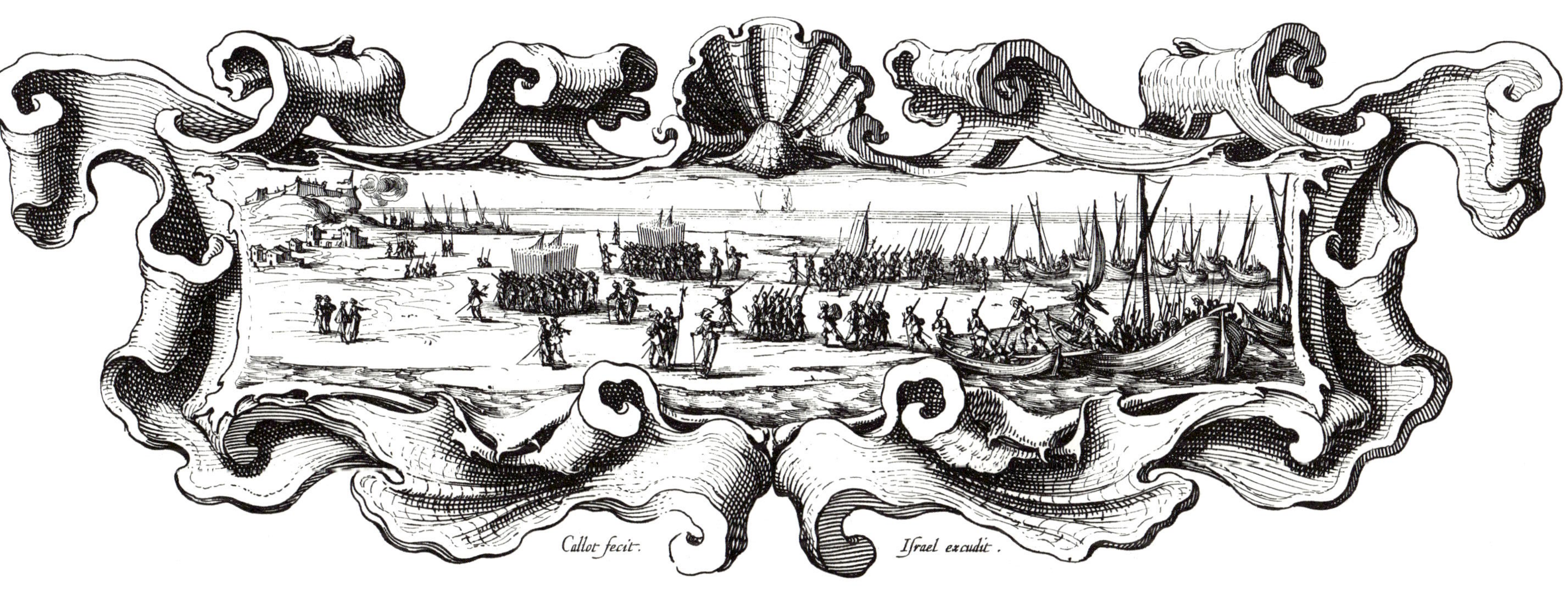

220 Disembarking of Troops. Etching, 1629. (Howard Daniel Collection)

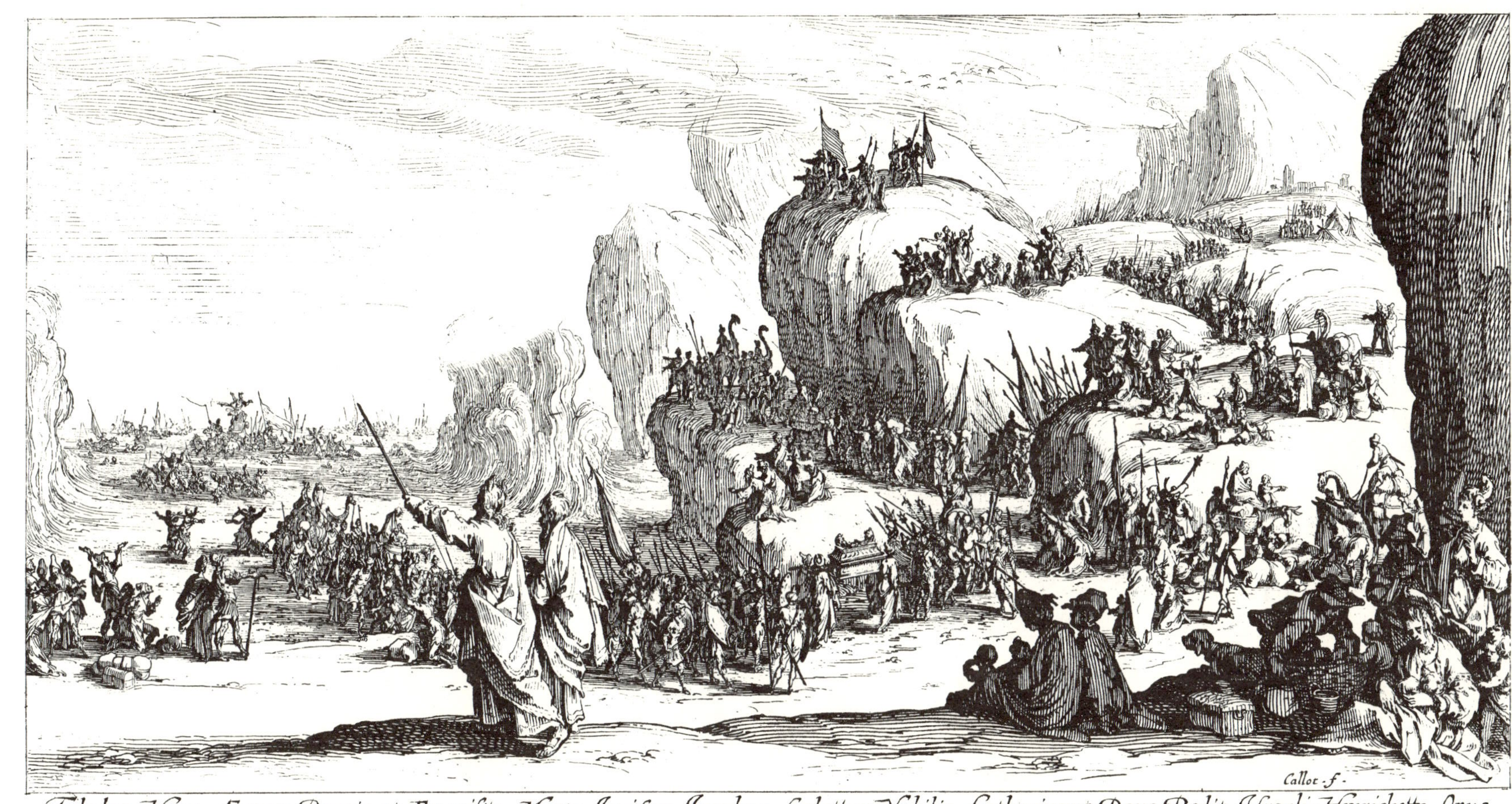

221 The Israelites Crossing the Red Sea. Etching, 1629. The inscription reads: "This copper plate, which he had elegantly engraved, was presented by Jacques Callot, a nobleman of Lorraine, as a very perfect work to Israël Henriet, best and sincerest of friends."

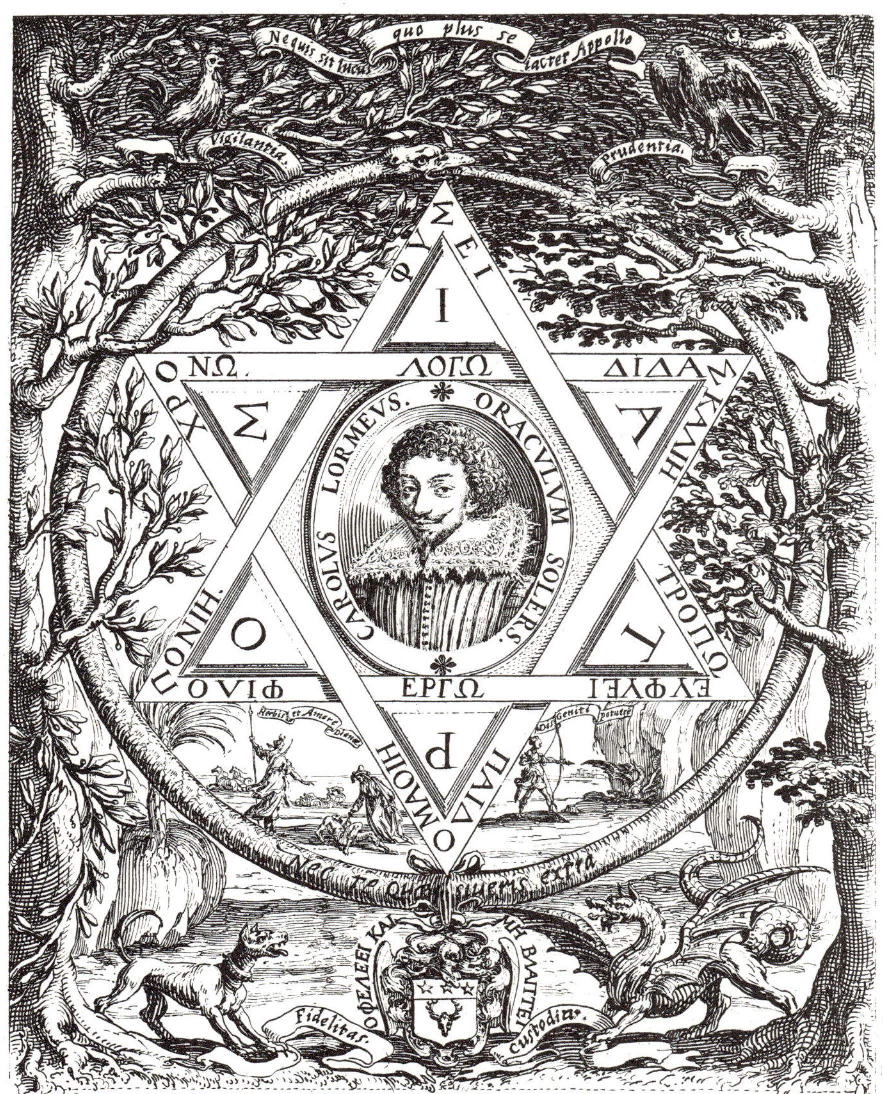

222 Portrait of Charles Delorme. Etching, 1630. The profusion of Latin and Greek inscriptions rehearse Delorme's titles and exalt his qualities of learning, industry and medical skill. (National Gallery, Washington, R. L. Baumfeld Collection)

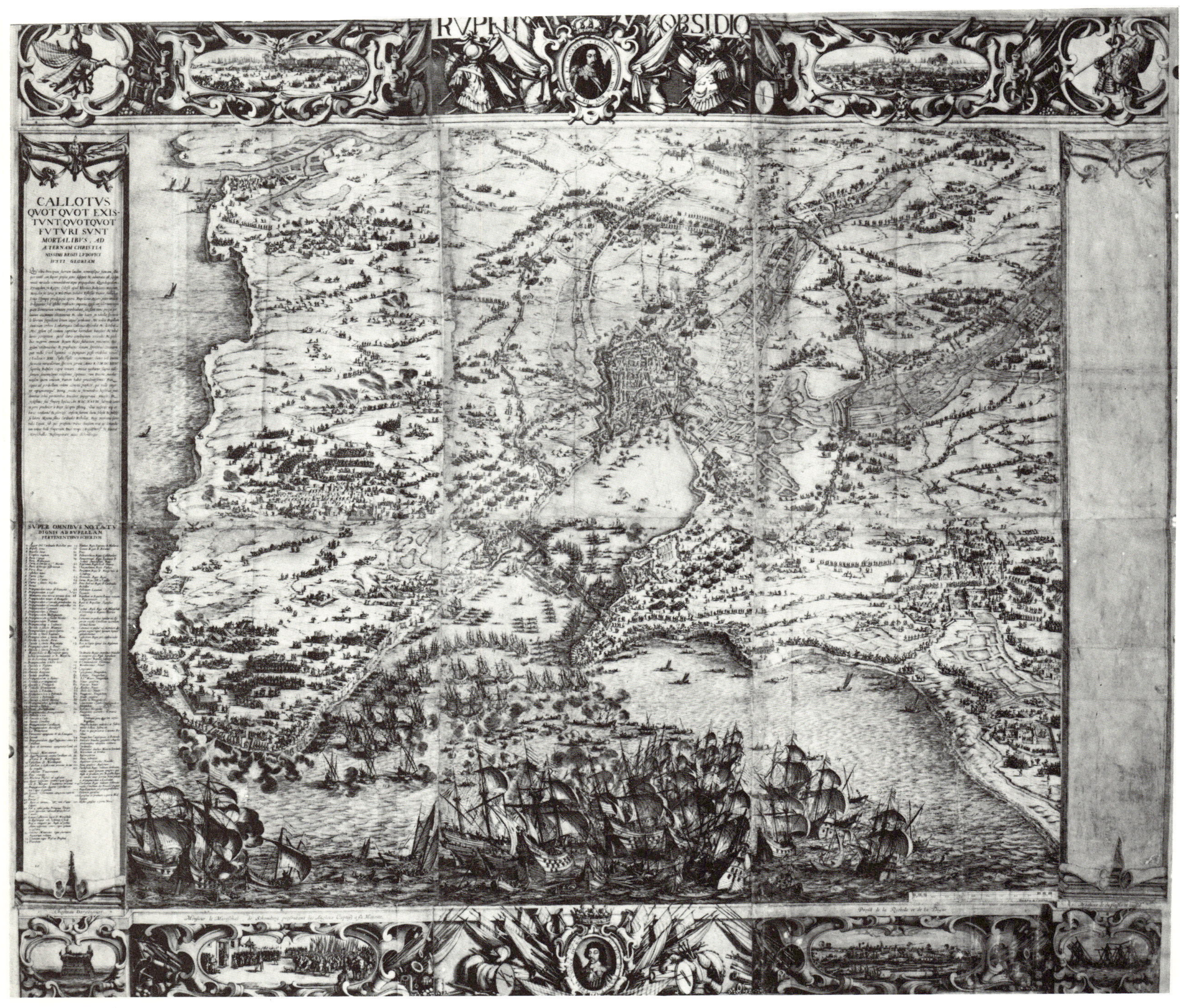

223 *The Siege of La Rochelle* [this 13-month siege took place in 1627 and 1628]. Consists of 6 etchings, plus borders with text and cartouches, some by other artists, 1631. Illustrations 224–226 show 3 of the 6 main parts. Illustrations 227–230 show border cartouches in which Callot had a hand. (Complete view, with variant borders, courtesy Trustees of the British Museum)

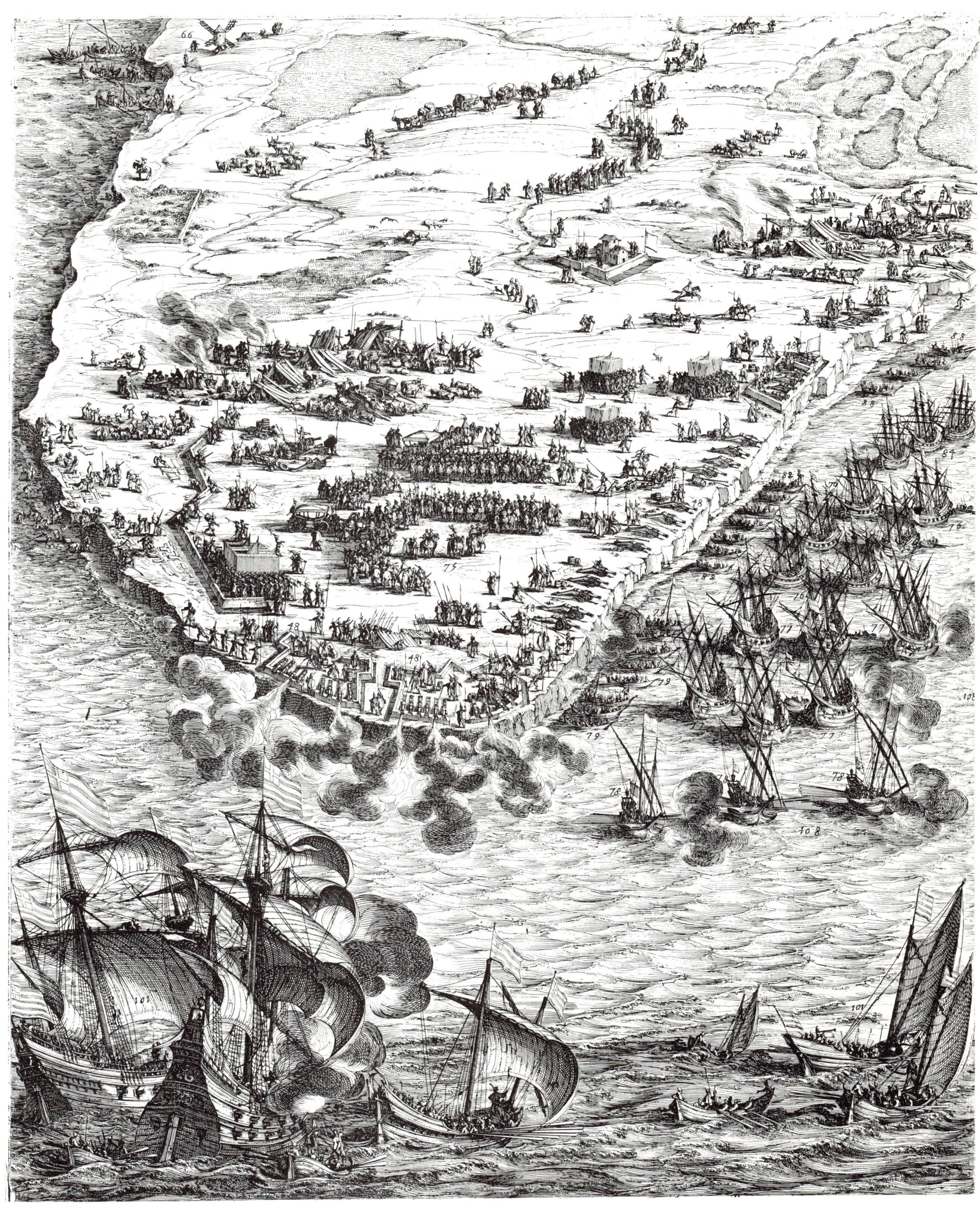

224 From *The Siege of La Rochelle*: the lower left section.

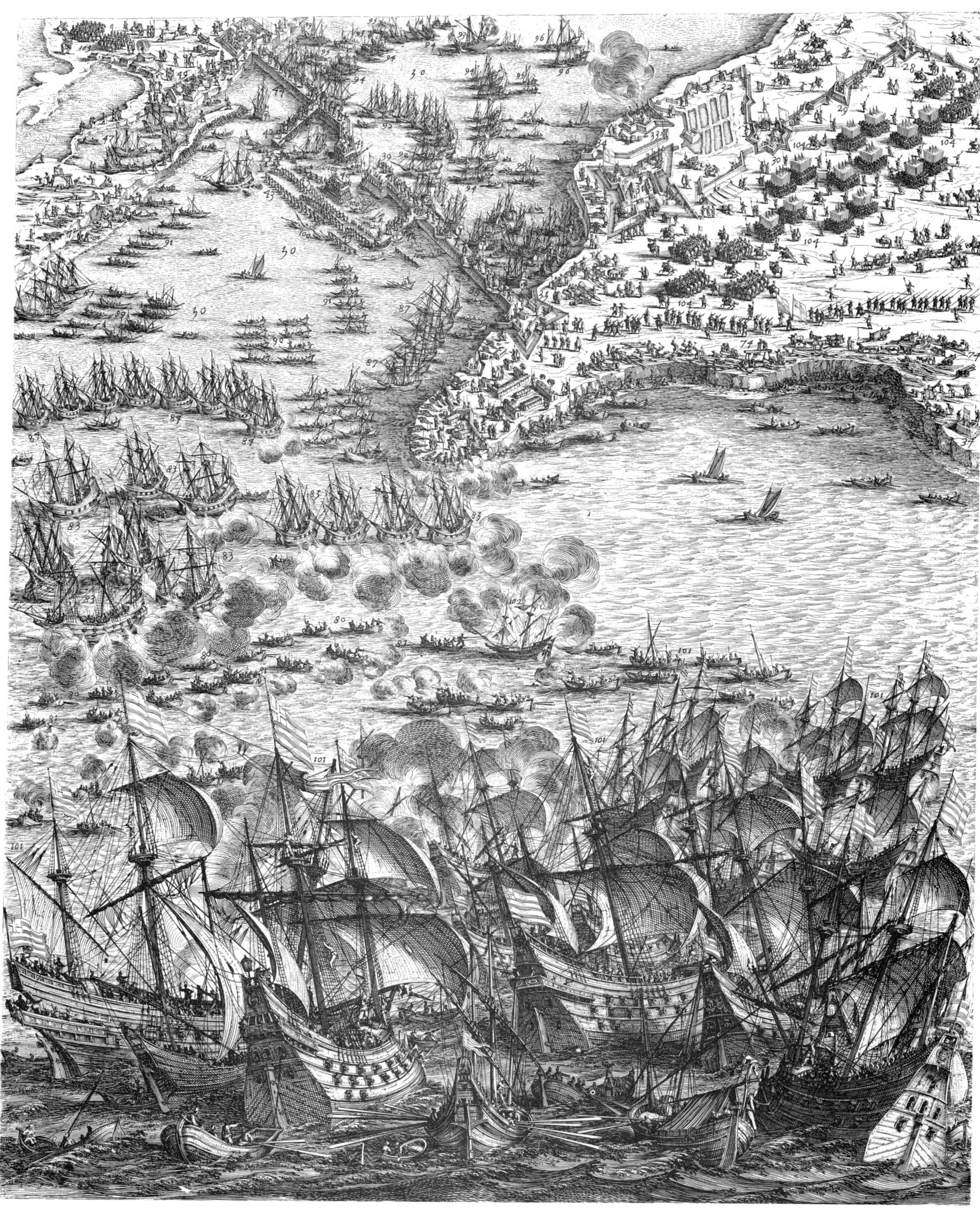

225 From *The Siege of La Rochelle*: the lower middle section.

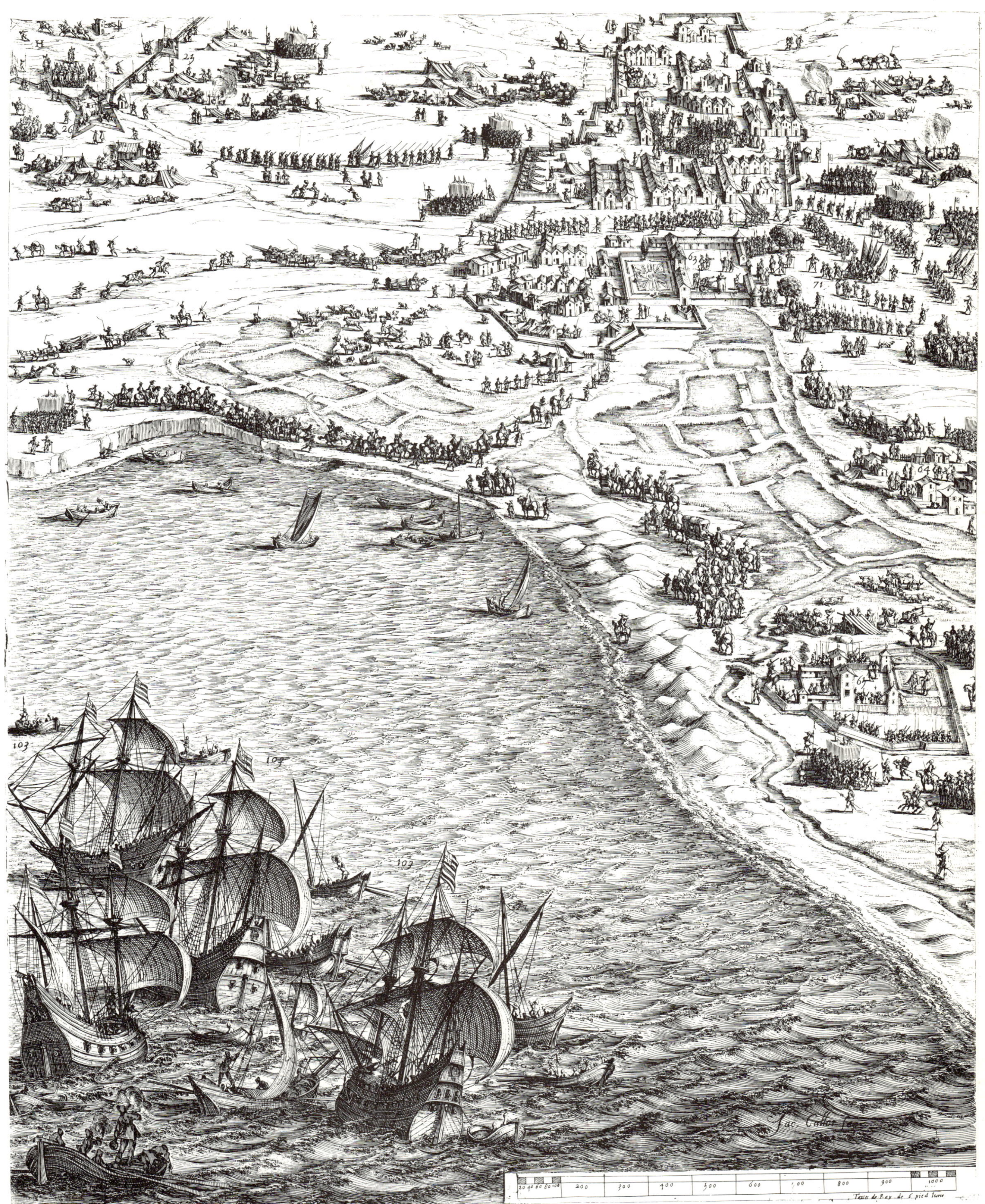

226 From *The Siege of La Rochelle*: the lower right section.

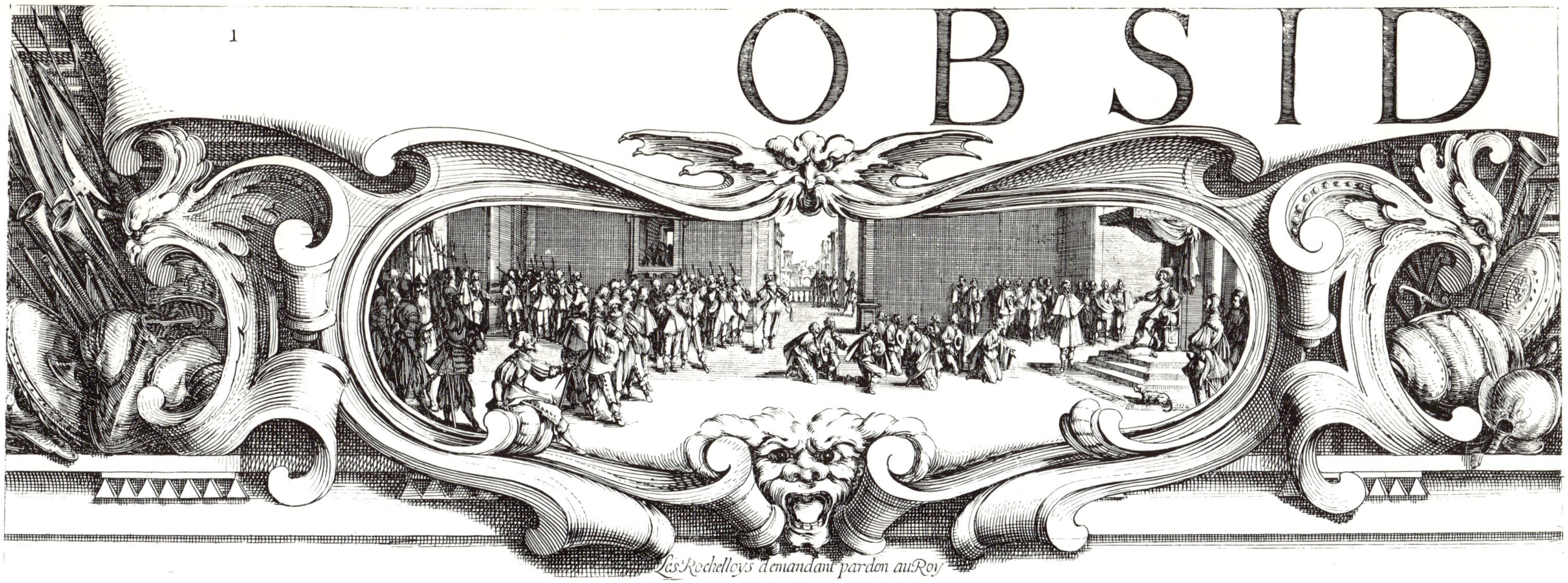

1

OBSID

Les Rochelloys demandant pardon au Roy

227 From *The Siege of La Rochelle*: "The Inhabitants of La Rochelle Asking Pardon of the King [Louis XIII]" (border cartouche). The scene (etched) is by Callot, the ornamental framework (engraved) by Abraham Bosse.

228 From *The Siege of La Rochelle*: "The King Enters La Rochelle" (border cartouche). The scene is by Callot, the ornament by Bosse.

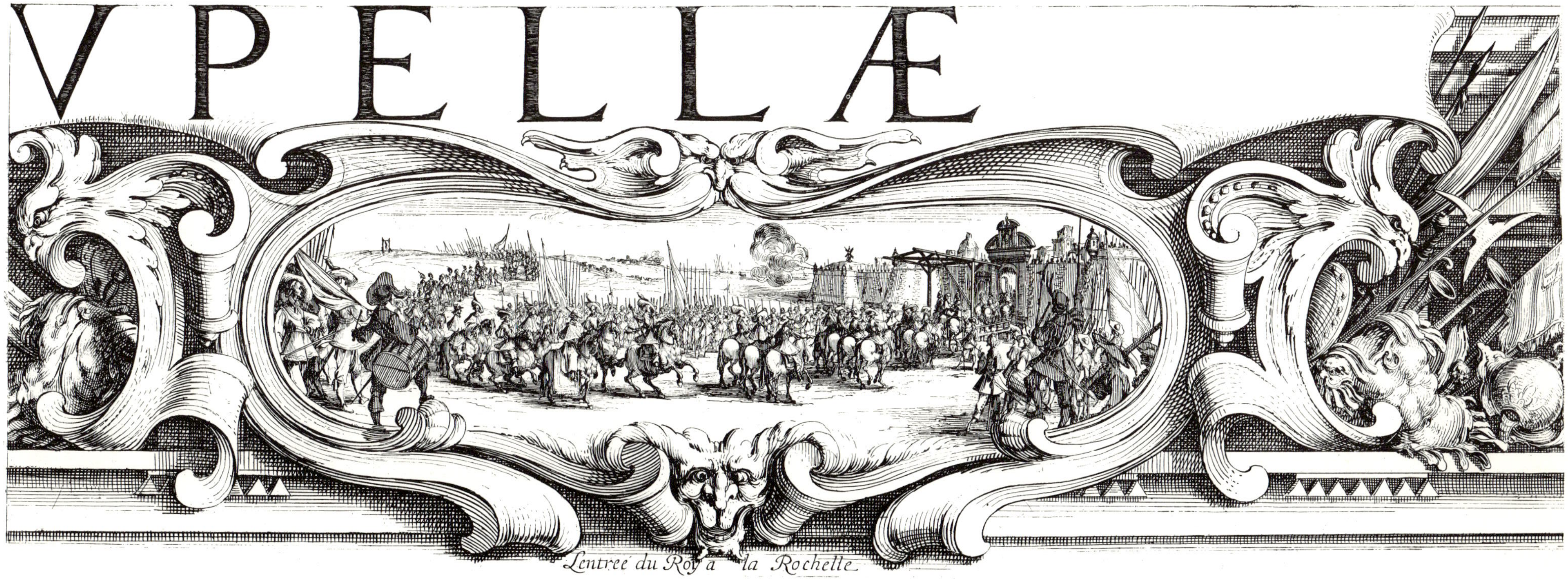

VPELLÆ

Lentreé du Roy a la Rochelle

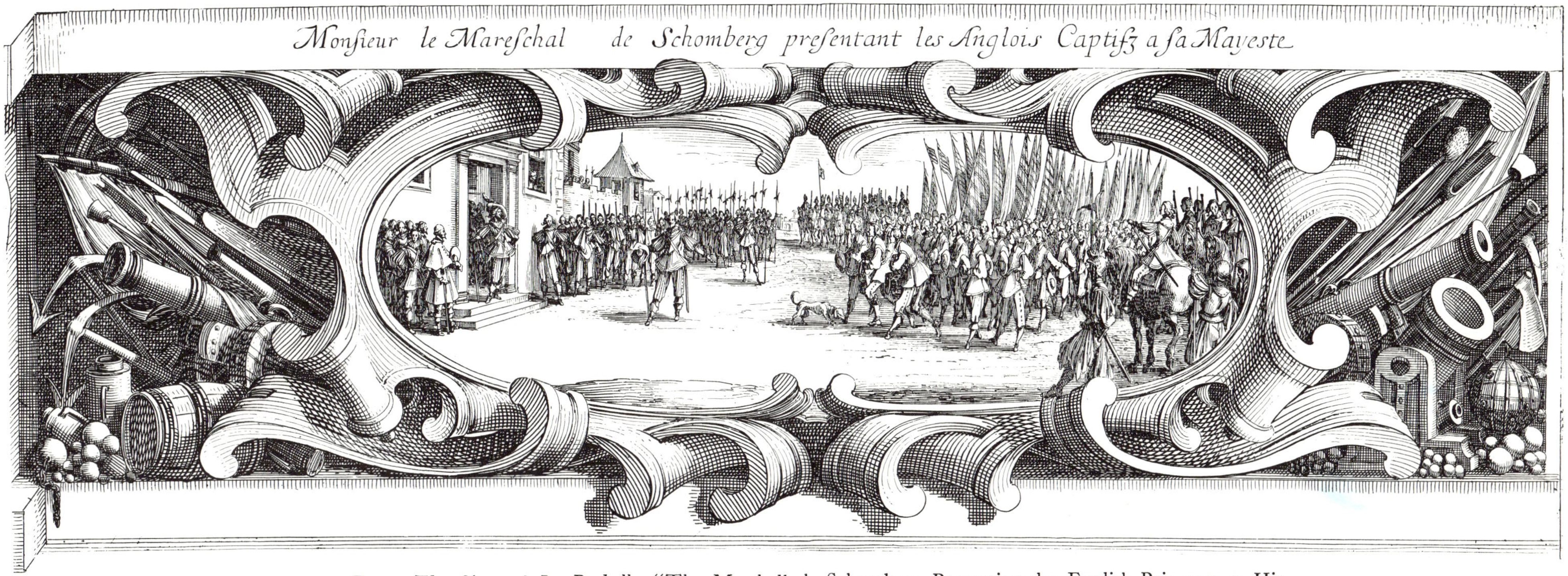

Monſieur le Mareſchal de Schomberg preſentant les Anglois Captifz a ſa Mayeste

229 From *The Siege of La Rochelle*: "The Marshall de Schomberg Presenting the English Prisoners to His Majesty" (border cartouche). Etched and engraved by Bosse or by Israël Henriet after a drawing by Callot.

230 From *The Siege of La Rochelle*: "View of La Rochelle and the Mole" (border cartouche). Etched and engraved by Bosse or Henriet after a drawing by Callot.

Profil de la Rochelle et de la Digue

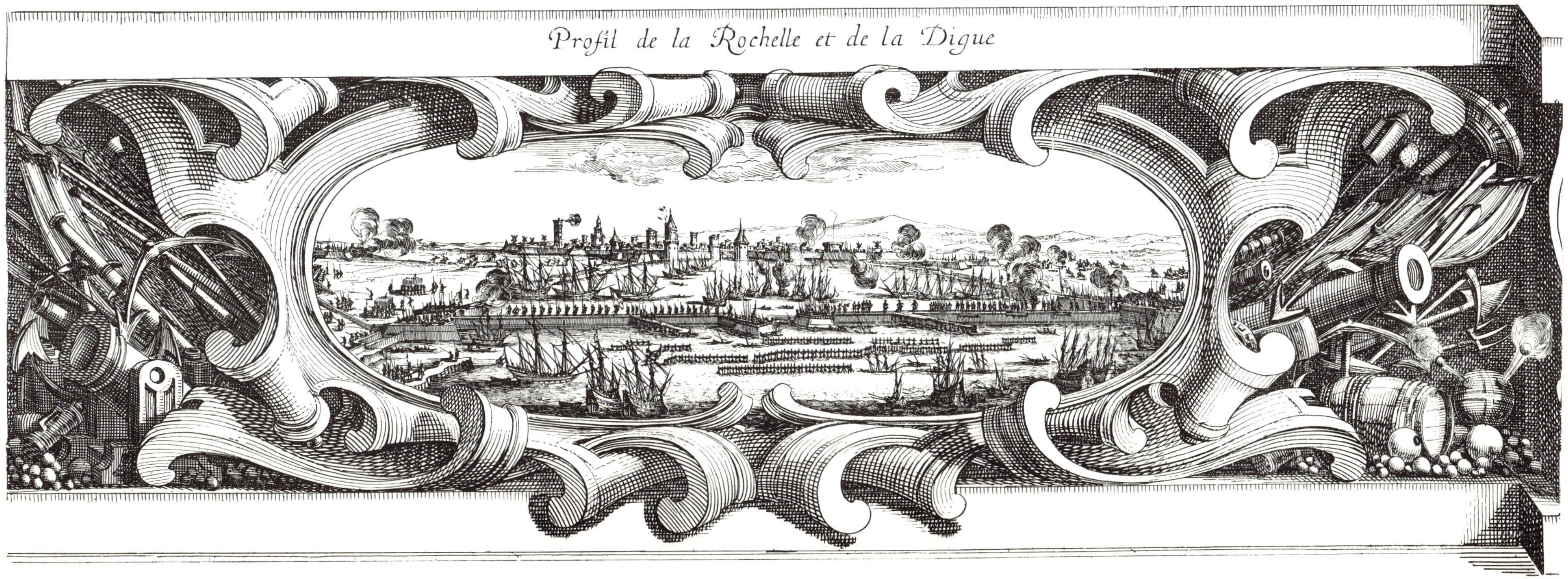

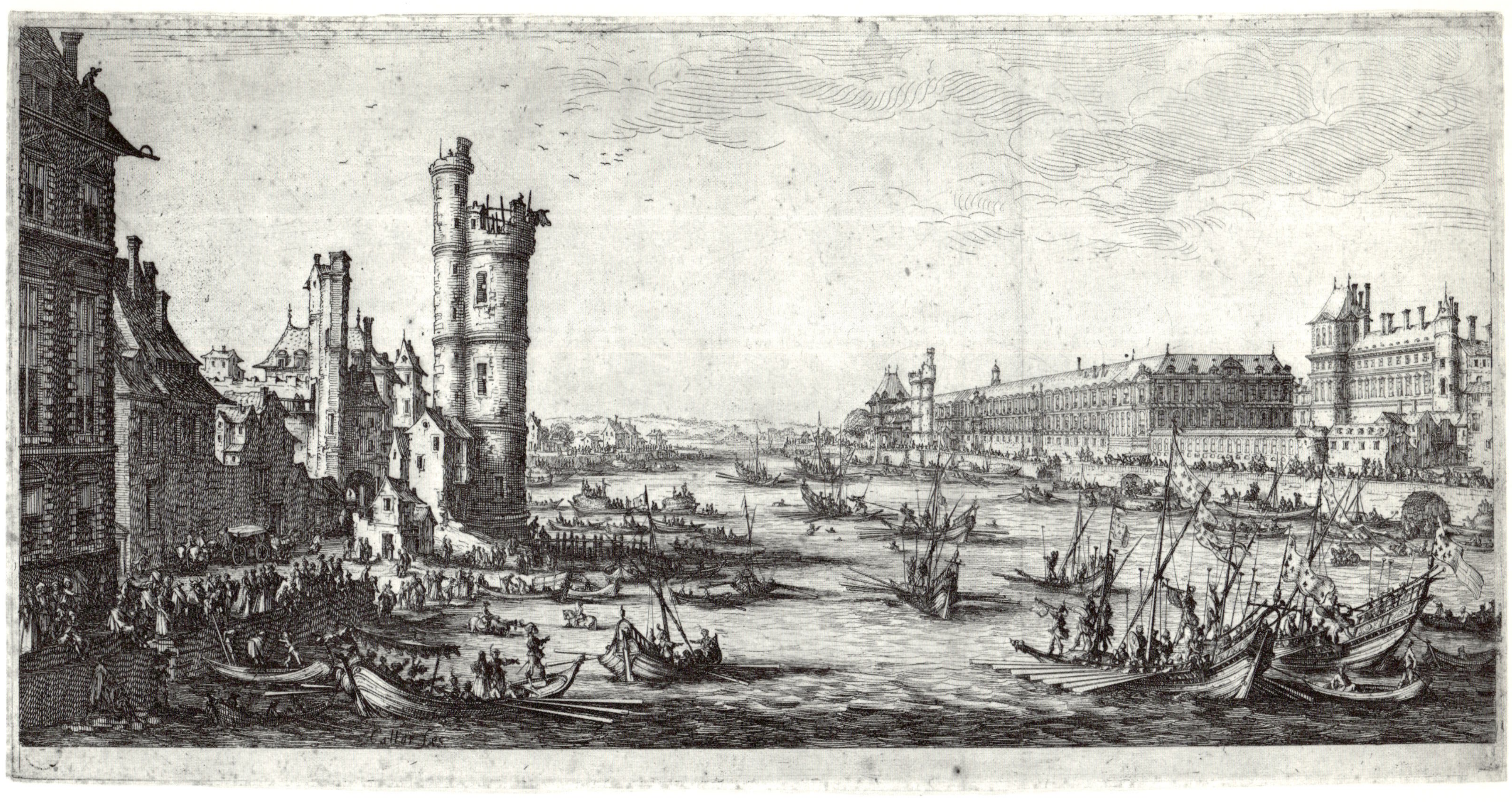

231 View of the Louvre, Paris. Etching (second state), ca. 1631/32.

238 & 239 From *The Images of All the Saints*, a series of 489 figures on 122 sheets, plus a frontispiece, etched during 1630's, published posthumously 1636.

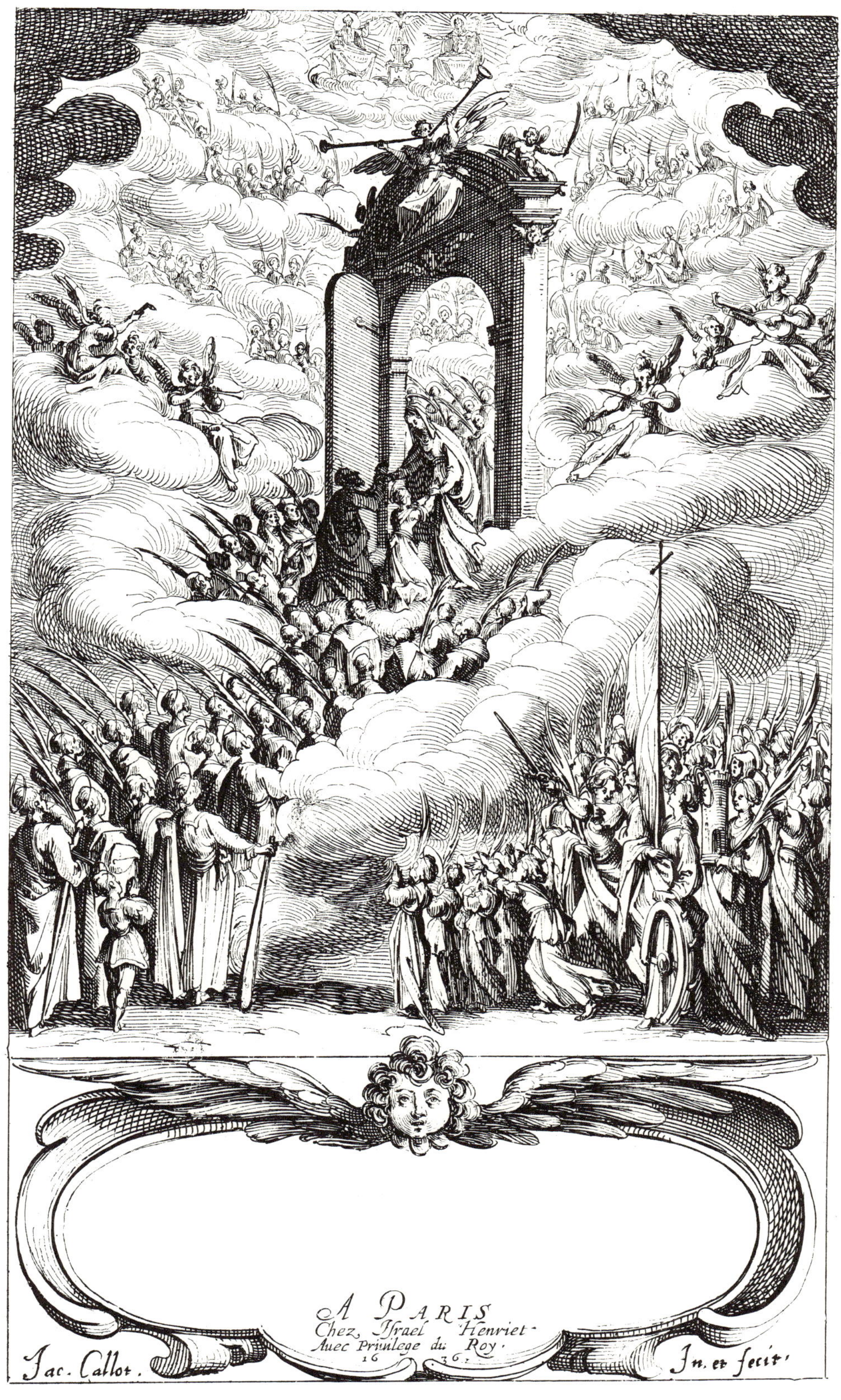

238 Frontispiece. A later state shows a biblical quotation inside the cartouche.

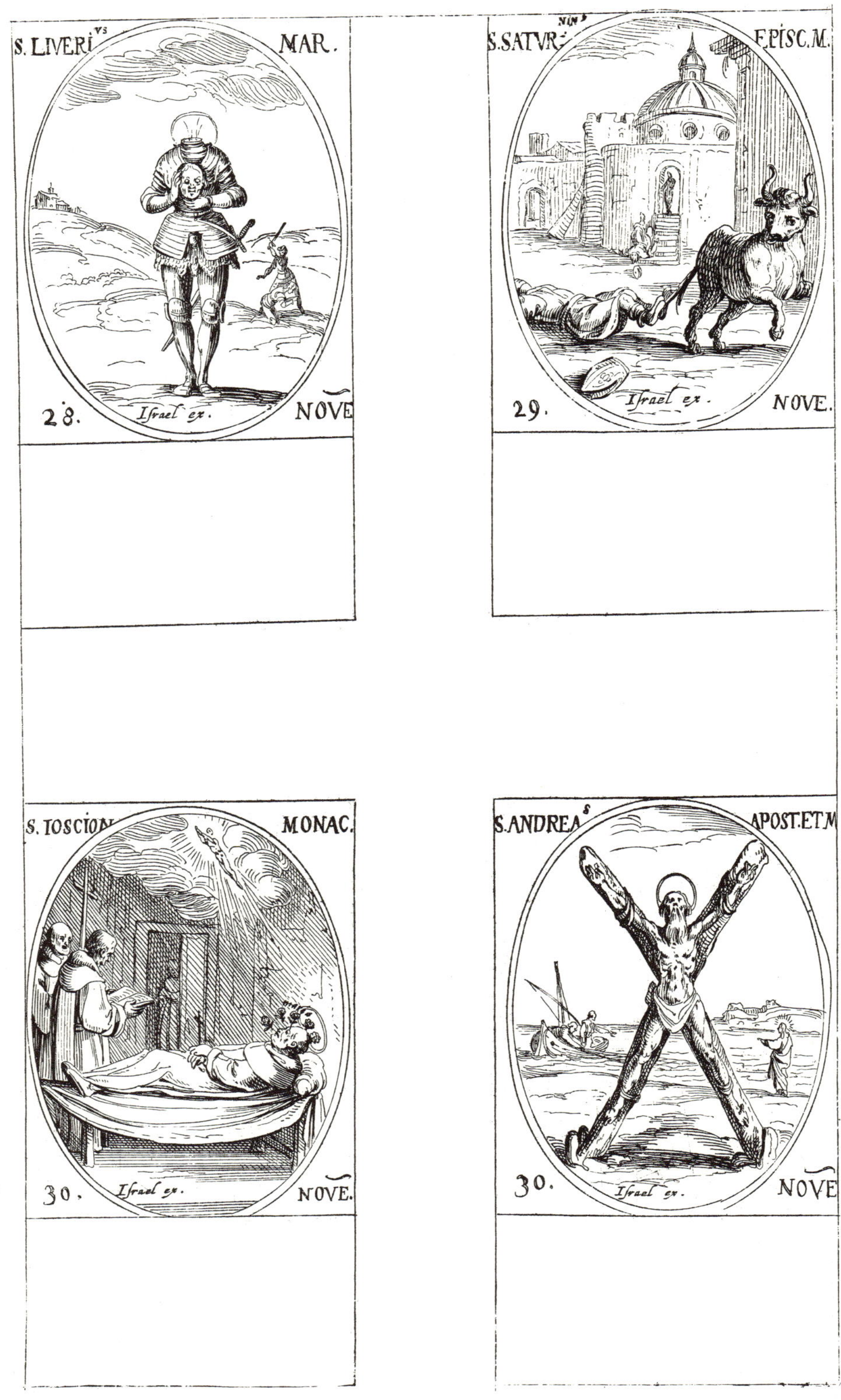

239 The last four saints of November: Liverius, Saturninus, Toscion and Andrew.

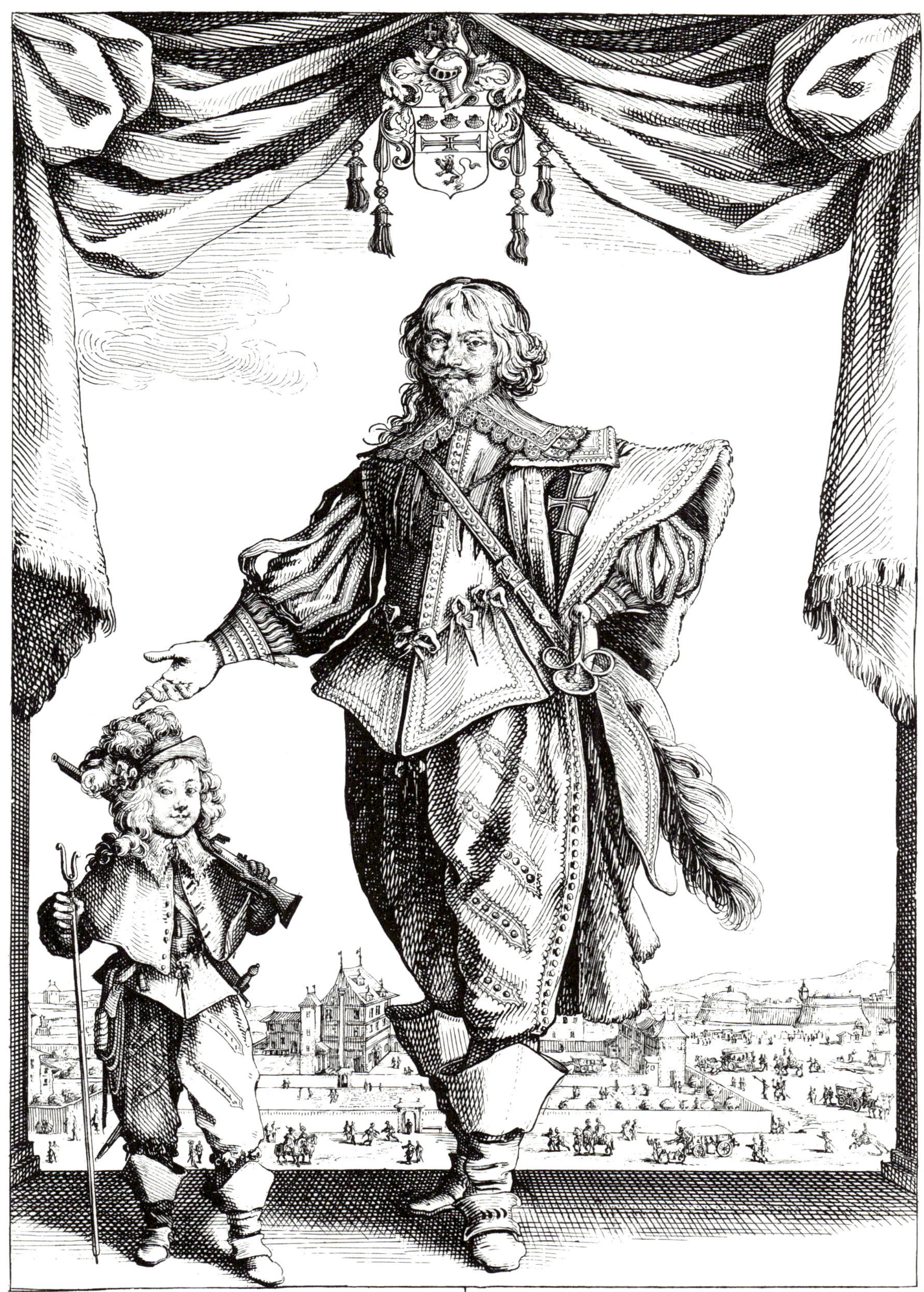

240 Portrait of the Painter Claude Deruet and His Son. Etching, 1632. The inscription at the very bottom reads: "To Claude Deruet, Esquire, Knight of the Order of Portugal, his faithful friend Jacques Callot." The poem is in adulation of Deruet.

241–243 From *The Savior, The Virgin and the Apostles* (the *Great Apostles*), a series of 16 etchings, 1631/32.

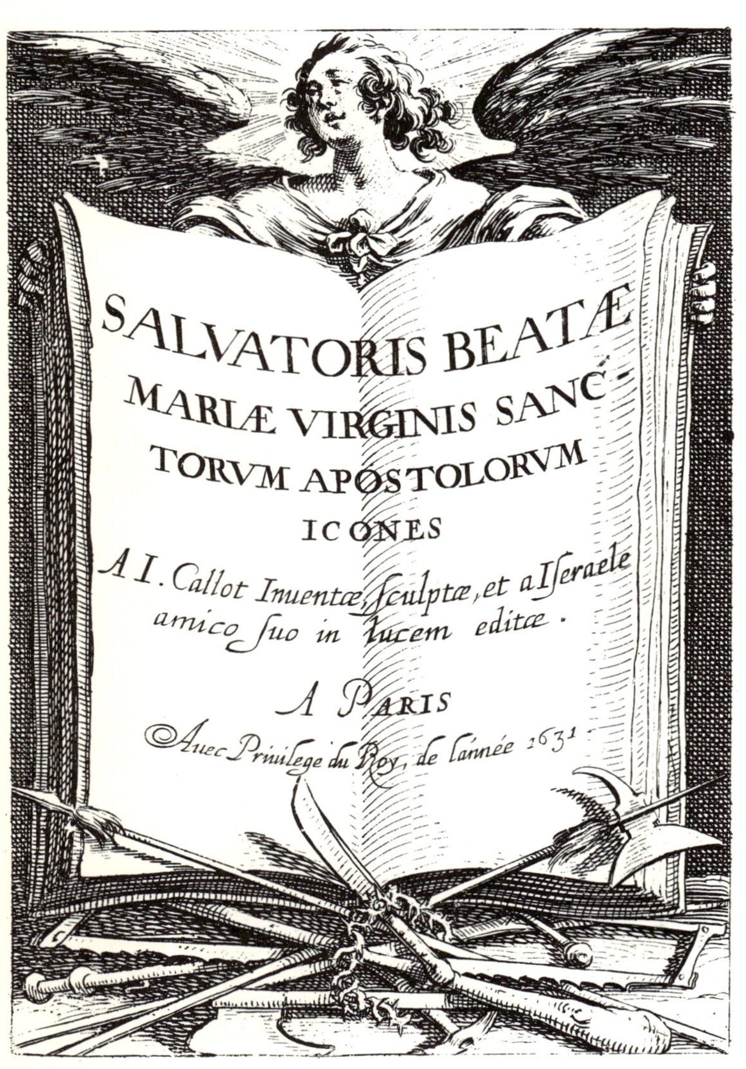

241 Title.

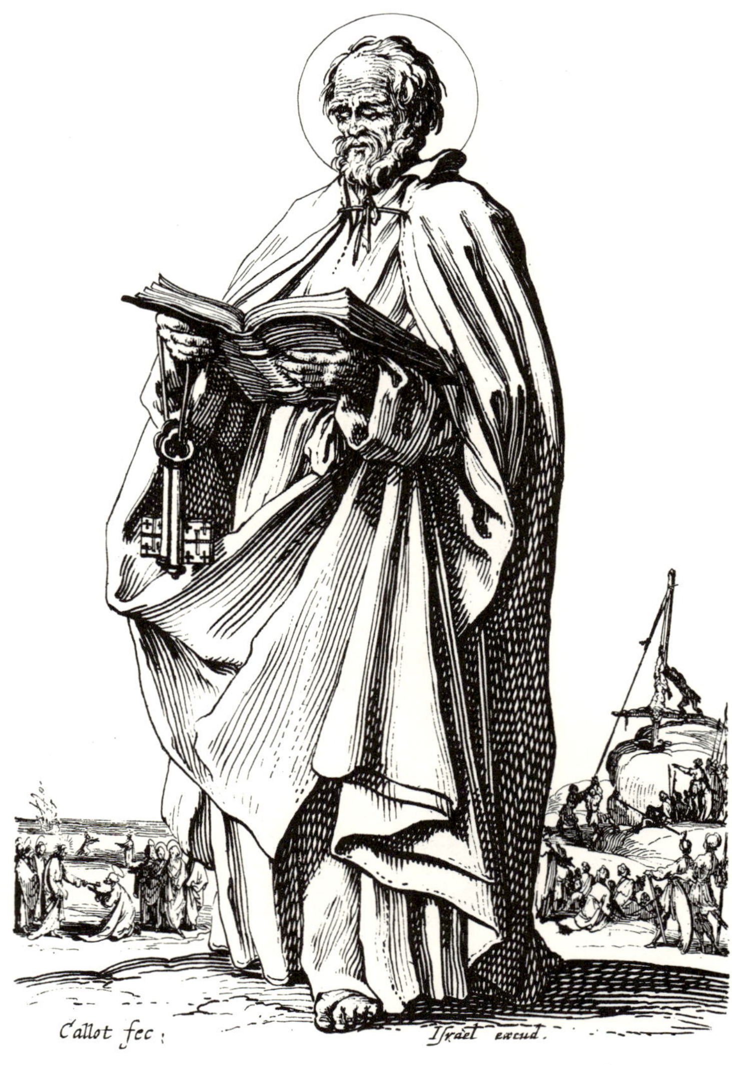

242 St. Peter, with scenes of Christ walking on the water and handing the keys to St. Peter, and the martyrdom of the saint.

244 & 245 *Two Cavalry Combats.*
Etchings, 1632.

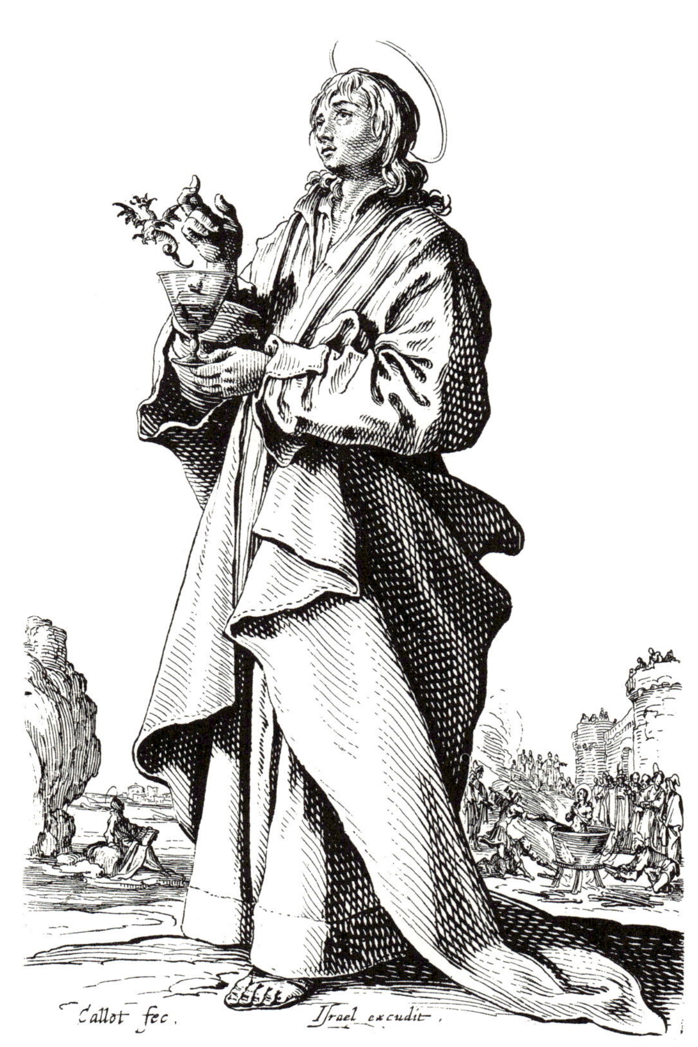

243 St. John the Evangelist, with scenes of the saint on Patmos and his martyrdom.

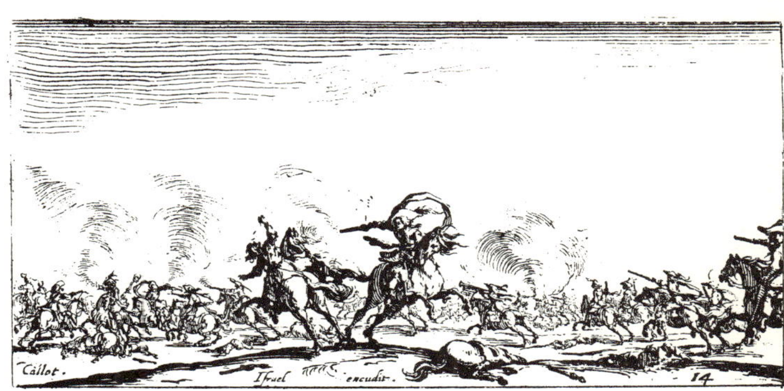

244 Combat with Pistols.

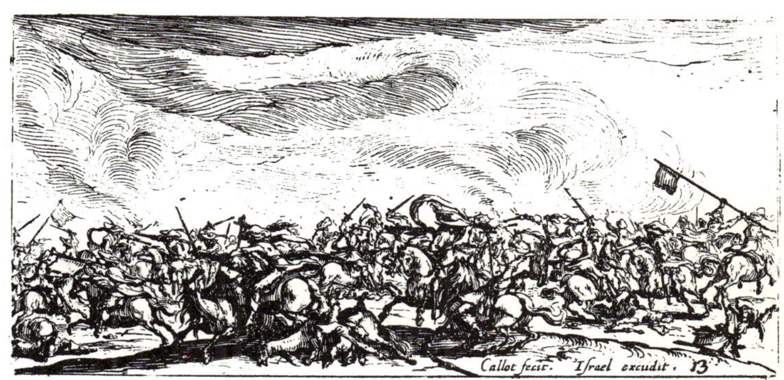

245 Combat with Swords.

246–258 The complete *Military Exercises*, a series of 13 etchings, done ca. 1632, published 1635.

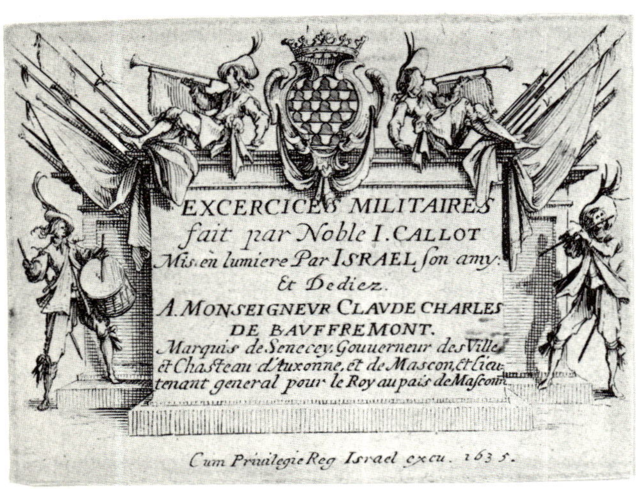

246 Title.

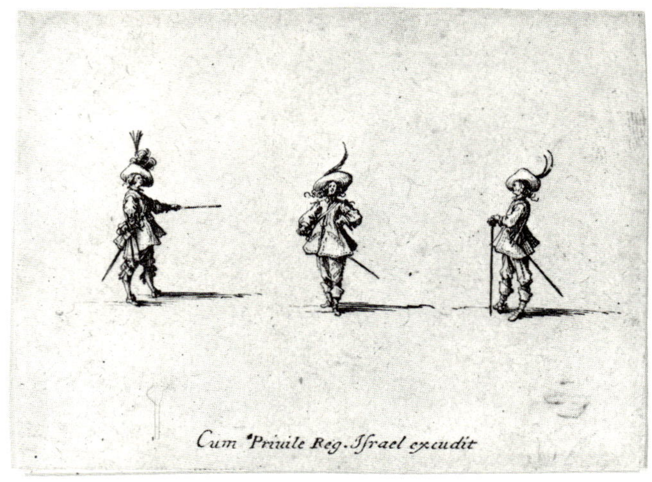

247 Unarmed Drill.

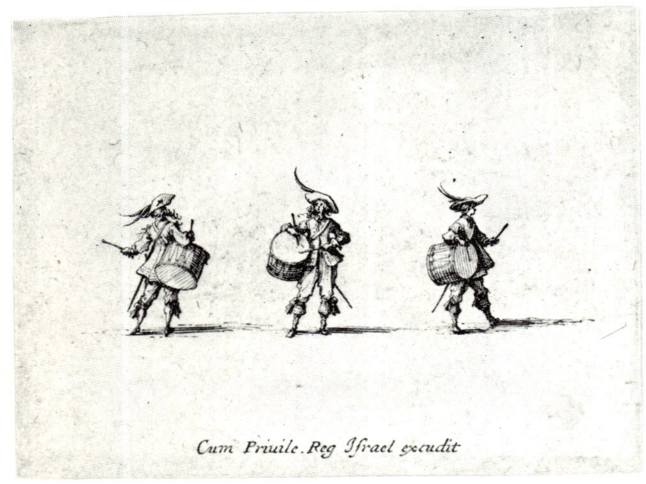

248 Drill with Drums.

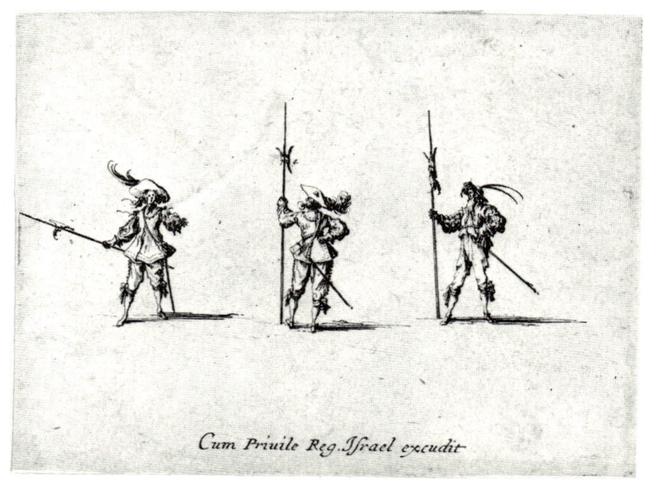

249 Drill with Halberds.

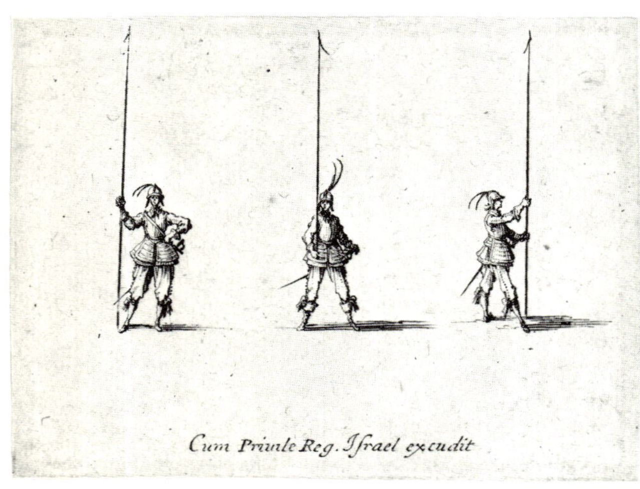

250 Drill with Raised Lances.

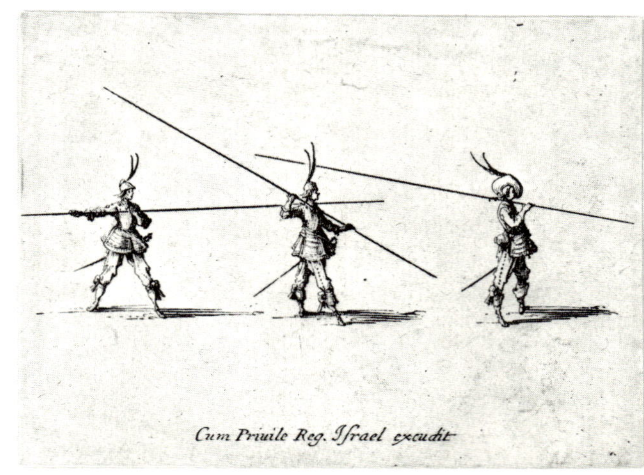

251 Drill with Tilted Lances.

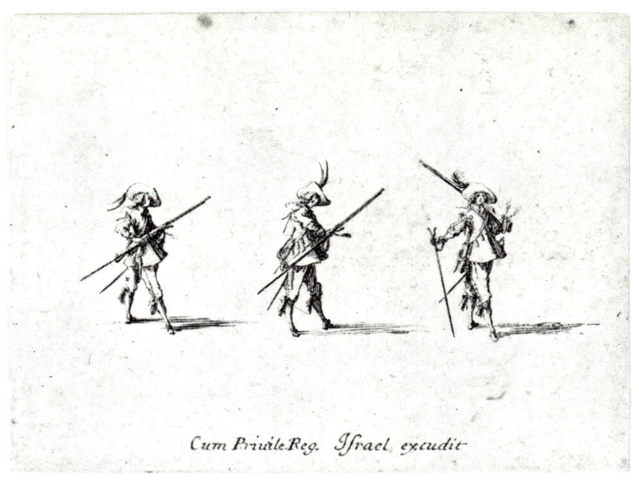

252 Drill with the Harquebus.

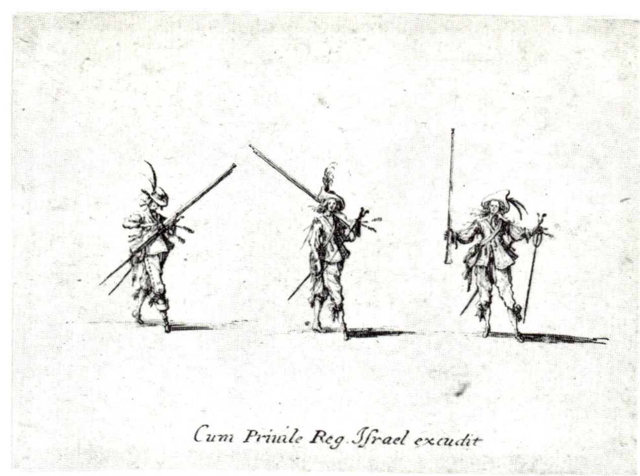

253 Drill with Shouldered Harquebus.

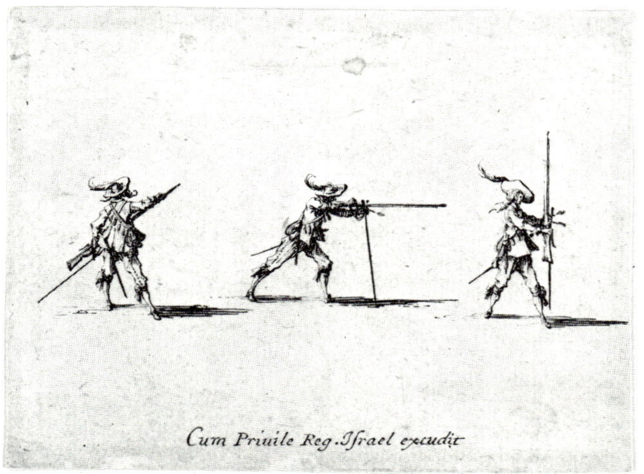

254 Preparing to Fire the Harquebus.

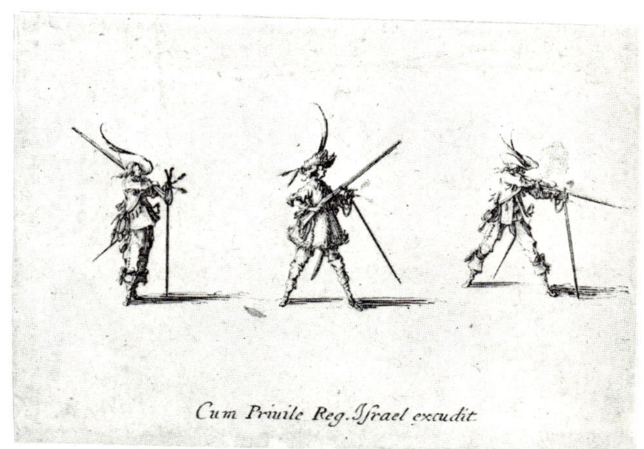

255 Harquebus Firing Drill.

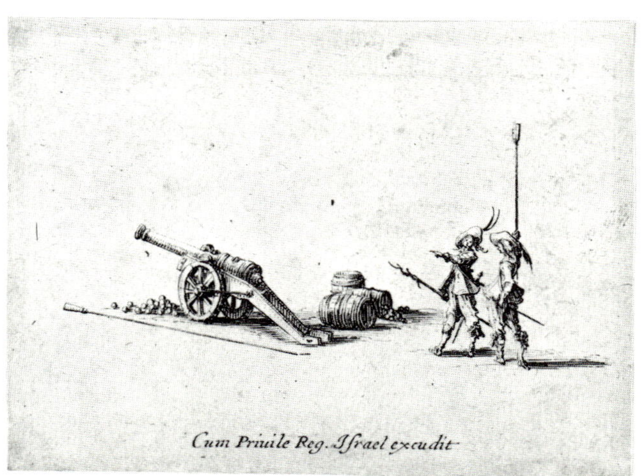

256 Preparing to Fire a Cannon.

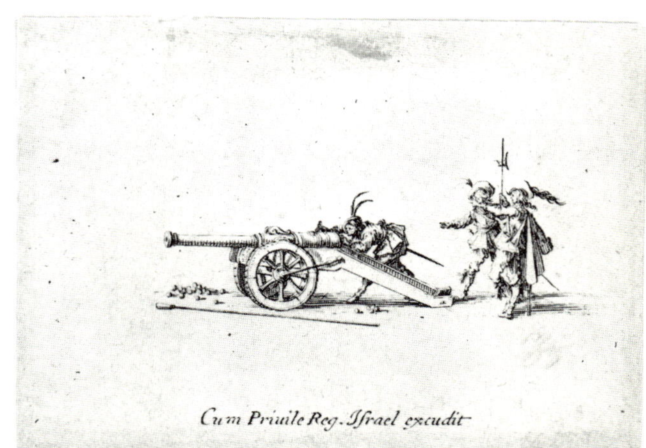

257 Loading the Cannon.

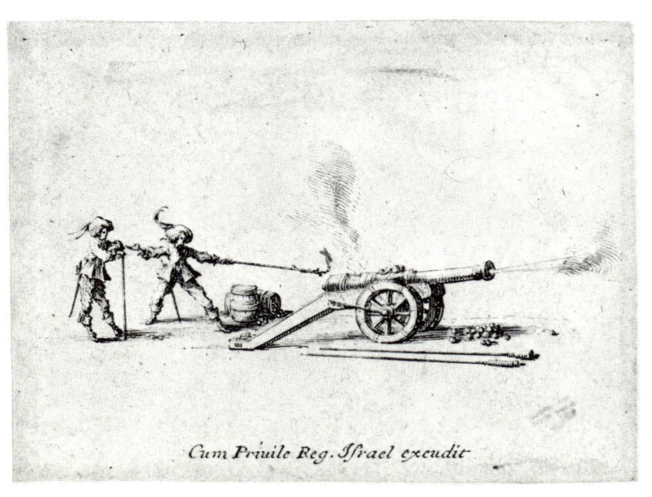

258 Firing the Cannon.

259–264 *The Miseries of War* (small format, *Misère de la Guerre*), a series of 6 etchings (not counting the title page by another artist), done ca. 1632, first published posthumously 1635.

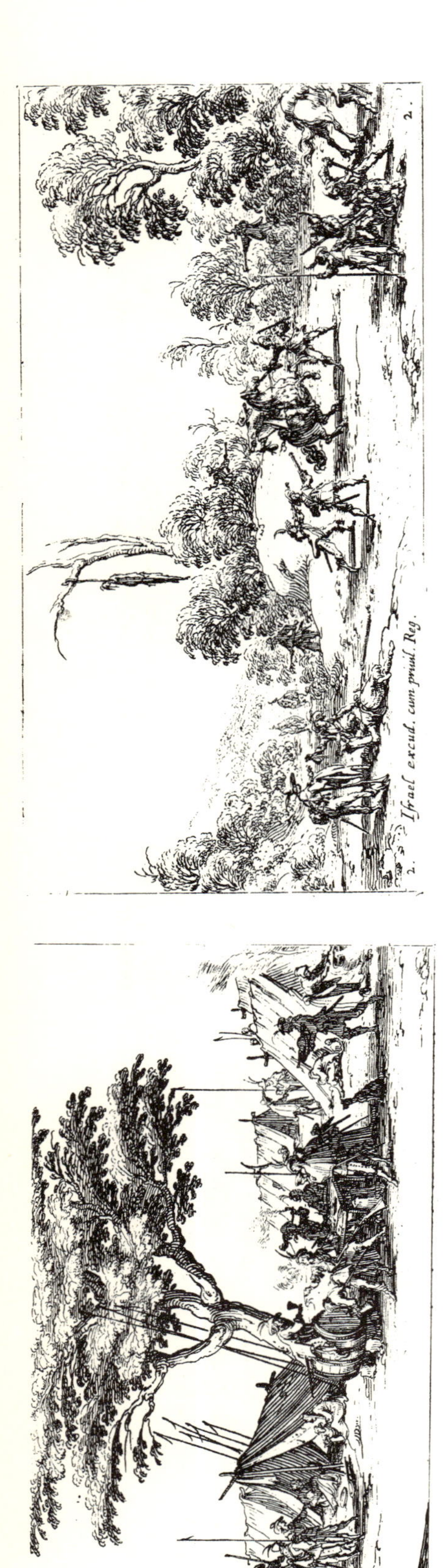

259 Camp Scene.

260 Attack on the Highway.

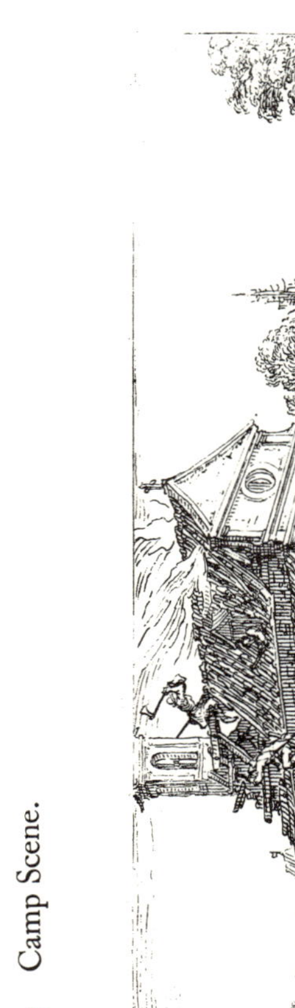

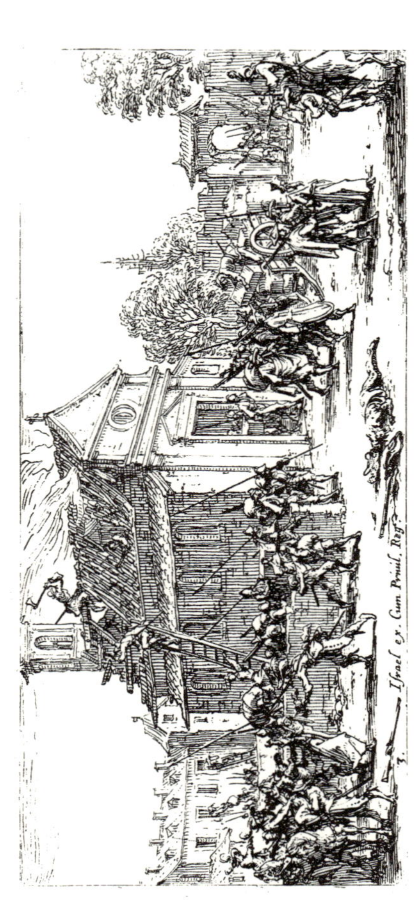

261 Destruction of a Convent.

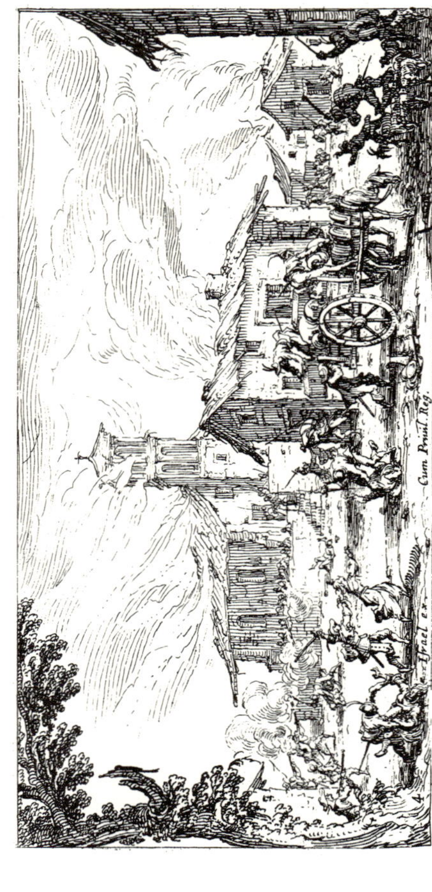

262 Plundering and Burning a Village.

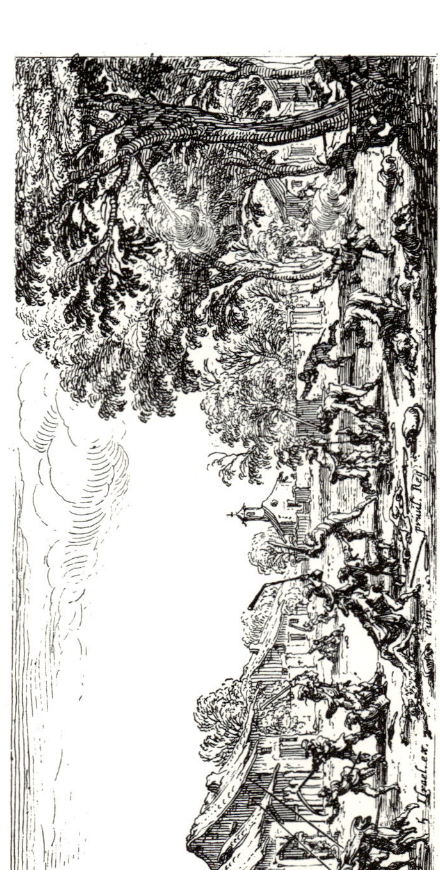

263 The Peasants Avenge Themselves.

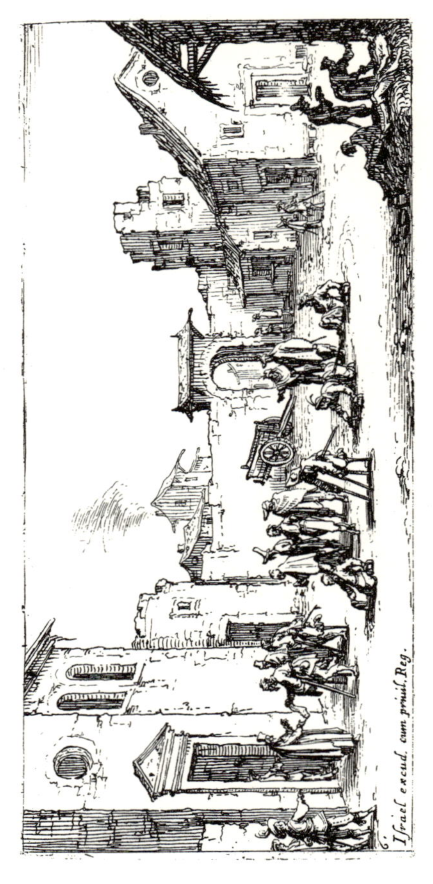

264 The Hospital.

265–282 The complete *Miseries of War* (large format, *Les Misères et les Malheurs de la Guerre*), a series of 18 etchings, 1633.

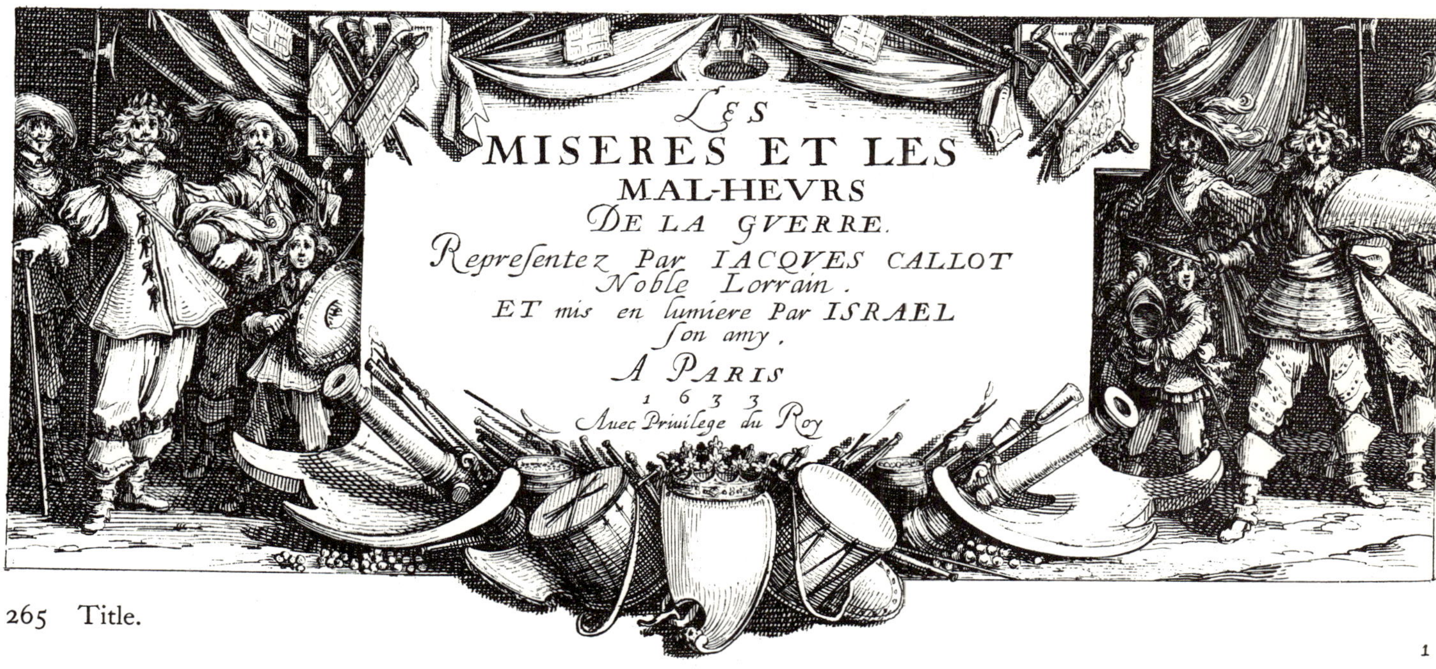

265 Title.

1

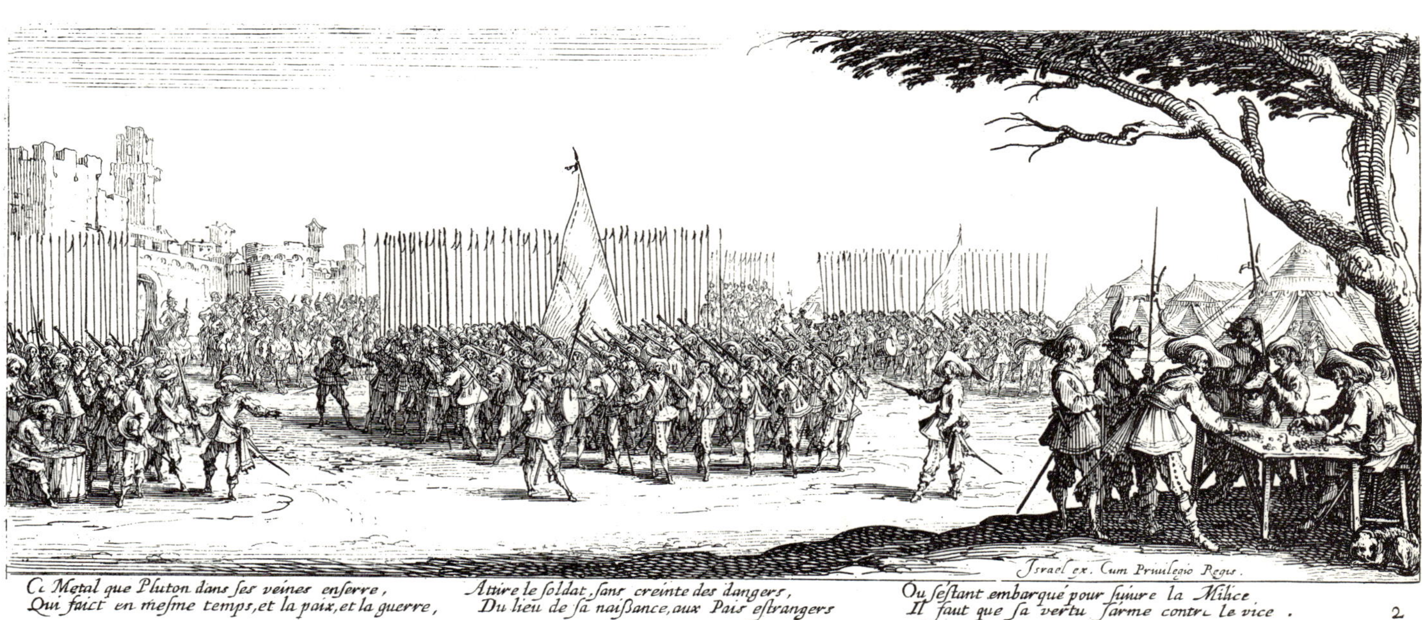

2

266 Recruitment of Troops. The poem reads: "That metal which Pluto encloses within his veins, which at the same time causes peace and war, draws the soldier, without fear of danger, from the place of his birth to foreign lands, where, having embarked to follow the military, he must arm himself with virtue to combat vice."

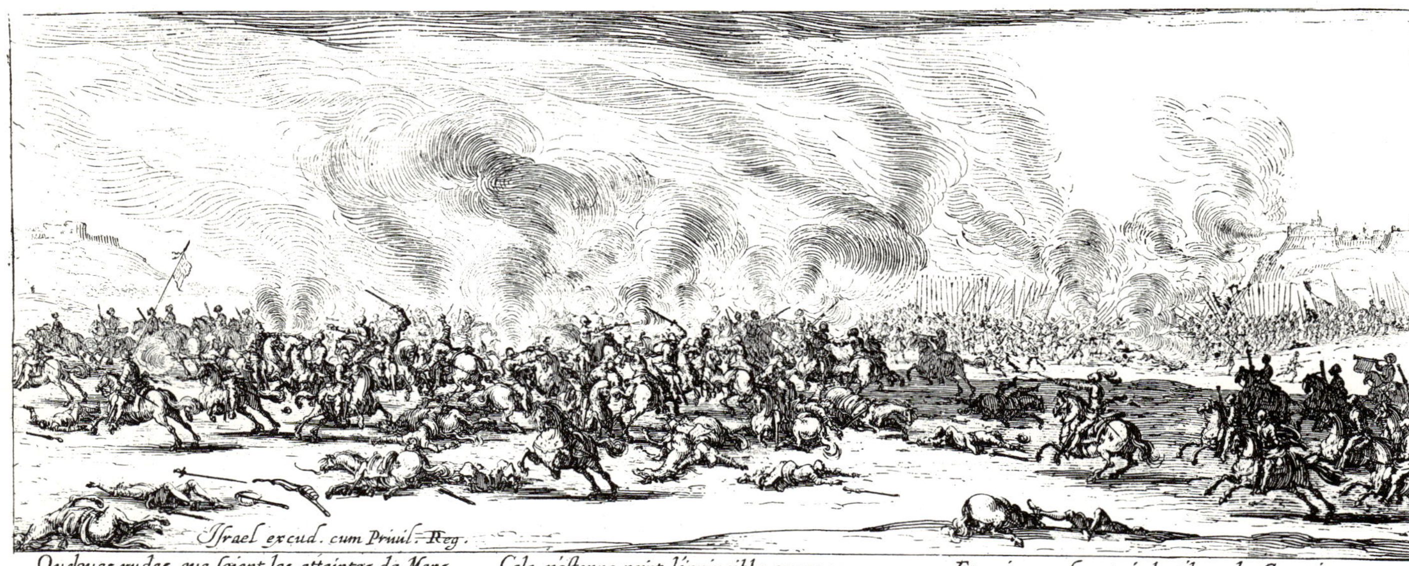

267 Battle Scene. The poem reads: "However rough may be the assaults of Mars and the blows that his arm strikes everywhere, that does not daunt the invincible courage of those whose valor can combat the storm, and who, in order to win the name of warrior, water their laurels with the blood of the enemy."

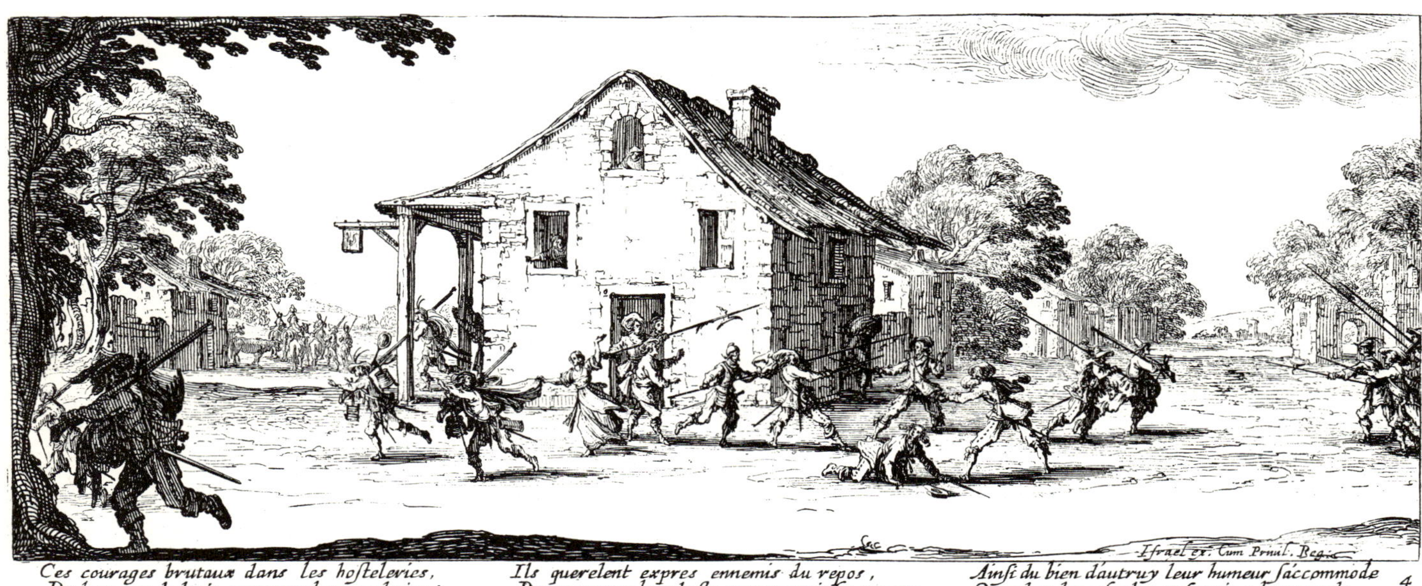

268 Scene of Pillage. The poem reads: "These brutal characters cloak their thefts at hostelries with the fair name of booty. Enemies of repose, they purposely pick quarrels to avoid paying the host, and seize even the mugs. Thus they take a fancy to other people's property when they have been made drunk and served as they desired."

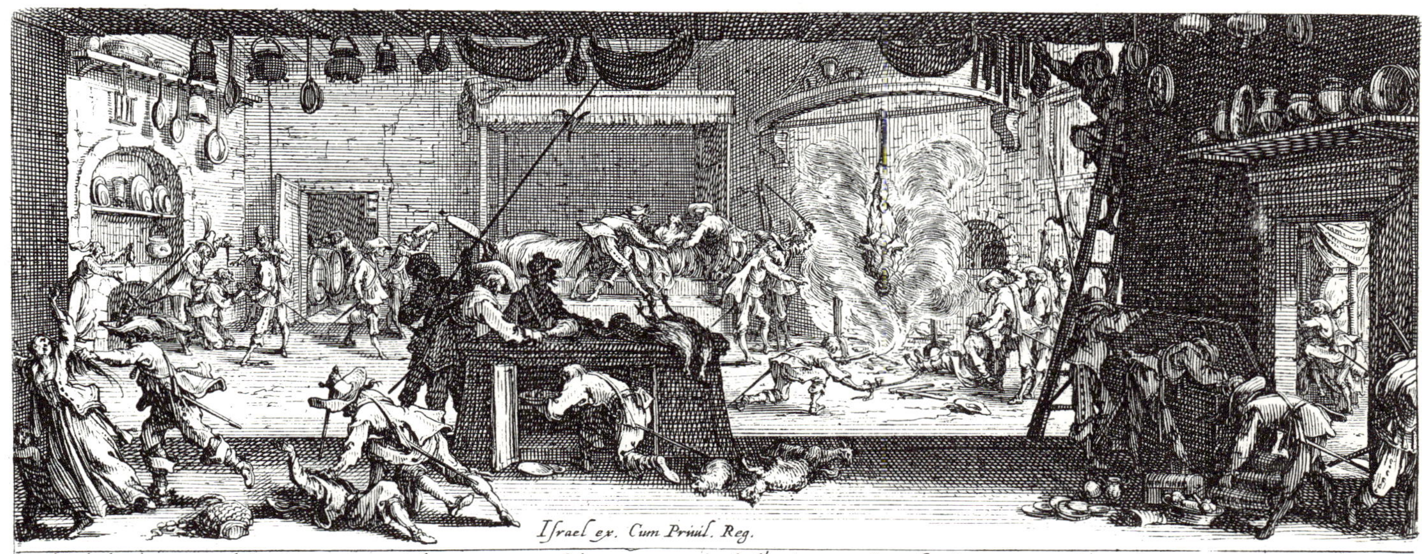

269 Plundering a Large Farmhouse. The poem reads: "Here are the fine exploits of these inhuman hearts. They ravage everywhere. Nothing escapes their hands. One invents tortures to gain gold, another instigates his accomplices to perform a thousand misdeeds, and all with one accord spitefully commit theft, kidnapping, murder and rape."

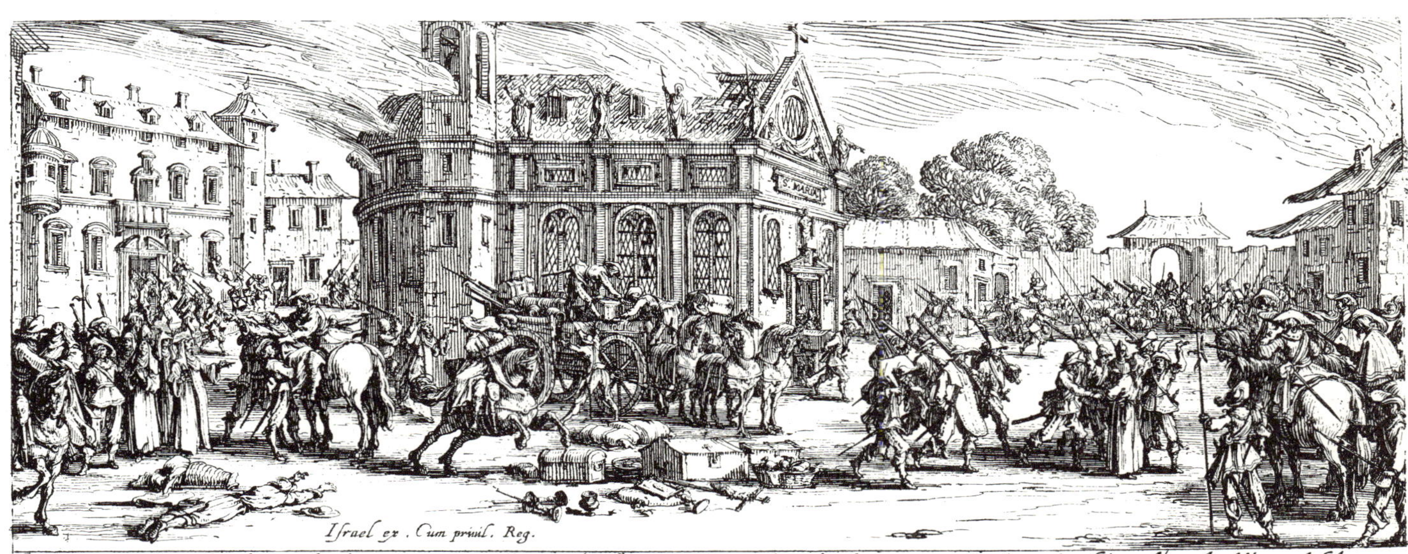

270 Destruction of a Convent. The poem reads: "Here, in a sacrilegious and barbarous action, these maddened, avaricious demons pillage and burn everything, ruin the altars, laugh at the respect due to the Immortals, and drag from the holy places the desolate virgins, whom they dare to carry off to be violated."

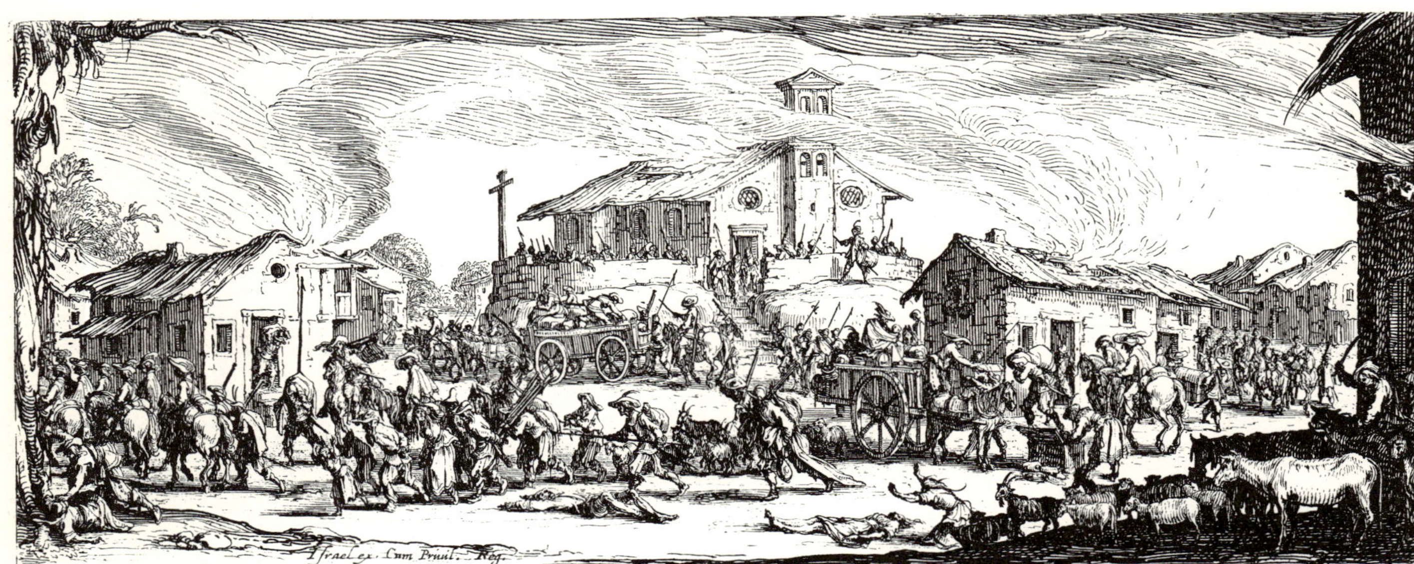

271 Plundering and Burning a Village. The poem reads: "Those whom Mars nourishes with his evil deeds, treat in this manner the poor country people. They take them prisoner, burn their villages and even wreak havoc on their livestock. Neither fear of the law, nor sense of duty, nor tears and cries can move them."

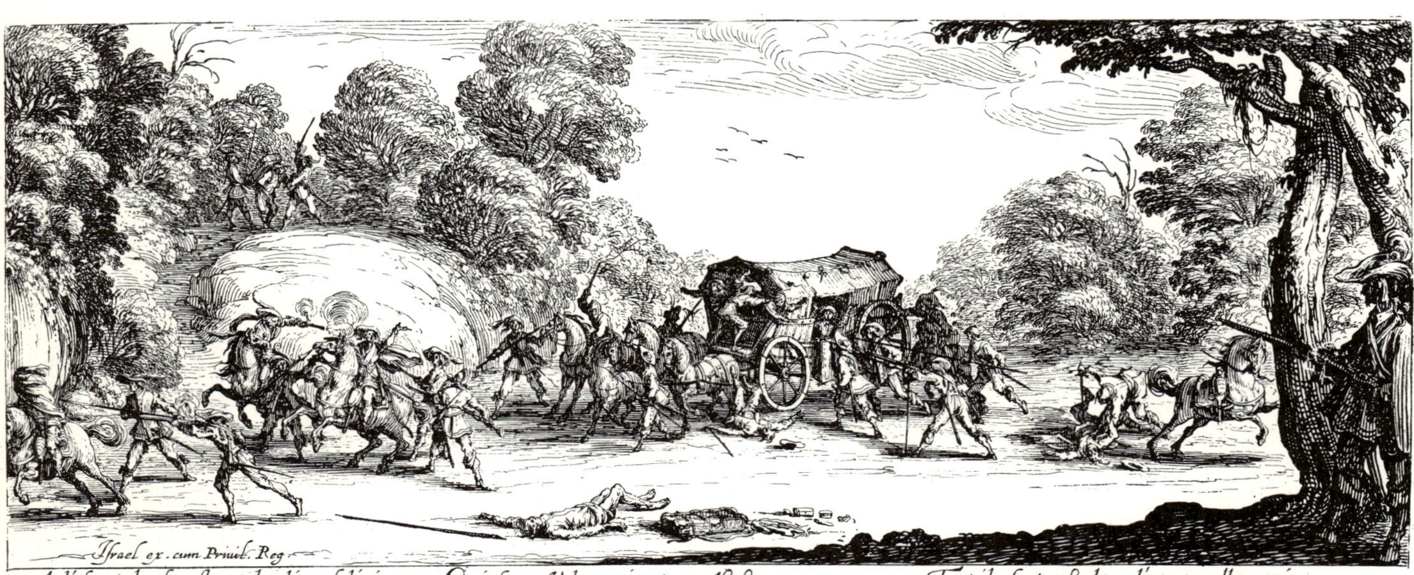

272 Attack on a Coach. The poem reads: "In the seclusion of forests and deserted places, quite far from military drill and discipline, these ignoble thieves lead the life of assassins, and their bloody arm deals only in robbery, so possessed are they with the cruel desire to take travelers' property and life."

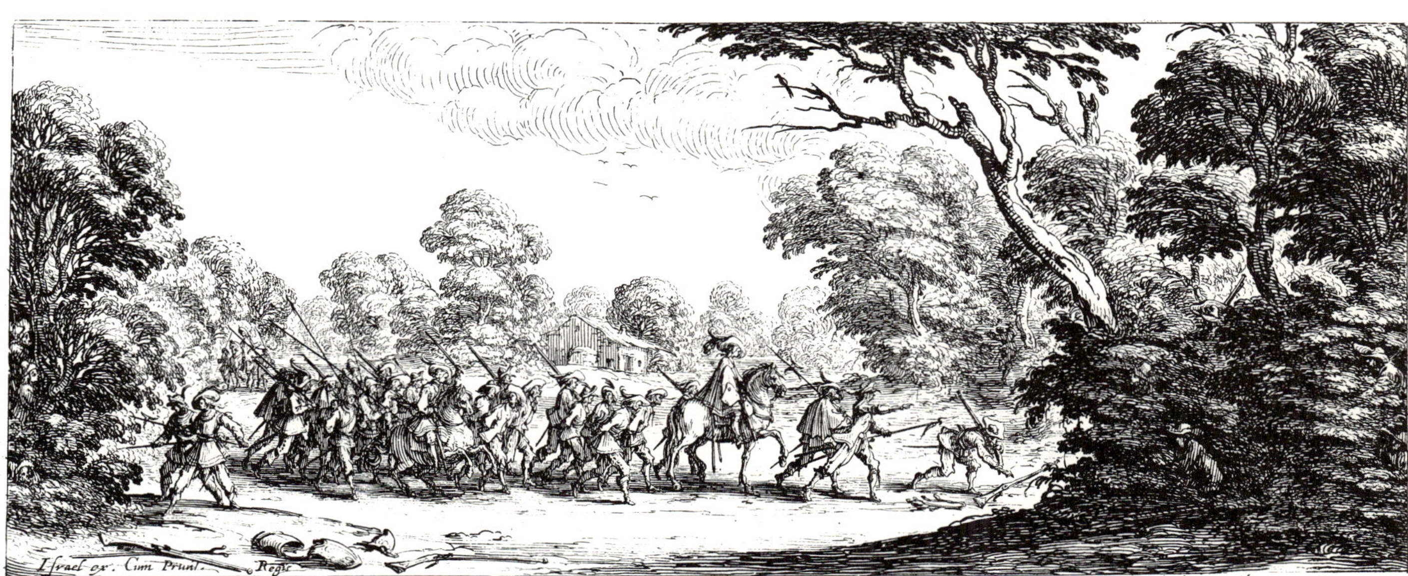

273 Discovery of the Criminals. The poem reads: "After the commission of several low crimes by these good-for-nothing enemies of glory they are sought everywhere with great diligence, and the camp provost marshal brings them back to quarters to receive, as they deserve, a punishment commensurate with their temerity."

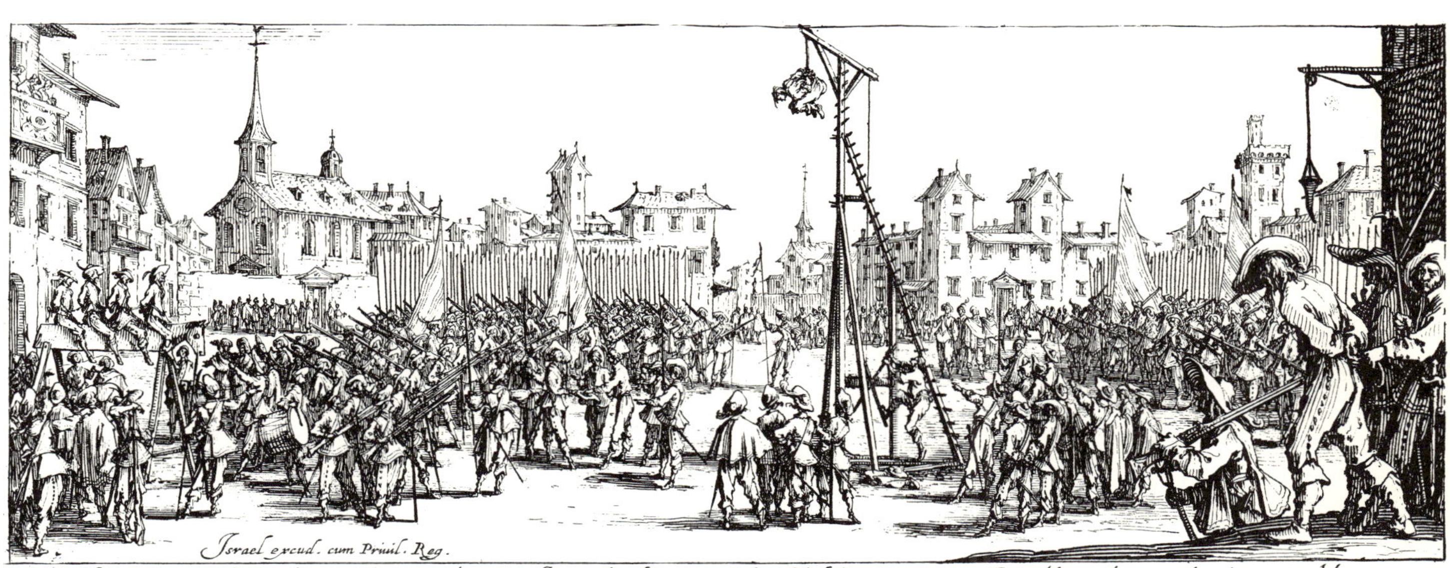

274 The Strappado. The poem reads: "It is not without cause that great captains have well-advisedly invented these punishments for idlers, blasphemers, traitors to duty, quarrelers and liars, whose actions, blinded by vice, make those of others slack and irregular."

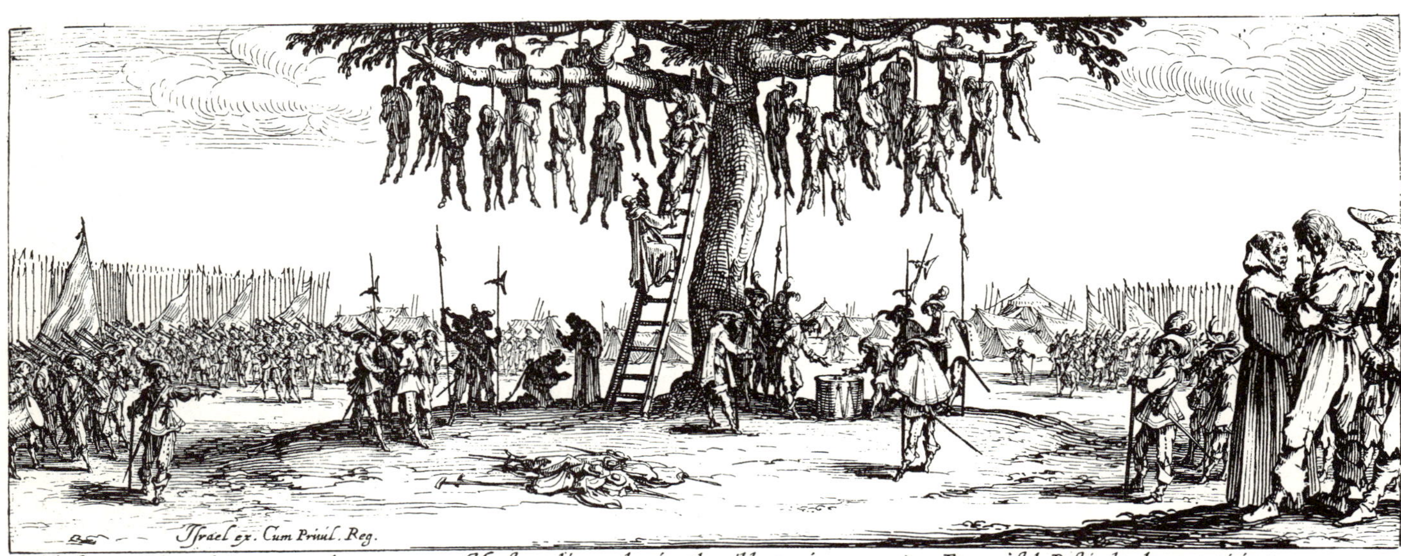

275 The Hanging. The poem reads: "Finally these ignoble and abandoned thieves, hanging from this tree like ominous fruit, show that crime (horrible and black spawn) is itself the instrument of shame and vengeance, and that it is the fate of vice-ridden men to experience the justice of Heaven sooner or later."

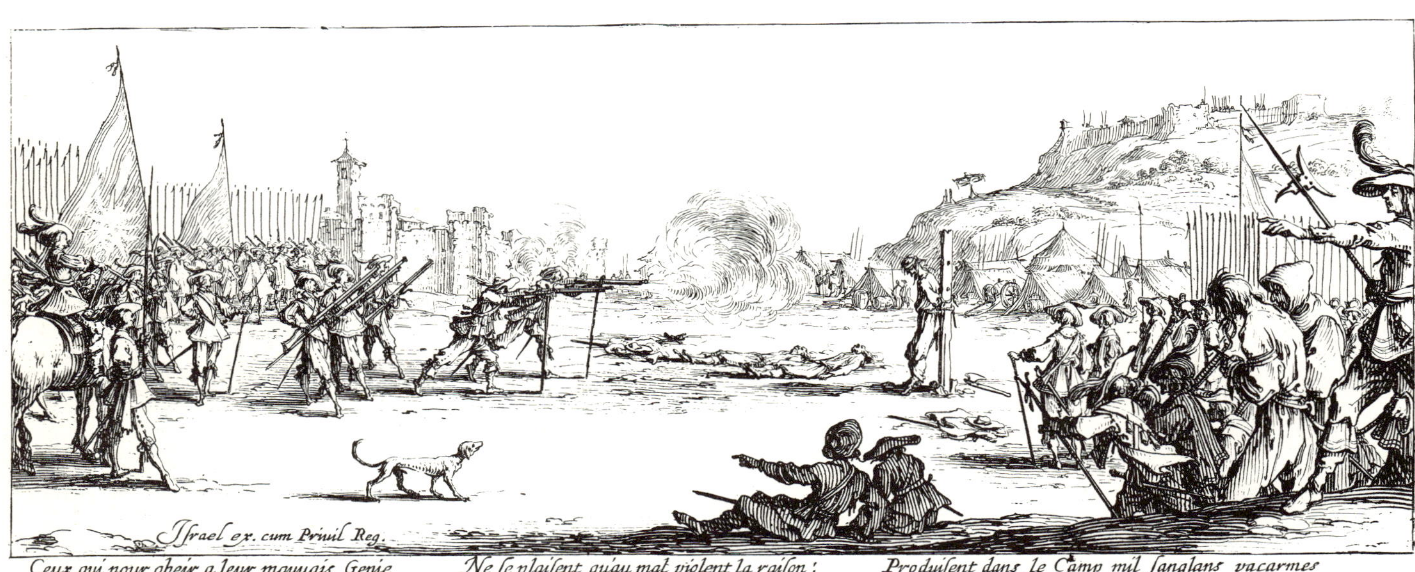

276 The Firing Squad. The poem reads: "Those who, in obedience to their evil genius, fail in their duty, use tyranny, desire only evil and violate reason, and whose treason-filled actions produce a thousand bloody uproars in the camp, are thus chastised and executed."

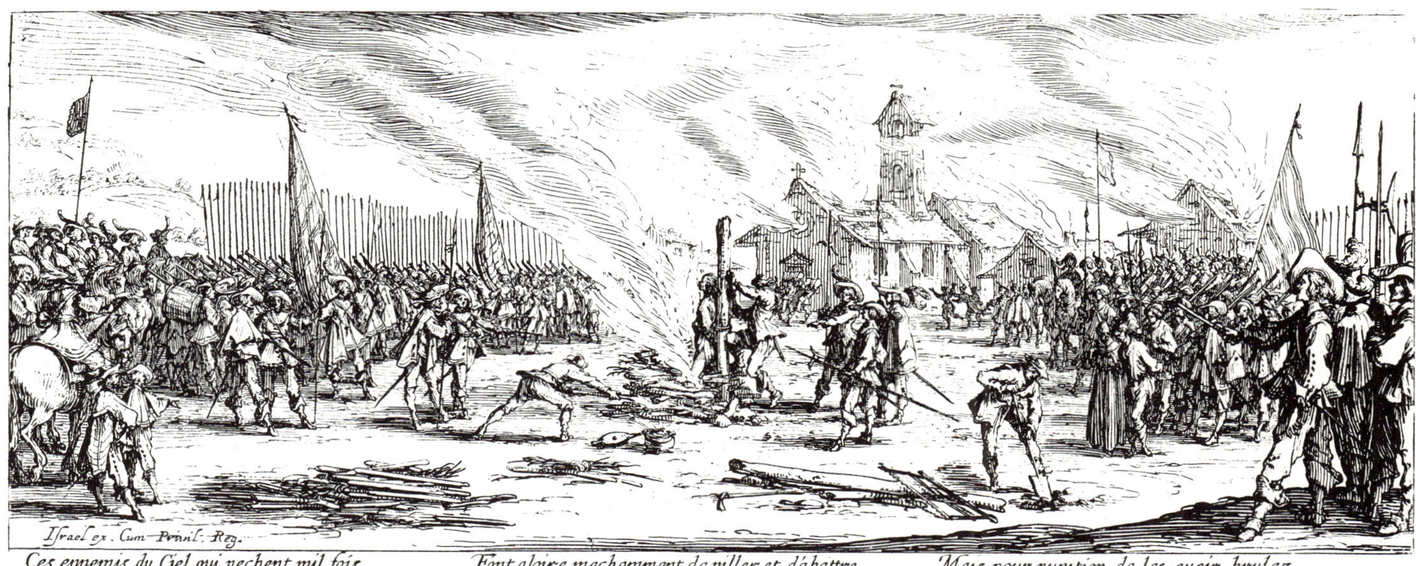

277 The Stake. The poem reads: "Those enemies of Heaven, who a thousand times sin against the holy decrees and divine laws, glory in spitefully pillaging and destroying the temples of the true God with idolatrous hand, but as punishment for burning them, are themselves finally sacrificed to the flames."

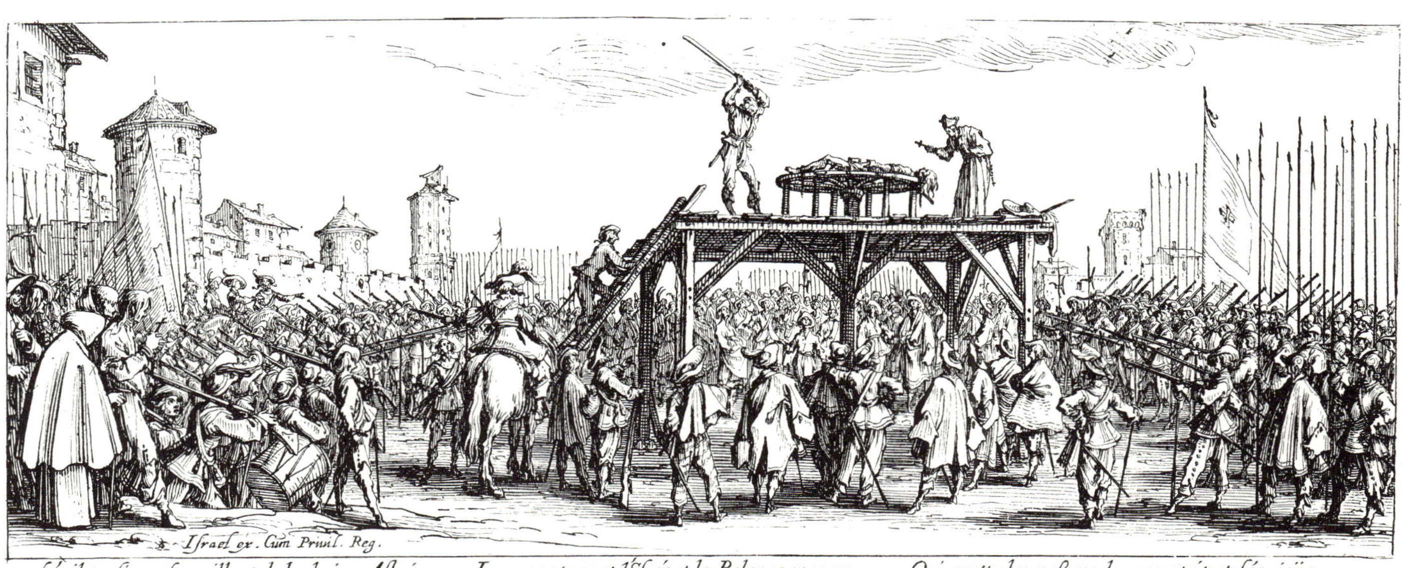

278 The Wheel. The poem reads: "The ever-watchful eye of divine Astraea [Justice] completely banishes mourning from a region when, holding the sword and scales in her hands, she judges and punishes the inhuman thief who awaits passersby in ambush, wounds them and toys with them, then becomes himself the plaything of a wheel."

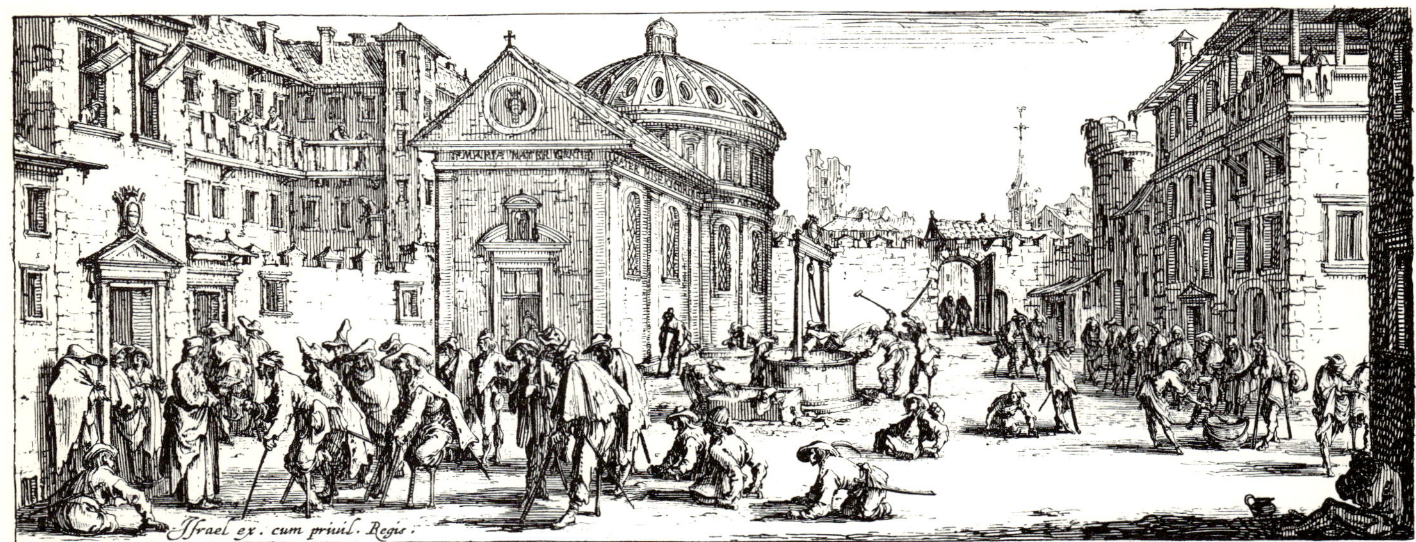

279 The Hospital. The poem reads: "See how the world goes, and how many misfortunes constantly pursue the children of the god Mars. Some, crippled, drag themselves along the ground. Others, more fortunate, receive promotion in war. Some die on a gallows by a fatal blow, and others go from the camp to the hospital."

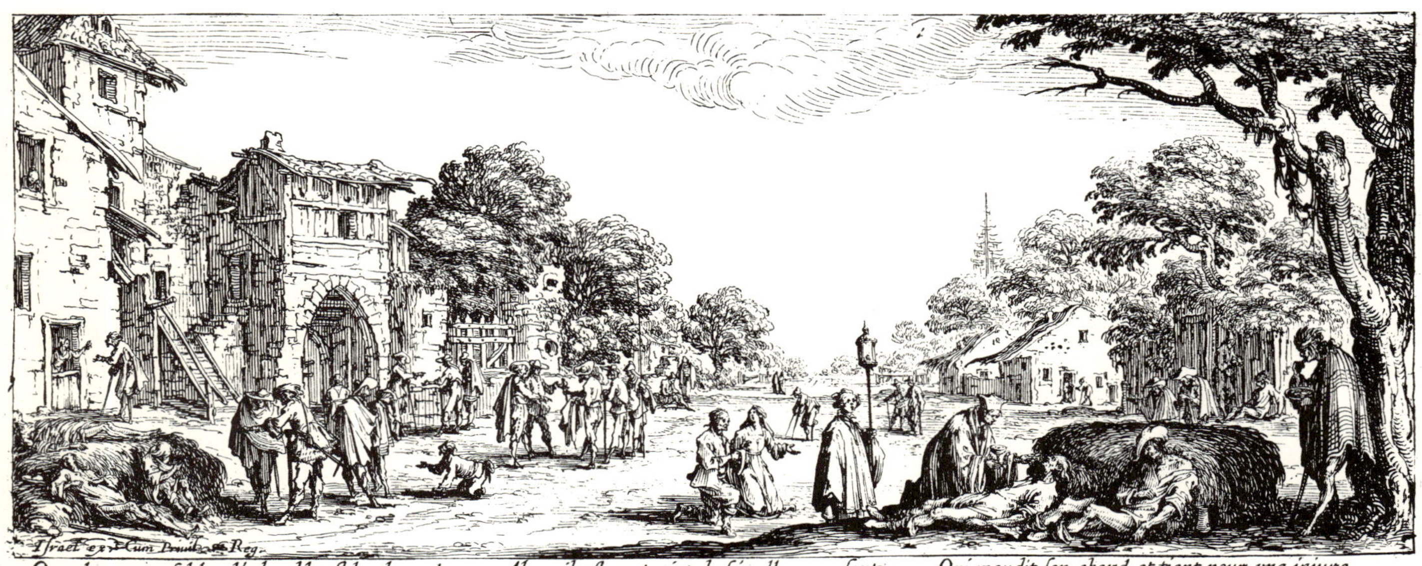

280 Dying Men by the Roadside. The poem reads: "How lamentable is the lot of the poor soldier! When the war is over, his misfortune starts again. Then he is compelled to go begging, and his poverty arouses the laughter of the peasant, who curses him when he asks for alms and considers it an insult to see before him the object of the sufferings he endures."

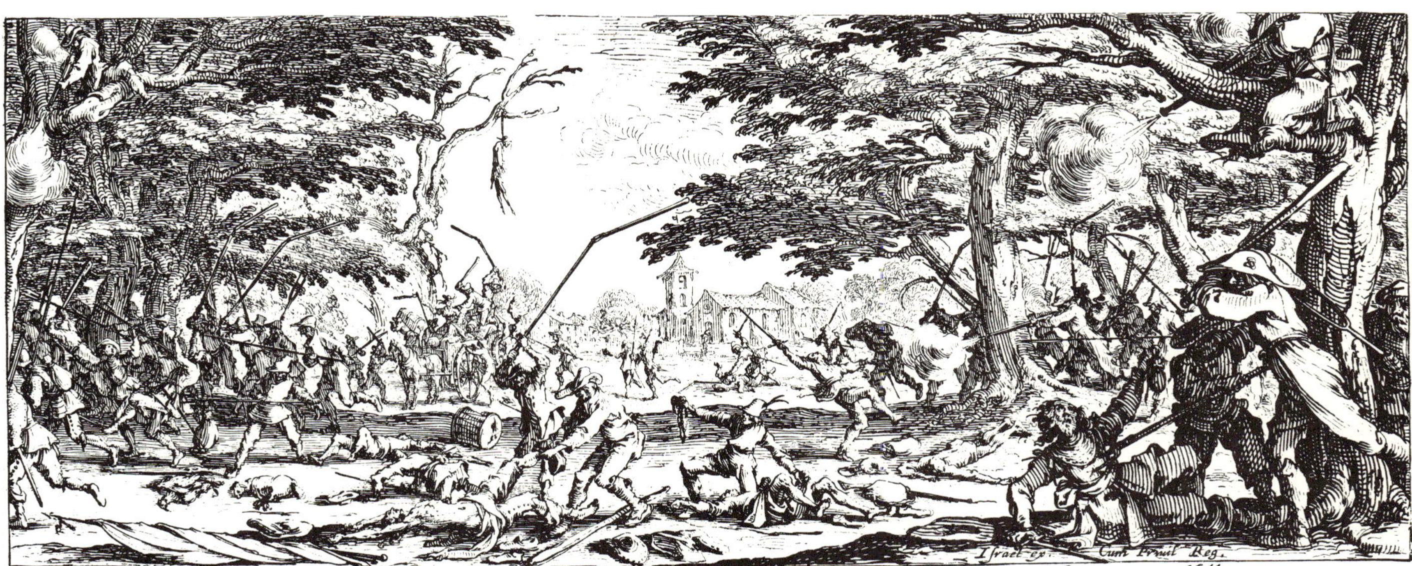

281 The Peasants Avenge Themselves. The poem reads: "After the soldiers have caused considerable destruction, finally the peasants, whom they have treated as enemies, await them in ambush in a secluded place, surprise them, kill them and strip them to their shirts, thus avenging themselves on these unfortunate men for the loss of their property, due solely to them."

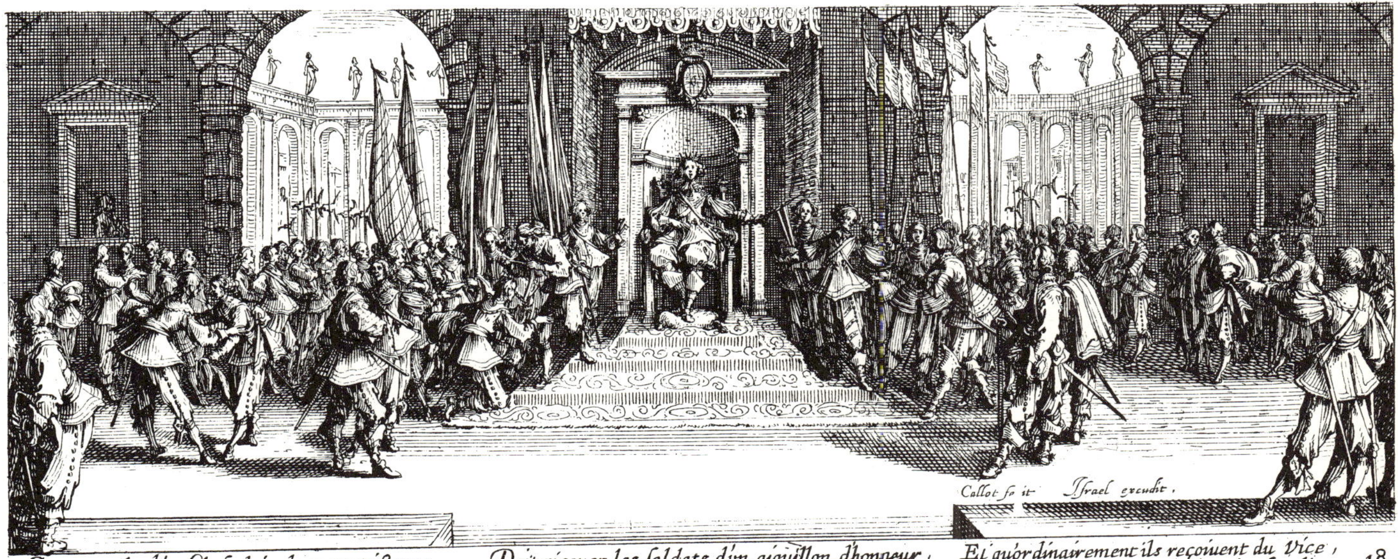

282 Distribution of Rewards. The poem reads: "This example of a grateful leader who punishes the evil and rewards the good, should prick soldiers with the goad of honor, since all their happiness depends on virtue and they ordinarily receive from vice shame, scorn and the most infamous punishment."

283 & 284 From *The Life of the Virgin*, a series of 16 etchings, ca. 1632/33.

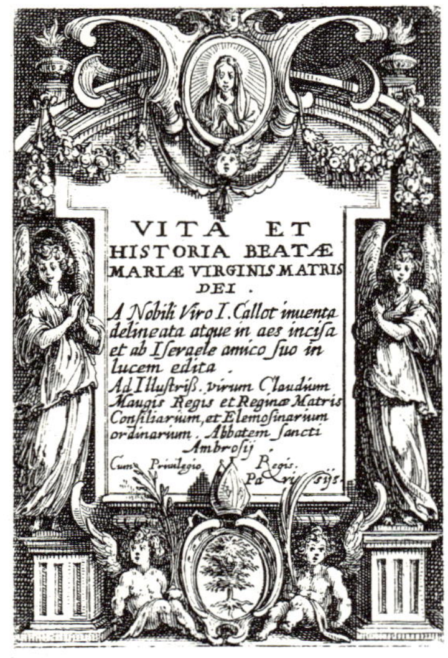

283 Title, with dedication to the royal almoner, Claude Maugis.

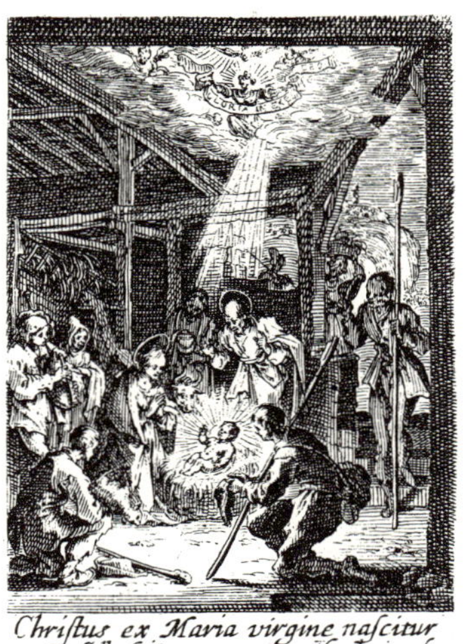

284 "Christ is born of the Virgin Mary."

285–298 The complete *Fantasies*, a series of 14 etchings, done ca. 1632, published 1635.

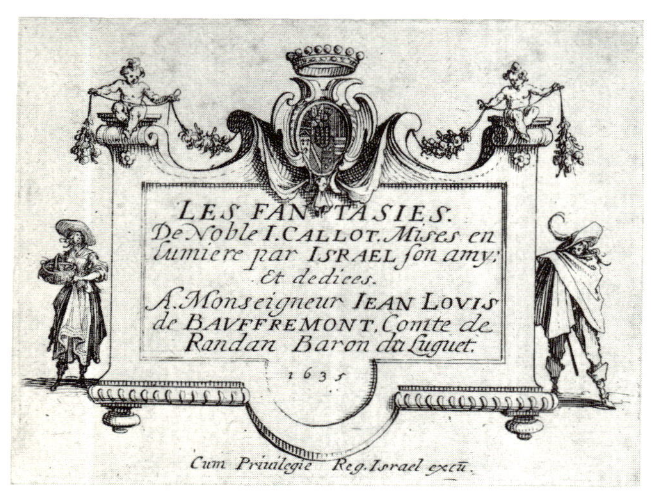

285 Title.

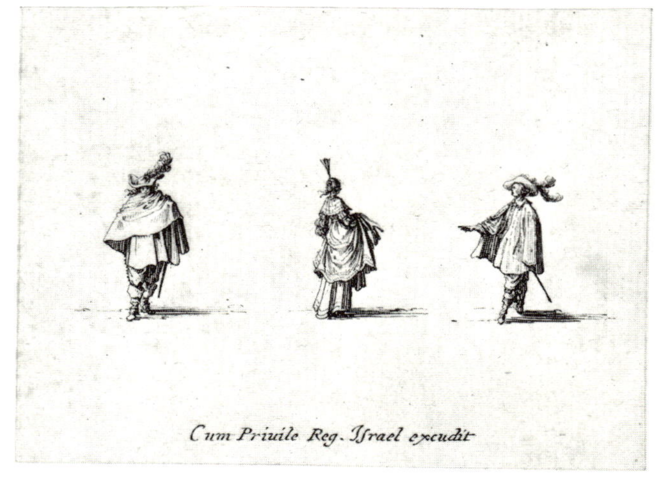

286 Lady with Dress Gathered Up, and Two Gentlemen.

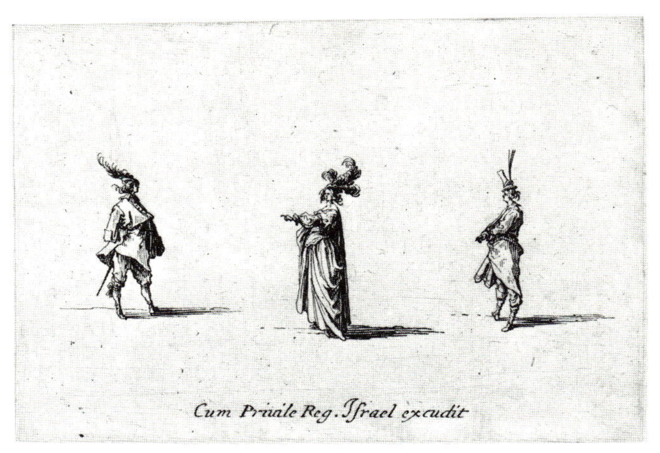

287 Lady with Plumed Hat, and Two Gentlemen.

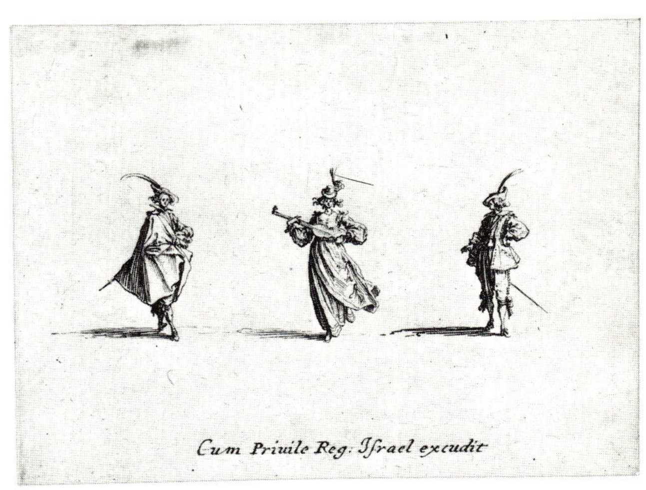

288 Lady with String Instrument, and Two Gentlemen.

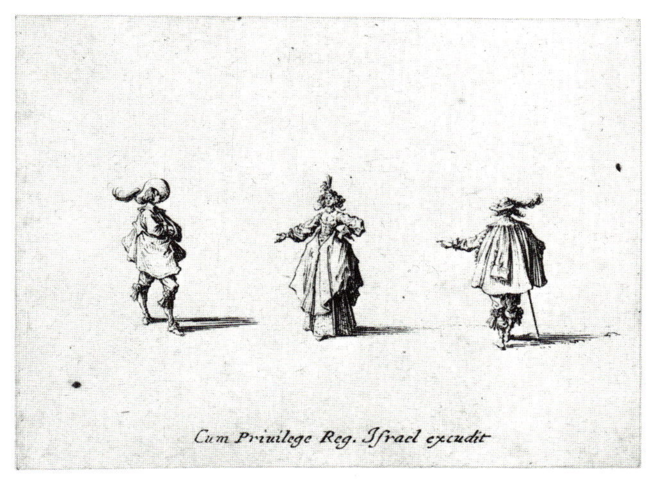

289 Lady with Outstretched Arm, and Two Gentlemen.

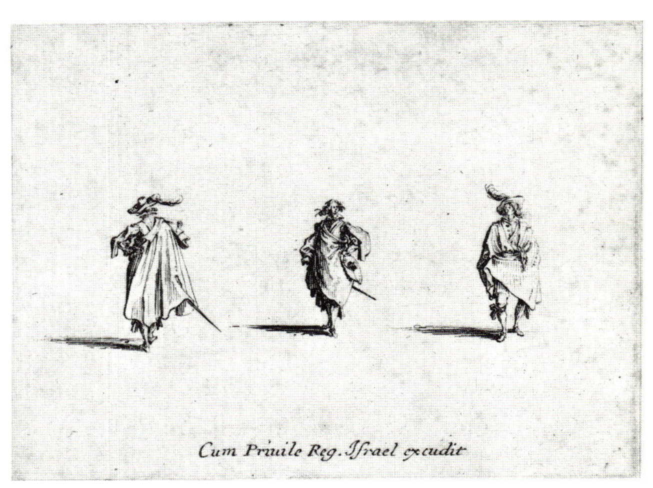

290 Three Gentlemen.

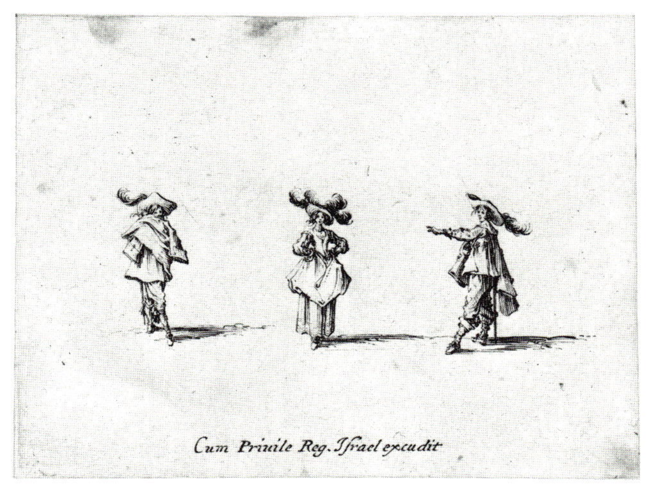

291 Lady with Large Plumes, and Two Gentlemen.

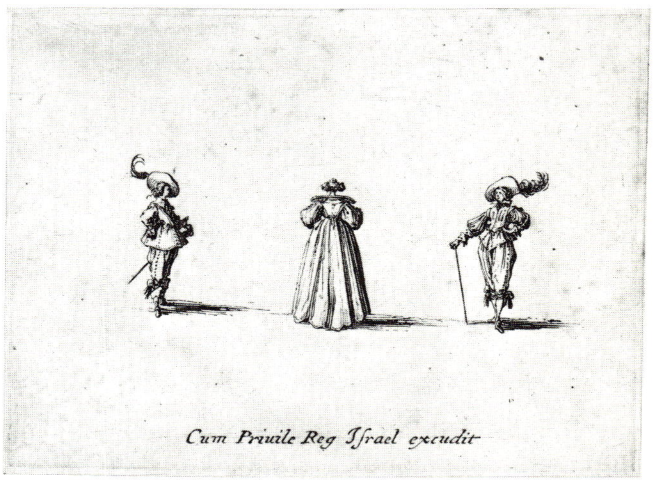

292 Lady Seen from Behind, and Two Gentlemen.

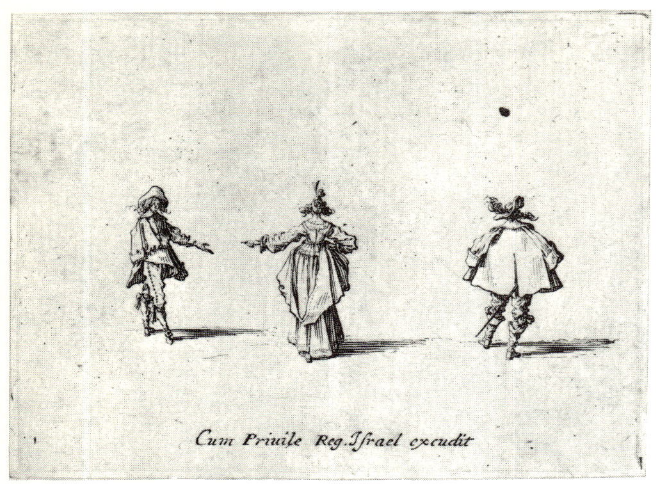

293 Lady with Outstretched Arm, Seen from Behind, and Two Gentlemen.

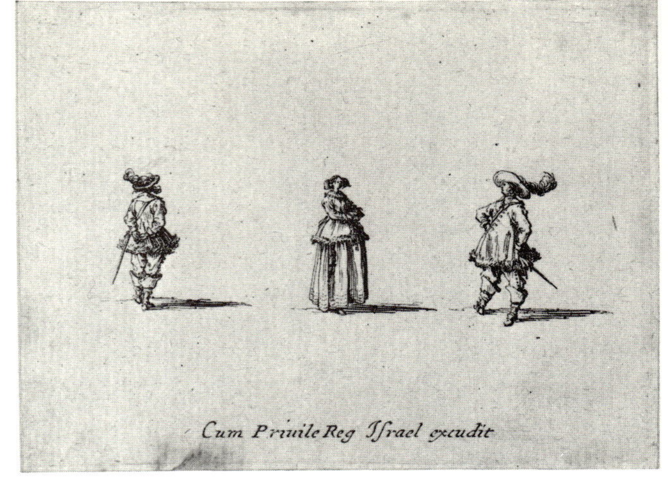

294 Lady with Arms Folded, and Two Gentlemen.

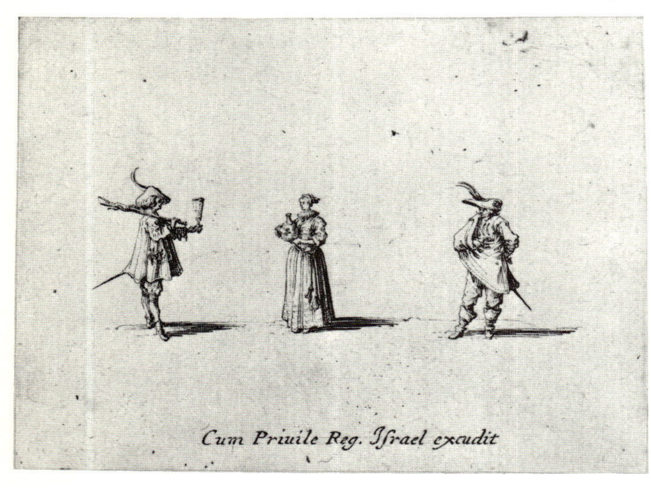

295 Lady with Wine Bottle, and Two Gentlemen.

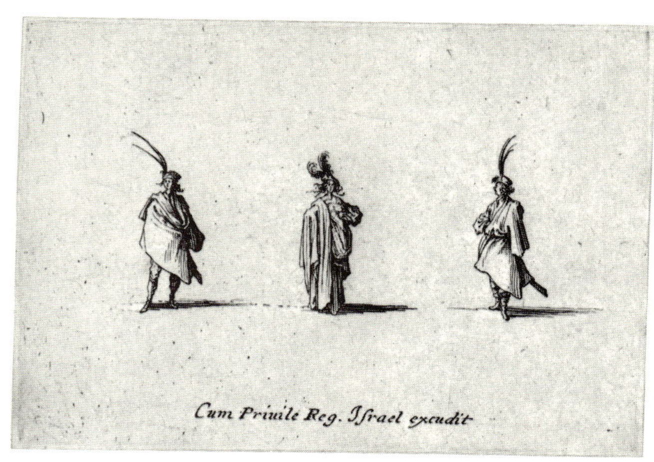

296 Lady in Long Cloak, and Two Gentlemen.

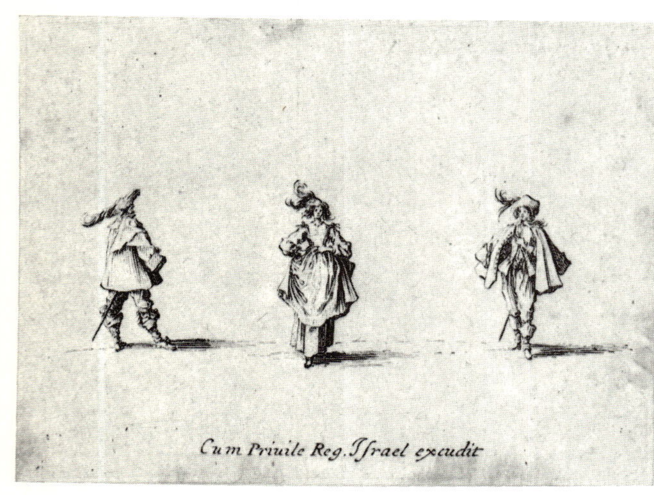

297 Lady with Plumes, and Two Gentlemen.

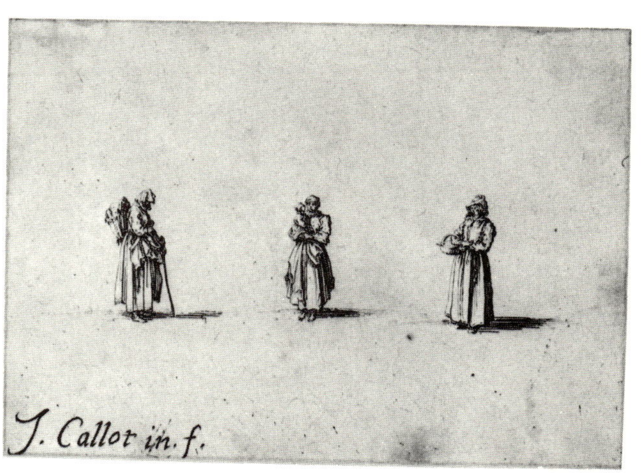

298 Three Women, One Holding a Child.

299–314 The complete *Small Apostles*, a series of 16 etchings, done in the 1630's, published 1635. (Courtesy Trustees of the British Museum)

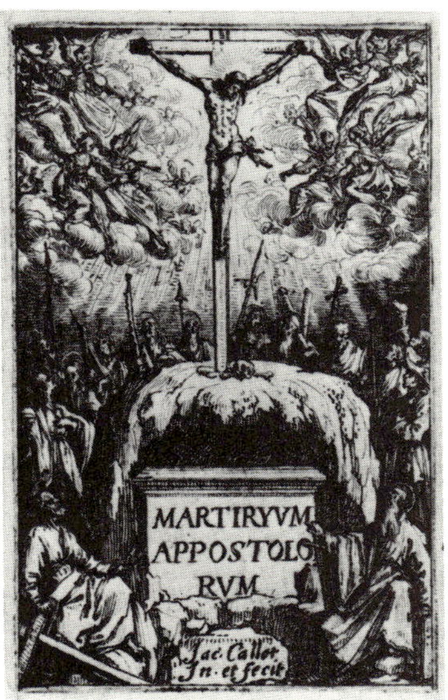

299 Title, "The Martyrdom of the Apostles."

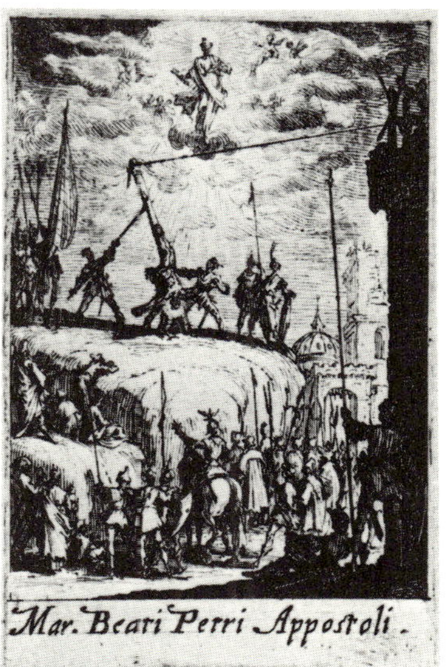

300 The Martyrdom of St. Peter.

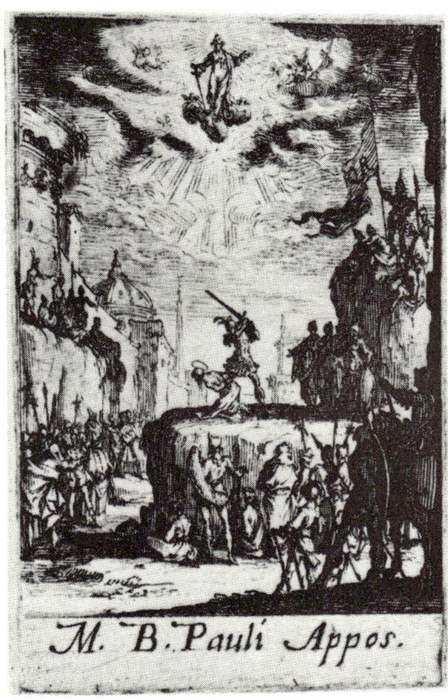

301 The Martyrdom of St. Paul.

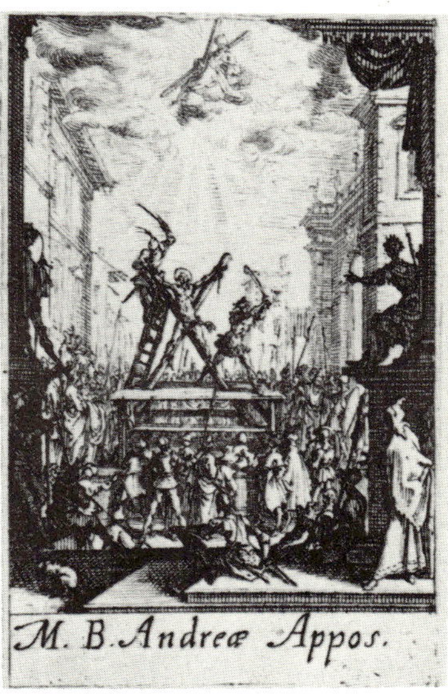

302 The Martyrdom of St. Andrew.

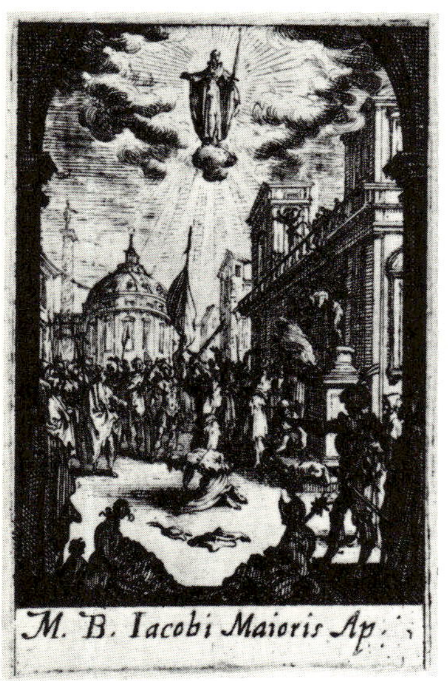

303 The Martyrdom of St. James the Great.

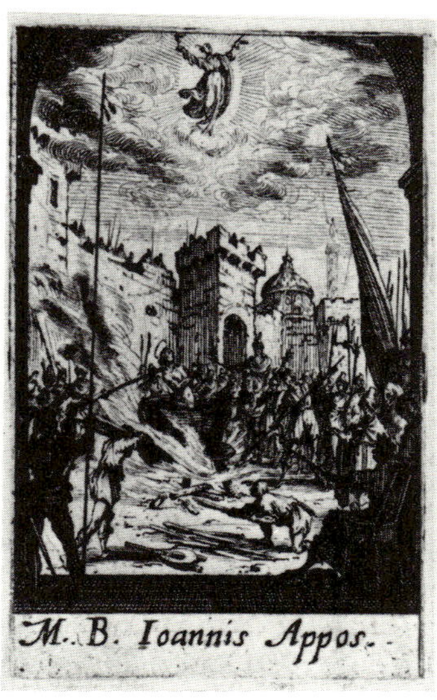

304 The Martyrdom of St. John.

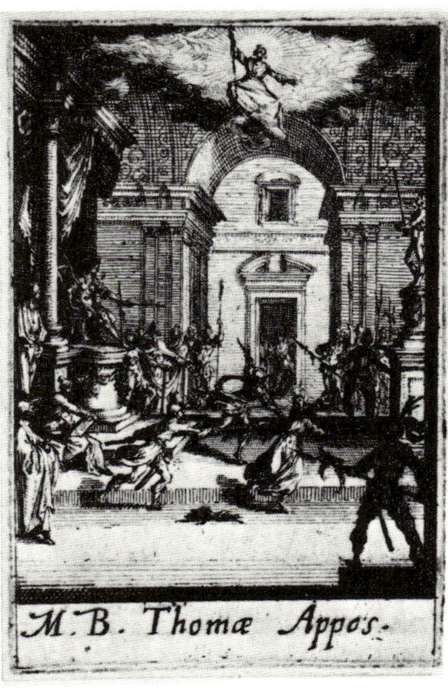

305 The Martyrdom of St. Thomas.

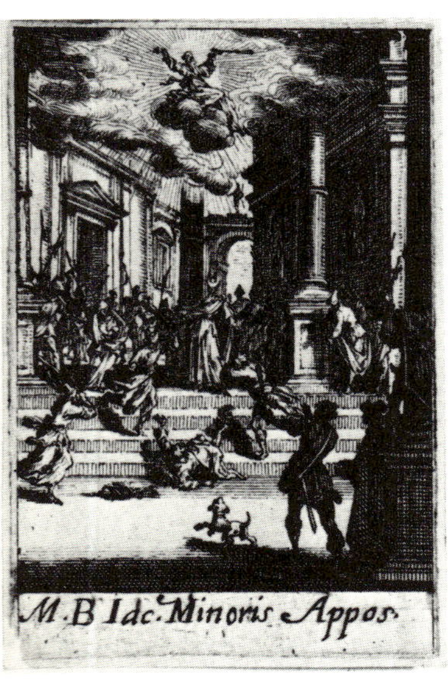

306 The Martyrdom of St. James the Less.

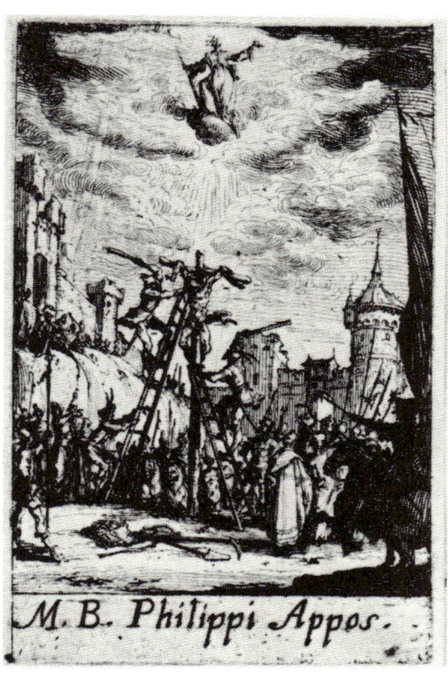

307 The Martyrdom of St. Philip.

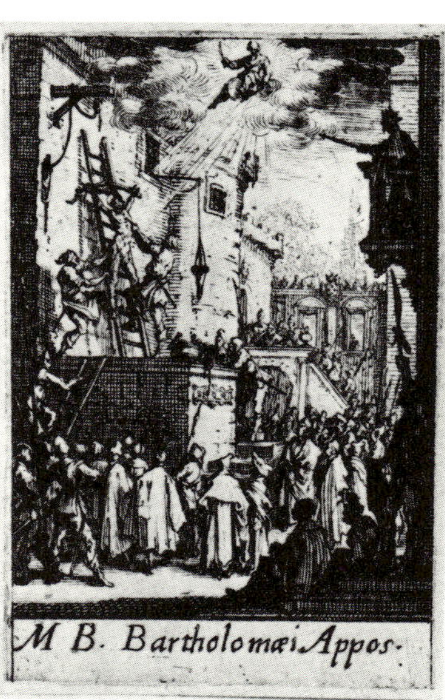

308 The Martyrdom of St. Bartholomew.

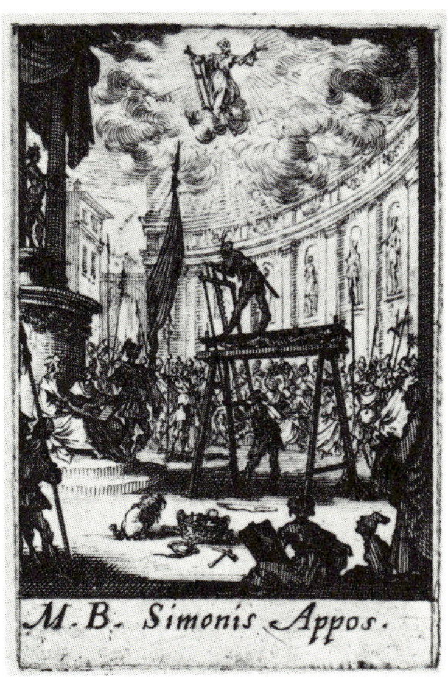

309 The Martyrdom of St. Simon.

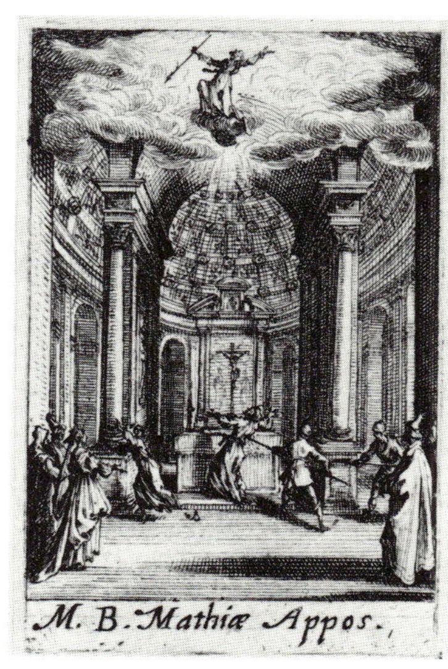

310 The Martyrdom of St. Matthias.

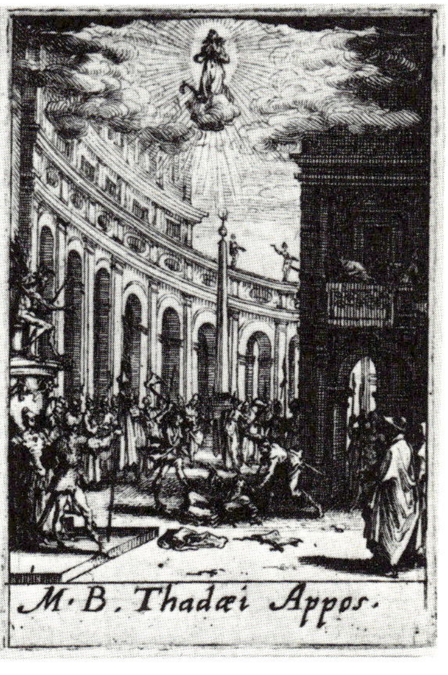

311 The Martyrdom of St. Thaddaeus.

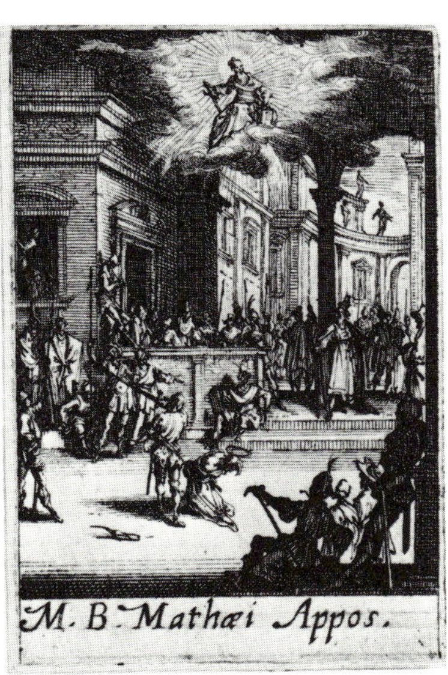

312 The Martyrdom of St. Matthew.

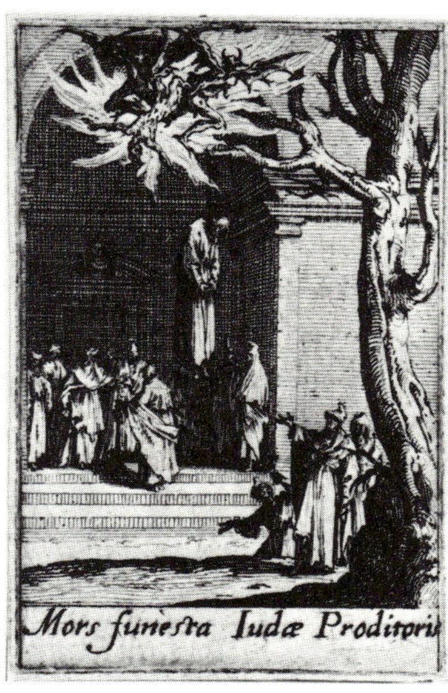

313 The Death of Judas.

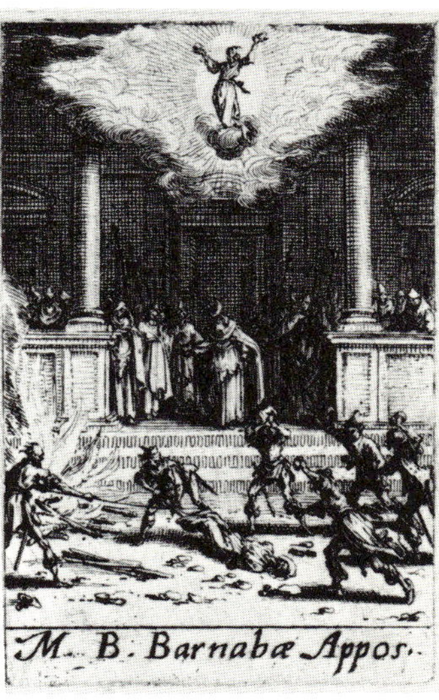

314 The Martyrdom of St. Barnabas.

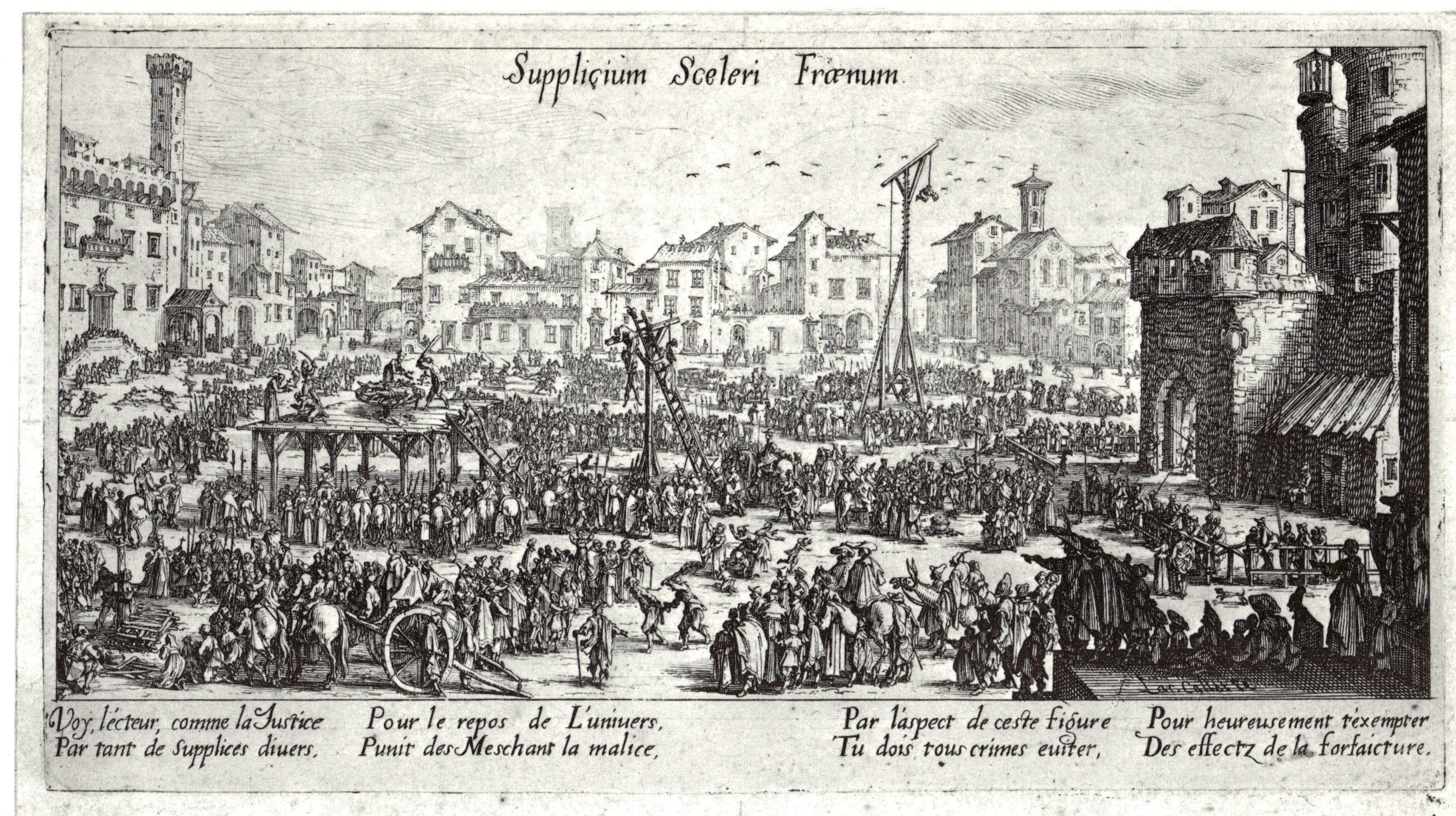

315 The Modes of Legal Punishment (Les Supplices, sometimes called The Tortures). Etching, ca. 1634. The Latin phrase at the top means: "Punishment, a curb upon crime." The French poem reads: "See, reader, how justice chastises the evil of criminals by so many varied punishments, for the repose of the universe. Looking upon this picture, you should avoid all crimes in order happily to escape the effects of wrongdoing."

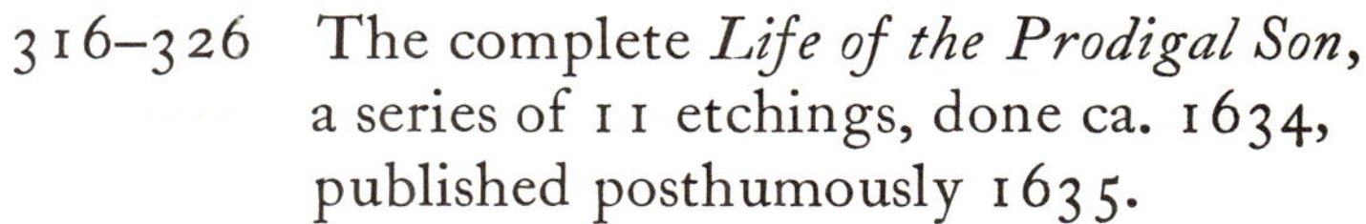
316–326 The complete *Life of the Prodigal Son*, a series of 11 etchings, done ca. 1634, published posthumously 1635.

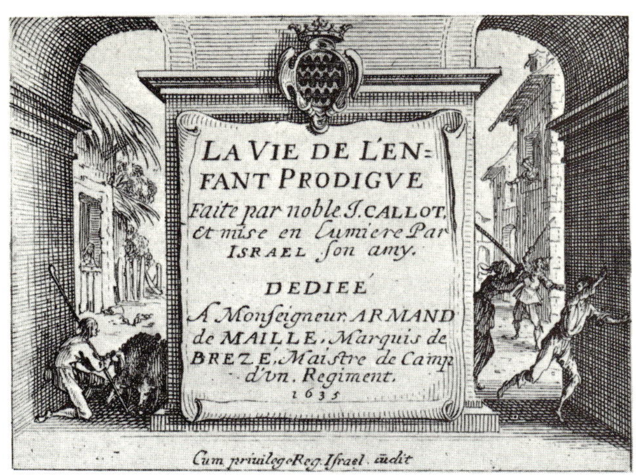

316 Title.

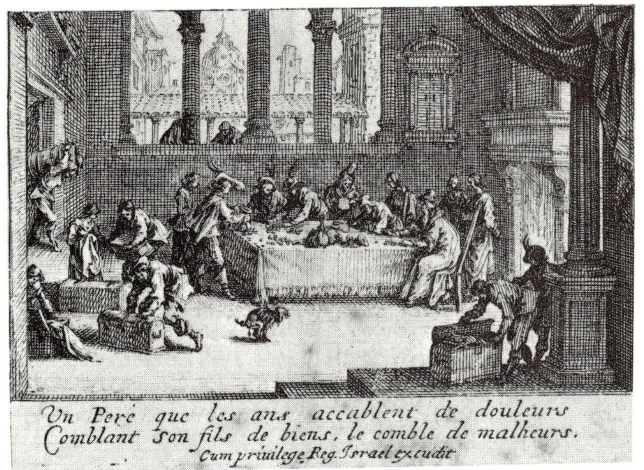

317 The Division of the Property. The poem reads: "A father whose great age overwhelms him with pains, loads his son with benefits, thus loading him with misfortunes."

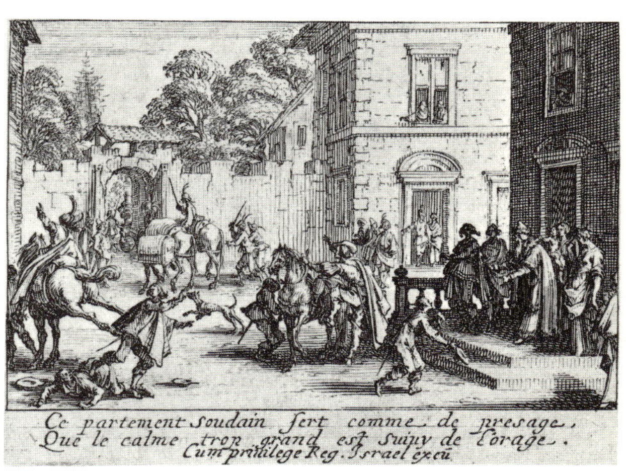

318 The Prodigal Son Leaves Home. The poem reads: "This sudden parting is like a presage that too great a calm is followed by a storm."

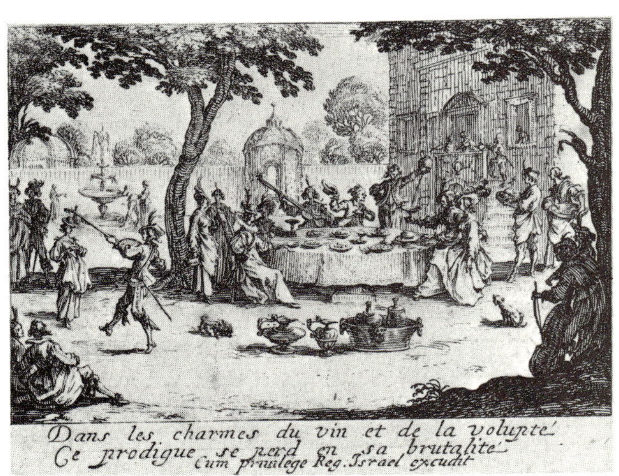

319 The Prodigal Son Squanders His Fortune. The poem reads: "In the charms of wine and pleasure this prodigal ruins himself in his bestiality."

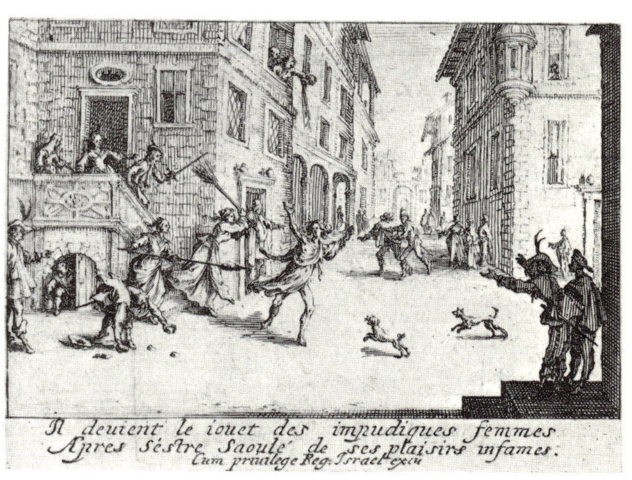

320 The Prodigal Son Reduced to Poverty. The poem reads: "He becomes the plaything of the shameless women after glutting himself with his vile pleasures."

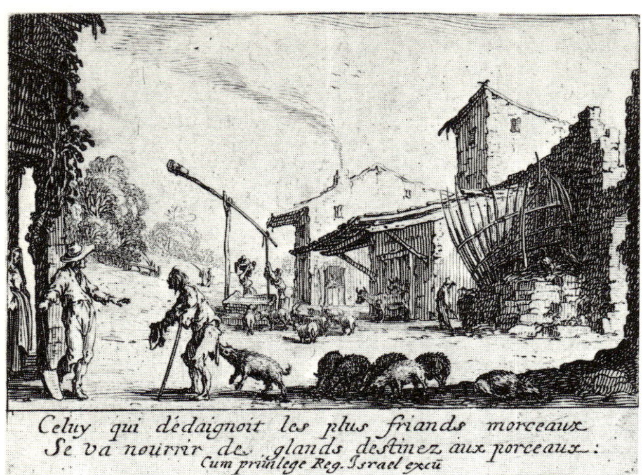

321 The Prodigal Son Becomes a Swineherd. The poem reads: "The man who spurned the tastiest morsels is going to feed on acorns meant for the pigs."

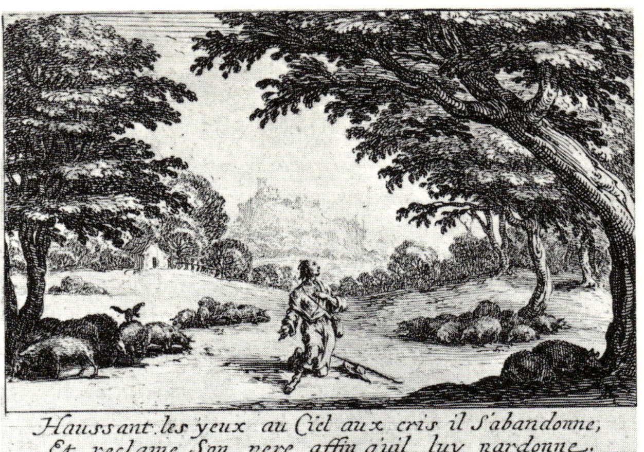

322 The Prodigal Son Repents. The poem reads: "Lifting his eyes to Heaven, he gives vent to cries and calls upon his father for forgiveness."

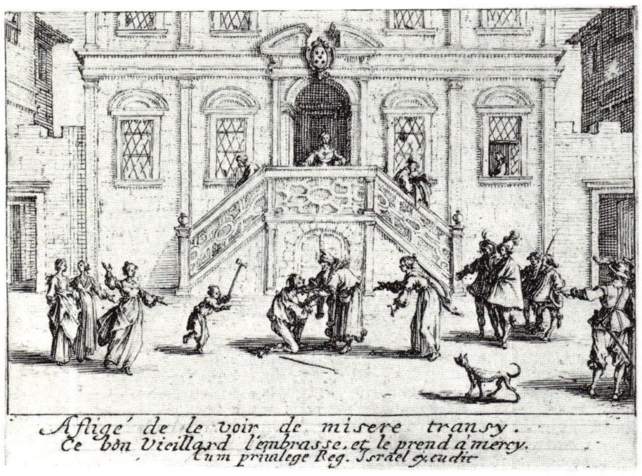

323 The Prodigal Son Returns Home. The poem reads: "Saddened to see him afflicted with poverty, this good old man embraces him and takes pity on him."

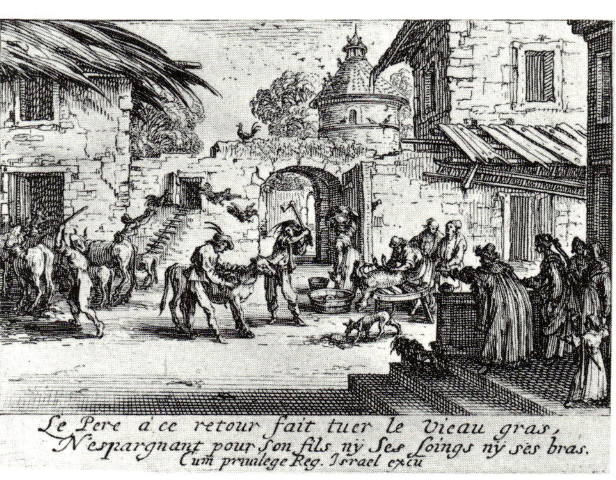

324 Killing the Fatted Calf. The poem reads: "Upon this homecoming the father has the fatted calf killed, sparing neither trouble nor effort for his son."

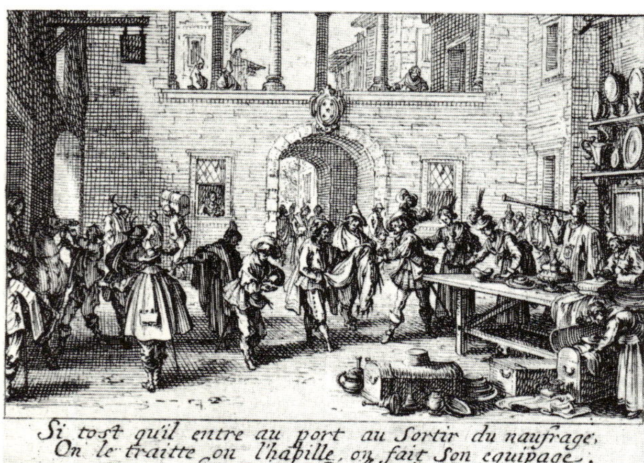

325 The Prodigal Son Newly Outfitted. The poem reads: "As soon as he enters port after his shipwreck, he is fed, clothed and fitted out afresh."

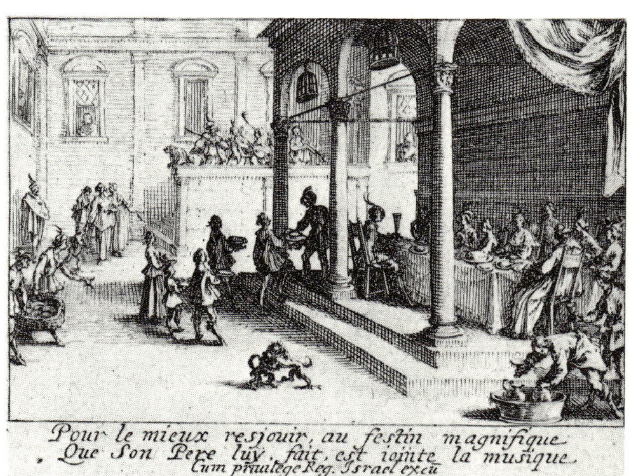

326 The Feast. The poem reads: "To give him more delight, music is played at the magnificent feast his father gives in his honor."

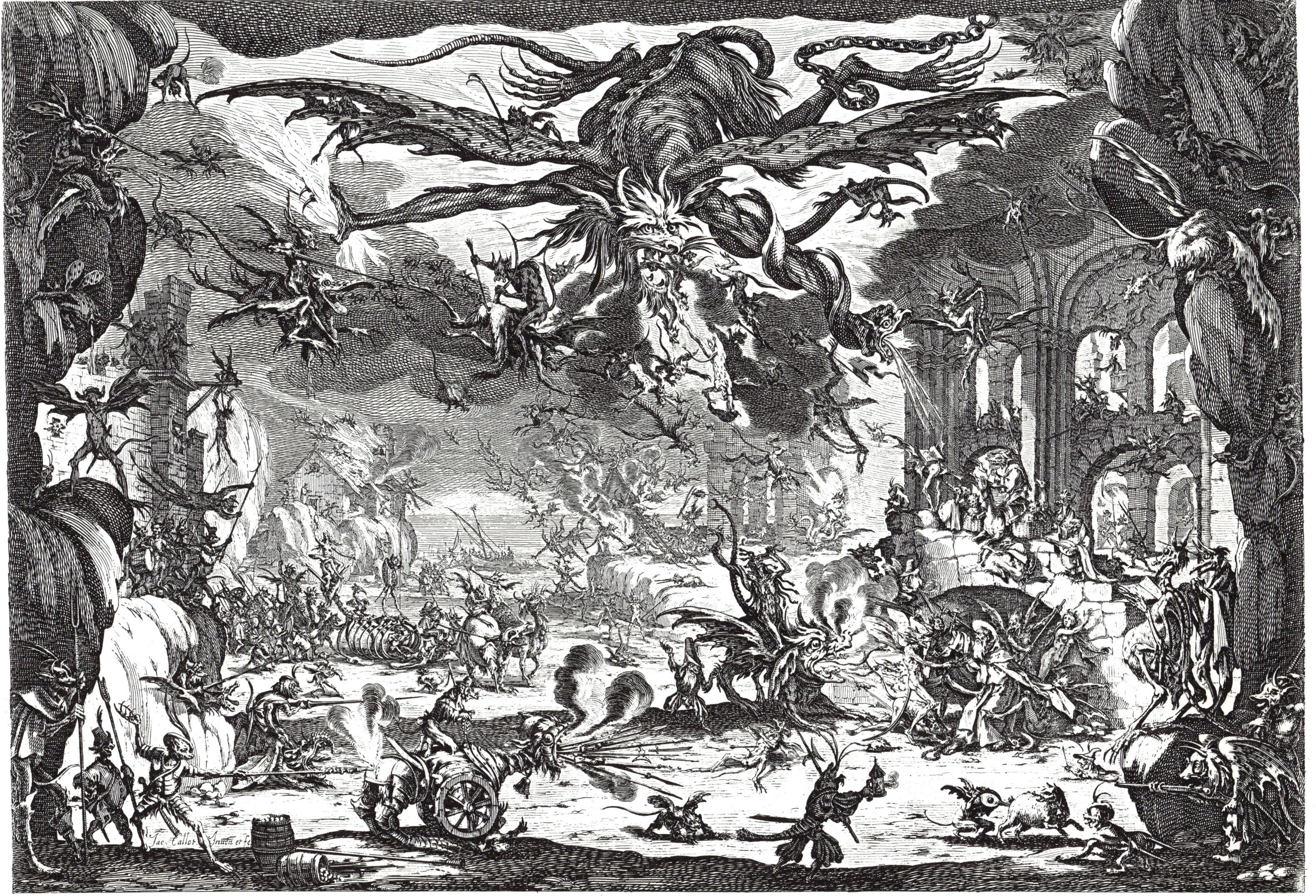

327 The Temptation of St. Anthony (second version). Etching, done ca. 1634, published 1635. The Latin inscriptions include a dedication to the French minister La Vrillière and a poem about the steadfastness of the saint in the face of all the monsters. (Howard Daniel Collection)

328–337 All 10 completed etchings of the series *The New Testament*, published posthumously 1635. (Courtesy Trustees of the British Museum)

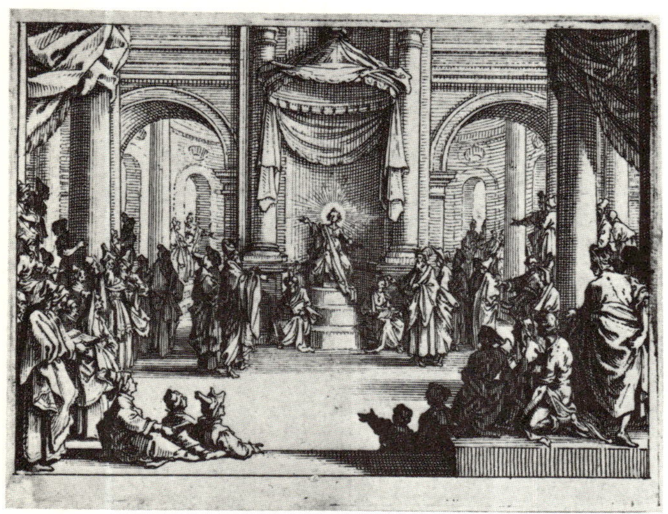

328 The Boy Jesus among the Doctors.

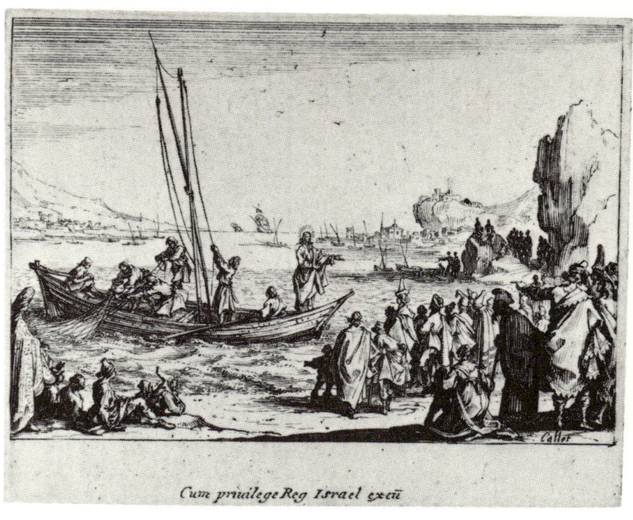

329 Jesus Preaching by the Sea.

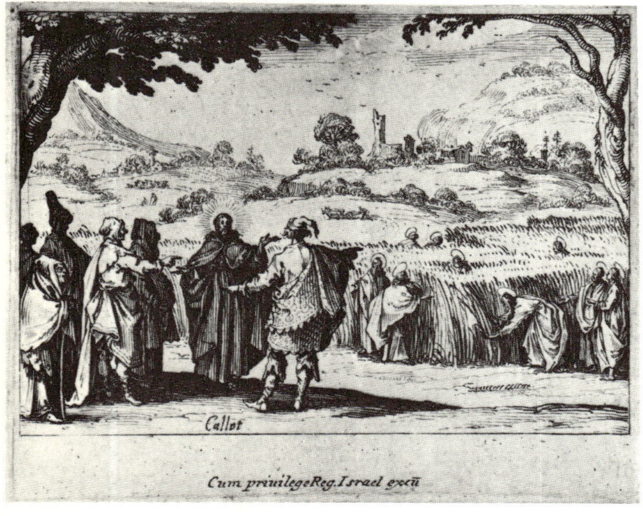

330 Jesus and the Pharisees.

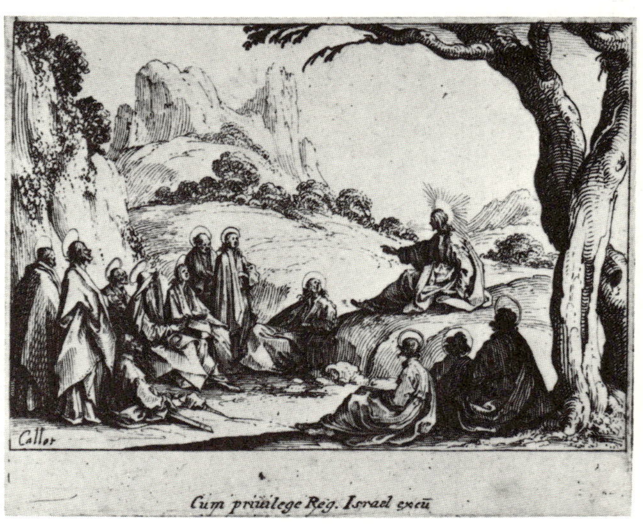

331 The Sermon on the Mount.

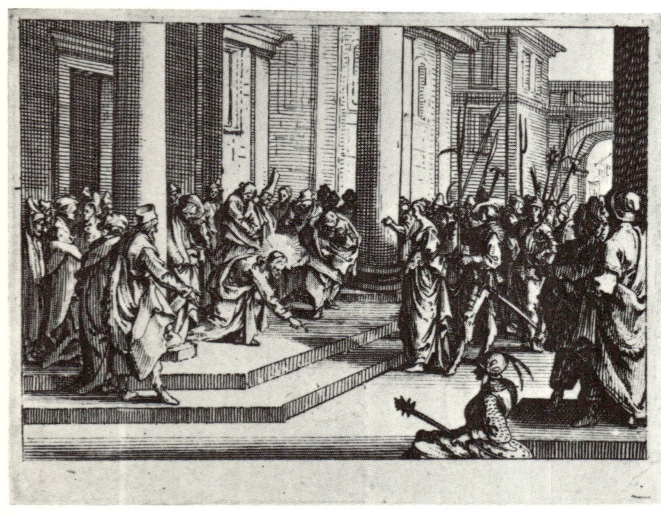

332 Jesus and the Adulteress.

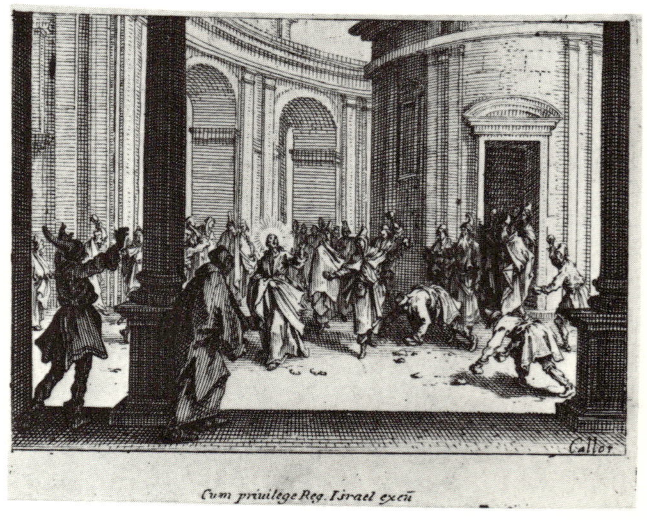

333 The Merchants Driven from the Temple.

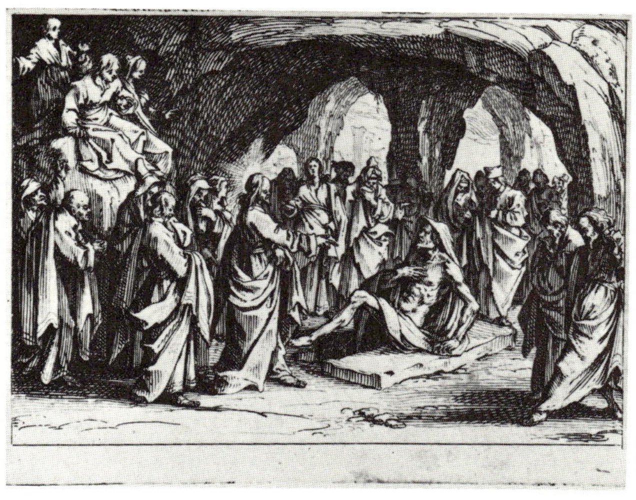

334 The Resurrection of Lazarus.

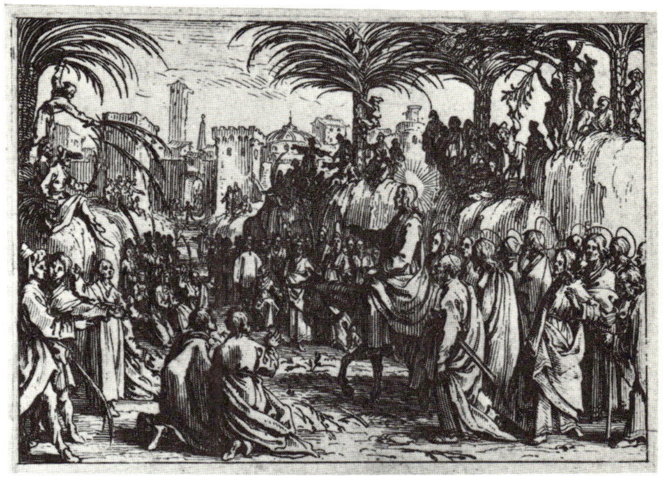

335 Jesus Enters Jerusalem.

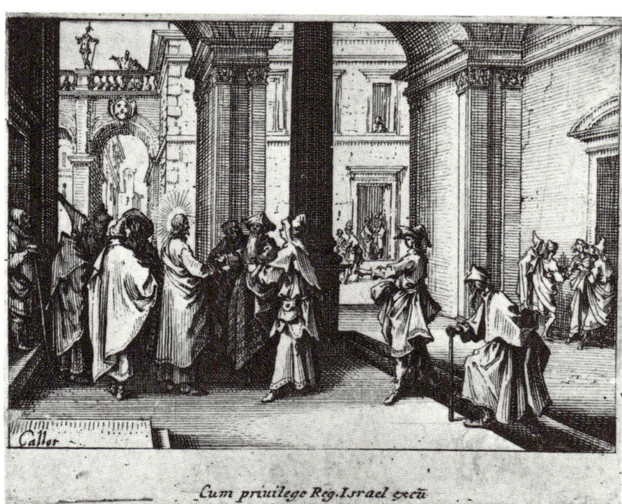

336 Jesus and the Doctors of the Law.

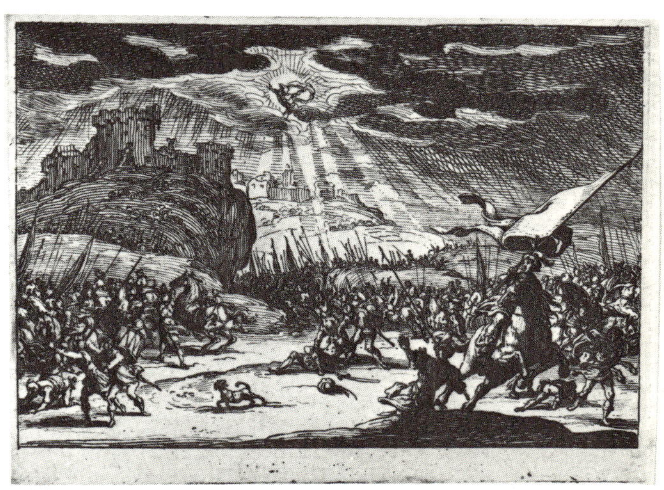

337 The Conversion of St. Paul.

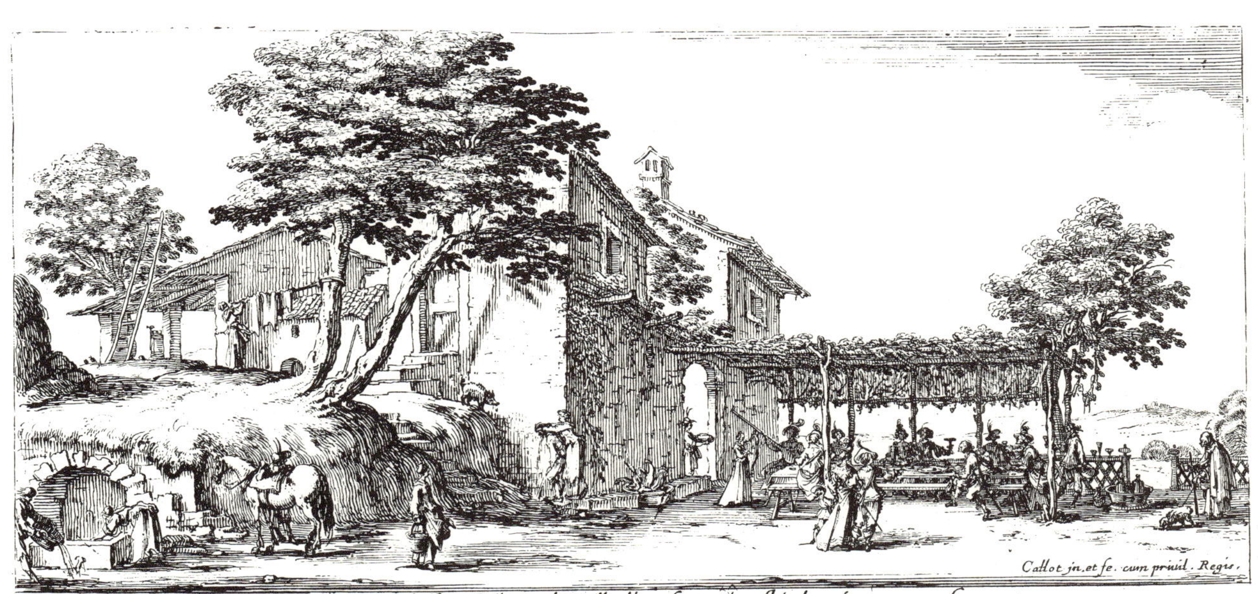

338 The Little Trellis ("La Petite Treille"). Etching, 1635. The inscription reads: "The late Callot's last plate, not etched until after his death." (National Gallery, Washington, R. L. Baumfeld Collection)